Internationalization, market power and consumer welfare

The study of industrial economics has been dominated in recent years by the USA. While there is a fund of theoretical and empirical knowledge relating to the US experience, this is not always relevant in the context of Europe. With its considerable national market the USA has developed competition policies that differ from those in the smaller economies of European countries.

This collection of essays looks at the market behaviour of an economy more open to international competition. The industrial organization of Sweden provides the ideal representation of smaller economies that can be applied to the other economies of western Europe.

The contributors apply different analytical approaches to assess direct and indirect forms of market power. Some papers draw on econometric cross-sectional models exploring the scope of market power and the role of international competition. Others look at specific markets investigating the formation of market power – its costs to consumers and the role of lobbying groups and the political sphere: case studies include the passenger car, white goods, pharmaceutical goods, food, textile and air transport markets. The book also contains papers that examine the role of competition policy towards restrictive practices and mergers in curbing market power and promoting economic efficiency.

This book will be of interest to all those studying industrial economics, international business and marketing as well as policy makers in the field.

Yves Bourdet is currently assistant professor in Economics at the Institute of Economic Research, University of Lund, and at the Stockholm School of Economics.

Internationalization, market power and consumer welfare

Edited by Yves Bourdet

Foreword by Dennis Mueller

London and New York

First published 1992
by Routledge
11 New Fetter Lane, London EC4P 4EE

Simultaneously published in the USA and Canada
by Routledge
a division of Routledge, Chapman and Hall, Inc.
29 West 35th Street, New York, NY 10001

Typeset in Times by
Columns Design and Production Services Ltd, Reading
Printed and bound in Great Britain by
Mackays of Chatham PLC, Chatham, Kent

British Library Cataloguing in Publication Data
Internationalization, market power and consumer welfare.
  1. Sweden. Industries. Competition
  I. Bourdet, Yves *1951–*
  338.604809485

  ISBN 0–415–06072–9

Library of Congress Cataloging-in-Publication Data
Internationalization, market power and consumer welfare /
  edited by Yves Bourdet : foreword by Dennis Mueller.
    p. cm.
  Includes bibliographical references and index.
  ISBN 0–415–06072–9 (hb)
  1. Sweden—Industries. 2. Sweden—Foreign economic
relations.
  I. Bourdet, Yves.
  HC375.I58 1991
  382′.3′09485—dc20

                         91–15097
                           CIP

Contents

List of figures   vii
List of tables   viii
List of contributors   xi
Foreword by Dennis Mueller   xiii

Part I Introduction

1 Market power and consumer welfare in open economies   3
  Yves Bourdet

Part II Concentration, efficiency and market power

2 Concentration, prices and profitability in the Swedish
  manufacturing industry   55
  Nils-Olov Stålhammar

3 Collusion and concentration in the Swedish
  manufacturing industry   87
  Nils-Olov Stålhammar

Part III International integration and multinational competition

4 The white goods industry   117
  Örjan Sölvell

5 The pharmaceutical market   145
  Bengt Jönsson

6 Competition and prices in the passenger car market   172
  Yves Bourdet

Part IV Producer behaviour, public policy and the market

7 Agricultural policy: old wine in new bottles 205
Ewa Rabinowicz

8 The textile and clothing market: towards a liberalization? 250
Eva Lindström

9 Economic regulation of domestic air transport in Sweden 274
Siri Pettersen Strandenes

**Part V Competition policy, market power and
    economic efficiency**

10 Policy toward market power and restrictive practices 299
Yves Bourdet

11 Competition policy and economic efficiency: efficiency
   trade-offs in industrial policy 337
Lennart Hjalmarsson

Index 358

Figures

2.1	Volume index of industrial production	73
2.2	Yearly change in price index of industrial products	74
5.1	Share of total drug sales 1972–88 for the twenty leading products in 1980	149
5.2	The Swedish pharmaceutical market	153
5.3	Millions of defined daily dosages (DDD) for Furosemide, distributed on different products, 1976–88	166
6.1	New registrations, 1968–88	174
7.1	Illustration of the consumer subsidy equivalent	208
7.2	Producer prices and world market prices	228
7.3	General price level, production costs, producer prices	229
7.4	Employment in agriculture (million man hours)	231
7.5	Milk production (thousand tonnes)	231
7.6	Investment in agriculture	232
7.7	Land values	232
7.8	General price level and food prices	239
7.9	Consumption of meat in kg per person (per annum)	239
8.1	The costs of a tariff for households	261
8.2	The effects of a trade policy discriminating amongst supplying countries	264
9.1	Travel frequencies: domestic travel with national carriers relative to population size, 1984	276
9.2	Ownership in the Swedish airline industry	281
11.1	Measures of technical efficiency and scale efficiency relative to a frontier production function	344
11.2	The size distribution of plants in a vintage model	348
11.3	The trade-off between productive and allocative efficiency	349

Tables

2.1	Sources and definitions of variables	65
2.2	Three-stage least squares estimates	66
2.3	The determinants of price change	77
2A	Concentration ratios at the four-digit level in the Swedish manufacturing industry	81
3.1	Industry profitability and concentration in 1965 and 1985	98
3.2	The implicit degree of collusion in 1965	100
3.3	The implicit degree of collusion in 1985	101
3.4	Determinants of the degree of collusion, 1965	106
3.5	Determinants of the degree of collusion, 1985	106
4.1	Market shares in the Japanese microwave oven market, 1978 and 1984	130
4A	Acquisitions made by Electrolux in the white goods industry, 1964–89	143
5.1	Sales in Sweden by the ten largest pharmaceutical firms, 1988 and 1978	147
5.2	Fifteen leading products, 1988 and 1978	148
5.3	Domestic and foreign companies' share of the pharmaceutical market, 1978–88	150
5.4	Import and export of pharmaceuticals between 1978 and 1988	150
5.5	Concentration ratios in 1988 and 1980 in two selected classification groups	152
5.6	Concentration ratios in 1988 and 1980, classification groups C2, C3, C7–9	152
5.7	The size of the three different markets in 1978 and 1988	155
5.8	Price index of pharmaceuticals and consumer price index	157

5.9   Price indices of domestic and foreign
       pharmaceutical specialities   158
5.10 Drug costs in relation to total health care costs and
       GNP in Sweden, 1978–88   158
5.11 Index on drug costs in current and fixed prices   .   159
5.12 International price comparison of 559 selected
       pharmaceutical specialities   160
5.13 Introduction of pharmaceutical specialities with
       and without NCEs in Sweden between 1960
       and 1988   161
5.14 Total number of domestic and foreign
       pharmaceutical specialities in Sweden at the
       beginning of each year   162
5.15 Data on life-time of pharmaceutical specialities
       registered between 1960 and 1979   163
5.16 Effective patent life for NCEs registered between
       1965 and 1987   164
5.17 Synonym competition among NCEs registered
       between 1960 and 1985 and not withdrawn from
       the market in 1986   165
6.1   Estimated income and price elasticities for new
       passenger cars   175
6.2   Distribution of new car sales by size–class,
       1974–88   176
6.3   Market shares and prices, 1988–9   177
6.4   Market concentration and import penetration,
       1960–88   179
6.5   Comparison of EEC directives and Swedish
       regulations for passenger cars with the regulations
       of the Economic Commission for Europe   184
6.6   Comparison of prices (net of taxes) of similar
       passenger car models   188
6.7   Pricing and exchange rate changes   191
7.1   Consumer subsidy equivalents, CSE   209
7.2   Welfare loss to consumers   209.
7.3   Market shares of farmer co-operatives in different
       sectors   235
8.1   Tariffs on textile products and industrial
       products   252
9.1   Effects of competition, Oslo–Stockholm air route   282
10.1 Number of cases examined by the Competition
       Commissioner, 1960–87   306

10.2   Distribution of cases examined by kind of outcome,
       1954–87   308
10.3   Restrictive practices examined by the Competition
       Commissioner and the market court, reported in
       the review of the competition authorities, 1970–87   309
10.4   Distribution of new agreements registered by the
       National Price and Cartel Board by kind of
       restrictive practices, 1947–87   311
10.5   Restrictive practices intensity and gross domestic
       product, 1960–87   315
10.6   Registered restrictive practices by kind of
       economic activity, 1971–87   319
10.7   Changes in the number of restrictive practices and
       in the resources of the Competition Commissioner,
       1960–87   321
10.8   Restrictive practices and merger intensities by
       kind of activity, 1971–87   324
10.9   Registered restrictive practices by kind of economic
       activity, 1971–87   327
10.10 Merger activity in Sweden, 1969–87   329
11.1   The number of MOS plants compatible with
       domestic consumption in six nations, c. 1967   343
11.2   Percentage cost reductions sufficient to offset
       percentage price increases for selected values of η 350
11.3   The value of m for different values of elasticity
       of scale   353
11.4   The value of m for different values of elasticity
       of scale when market shares differ between firms   354

Contributors

Yves Bourdet, Assistant Professor, Institute of Economic Research, University of Lund and Department of International Economics, Stockholm School of Economics.

Lennart Hjalmarsson, Professor of Economics, Department of Economics, University of Gothenburg.

Bengt Jönsson, Professor of Health Economics, Department of Health and Economics, Stockholm School of Economics.

Eva Lindström, Economist, Ministry of Finance, Stockholm.

Dennis Mueller, Professor of Economics, University of Maryland.

Ewa Rabinowicz, Associate Professor, Department of Economics and Statistics, The Swedish University of Agricultural Sciences, Uppsala.

Örjan Sölvell, Assistant Professor, Institute of International Business, Stockholm School of Economics.

Nils-Olov Stålhammar, Research Fellow, Department of Economics, University of Gothenburg and Case Western Reserve University.

Siri Pettersen Strandenes, Assistant Professor, Norwegian School of Economics and Business Administration, Bergen.

Foreword

Both theoretical and empirical research in the industrial organization/ industrial economics field have been dominated for some forty years at least by work from the United States. This domination is apparent in varying degrees in some other fields, but seems much more pronounced in industrial economics than it is in, say, international trade or macroeconomics. Just why this should be so is not obvious. Indeed, it may have been largely chance that Joe Bain happened to be an American, and happened to be the person who defined the field and its research agenda for nearly a generation, and that the author of the field's first encyclopedia of knowledge, F.M. Scherer, was also an American. Whatever the explanation, the facts are what they are. The consequence is that students of industrial organization in many countries often know more about how particular industries and companies are organized in the United States than they do about how they are organized in their own countries.

This historical development of the field has two important negative consequences. First, to the extent that factors which differ across countries have important effects on the performance of certain markets, generalizations about, say, the effects of certain public policies toward business, based upon the United States' experience, may be misguided, and could lead to the selection of inappropriate policies and avoidable welfare losses. Second, it slows the growth in our understanding of market phenomena. We have learned about the effects of scale economies on industrial concentration in a country with large, typically national markets. We know little about their effect in small or balkanized economies. We have a plethora of studies of the relationship between market concentration and profitability in a closed economy; we have very few studies of this relationship in an open economy.

There exists, therefore, a great need for more theoretical and empirical industrial economics focusing on institutions and markets in other countries. The chapters in this book, therefore, are a welcome addition to the field.

Sweden is a country which is both much smaller and more open to international competition than is the United States. Indeed, Sweden and its relationship with the world economy might better be compared to Ohio and its relationship with the US national economy, rather than with the United States and the world economy. It is also a country, luckily, with sufficiently good data to allow a sophisticated analysis of its industrial structure. The chapters that follow present such an analysis.

The book commences with a broad review of the structure–conduct–performance paradigm by Yves Bourdet (Chapter 1). Bourdet extends the analysis to integrate the consequences of international competition and then shows the relevance of the paradigm to issues of consumer welfare and consumer protection policy.

The next two chapters by Nils-Olov Stålhammar present empirical estimates for Sweden of some of the most basic relationships studied in industrial organization. In Chapter 2 a (weak) positive relationship is found between industry concentration and the rate of return on total capital. Some support for the administered price hypothesis, that prices change more slowly in concentrated markets, is also presented. The concentration–collusion–profits hypothesis receives rather marginal support in Sweden, both because the concentration variable has low explanatory power in the returns on capital equation, and is statistically insignificant in the price–cost margins equation.

In Chapter 3, Stålhammar pushes beyond the standard, simple linear concentration–profits equation and attempts to estimate conjectural variations or the degree of co-operation in an industry. As such, these estimates help quantify the significance of oligopolistic interdependence across industries. Stålhammar estimates mean values of co-operation that come much closer to what one would expect under the effectively independent behavioural assumption employed by Cournot than to what one would expect from perfect collusion. Foreign trade has a significant effect enhancing competitive performance as one might expect that it would.

Part III contains three case studies of industries in which competition is international in nature. The white goods industry represents a particularly good example for close examination, since one of the world's leaders, Electrolux, is based in Sweden. Örjan

Sölvell in Chapter 4 describes how this market leader both copes with international competition at home, and becomes itself an increasingly internationalized firm.

There are some features of the pharmaceuticals market in Sweden that make it different from that existing in many other countries. In particular, the Apoteksbolaget, the state-run national chain of pharmacies, has a monopsony of the purchases of pharmaceutical products. Since patent protection often grants pharmaceutical manufacturers monopoly power, the market for many pharmaceutical products in Sweden resembles a bilateral monopoly. Although differing from other countries in this respect, Sweden is not alone in having a separation between the person prescribing a drug and the person (agency) paying for it. This separation results in the same kind of insensitivity to price as in other countries. These and other characteristics of the Swedish pharmaceuticals industry are described by Bengt Jönsson in Chapter 5.

As with white goods, the passenger car market is one in which there is much international competition, but it is also a market in which Sweden has one of the dominant companies. Yves Bourdet's chapter on passenger cars (Chapter 6) indicates that international competition has not succeeded in making Sweden's car market fully competitive, and presents some estimates of consumer welfare losses in Sweden due to higher than competitive car prices.

Part IV of the book examines Sweden's experiences in regulating other sectors of the economy. Chapter 7 by Eva Rabinowicz describes Swedish experience within the agricultural sector over the last generation. As in all other developed democracies, Sweden's farmers have formed a successful interest group that has helped to raise the prices of agricultural products considerably, and thereby has produced large welfare losses for Swedish consumers. Rabinowicz both presents estimates of the magnitude of these welfare losses, and discusses the latest set of reforms with which Sweden hopes to rectify the situation.

While agriculture is a rather unsurprising case of successful interest group lobbying for protection, the same cannot be said of the next case study of Swedish intervention in the marketplace written by Eva Lindström (Chapter 8). One might have expected that textiles and clothing, like many other markets in Sweden, would have appeared in this book as an example of how the famed 'partnership' between government, business and labour produced a rationalization and modernization of production, accompanied by a rapid exodus of Swedish workers and capital to other sectors.

Instead, it appears as an example of how powerful interest groups can use government, in this case through a combination of tariffs, quotas and subsidies, to achieve their private ends. For example, the ratio of tariffs on textiles to tariffs on industrial products is less than two to one for the EEC and more than three to one for Sweden. Lindström describes some policy changes in Sweden that may change the outcome.

The third example of Swedish regulatory policy is domestic air transport described by Siri Pettersen Strandenes in Chapter 9. Air transport has been, and still is in most countries, a heavily regulated market. Estimates of welfare losses from such regulatory policies have been quite large. Strandenes describes the complex pattern of regulation in Swedish air transport and then describes and discusses various auction-model reforms that have been proposed to reduce the social costs of regulation.

The concluding section of the book, Part V, contains two broader essays on regulatory policy. Yves Bourdet in Chapter 10 reviews Sweden's experience with antitrust policies as they pertain to collusive agreements, mergers and vertical restraints. Lennart Hjalmarsson in Chapter 11 deals with industrial policy which, as he notes, might also be described as *pro*trust policy. The presumption in Sweden with respect to industrial policy has been to encourage mergers in the hope of obtaining larger firms, which could better exploit scale economies, better develop new products and processes, and more generally withstand better the 'perennial gale' of international competition. Hjalmarsson shows how one can model and measure the trade-off between dynamic efficiency gains from scale economies and cost reductions against the static welfare losses of market power.

As this brief synopsis hopefully reveals, the chapters of this book present a rich mosaic of information related to industrial economics with particular reference to Sweden. They range from detailed accounts of performance in particular markets to more general questions of consumer welfare loss measurement, and the effects of competition policy. In short, they provide something of interest for everyone in the industrial economics field.

Dennis Mueller
University of Maryland

Part I
Introduction

1 Market power and consumer welfare in open economies*

Yves Bourdet

INTRODUCTION

Two issues related to power have received particular attention by economists: the power over companies and the power over markets. The first issue concentrates on the changes in the structure of ownership and control in the economy. It is concerned not with the exercise of power *per se*, but rather with changes in the ability to exert power. The second issue deals with actual influence, i.e. with the way in which power is wielded. It is concerned with firm behaviour and the way firms affect competitive conditions and prices in a market or a set of markets. This is the theme of this book.

Market power has commanded less space on the research agenda over the last two decades, one reason being that the opening up of economies to international trade has been assumed to work as a straitjacket on non-competitive behaviour. However, several factors suggest that this view has to be revised. The limited number of firms in many industries, such as the motor vehicle, pharmaceutical and white goods industries, and the wave of mergers over the past decade indicate that market power may still be a problem for consumer welfare even in open economies. The influence of organized groups on public policy and, indirectly, on prices in sectors like agriculture, textile and air transport confirms further that market power, broadly defined to integrate the result of lobbying activities, has not disappeared with the internationalization of industrial economies.

The present chapter focuses on *market power and consumer welfare in open economies*. Its purpose is to examine the meaning, the determinants and the effects of market power and to delimit research topics of interest. The chapter is divided into eight parts. After an introduction, the second section presents the concept of market power and relates it to the different definitions of power existing in social science. The third part surveys traditional theories of market power in economics. It shows how different market forms affect the exercise of market power. Another aspect examined in this section is the cost to society of market power. In the fourth part, we take up the difficulties faced in carrying out empirical studies of market power in economics. Attention is focused on the relevance of concentration as a proxy for market power and on the role of barriers to entry. In the fifth part, the effect of the liberalization of trade since the Second World War on actual market power and economic research in this area is examined. The sixth part deals with the way in which the interaction between producers and the public sector influences market conditions and prices. The seventh part examines the government policies aimed at curbing market power and the changes in view concerning these policies that recent developments in the theory of market power have suggested. Finally, in the last section, an investigation is made of which markets are worth studying in an open economy because it is there that market power is most likely to be present. An additional selection criterion used is to put emphasis on those markets that are of significant importance for citizens' living conditions. In this last part, we also raise several crucial issues that will be examined in other chapters of this book.

WHAT IS MARKET POWER?

What do economists mean by market power? Market power denotes the degree of discretion of a firm (or group of firms acting jointly) in affecting price and competitive conditions in a market. This influence is not temporary. Further, it can be either *direct* or *indirect*. In the former case, exercise of power is achieved in the marketplace where the firms have control over price and quantities sold. In the latter case, it is achieved through influence over public policy affecting issues of interest for firms, such as price, barriers to entry or trade policy in the larger sense of the phrase.

It is the results rather than the causes and means involved which are decisive for the existence of market power. Market power is defined in terms of its effects, i.e. when a firm (or group of firms) is able to charge a price that is higher than that arising from a competitive market and, hence, gain an economic advantage at the cost of consumers or/and other firms. An important aspect of the definition is the implicit reference to perfect competition where price, which is determined by the free play of supply and demand, is beyond the control of firms. When competitive conditions prevail in a market, individual firms cannot depart from competitive behaviour and competitive prices for fear of losing their customers and of being driven out of business. Market power does not exist in such cases or, at least, does not last. Competition is the main restriction on market power.

Another important aspect of the definition concerns the concept of market. This issue is of crucial importance when it comes to the analysis of market power and it is no wonder that it has been debated at length.[1] The concept of market determines the products to be included in a specific market and, consequently, the firms that compete in this market and the degree of competition prevailing among them. In other words, the market concept delimits the boundaries within which market power may be exercised. Although the term 'market' is widely used in economics, there is no simple and well accepted definition to which this term can be applied.[2] In the present chapter, a market is said to consist of all the products that are substitutes. Using the language of economists, this definition means that the cross-elasticities of demand between each pair of products that belong to a market have high positive values and that the cross-elasticity of demand between each of these products and every other product is low.[3]

For the sake of completeness, the time dimension of market power should also be discussed briefly. Market power does not exist if, within a relatively short time, other firms can enter a market dominated by one firm and force it to adopt competitive behaviour and a lower price. In such a case, firms can be said to benefit from temporary market power. This gives rise to excess profits and may be the result of factors such as imperfect information, innovation and cheaper methods of production. It should be stressed that temporary market power disappears as soon as a new entry occurs in the form of firms that produce substitute products and that use rather similar techniques of production and possess the same information. Note that this form of market power, and the excess profits that it generates, constitutes one of the main incentives for firms to innovate and improve product quality. It allows them to reap the rewards of their innovative activity. Firms that benefit from it generally fear the entry of competitors and take care of their customers. Joseph Schumpeter regarded it as the main dynamic factor behind economic development.[4] Its temporary nature and its positive effects on economic growth are the main reasons behind its omission in empirical studies of market power in economics.

One of the most debated issues regarding power concerns its definition. In social science, there are several definitions that emphasize different features of the way power is distributed and wielded in society.[5] Those definitions that seem most important to the understanding of power explain it in terms of (1) influence between two or more actors (2) causality or ability to impose one's will on someone else and (3) the conditions that make easier its exercise. The first definition states that power is a relationship between two or more actors. In respect to market power, the actors are the firm(s) and the consumers and the relation is the exchange between them in a market. If the firms and the business associations that represent them advance their interests indirectly, i.e. through an influence on trade policy or regulatory measures, it becomes necessary to bring into the analysis a third actor, the authorities or the public sphere. The second definition concentrates on the ability of someone that benefits from power to impose his will on someone else. In terms of market power, this means that a firm, by charging a higher price, excludes from the market those consumers unwilling to meet this higher price and forces customers to buy a product at a price that is higher than that prevailing under perfect competition.

The definition of market power given above fits well with the first two definitions of power but less well with the third one. An underlying reason is that the latter definition emphasizes those factors that promote or inhibit the ability to exert market power, but ignores the *exercise* of power *per se*. Note, however, that many empirical studies of market power have focused exclusively on these conditions. The different analyses of concentration carried out in OECD countries during the past three decades are illustrative examples of such an orientation.[6] This issue will be further discussed in the following sections, especially in the section devoted to concentration, barriers to entry and market power.

In discussions of power in social science, two questions often arise. First, why do actors strive to exercise power? Second, how can power be measured? As will be shown in the following sections, it is economic motives which explain why firms attempt to charge a price that is higher than the competitive price. Profit maximization is the most common of these motives. Other motives, that are not contradictory with the profit maximizing motive, are the efforts made by some firms to live a quiet life or by some threatened producers to survive. In other words, firms exercise market power because it results in larger profits or because it gives them some form of economic advantage.

An answer to the second question is crucial since the impossibility, or great difficulty, of measuring power is one of the major objections raised against studies of power in social science. Market power is defined by opposition to competition. Lack of market power characterizes situations where competitive conditions prevail. It seems, therefore, natural to measure market power by the difference between the price outcomes of competitive and noncompetitive situations. Note, however, that a difficulty arises from the fact that, in most cases, the competitive situation is not observable. This problem will be discussed in the following sections.

MARKET POWER AND ECONOMIC WELFARE: THE CONVENTIONAL WISDOM

Once market power is defined, the question which arises is what are the main theoretical approaches to the subject of market power? In this section, we will concentrate on conventional theories of market power in economics. When perfect competitive conditions prevail in a market, firms have no control over price; there is no market power. Price is determined by the anonymous forces of total demand and total supply and firm behaviour is constrained by the 'power' of the market. The lack of persistent market power in perfect competition explains why market power is often defined by reference to perfect competition. To put it another way, perfect competition constitutes a norm and market power constitutes a deviation from the norm. A brief description of the characteristics of this norm is, therefore, necessary to the understanding of market power. Just as important as studying market power is studying *lack* of market power, i.e. perfect competition.

A perfectly competitive market is composed of many individual firms that cannot influence the market price. Firms are price takers. They expand their production until they reach the output where their marginal costs equal the market price. Any attempt by one (or several) of them to raise the price over the going price leads to a complete desertion by buyers, since it is assumed that the product is standardized and perfect information exists. Further, there is no point in an individual firm lowering the price because its whole production can be sold at the going price. Two other main conditions are required for perfect competition to prevail and to last in a market: many buyers and an absence of barriers to entry. The former condition implies that buyers cannot influence the competitive price, while the latter means that established firms cannot depart from competitive behaviour for fear of a new entry.

Each market consists of a certain number of sellers. This number is usually regarded as the main indicator of the intensity of competition. It determines the market form. As stated above, the presence of many sellers characterizes perfect competition. On the contrary, the presence of only one seller (monopoly) or a few sellers (oligopoly) characterizes imperfect competition. To begin, let us consider the monopoly case.[7]

Highly different factors of an institutional and economic nature explain the presence of a monopoly in a market. For example, it can be the result of public policy that grants one firm the exclusive right to sell a product and, hence, prevents other firms from entering the market. The imposition of a prohibitive tariff against imports or the existence of substantial transport costs can achieve the same result by insulating a national or a regional market. Among the economic factors, the existence of large economies of scale is the most common. This form of market structure, which is called natural monopoly, occurs when one firm can produce the whole output of the industry at lower cost than could two or more firms. Another factor of importance is the exclusive control by one firm over an input or a technique of production.

By definition, the monpolist totally controls the supply of a product that does not have any near substitute. (The value of the price cross-elasticity of demand between its product and every other product is near zero.) Unlike firms acting under perfect competition, the monopolist is a price maker. He can raise price by restricting output. The absence of substitute products means that he does not fear competition from other firms. He will select the output where marginal cost equals marginal revenue. This is the output that maximizes his profits. Any other output, smaller or greater, results in lower profits.

The output chosen by the monopolist is smaller than the perfectly competitive output. This has two important implications. Compared with the perfect competition situation, the monopoly output/price policy generates an income transfer from consumers to the monopolist. Customers are forced to pay a price that is higher than the price prevailing under perfect competition. Further, the monopoly behaviour implies that some customers cannot buy the product in question. They are priced out of the market. They suffer a loss that is not offset by any gain to the monopolist. This loss is called the deadweight welfare cost or allocative inefficiency cost (or

Harberger triangle). According to conventional theory, it is the net cost to society of monopoly.

It should be stressed that the monopoly case has very little empirical relevance. Very few real world markets are dominated by only one firm. On the other hand, most markets are dominated by a few sellers. To put it another way, oligopoly is the predominant market form in modern economies. It is in particular true for most industrial markets where production can only be carried on economically if conducted on a fairly large scale. This stems from the nature of technology and cost in industry. Actually, the decline in average cost as output rises implies that only a few firms can produce the total output sold on the market at the lowest average cost. Another factor behind the oligopolistic structure of many industries is the desire of already technically efficient firms to acquire market power through mergers and takeovers.[8]

The nature of interdependence between oligopolists that wish to collude is the central point when it comes to output and price determination. Joint-profit maximization is reached when oligopolists act together as a monopolist. In such a case, the price/output and social cost outcome is the same as in the monopoly case. Although beneficial for the entire set of firms in a market, joint-profit collusion is likely to last only under very special circumstances. There is a strong incentive for individual oligopolists to break a collusive agreement. If one of them succeeds in lowering his price without bringing about any reaction from competitors (secret price cutting), he will gain larger profits than by conforming to the agreement. This suggests that a high degree of instability is very likely to characterize oligopoly.[9]

Thus, policing a collusive agreement among oligopolists is essential to its existence.[10] In other words, a collusive action cannot last without some form of control. Yet this may be difficult for several reasons. First, price/output agreements between firms are forbidden by law in industrial countries. Second, policing an agreement may be an impossible task if the number of oligopolists is large. The larger the number, the more difficult it is to detect secret price cutting and to find and maintain common ground. In short, the larger the group, the looser the oligopoly will be. The size distribution of sellers may also affect the feasibility of collusion. For example, tacit forms of collusion, such as price leadership, are expected in markets composed of one or two very large firm(s) and small fringe firms. This is all the more likely if the very large firm(s) has indulged in predatory price cutting in the past. Note that in such a case, the price is lower and the output larger than under monopoly but, of course, the price is higher and the output smaller than under perfect competition.

Up to this point, we have concentrated on factors that are expected to most influence the likelihood of collusion in oligopoly and its price and output outcome. It should be noted that other factors as well, such as the conditions of entry into the industry, cost differences between firms and the price elasticity of demand, affect the level of collusive prices under oligopoly.

A conclusion to be drawn from this brief review is that no general theory of oligopoly yet exists.[11] There are only models that apply to different types of oligopolies and that present a range of indeterminacy between the monopoly and competitive solutions. A central result is that the market power of an oligopolist is less than that of monopoly. Another result is that the social cost of oligopoly is of the same nature but, in most cases, less important than that of monopoly.

So far, the analysis has dealt with standardized (or somewhat standardized) products. At first sight, this seems a strong limitation because one of the main features of most industrial and service markets is product differentiation. Economists call monopolistic competition a form of market characterized by product differentiation and numerous sellers. The fact that products are good, but not perfect, substitutes means that each firm faces a downward sloping demand curve. In other words, product differentiation confers on each firm some degree of discretion over its price. The large number of producers under monopolistic competition is the result of low barriers to entry, in the form of limited opportunities for economies of scale and small initial capital requirements.

For our discussion, an important question is: to what extent can the monopolistic firm achieve market power and raise its price? In order to maximize profits, the monopolistic firm chooses the output (and price) where marginal cost equals marginal revenue. If this output/price combination results in excess profits, i.e. profits after the opportunity costs have been taken into account, new entrants will be attracted into the business because of the low entry barriers. The new entrants will dilute the excess profits as well as the market share of the monopolistic firm. The latter will select an output where marginal cost equals marginal revenue and where no excess profits are earned. At this point, profits are still maximized, since any other point on the demand curve will leave the monopolistic firm operating at a loss, but the solution is technically inefficient because price is above marginal cost.

Entry conditions limit considerably the exercise of market power by monopolistic firms. To put it another way, the very existence of market power in differentiated markets with low barriers to entry is questionable. The relevance of monopolistic competition for the understanding of the working of real world markets can also be questioned since most differentiated industries, except service industries, are characterized by large opportunities for economies of scale and few producers. The latter characteristic is all the more common when the markets and the countries considered are relatively small. Obviously, the key feature of such markets remains oligopolistic interdependence.

From this brief review of the conventional price and allocation theory under differing market conditions, one can note that market power results in a social cost. This is the main reason put forward by economists to combat it. However, several authors have questioned the conventional wisdom. Criticism has been directed toward, on the one hand, the size and the nature of social costs and, on the other hand, the very existence of market power.

As stated above, consumers that are priced out of the market by non-competitive practices suffer a loss that is the net cost to society of market power. Besides this cost, market power results in a transfer from consumers, that remain in the marketplace, to producers. A first criticism argues that the existence of an opportunity to achieve this transfer will attract resources into activities whose purpose is to obtain market power.[12] Examples of such activities are lobbying efforts to obtain legislation that regulates entry or some form of protection against foreign competition. The resources devoted to such activities could instead have been used elsewhere in the economy to produce goods. Thus, these activities have a cost that is equal to the return that these resources could have earned in their best alternative use (opportunity cost). This opportunity cost is a social cost as well. Obviously, it should be added to the so-called deadweight welfare cost of market power.

A second criticism argues that the welfare cost is not sufficient as a measurement of inefficiency. Incentives for cost reductions are lacking when firms enjoy an insulated market position. For example, the oligopolistic umbrella protects high-cost producers that would be eliminated in a competitive market. The absence of competitive pressures on firm profits does away with incentives to keep costs to a minimum and results in X-inefficiency, i.e.

organization slack and waste. Harvey Leibenstein is the economist who contributed most to the introduction of this concept in economics.[13] According to him, the X-inefficiency costs of market power are significant while the allocative inefficiency costs are trivial. Unfortunately, this statement cannot be verified because, as a result of difficulties of measurement, there is very little quantitative evidence on the extent of X-inefficiency under non-competitive market conditions. Nevertheless, the existence of X-inefficiency is substantiated by several individual industry studies that show that costs rise above necessary levels in the absence of competition.[14]

The allocative inefficiency cost of market power is measured in static terms in the conventional approach. In addition, it is important to examine the conditions for industrial innovation, i.e. to provide a measure of the effects of market power in terms of dynamic efficiency. Product innovation is one of the principal dimensions of competition. In markets characterized by intensive competition, there are strong incentives for firms to innovate in order to survive and to reap high temporary profits. On the other hand, in markets characterized by monopolies and collusion, the introduction of new technology and new products is less stimulated. Absence of competitive pressures and high product prices allow obsolete production units to survive and delay the introduction of new technology. In short, market power is very likely to result in significant dynamic inefficiency costs that are not taken into account by static welfare theory.[15]

A third criticism directed against the conventional approach concerns the emphasis put on the number of firms as the main determinant of the intensity of competition. The Theory of Contestable Markets argues that the nature of competition depends on a variety of other factors.[16] Among the latter, the presence of sunk costs is decisive. Sunk costs are investments in production capacity, R&D or advertising that are irreversible. Such investments have no alternative use and are lost for the firm that drops out of business. Generally, sunk costs are more important in industry than in the service sector. Sunk costs must be committed by entrants but not by established firms. They create an asymmetry between potential entrants and established firms. Hence, they deter entry, relax the perfect competition straitjacket and provide established firms with market power.

On the other hand, the absence of sunk costs means that the market is perfectly contestable.[17] By this is meant that the threat of entry forces the established firm(s) to adopt a price just equal to marginal cost. Potential entry imposes efficiency upon a market regardless of the number of established firms. This implies that even under monopoly conditions, markets behave competitively in the absence of sunk costs. The conclusion which emerges from this theory is that the degree of competition is underestimated by conventional theory. Competition is determined by the number of firms which are established in a market as well as by those firms which can contest this market. In other words, the market consists of more than the firms actually selling in the market.

CONCENTRATION, BARRIERS TO ENTRY AND MARKET POWER: THE TRUNCATED PARADIGM

One of the main objections raised against studies of power in social science concerns difficulties of measurement. This is of course all the more prejudicial when it comes to empirical studies of power. As stated above, prices are forced down towards costs under perfect competition. A natural measure of market power is therefore the difference between the price that results from the exercise of market power and the marginal cost. This measure is known as the Lerner index and is equal to $(p - mc)/p$.[18] The use of this index in empirical studies in economics is subject to the same kind of criticism raised against other studies of power in social science.[19] It presents quasi-insurmountable difficulties of measurement: while the market price is observable, the marginal cost of the firm is unknown and the firm has no interest in reporting it. Further, because of the lack of competitive pressures, we may expect the actual marginal cost to be higher than that under perfectly competitive conditions. The incentives to be X-efficient and to minimize costs increase with the intensity of competition.

Empirical studies have attempted to circumvent the measurement difficulty by focusing on the level of concentration and the height of barriers to entry.[20] Concentration is considered the most important factor in determining market power. It measures the level of actual competition in a market. The height of barriers to entry is a complementary explanatory factor. It is regarded as an indicator of the intensity of potential competition. Note that concentration and barriers to entry are not independent of each other. High barriers deter entry and bring about concentrated market structures while low barriers promote entry and competitive market structures.

The field of industrial economics is concerned with the functioning of competition and the welfare effects of real world markets. Empirical work in this field has been largely directed to the task of searching for market power. Factors, such as concentration, that are expected to facilitate the exercise of market power have remained the central theme of this field since its creation in the 1930s.[21] However, focusing exclusively on concentration (or other dimensions of market structure) and its determinants is not enough. Market should be judged by their performance, not by their structure.

Concentration provides information on the number and the size distribution of firms. For example, a high level of concentration means that a few firms account for the bulk of market supply. In such a market, the sellers are very likely to recognize their interdependence and collude in order to mould competitive conditions and achieve a higher price. This outcome is all the more likely when barriers to entry are high: the higher they are, the more difficult entry and the lower the degree of potential competition. Hence, the focus of attention on concentration in industrial economics is based on the assumption that a high level of concentration correlates with market power, regardless of whether a high level of concentration is in fact synonymous with market control. The question which arises is of course whether this assumption is justified. This issue has been scrutinized by both theorists and applied workers.

The former have attempted to see whether there is a theoretical relation between concentration and market power by relating diverse measures of concentration to some index of market power. For example, the Lerner index was related to the concentration ratios by Saving, to the Herfindahl concentration measure by Cowling and Waterson and to the entropy measure by Encaoua and Jacquemin.[22] It is worth stressing that the demonstrations are based on a strict (Cournot-like) assumption about the behaviour of firms: each firm assumes that a change in its output has no influence on the output of other firms. Another strict assumption is the existence of effective barriers to entry, so that the established firms do not concern themselves with the effects of higher profitability on entry. The main result that emerges from these models is that the degree of market power is positively related to the level of concentration and inversely related to the value of the price elasticity of demand. Another basis result is that the level of concentration cannot be regarded as a determinant of performance. Concentration and performance, as measured by the Lerner index, are determined simultaneously and concentration is rather an approximation than a determinant of the level of performance.[23]

Applied workers have explored the relation between concentration and market power within the framework of the structure–conduct–performance paradigm. A behavioural and causal relation between structure and performance is the core of this paradigm. Concentration is considered the main dimension of structure and the main determinant of performance: attempts to exercise market power are likely to be more successful in industries that are highly concentrated. Since the pioneer work of Bain in 1951, many empirical studies based on cross-section econometric research have been conducted to test this hypothesis.[24] Their main conclusion is that concentration generally has some, albeit not a substantial, positive effect on profitability. Although the methods, the variables and the nature of the investigated relationship differ, the great majority of studies show that highly concentrated industries exhibit higher rates of return than less concentrated industries. Most of the studies are concerned with the US economy. Nevertheless, the few studies of British and other west European industries give a broadly similar picture.[25]

This kind of study now seems much less common in the field of industrial economics than it was a decade ago. The main reason for this shift in interest is the strong criticism that such studies have been subjected to over the past decade. Three main criticisms have been put forward: deficient measures of concentration, erroneous interpretation of the statistical results and questionable focus of attention on concentration as the main predictor of market power.

In regard to the first criticism, most of the empirical studies have relied upon concentration ratios as the main indicator of market power, largely because those ratios are easily available. The most widely used is the CR4, i.e. the accumulated share of the first four firms.[26] Undoubtedly, this choice challenges the results because concentration ratios fail to reflect accurately the two major dimensions of market structure, number and size inequality of firms. These two dimensions are more adequately captured by other concentration measures, such as the Herfindahl and the Rosenbluth indices. Note, however, that the few studies using the Herfindahl index provide a similar picture of the relation between structure and performance.[27] During the 1970s, efforts were made to develop more comprehensive measures of concentration.[28] They came to an end in the early 1980s when industrial economists became aware of the fact that progress toward a better understanding of market power is not achieved through an increased sophistication of the concentration measures.

Concentration measures used in empirical studies of the concentration–profitability relationship suffer from another important shortcoming. They are concerned with industry structure, i.e. with the shares of domestic production, and ignore the role of imports and exports.[29] In most cases, these measures underestimate the degree of competition prevailing in markets subject to international competition. This is in particular true in western Europe because of the high degree of trade exposure. Obviously, the use of biased concentration measures in statistical tests of the relationship between structure and performance affects the regression results and casts doubt on the conclusions to be drawn from them.

The second criticism emphasizes the erroneous interpretation of what has been observed in empirical studies. It is argued that the positive relationship between concentration and profitability is not evidence of market power, but of large firms' efficiency.[30] Innovation, or some other form of differential advantages, in some firms in an industry brings about an increase in both their market shares and their rates of return. The higher degree of concentration and profitability in some industries is due to the larger proportion of successful firms. In order to see whether it is efficiency or market power that is at work, Demsetz compared the rates of return of small firms in concentrated and non-concentrated industries.[31] If collusion is at work, small and medium firms in concentrated industries should exhibit a higher rate of return than corresponding firms in non-concentrated industries. On the other hand, if efficiency is at work, no significant differences between these firms' rates of return should be observed. Demsetz found no correlation between the rates of return of small and medium firms and the concentration of the industry these firms occupy. He rejected, therefore, the collusion explanation. This view was further supported by other studies.[32] Another argument advanced in these studies is that high profits in concentrated industries do not persist through time. High profits only reflect the temporary (Schumpeterian) market power of successful firms. They are the rewards of their innovative activity. The main conclusion that emerges from this criticism is that, although market power may play a certain role, efficiency is the main factor behind the high rates of return observed in highly concentrated industries. Another conclusion is that disentangling the relative importance of efficiency and temporary market power in high profits is an impossible task.[33]

The third criticism is of the focus on concentration as the main determinant of market power to the neglect of other dimensions of market structure. The price policy of established firms is also influenced by the height of barriers to entry and the intensity of potential competition. Many empirical studies have, therefore, integrated proxies for barriers to entry.[34] The above suggested fact that the height of barriers to entry is a determinant of concentration raises, however, serious difficulties for regression analysis. It is clear that the inclusion of both concentration and barriers to entry as explanatory variables of performance on the right-hand side of a single equation makes difficult the interpretation of the regression results.[35]

Scrutiny of the conditions of entry is the main feature of recent research in industrial economics. The pendulum seems thus to have swung in favour of the importance of barriers to entry and against the importance of concentration in analysing market power. The height of barriers to entry provides established sellers advantages over potential entrants. It determines the extent to which the former can persistently raise their prices above the competitive level and earn excess profits without attracting the latter. In short, it gives established firms some degree of market power. In his seminal work on conditions of entry, Bain identified three main types of entry barriers: absolute cost advantages, product differentiation and economies of scale.[36] Absolute cost advantages for established firms can arise from factors such as patent protected production, lower interest charges or favourable location. Whatever their source, such cost advantages permit existing firms to charge a price up to the unit costs of the potential entrants without inducing entry.

The second type of barrier to entry identified by Bain is product differentiation, where new firms bear higher selling costs because of consumer preferences for the established products. To put it another way, new firms that want to break into a market suffer a cost differential relative to the established firms. The latter can thus charge a price up to the unit costs of the potential entrants without inducing entry. Product differentiation exists whenever rival products are not viewed as perfect substitutes. Bain regarded it as the most important barrier to entry.[37] No doubt product differentiation and buyer loyalty have several sources. Bain identified uncertainty about the quality of new products as the main one.[38] If this is the only one, product differentiation barriers should first diminish and then vanish after a period of years during which the new products gain buyer loyalty.

Most of the empirical work during the 1960s and 1970s has focused on another source of differentiation, advertising.[39] The discussions of its role as a barrier to entry have been dominated by controversies. Some economists support the view that intense advertising leads to consumer loyalty and creates substantial barriers to entry. Numerous cross-section studies were made during the 1960s and the first half of the 1970s to illustrate this view.[40] They concluded that advertising intensity and profitability are positively related. The results were, however, intensely questioned by other economists who argued that they were due to statistical biases and to an inverse direction of causality between advertising and profitability.[41] They further argued that advertising has exactly the opposite effect on entry conditions and the exercise of market power. By providing information on new products, it permits new firms to grow rapidly and limits the room for manoeuvre for established firms. Today the debate is still going on. Yet three provisional points seem to emerge. First, advertising is not the main source of product differentiation. There are other factors whose effects on purchase behaviour and buyer loyalty is decisive.[42] Second, several models show that over-investment in advertising by established firms under pre-entry conditions does not create a barrier to entry.[43] Third, the nature of consumer response to advertising varies between markets and depends upon product traits and market attributes.[44] By implication, the impact of advertising – if any – on entry barriers is dependent upon the market examined.

The third main type of barriers to entry is economies of scale. The existence of large-scale economies relative to the total market implies that entry at the least-cost scale will add significantly to market supply. Entry will thus depress market price if the existing firms do not reduce their output by an amount equal to the production of the newcomer. If, as assumed by Bain, established firms do not reduce their output, the price may fall below the entrant's unit costs and entry will prove to be unprofitable.[45] In case potential entrants anticipate this impact on price, it is clear that economies of scale act as a barrier to entry and that existing firms can secure prices above minimal average costs without attracting new firms. The scale economies/entry barrier argument has been largely discussed since its first formulation by Bain in the 1950s. An extreme position is taken by Stigler who argues that scale economies do not constitute a barrier to entry because there is no cost difference between established firms and an entrant that has invested in an efficient plant, i.e. on a least-cost scale.[46] A rather similar view is supported by the Theory of Contestable Markets.[47] Nevertheless, a less extreme position emerges from other recent research. Central to the argument on scale economies as the basis of barriers to entry is the assumed reaction of established firms. Bain assumed a Cournot-like behaviour where established firms do not react to new entry, i.e. do not reduce their output after entry. The introduction of more rational hypotheses in recent research tends to support the view that scale economies act as a barrier to entry. For example, Spence argues that entrants may be deterred if established collusive firms build enough capacity to produce the competitive output and threaten to use it if entry occurs.[48] A rather similar conclusion is reached by Dixit.[49] He shows that established firms can deter entry by making irreversible decisions in the form of excess capacity before potential entrants appear. Another basic point that emerges from recent research is that barriers to entry erected by large opportunities for scale economies are of limited quantitative importance.[50]

To identify the presence of market power, empirical analyses have concentrated on diverse dimensions of market structure that are expected to facilitate its exercise. In a second stage, these dimensions, in particular concentration, have been related to some proxy measure of market power. Deficient measures and data, hardly surmountable statistical biases, and erroneous interpretation due to the lack of adequate theoretical guidance seem to have produced misleading results. An important consequence is that empirical research in industrial economics prior to the end of the 1970s has exaggerated the extent of market power.[51] Market power is probably not so widespread in real world markets in industrial countries. Another consequence is an exaggeration of the role of concentration and of the height of the barriers to entry in non-competitive activity. Among the latter, absolute cost disadvantage seems to be most deterring for potential entrants. Note that this barrier to entry often has an institutional origin.

Surveys of empirical studies on the determinants and effects of market power show that their number is much less in western Europe than in the United States.[52] Further, they indicate that market power has become a less popular object of economic research over the past two decades. One of the reasons behind this last fact is probably the recent theoretical developments in the analysis of market structure. In the next section, another reason for this shift in the focus of economic studies will be examined.

INTERNATIONAL INTEGRATION AND MARKET POWER: THE COMPETITIVE STRAITJACKET

Trade liberalization is one of the factors that most contributed to the shape of industrialized economies after the Second World War. The different 'rounds' of world-wide tariff negotiations under the auspices of the GATT and the formation of an enlarged free trade area for industrial products in western Europe have resulted in a continued and very significant decline in tariff levels.[53] By the mid-1980s, the tariff levels on industrial products of the industrialized countries had shrunk to 4.3 per cent in the United States, around 6 per cent in the European Community and 5 per cent in Sweden.[54] By the same date, tariffs on intra-European trade in industrial products had been completely removed.

The suppression of most quotas during the 1950s and the early 1960s and the rapid decline in tariff protection since then have fostered a rapid expansion of international trade. Trade has grown faster than production.[55] The tendency has been particularly striking in western Europe as a result of the formation of the EEC and EFTA. This may be seen in the high degree of openness, as measured by the ratios of total imports to total domestic consumption, and of total exports to total domestic production. Today these ratios amount to around 30 per cent in most west European countries.

How have such changes in the international environment affected the attempts of firms to exercise market power? Trade expansion is responsible for a wide integration of national markets. An opening up to trade and a rise of imports are synonymous with new entry into domestic markets. In other words, trade liberalization means a rapid increase in the number of firms in domestic markets and a higher degree of competition. This rapid increase is partly due to the fact that the usual barriers to entry do not impede foreign entry. Unlike domestic entrants, foreign firms face neither the economies of scale nor the absolute cost disadvantage barriers to entry. Furthermore, they already benefit from a well-established brand image abroad and may thus be better equipped to overcome the brand loyalty barrier to entry. In contrast, however, they face additional barriers to entry in the form of transportation costs, information obstacles, national consumer loyalty and other impediments to trade.

The removal of trade barriers improves market performance by constraining the pricing behaviour of domestic firms. In most cases, it implies that the world competitive price will prevail in the domestic markets after the opening up to trade, except for transport costs and search costs. Thus, firms that displayed differing degrees of market power prior to the opening up to trade can no longer exercise this market power for fear of being driven out of business. Each firm becomes a price-taker on its own domestic market and one more competitor in the world marketplace.

Existing evidence tends to support the view that import competition effectively limits the degree to which firms are able to secure market power. Indeed the overwhelming majority of statistical studies show that import competition exerts a negative and significant effect on industry profit rates.[56] For example, Pagoulatos and Sorensen showed that import competition tends to reduce the price–cost margins of the manufacturing sector in Belgium, France, the Netherlands and West Germany.[57] Similar results were obtained by Turner, Hutchinson, Wahlroos and Jacquemin *et al.* for the United Kingdom, Ireland, Finland and Belgium respectively.[58] Although Canada and the United States are much less exposed to international trade than west European countries, the same significant negative relationship has been found there between import penetration and profitability.[59]

Taken together, all these results seem robust and rather convincing. The failure of the used import/domestic consumption ratio to accurately model the actual strength of import competition throws, nevertheless, some doubt on them. Growing import penetration is not only responsible for a large increase in actual competition but also for a tremendous increase in potential competition. For example, the absence of foreign competitors in a certain number of domestic markets that are not protected against imports does not mean that competition is absent. In such markets, domestic firms fear the entry of foreign competitors and should be sensitive to customers. Their markets are highly contestable and their prices brought down to competitive levels. Therefore, an accurate measure of the intensity of import competition is the elasticity of foreign supply with respect to domestic market price. The use of the import/sale ratio in empirical studies underestimates this intensity and has, probably, biased the results. Another source of error is the inclusion of captive imports, that is, imports by domestic producers, in the import/sale ratio.[60] Obviously, such imports should not be considered because they are controlled by domestic producers and, therefore, do not exert any competitive pressure on them.

A second conclusion emerges from the above studies. The results are, however, disparate and this conclusion should be regarded as tentative. Import competition and seller concentration interact to explain price–cost margins.[61] In other words, import competition seems to affect profitability only in highly concentrated sectors. In other sectors, prices seem to be forced down towards their competitive level by purely domestic competition.[62]

Increased export involvement is another side of trade expansion. The question which arises now is whether export opportunities affect the behaviour of firms that displayed some degree of market power prior to the opening up of trade. Two main cases exist. If the exporting firms cannot discriminate betwen the domestic and foreign markets, the opening up to trade will eliminate domestic market power in the same way as the discipline of import competition.[63] Firms cannot charge a price on export markets that is higher than the competitive world market price. Assuming that exporting firms cannot prevent arbitrage-induced reimports of their own products, they are now forced to behave as competitive firms on their home market as well. On the other hand, if the exporting firms are allowed to discriminate between home and foreign markets, exporting activities will not limit domestic market power. In this case, the degree of departure from competitive prices at home will depend on the demand elasticities in the domestic and foreign markets. Several factors may give firms the opportunity to discriminate: tariff or non-tariff barriers to trade, strict control over their distribution network abroad, asymmetric transport costs, imperfect information or any other form of obstacles to reimport.

Actual statistical results provide disparate evidence on the impact of export activities on domestic market power. The majority of empirical studies found a negative and significant influence of exports on industrial profitability in Canada, France, Italy, Finland and West Germany.[64] Such results can be interpreted to mean that participation in foreign markets dilutes domestic market power.[65] There are, however, other studies whose results run counter to this conclusion. These studies, concerned with Belgium and Britain, exhibit a positive relationship between the rate of exports and the profit margin in the manufacturing sector.[66] A lower degree of monopoly power in the manufacturing sector of these two countries before the opening up to trade and a strong sales increase effect of exports on profitability were put forward to explain this conflicting result. Taken together, the tentative conclusion which emerges is that exports have a certain, albeit not substantial, dampening effect on market power.

A third dimension of the integration of national economies in a world-wide economic system is foreign investment (or multinational activity). This dimension gave rise to heated controversies and intense debates during the 1960s and the early 1970s when US investments were growing in western Europe. The very significant decline of US investments over the past decade and the growth of European investments in the United States during the same period have put an end to much discussion.[67] Contrary to trade expansion, the growth of foreign investment is not the result of the abolition of trade obstacles. It has multiple causes that have been extensively analysed in the economic literature.[68] Impediments to trade, the necessity to adapt the product to local taste, production facilities in the host country, large multi-plant economies of scale, management skills, process and product patent, and other such intangible assets are the factors advanced to explain it. These causes are not our concern as long as they do not influence the effect of foreign investment on market power. Factual observation indicates that oligopolistic and product differentiated industries are the main recipients of foreign investment.[69] As suggested in former sections, competitive pressures are most needed in those industries where there are a priori risks for non-competitive corporate behaviour. This suggests that foreign investment adds a degree of rivalry and competition that could not come from imports. Hence, it probably limits the degree to which domestic firms are able to secure market power.

To test the influence of foreign investment on market power, as measured by profitability, is a difficult task. According to most scholars, foreign investment is a means of internalizing the returns to ownership-specific assets in the presence of significant transaction costs.[70] If true, this suggests that the presence of multinational firms in an industry may both result in high profits and add a degree of rivalry and competition. This may explain some of the unconvincing and disparate results yielded by empirical research. For example, Caves showed that the proportion of the sales of an industry controlled by foreign subsidiaries affects negatively, albeit not significantly, profitability in Canada.[71] A more recent study further illustrated the absence of a direct and unambiguous causal relation between the prevalence of foreign investment and the level of profitability in Canadian industries.[72]

The conclusion to be drawn thus far is that trade liberalization and the integration of national markets have considerably restrained the exercise of market power in the western world. This is definitely true for import competition and probably true for export opportunities and foreign investment. This conclusion is without doubt the main factor behind the lack of attention given to the concept of market power and the very limited number of empirical analyses of market power, especially in western Europe.

The impact of trade expansion and internationalization on competitive conditions is one of the so-called dynamic effects of international integration. Like the dynamic efficiency put forward by Joseph Schumpeter and discussed above, this effect is difficult to measure. This is one of the main reasons behind the small number of empirical studies that attempt to capture its overall role.[73] According to some authors, the dynamic competitive welfare gains are much larger than the static gains of trade expansion.[74] Though this is a debated issue, it is obvious that the dynamic competitive factors affect economic welfare considerably. As illustrated above, international integration restrains market power. It forces firms to adopt a competitive behaviour and brings down prices to competitive levels. Further, it provides an ideal economic climate for innovative activity and economic growth.[75]

The role of dynamic competitive effects should be specially important in industries in which only a small number of firms existed prior to the start of the integration process. This kind of industry structure should be more common in small countries and in industries with large economies of scale: the smaller the country and the larger the economies of scale in an industry, the larger the dynamic competitive gains will be when trade is liberalized. In most branches, the economies of scale are large only in the context of the domestic market but not relative to the world market. Sizeable opportunities for scale economies are therefore unlikely to give rise to high concentration and collusive behaviour at the world level.

The analysis has cast a favourable light upon the impact of international integration on market power. Indeed theoretical and empirical indications show that integration reduces the loss of efficiency due to market power. This reflects the opinion of the great majority of economists who came to regard markets as having become competitive as markets broadened to international scope. Nevertheless, such a view should be somewhat corrected since there is another side of the story. There can be 'market failure' in the international economy. First, growing internationalization, in the form of import penetration or multinational firm entry, may provoke defensive mergers among national firms, tighten the interdependence of oligopolies and facilitate collusive behaviour. Second, a certain number of industries at the world level are dominated by a small number of firms (or actors) whose actions may result in non-competitive prices. The policy of the OPEC countries is the most illustrative example of such a world-wide agreement designed to restrict competition. Third, there are a certain number of non-tariff obstacles to trade that build a form of cordon sanitaire around the domestic markets and allow domestic firms to exercise their market power. The extent of these non-tariff barriers has grown over the past fifteen years, contributing to further isolate domestic markets from the discipline of foreign competition.

The interaction between politics and corporate behaviour is often put forward to explain the emergence of these non-tariff trade barriers. In the next section, we will concentrate on this interplay and see how it affects market conditions and prices.

PRODUCER BEHAVIOUR AND REGULATORY POLICY: THE POWER OVER MARKETS

Over the past three decades, international liberalization and the integration of national economies in a world-wide economy have run parallel to the growth of the public sector. This tendency has been particularly marked in the relatively small west European countries.[76] Whether the growing interventionism is a sort of response to internationalization is beyond the scope of this chapter. Whatever the answer to this question, it is clear that the growth of government intervention in domestic economies has profoundly modified the rules of the game. A new actor, the public sphere, has been given an important and increasing role in the functioning of competition in the marketplace.

Not surprisingly, this change in the institutional setting has been reflected in theoretical research in social science. An illustrative example is the social-organization theory developed by Hernes in the Norwegian Commission of Power.[77] The main merit of this theory is that it extends the dominant paradigms in social science and economics to encompass the interplay between markets, interest groups and politics. Note, however, that the analysis of market power in the Norwegian Study of Power did not make use of this approach to understand the way organized interests obtain and secure market power.[78]

In recent years, economists have also shown a growing interest in the interaction between markets and politics. Rent-seeking can be considered the main manifestation of this growing interest.[79] A central point of this approach is the emphasis put on the interaction between organized producers and the political sphere within the framework of a political market for regulatory measures. Such measures are demanded by particular groups of firms and their associated interest groups in order to get control over supply and to achieve a higher price (or some form of price regulation). They are supplied by politicians and government bureaucrats. Contrary to what is argued by conventional theories of market power, output restriction is not achieved solely by the collusive producers in most real world markets. Market power is secured through regulations and other forms of legal barriers that impede entry and retard the rate of growth of new firms.[80] One implication of this process is that a certain number of decisions are shifted from the market to the political and bureaucratic spheres.

Whatever the political process by which these regulations are achieved, in most cases, they deserve the interest of profit-seeking producers. Regulations and other forms of barriers to entry lead to a price that is higher than the price in absence of public intervention. Hence, they price certain customers out of the market and force the remaining ones to pay a higher price. The former suffer a loss that is a cost to society of this form of market power. The resources used to finance lobbying and organization costs to obtain regulatory measures might have been used to produce goods and services elsewhere in the economy. Thus, they are socially wasteful and add further to the cost to society. This cost is usually spread over a large number of consumers. The high costs of organizing such large groups of consumers, and the fact that the outcome of interventionist policy is of far greater importance to the producer than to the consumer, prevent collective action by consumers from trying to influence public policy in the opposite direction. Note that the decisive role of the public sector implies that this form of market power is enforced with much more coercive power than the collusive producers could exercise privately.

The opportunities given to producers to influence the institutional framework is sometimes called extra-market power. Although the most fruitful theoretical analyses are of American origin, it is generally believed that extra-market power is more important in governing west European economies than it is in the US economy.[81] This may be due to the larger relative size of the public sector in western Europe and the fact that the intensity of rent-seeking activity is directly related to the scope of government intervention in the economy.[82] The question that now arises is what are the factors that facilitate the exercise of this form of market power? This main question can be divided into two sub-questions. First, why are some industries more active in seeking and securing protection and regulation? Second, what are the factors that tend to concentrate public policy to certain industries and interest groups? The reasoning will be mainly illustrated by measures whose purpose is to shelter the domestic markets from world markets, mainly because they are the most effective means to secure domestic market power in open economies.

The attempts of industry to influence public policy depend upon the benefits expected from intervention and the costs of achieving collective action. More precisely, an industry tends to invest in collective action up to the point where the marginal cost of further organized action equals the marginal gains from influencing public policy in its favour. This implies that the likelihood of collusive action depends upon factors that affect its cost–benefit ratio.

The most important cost-related factor is undeniably the number of producers. In industries with only a few firms, it is relatively easy to organize collectively. Co-ordination costs are low. In such industries, firms are very likely to recognize their interdependence and to organize in order to influence market conditions. This can be achieved either through the introduction of special trade barriers or of regulations. The first kind of measure is directed towards foreign competitors, while the second is directed towards foreign as well as domestic potential rivals. Both measures result in a price that is higher than the price prevailing without public intervention. According to Olson, this higher price, i.e. the achievement of market power, can be regarded as a public good since it benefits all sellers in the market.[83]

In many cases, the success of lobbying activity depends upon the degree and form of organization of producer interests. These in turn are dependent upon the number of firms in the industry.[84] The greater the number of firms in an industry, the more difficult it is to form a common interest organization and the less successful lobbying activity is likely to be. On the contrary, the smaller this number, the easier it is to form a common interest organization and the greater the opportunity to secure entry prevention will be. The reason for this is that free-riders are less likely to exist and to deter collective action in the latter case since the incentive to be a free-rider increases with the size of the group. When numbers are small, it is impossible for one or a few firms to adopt a non-cooperative strategy without being detected and sanctioned by other firms.[85]

Historical experience suggests that some large groups also benefit from a high degree of business organization. The agricultural sector is without doubt the most obvious example. An explanation of this apparently contradictory result has been put forward by Olson.[86] Large groups can organize, provided that they can secure selective incentives for members that act to advance the group interest. These incentives may be positive or negative. In the latter case, they take the form of sanctions for non-organized members.[87] Historical evidence indicates, nevertheless, that large groups do not organize spontaneously. It takes time for their professional associations to emerge.[88] According to Olson, an external shock, like an economic crisis or a rapid increase in imports, is necessary for large group members to become aware of their common interests and act collectively.

Although less important, there are other factors that affect the lobbying efforts of an industry.[89] For example, geographic concentration lowers co-ordination costs among producers and improves their ability to organize collectively. Another factor may be the presence of a large proportion of unskilled personnel in the industry's work-force. Their greater difficulties in finding new jobs implies that they add to the management's demand for intervention and increase lobbying activity. On the other hand, there are factors that act in the opposite direction. For example, industries that export a large share of their output are less likely to organize and to lobby for protection for fear of retaliation by foreign countries. Industries that use the regulated product as an input in their production would also be unlikely to support lobbying for protection.

As stated above, the attempts of some industry to influence public policy depend upon the costs of securing collective action and the benefits expected from intervention. Thus, factors that influence the rewards of collective action also influence its likelihood. One of these factors is the price elasticity of demand for the product. Only when this elasticity is low will the industry try to use the state for its purpose. The reason for this is that price changes induced by entry barriers will be very profitable for the industry in such a case. Another factor may be the extent of import competition. The larger the degree of import penetration and the higher the foreign supply elasticity, the more profitable it will be for the industry to have public intervention to limit foreign entry.

Up to now, we have been concerned with the factors that induce organized producers to demand protection against entry. As suggested above, the extent of public assistance also depends upon the factors that induce politicians and bureaucrats to supply entry preventive measures.[90] In each democracy, governments are subject to the re-election constraint. This is true even if governments are assumed to pursue ideological goals. The fear of losing political power encourages governments to undertake policy measures that increase the number of their voters. Clearly, this is a first priority for weak political majorities. The costs of protecting an industry in terms of voters are, in most cases, small because consumers are not organized and the price effect on the item protected is rather diffuse for them. On the other hand, the political benefits may be substantial if the industry that demands protection is large in terms of employment and is a significant government supporter.

Politicians are not the only suppliers of protection. Many protective measures are formulated and implemented by bureaucrats. These measures are mainly of a non-tariff nature (technical rules, administrative practices, etc). Bureaucrats are considered to supply systematically more protection than politicians.[91] They are more devoted to industrial lobbies and interest groups and less dependent upon anti-protection interests. This is partly due to the fact that they are organized along industry lines and are in office to serve an industry or an economic sector. Moreover, unlike politicians, they are not responsible to voters, and thus consumers, for their decisions.

It should be noted that the various determinants of the demand and supply of regulation discussed above do not cover all the forces that shape regulations in a particular country over time. First, it is generally admitted that a deterioration of economic conditions (low rate of growth, bad balance of trade or huge public deficits) increases the supply of protection.[92] The experience of the past decade, i.e. the emergence of the New Protectionism, tends to support this argument. Second, it seems clear that country-specific factors also affect the demand and supply of protection. Examples of such factors are different trade-off relationships between government and industry, different political systems, different divisions of responsibility between government and bureaucrats for trade policy and the presence in some countries of state-owned firms.

The analysis thus far suggests that there are incentives for producers, and often the capacity, to further their interests and secure their market power through the political system. It further suggests that there are also incentives for governments, and the capacity, to further their interests through the economic system. On a priori grounds, we may thus expect the existence of an interplay between markets and politics that affects market conditions and prices through regulations and legal barriers to entry. The question is now whether evidence collected in real world markets substantiates this theory.

Empirical literature on the interaction between organized interests and the public sphere has grown rapidly over the past decade. It can be divided into two main types of study. First, there are many studies of individual markets and industries that examine the way organized interests influence public policy in order to get control over supply and to regulate price formation.[93] Most of these studies are concerned with highly regulated sectors, like agriculture, which are large in terms of employment and where producer interests are well organized, import penetration important and the price elasticity of demand rather low. Because of the complicated nature of most regulations and of their industry-specific nature, these studies provide much insight into the complex way in which the different actors interrelate in the decision-making process. Without doubt, such studies are very appropriate to show how complicated regulations combined with trade barriers secure the dominance of producers in the marketplace.

The second type of study is of a cross-sectional nature. These studies are mainly concerned with the interplay between organized producers and the public sphere in erecting trade barriers.[94] On the whole, the four main conclusions that emerge from these studies support the politico-economic approach discussed above. First, industries with few firms and large numbers of employees benefit from a higher degree of protection. In other words, they are more able to use the state for their purposes. Second, low-wage industries and import-competing industries tend to receive more protection. Third, consumer goods industries are more protected than other industries. This reflects, *inter alia*, the difficulties for consumers to organize effectively in such industries because of their large number.[95] Fourth, industries that benefited from high rates of tariff protection prior to the Kennedy Round now benefit from high non-tariff protection.[96] Obviously, these industries are more able to influence regulatory policy.

Hence a crucial point which emerges from economic studies that integrate the public sphere into their analysis is that public policy often contributes to further the exercise of indirect market power by well-organized producers. An opposite effect can be expected from another form of government policy, namely competition policy, whose purpose is to combat market power. In the next section, we will turn to this issue.

MARKET POWER, PUBLIC POLICY AND CONSUMER PROTECTION: THE LIMITS OF VOICE

Consumers dissatisfied with the price-quality characteristics of a product can express their preferences by either exit or voice. If the market is competitive and the degree of product loyalty low, exit is the dominant option: consumers decrease their purchases of the product and shift to that of another seller.[97] Exit acts as a constraint for firms in competitive markets and secures market efficiency. It expresses the anonymous power of the market over individual firms. Another function of exit is to provide firms with information about consumer preferences for their products and to act as a mechanism of recuperation by inducing recovery on their part. In contrast, if monopoly or collusive behaviour prevails, the exit option is unavailable and the voice option becomes the only recuperation and complaint mechanism. Voice works as a substitute for exit.

Product differentiated markets are characterized by the presence of a non-negligible degree of product loyalty which limits and postpones exit. In such markets, each firm faces a downward sloping demand curve and exit and voice are combined in different proportions. The intensity of the voice option depends mainly upon the availablity of exit. It also depends upon the number of buyers and their ability to take up the voice option. The larger this number, the more difficult it is for buyers to combine for collective action and the less likely that they will be convinced that voice will be effective. A third determinant is the readiness of buyers to complain to express their preferences and of the presence of institutions that can channel complaints effectively.[98] Competition policy can be regarded as a channel for such complaints that minimizes co-ordination costs and improves information about market prices.

The need for competition policy depends upon the availability of exit. Trade liberalization makes it less necessary. It promotes competition and increases the number of firms in the marketplace. It puts pressure on domestic firms by facilitating the exit option. Without doubt, it can be considered the most effective competition policy. An implication is that, on a priori grounds, competition policy is likely to be concerned with only a relatively few aberrations in open economies. These aberrations can be of two sorts. First, it can be those markets that are composed of a small number of firms at the international level and where firms have recognized their interdependence enough to raise their prices significantly above their costs. Second, it can be those markets that are protected against foreign competition by some form of regulation or high transport costs.

One of the motives for studies of market power is the desire to be policy-relevant, i.e. to provide public policies with adequate theoretical guidance. Economic theory points out that market power is harmful to consumers. It prices some customers out of the market and forces others to pay a price that is higher than the competitive price. This cost, the so-called deadweight triangle, is not the only cost. Market power results in other less identifiable costs that were analysed in the previous sections. A main conclusion to emerge from the economic literature is that market power results in social costs whose existence is undeniable although their size can be debated. The function of competition policy is to curb market power in order to remove its harmful effects to consumers. The welfare gains of this policy stem mainly from the elimination of the different social costs.

A limitation of the preceding analysis is that it concentrates on only one sector of the economy and ignores the state of competition in other sectors. This shortcoming, which is common to all partial-equilibrium models, is of crucial importance when it comes to competition policy: it is unclear whether competition policy directed towards one sector will improve or decrease welfare when other sectors are themselves non-competitive.[99] Actually, an economic benefit in a partial-equilibrium framework may be transformed into a loss in a general-equilibrium framework. If non-competitive conditions prevail in other sectors, a policy that restores competition in only one sector may lead to too many resources in this sector, may further contract production in other sectors and may be detrimental to economic welfare. According to the theory of second best, a situation in which more, but not all, of the optimum conditions are fulfilled – perfect competition in every market – is not necessarily superior in welfare terms to a situation in which fewer conditions are fulfilled.[100] Note that this also implies that there is no a priori criteria to evaluate the impact of competition policy in a second best world. Public policy generally ignores this fact. It considers that moves towards perfect competition in a market lead to welfare improvements. In other words, it assumes that changes in this market have negligible implications for most other markets. Although the attitude of economists has varied over time, it should be stressed that second best considerations *per se* have rarely led to *laissez-faire* recommendations on their part when clear non-competitive practices prevail in one market.[101] One reason for this is that the second best nihilism is only based on the allocative costs of market power. It ignores other social costs, such as the opportunity costs of lobbying activities and the X-inefficiency costs, whose elimination is probably beneficial to society. Note, also, that anti-competitive practices lead to an income transfer that may in itself be regarded as undesirable from a welfare standpoint.

Once the purpose and welfare effects of competition policy have been examined, we can now turn to its modes of enforcement. Competition policy is usually divided into two sub-policies, merger policy and restrictive business practices policy. Both aim towards limiting the degree to which firms are able to secure market power. Put differently, their main objective is to police tendencies towards monopoly and collusion. The first sub-policy concentrates on structure while the second is mainly concerned with market conduct.

Merger policy tries to prevent the growth of already large firms to dominant positions. The focus of attention is principally on horizontal mergers which are considered to most enhance the exercise of market power. Since the main purpose of competition policy is to improve social welfare, merger policy should also consider the efficiency gains of mergers through the exploitation of scale and transactional economies. This procedure is associated with the pioneering work of Williamson in 1968 and is known as the trade-off analysis.[102] The basic point of this analysis is to weigh the efficiency gains of mergers against its anti-competitive costs for netting out the welfare gain or loss of a merger. The great majority of economists regards the trade-off approach as adequate theoretical guidance for merger policy. However, there are conflicting opinions concerning the evaluation of social costs. Williamson considers the deadweight triangles the only costs to society of mergers leading to dominant positions.[103] Other economists have put forward other non-negligible costs. The opportunity costs of lobbying activities are social costs as well.[104] Market power generally inflates costs and results in X-inefficiency.[105] Unambiguously, such costs should also be taken into account. Note further, that recent theoretical developments in industrial economics question the anti-competitive behaviour of concentrated market structures (and of large-scale mergers that lead to them) and, thus, the very existence of social costs.[106] When sunk costs are mininal, that is mainly in the service sector, markets are contestable and merger activity is unlikely to bring about non-competitive practices and social costs.

Although it was only at the end of the 1960s that the trade-off approach received its theoretical consecration, merger policy has always been based on,an intuitive trade-off 'rule of reason'. This is in particular true in western Europe where the perceived efficiency gains of mergers have been regarded as more important than the detrimental and more uncertain anti-competitive effects. Such a result is a priori surprising because of the rather tight anti-merger legislation in western Europe and because efficiency considerations are given a trivial role in this legislation.[107] Three factors can be put forward to explain this result. First, efficiency gains were, and still are, expected to be large in western Europe because of the small and inefficient size of many European firms.[108] This fact explains why priority has been accorded to merger-promoting industrial policy, in particular during the 1960s, at the expense of antitrust policy.[109] Note, however, that the conventional wisdom on the inefficient size of European firms has been questioned by empirical studies of the size of plants and by analyses of the role of efficiency in merger activity.[110] Second, the high degree of trade exposure of west European industries is expected to act as a perfect competition straitjacket for individual firms and to police tendencies towards the achievement of market power. A third factor may be the greater influence of producers on public decisions in western Europe, the desire on their part to obtain some further degree of extra-market power and the high costs in relation to the benefits for consumers in obtaining information about a merger and in resisting it.[111]

Policy against restrictive practices constitutes the other part of competition policy. Its main purpose is to prevent undesirable market conduct and the exercise of market power. Its main task is to detect and sanction collusive agreements, such as price-fixing, price leadership, restriction of production, allocation of markets, dumping and predatory pricing. Apart from obvious (easily observable) anti-competitive practices, this task is, however, not so simple as it appears at first sight. A first difficulty arises from the virtual absence of a well accepted and coherent theoretical framework around which policy towards restrictive practices can be designed. Oligopoly is the dominant market form in the real world. In such a market, economic theory tells us that it is difficult to determine when producers recognize their oligopolistic interdependence sufficient to raise their prices significantly above their costs. For practitioners in charge of competition policy, this implies that it is very difficult to say whether observable oligopolistic prices are collusive prices. No doubt the lack of perfect knowledge about the process of price formation contributes to create points of disagreements among practitioners over the existence and the nature of restrictive practices. These points of disagreement concern mainly the definition of market boundaries, the restrictive character of exclusive distribution agreements between producers and dealers, and the anti-competitive nature of certain pricing policies, e.g. price discrimination and price leadership.[112] The second difficulty encountered in the enforcement of restrictive practices laws arises from the lack of reliable information on costs. As indicated above when measures of market power were discussed, such information is necessary to substantiate the existence of restrictive practices. A third difficulty concerns the interpretation of excess profits (as compared to other branches) and the lack of knowledge about the ultimate welfare effects of the various policies actually pursued. Are excess profits the manifestation of market power or of the efficiency of large firms? If the latter explanation is the correct one, a tight competition policy that forces firms to charge lower prices might have undesirable effects on dynamic efficiency. It might prevent firms from appropriating returns from innovations and thus eradicate incentives to innovate. In respect to policy towards anti-competitive practices, all this taken together points out that it is easier to argue against rather than for policy proposals.

All national legislations prohibit collusive agreements that restrict competition and are harmful to consumers.[113] Large differences exist, however, in their enforcement in western Europe. Among the large countries the United Kingdom and, to a lesser extent, West Germany have the tightest restrictive practices policies and enforcement apparatus.[114] In spite of this, relatively few anti-competitive cases have been brought to court in these two countries.[115] Other large west European countries have broadly a lenient policy towards anti-competitive business practices.[116] This is likely to be the result of different relationships between the industry and the state, of different industry characteristics (number of firms, presence of state-owned firms, etc) and of different views about the virtues of competition. The high degree of trade exposure of small countries, like Sweden, reduces the scope for competition policy. This does not mean that restrictive practices are absent in such countries. For example, no less than 200 anti-competitive cases were examined in Sweden in 1986.[117] Among them, only seven were brought to court. The others were remedied through negotiations between the Competition Ombudsman and the firms involved in restrictive practices. The most common of these practices was refusal to supply dealers, followed in order of importance by mergers, different forms of price co-operation and price discrimination.

In addition to its effects on observable non-competitive business conduct, historical experience indicates that policy towards restrictive practices might have had a deterrent effect on producer attempts to collude.[118] Although this is not a demonstrable proposition, it is likely that this portion of competition policy has reduced the frequency of conspiracy and other restrictive practices. Note, however, that a less clear-cut result is suggested by recent research in industrial economics. A tight policy towards 'predatory' pricing, i.e. price below marginal cost, may only lead firms to shift to another entry-preventing instrument.[119] In some cases, it may result in over investment and be welfare decreasing. According to Spence, established firms face a trade-off between prior investment to deter entry and aggressive pricing policy after entry.[120] If competition policy prohibits the second alternative, it is likely that established firms will instead make excess pre-entry investment in production capacity, advertising and new products in order to deter entry.

In the former section, we discussed the role and logic of indirect market power. Further, we argued that the scope of indirect market power has increased over time, as a result of the growing involvement of government in economic life, and that it is enforced with much more power than the collusive producers can exercise privately. Exit is prohibited. Producers who secure protection and influence the terms at which they sell goods and services through non-tariff barriers or government regulations may do so, without fear of competition laws. This form of market power is not a matter for competition policy! The reason behind this stems from the potential conflicts among the various objectives of government intervention. In this case, the conflict is between competition policy and regulatory policy. The latter was illustrated in the previous section, where we showed that there are political reasons for governments to help firms and industries to secure market power positions by, for example, limiting import penetration.

Another source of conflict may be industrial policy and the desire to promote exports. Monopolists or collusive oligopolists who can discriminate between the domestic and foreign markets export a larger share of their production.[121] This implies that governments that want to promote exports may be willing to provide firms with some degree of domestic market power. A final example of the potential conflicts between government objectives is that of price control policies, which have been applied in several countries in order to combat inflation. The Swedish experience shows that these policies have furthered co-operation among producers and distorted competition.[122] These three examples support the view that, in many cases, the promotion of competition on the domestic markets and the maximization of consumer welfare may not be a government priority. Market power is tolerated if it brings government some form of benefit. No doubt there are government measures that create market power where it did not previously exist.

The purpose of competition policy is to encourage a system of competitive markets and to enhance consumer welfare. Potential conflicts between the different objectives of public intervention, lack of perfect knowledge about the process of price formation under less than competitive conditions and about the ultimate welfare effects of market power, and points of disagreements over the enforcement of restrictive practices regulations cast some doubt on the adequacy of competition policy to effectively combat market power. The voice option, as it is reflected by present competition policies, is not enough to achieve the desired competitive outcomes. Unambiguously, the availability of exit is a better safeguard against market power. In order to secure consumer protection, theoretical and empirical considerations militate in favour of a combination of competition and free-trade policies that gives a much greater place to the latter.[123] This is a widely accepted belief of economists.[124]

MARKET POWER IN THE OPEN ECONOMY: DESIGN FOR RESEARCH

The aim in writing this chapter has been to provide an analytical background against which to set the empirical pieces of evidence that will follow. A certain number of topics that have dominated past and recent economic research on the origin, logic and impact of market power have been focused upon. In this final section, a certain number of crucial issues that may further contribute to the understanding of market power in modern economies will be briefly examined. It is hoped that the empirical studies that follow in the succeeding chapters will shed some light on these issues. Their focus is on the Swedish economy, even if comparative aspects are not absent. In this final section, we also discuss the sectors and markets of the Swedish economy that these studies investigate.

A first issue concerns the role of concentration. As indicated in the section on market power and economic welfare (pp. 7–13), the role devoted to concentration in the emergence of market power seems to have been exaggerated. Both theoretical and empirical evidence tends to support this view. In spite of this, the role of concentration is often addressed in the public debate. This fact, plus the absence of a well accepted alternative paradigm, militates in favour of further research and against the definitive rejection of cross-sectional studies of the concentration–profitability relationship. Empirical studies should attempt to answer three main questions. The first is whether concentration has increased over the past decades. In view of the high degree of trade exposure of the Swedish markets, accounting for foreign trade is necessary to such a study. (There is, however, a reason for the focus of attention on industry concentration instead of market concentration. As illustrated in the section on producer behaviour and regulatory policy (pp. 25–31), a high level of industry concentration seems to facilitate the exercise of indirect market power.) The focus of attention on concentration is only interesting if a positive relationship exists between market concentration and market power. A second task of empirical studies is thus to see whether the level of profitability can be related to the level of concentration in the Swedish industrial sector. A third task is to analyse whether the existence of a positive relationship is a manifestation of the presence of market power. (Note that the importance of sunk costs in industry means that industrial markets are far from being contestable.) As argued in this chapter, much attention must be given to the formulation of the model used to test the relationship, to the accounting for international competition and to the interpretation of the statistical results. The two chapters in Part II of this book address these questions and provide much information on the complex relationship between structure and performance in an open economy.

A second issue is the international dimension of competition. In the section on international integration and market power (pp. 20–5), it was argued that international competition acts as a competitive straitjacket for domestic firms. It is also indicated that this might not hold for industries composed of only a small number of firms at the international level. This is a crucial topic. Empirical evidence about the oligopolistic interaction at the international level is fragmentary and inconclusive. This interaction is likely to vary according to the nature of the industry and the institutional context. It should be more common in mature industries, where it is likely to give rise to market inter-penetration behaviour and intra-industry trade,[125] than in industries that have only reached the introduction or growth phase. Furthermore, oligopolistic interaction is likely to be different in industries based on natural resources and in foot-loose industries, where entry is much easier and products differentiated. The purpose of empirical studies will be to substantiate these aspects, to acquire some knowledge of how entry deterrence is managed by firms and how markets are segmented, and to see how all this affects competitive conditions and prices in various markets of the Swedish economy. Another purpose will be to study whether such oligopolistic industries are organized at the international level and to examine the institutional ways in which groups of firms acquire and maintain positions of market power. No doubt this issue is highly topical due to the increasing integration of the west European economies and because of the growing role in this area of an institutional framework, the EEC Commission, which has opened up opportunites for different forms of rent-seeking. Case studies seem to us the most appropriate method to capture these features because industries and markets are far too complex and varied to permit cross-sectional studies and to derive general rules.

This raises the question regarding which sectors of the Swedish economy should be analysed? A priority should be to concentrate on those markets that most affect private consumption rather than evaluate the general scope of market power in the economy. Many durable consumer goods are produced by oligopolistic firms in mature and differentiated industries. These goods account for a non-negligible share of private consumption. The studies in Part III of this book concentrate on the white goods, the pharmaceutical and the passenger car industries. The analysis of corporate behaviour in these industries permit one to illustrate oligopolistic interaction at the international level.

In the preceding sections, we have shown that market power takes a variety of forms and can be gained in many ways. Note that we have deliberately shifted the discussion from direct to indirect market power as the discussion proceeded. This is mainly due to the fact that the latter kind of market power has become more important because of the growing role of government in industrial economies. This institutional change has opened up opportunities for pressure groups that did not exist prior to the Second World

War. Another factor behind the relatively more dominant role of indirect market power has been the increasing integration of the Swedish economy in the world economy over the past three decades. As suggested on pp. 20–5, direct market power has become less of a problem as markets have broadened to international scope. Hence, the third issue is that of indirect market power. It is concerned with the interplay between organized producers, interest groups and the political sphere in affecting market conditions and prices.

The main purpose of the empirical studies in Part IV of the book is to provide some insight into the ways in which individual firms and groups of firms affect quantities and prices through regulations. As pointed out above, empirical studies of individual markets should preferably focus on those markets that most affect living conditions. In respect to the present issue, another criterion of selection is to concentrate on those markets where the interplay between politics and organized interests is at work. The agricultural and food sectors are unavoidable examples since they account for an important share of family budgets and are characterized by active pressure groups and extensive political intervention. The poor performance of Swedish food markets in terms of prices, as compared with corresponding (west European) markets, further justifies this choice. Obviously, the textile industry is another candidate because it also fulfils these two criteria. A third example is the airline industry where there is an interplay between organized producers and politics to control entry and regulate prices.

Another priority should be to determine the opportunities that exist for citizens, individually or in groups, to influence market power and their living conditions. This raises the question of competition policy and the way this may influence consumer welfare. This is the topic of the two chapters in Part V. Two issues are examined. The first concerns the way competition policy is enforced. Several questions can be raised to delimit this issue. How have the resources of the Swedish competition authorities been utilized? What kinds of non-competitive cases have characterized its enforcement efforts? Have more resources been devoted to structure cases or to conduct cases? Has the mix of cases changed over time as a result of changes in trade exposure? What other factors determine this mix? On a priori grounds, the most likely candidates are the size of the welfare effects, the chances of success of the enforcement procedure and the cases that maximize the budget of the Commission. Another significant question is whether it is possible to relate anti-competitive cases to the characteristics of the industries prosecuted, e.g. the degree of trade exposure, the degree of concentration, the nature of the product, etc? Such questions cannot be answered solely on the basis of a priori reasoning. Obviously, the answers lie in an empirical analysis of the policy of the Swedish Monopolies and Restrictive Practices Commission. A conclusion to be derived from such an analysis concerns the suitability of the Commission to attack economic ills, to effectively channel voice and to secure consumer protection.

The relation between competition policy and economic efficiency constitutes another crucial issue that is examined in Part V. Empirical knowledge is needed on the trade-off between social costs and efficiency gains from increased concentration and on the factors that influence it. In particular more information on the extent of economies of scale from a *dynamic* perspective is necessary for an evaluation of the social costs at stake. No doubt the answers given to these questions are highly relevant to the formulation of competition policy, in particular anti-merger policy, and to consumer welfare.

NOTES

* Thanks are due to Stephen Martin, Dennis Mueller, Inga Persson and Nils-Olov Stålhammar for their comments and suggestions on a preliminary version.

1 Bain (1950), ch. 14 and Shepherd (1979), pp. 173–7.
2 See, for example, Nightingale (1978), pp. 31–40.
3 Shepherd (1979), pp. 173–7.
4 Schumpeter (1942), *Capitalism, Socialism and Democracy*, New York: Harper, especially pp. 83–106.
5 See e.g. Lukes (1974), Boulding (1989), ch. 1 and Perroux (1974), ch. II.
6 OECD (1979). A Swedish example is the concentration study made during the second half of the 1960s (SOU (1968:5)). Still another example is the concentration study made in Norway within the framework of the Norwegian Commission of Power (NOU (1978)).
7 For a more complete description of the conventional approach, see any textbook in microeconomics.
8 Several empirical studies of mergers have shown the importance of this motive. See, for example, De Jong (1976), pp. 95–123, and George and Silberston (1976), pp. 124–42.
9 Instability in oligopolistic market structures is confirmed by real world experience. This shows that, in such markets, periods of intense competition generally alternate with attempts to control and regulate sales. The breakdown of most cartels in raw material world markets

constitutes the most illustrative example of the fragility of oligopoly. See, for example, Nappi (1979), pp. 178–9 and 185–8.

10 On this aspect, see Stigler (1964).

11 For a survey of the different models of oligopoly, see Scherer (1980), chs 5–8.

12 On these aspects, see the pioneering work of Tullock (1967) and Posner (1975).

13 Leibenstein (1976), pp. 29–47.

14 Scherer (1980), pp. 464–6 and Shepherd (1979), pp. 378–81.

15 A counter-argument is that only enduring market power allows for larger profits, significant R&D investments and innovation. See Galbraith (1956), pp. 86–7.

16 Baumol, Panzar and Willig, *On the Theory of Perfectly Contestable Markets* in Staglitz and Mathewson (1986), pp. 339–65 and Jacquemin (1985), ch. III.

17 Empirical research suggests that sunk costs are ubiquitous for real world firms and that the conditions for perfect contestability are very rarely satisfied. See, for example, the analysis of the airline market, which the advocates of the Theory of Contestable Markets consider one of the best examples of a contestable market (Hurdle *et al.* (1989), pp. 119–39).

18 Lerner (1934).

19 Other measures of market power, such as the Rothschild, Papandreou and Bain indices suffer from the same practical problems. See Asch (1970), pp. 138–47.

20 On these aspects, see the pioneering work of Bain (1954), pp. 15–39.

21 On the history of the field of Industrial Economics, see Shepherd (1979), pp. 13–25.

22 Saving (1970), Cowling and Waterson (1976) and Encaoua and Jacquemin (1980). See also Simonin (1980).

23 Jacquemin (1985), p. 64.

24 Bain (1951). Surveys of statistical studies on the relation between concentration and some dimension of performance, in most cases profits, are available in Weiss (1971), Scherer (1980), ch. 9, Shepherd (1979), ch. 13, Sawyer (1981), ch. 6 and Schmalensee (1989), ch. 16.

25 See, for example, Sawyer (1981), pp. 94–7, Jacquemin and De Jong (1977), pp. 142–4, Jenny and Weber (1974), pp. 117–34, and Cars (1975), ch. II.

26 Sawyer (1981), pp. 92–3 and 98–9 and Weiss (1974), pp. 204–15.

27 See Sawyer (1981), pp. 92–3.

28 See, for example, Marfels (1974), Marfels (1975), Linda (1976) and Schmalensee (1977).

29 For a survey of concentration studies in OECD countries, see OECD (1979).

30 Demsetz (1973), pp. 1–9, Demsetz (1974), pp. 164–84, and Demsetz (1982), pp. 32–6.

31 Demsetz (1974), pp. 177–81.

32 See Brozen (1973), pp. 59–70 and Peltzman (1977), pp. 229–63.

33 See Peltzman (1977), pp. 229–63. In a recent study, it is shown that concentration and efficiency constitute complementary rather than

competitive explanations of higher profits (Martin (1988)).
34 Sawyer (1981), pp. 92–3 and 98–9 and Weiss (1974), pp. 204–15.
35 Severe criticism was also raised against the barriers to entry variables used in empirical studies. It was in particular directed toward the advertising–sales ratio, as a measure of product differentiation, and the average size of the largest plants divided by total output, as a measure of economies of scale.
36 Bain (1956) and Bain (1968), pp. 252–69.
37 Bain (1956), p. 216 and Schmalensee (1986), p. 387.
38 Bain (1956), ch. 4 and Schmalensee (1982), pp. 267–77.
39 See Comanor and Wilson (1974), ch. 4, Comanor and Wilson (1979) and Shepherd (1979), pp. 369–71.
40 Sawyer (1981), ch. 7, Comanor and Wilson (1979) and Mann (1974), pp. 137–56.
41 Brozen (1974), pp. 115–37. Typically, simultaneous equation studies show a positive impact of advertising on profitability (see for example Martin (1979)).
42 Schmalensee (1982), p. 278.
43 Schmalensee (1986), pp. 385–92.
44 Schmalensee (1982), pp. 277–8.
45 On the relation between economies of scale and barriers to entry, see Scherer (1980), pp. 244–5.
46 Stigler (1968), pp. 67–70.
47 Baumol, Panzar and Willig, *On the Theory of Perfectly Contestable Markets* in Stiglitz and Mathewson (1986), pp. 339–65.
48 Spence (1977), pp. 534–44, and Spence (1981), pp. 51–60.
49 Dixit (1980), pp. 20–32.
50 Schmalensee (1981), pp. 1235–6.
51 For a conflicting view, see Cowling and Mueller (1978).
52 Sawyer (1981), pp. 90–102 and Scherer (1980), ch. 9.
53 See, for example, Bhagwati (1988), pp. 3–4.
54 Deardorff and Stern (1983), p. 606.
55 See, for example, Beenstock and Warburton (1983), pp. 130–5.
56 For a survey of empirical studies, see Pagoulatos and Sorensen (1980), pp. 308–12 and Caves (1979), pp. 55–8.
57 Pagoulatos and Sorensen (1976a), pp. 255–67.
58 Turner (1980), pp. 155–66, Hutchinson (1981), pp. 247–67, Wahlroos (1980), ch. 3, and Jacquemin *et al.* (1980), pp. 131–44.
59 Esposito and Esposito (1971), pp. 343–53, Pagoulatos and Sorensen (1976b), pp. 45–59, Pugel (1980), pp. 119–29, Caves *et al.* (1980), ch. 9, and Marvel (1980), pp. 103–22.
60 Captive imports have grown rapidly over the past decade. Their extent varies widely from market to market. For an example concerned with the west European passenger car markets, see Bourdet (1988), p. 63. On this issue, see also Geroski and Jacquemin (1982).
61 Caves *et al.* (1980), ch. 9, Jacquemin *et al.* (1980), pp. 131–44, Pugel (1980), pp. 119–29, and Turner (1980), pp. 155–66.
62 Another reason for the tentative nature of this conclusion is the deficient measures of concentration used in these studies.
63 See, for example, Caves and Jones (1985), p. 168.

44   *Internationalization, market power and consumer welfare*

64 For brief surveys of the empirical literature, see Caves (1979), pp. 59–60, and Jacquemin (1982), p. 84.
65 Pagoulatos and Sorensen (1976a), pp. 262–6, Jenny and Weber (1974), pp. 126–30, Caves *et al.* (1980), ch. 9, Neuman *et al.* (1979), and Wahlroos (1980), ch. 3.
66 Caves and Khalilzadeh-Shirazi (1977), pp. 111–28, and Geroski (1982).
67 On changes over time in US investments abroad, see Ruffin (1984), pp. 240–5.
68 See, for example, Caves (1971), pp. 1–27, SOU (1975:50), pp. 105–73, and Caves (1982), ch. 2.
69 Caves (1971), pp. 8–13, and Pagoulatos and Sorensen (1980), pp. 312–15.
70 Ruffin (1984), p. 248.
71 Caves (1974), pp. 178–84.
72 Caves *et al.* (1980), 241–3.
73 See Robson (1980), pp. 31–2 and Scitovsky (1958), pp. 123–30.
74 Leibenstein (1976), ch. 3.
75 Zimmermann (1987), pp. 84–5.
76 Katzenstein (1985), pp. 47–70.
77 For a presentation, see Gorpe and Hägg (1983), pp. 141–55.
78 NOU (1978:33).
79 For an introduction, see Buchanan, Tollison and Tullock (1980).
80 Stigler (1971), pp. 3–6.
81 See, for example, Jacquemin and de Jong (1977), p. 156, and Hollingsworth and Lindberg (1985), p. 224.
82 Buchanan (1980), p. 9.
83 Olson (1982), p. 19.
84 Olson (1965), p. 143.
85 On the free-rider principle, see Mueller, pp. 14–18, and Stigler (1974), pp. 359–65.
86 Olson (1965), p. 51.
87 For an example of negative selective incentives, see Bolin, Meyerson and Ståhl (1986), pp. 72–3.
88 Olson (1983), p. 17.
89 See Pincus (1975), p. 758, Anderson and Baldwin (1981), pp. 5–9, Frey (1984), pp. 24–31, and Baldwin (1982), pp. 263–78.
90 See Baldwin (1989), Frey (1984), pp. 32–4, and Anderson and Baldwin (1981), pp. 10–13, Baldwin (1982), pp. 267–73.
91 See Messerlin (1981), pp. 480–7, and Frey (1985), pp. 148–9.
92 Takacs (1981), pp. 687–93.
93 See, for example, Hedlund and Lundahl (1985), and Bolin, Meyerson and Ståhl (1986), Cable (1983), Bourdet (1988), Verreydt and Waelbroeck (1982), pp. 369–93.
94 Anderson and Baldwin (1981), pp. 17–20, Frey (1985), pp. 149–55, Lundberg (1981), pp. 12–16 and Messerlin (1982), 1003–14.
95 Marvel and Ray (1983), pp. 190–7.
96 Ibid.
97 Hirschman (1970), chs 2 and 3.
98 Ibid., p. 43.
99 Jacquemin and de Jong (1977), pp. 139–40, and Asch (1970), pp. 114–17.

100 Asch (1970), pp. 115, and Lipsey and Lancaster (1956), p. 301.
101 Swann (1979), pp. 102–3.
102 Williamson (1968), pp. 18–36, Williamson (1977), pp. 237–71, and Cowling *et al.* (1980), pp. 16–39.
103 Ibid.
104 Posner (1975), pp. 71–94.
105 Swann (1979), p. 138.
106 Baumol, Panzar and Willig, *On the Theory of Perfectly Contestable Markets* in Stiglitz and Mathewson (1986), pp. 339–65.
107 Walsh and Paxton (1975), chs 6 and 7, OECD (1984b), pp. 11–49.
108 For a Swedish illustration, see Hjalmarsson (1976).
109 Bourdet (1988), pp. 98–103.
110 Scherer *et al.* (1975), p. 382, Scherer (1974), pp. 186–90, Cowling *et al.* (1980), pp. 369–72, and Mueller (1980), pp. 323–4. A slightly different opinion on the role of economies of scale as a determinant for mergers emerges from a study of merger activity in Sweden. See Rydén and Edberg (1980), pp. 205–6.
111 See Scherer (1974), pp. 181–97, Arndt (1976), p. 46, and Schmidt (1981), p. 503.
112 For an illustration of the disagreements between lawyers and economists over competition policy, see Katzmann (1980), ch. 4, and Stigler (1982), pp. 1–11.
113 Walsh and Paxton (1975), chs 6 and 7.
114 Sawyer (1981), pp. 245–9, and Schmidt (1981), pp. 491–503.
115 Ibid.
116 Jenny and Weber (1975), pp. 597–639, and Bianchi (1981), pp. 449–64.
117 SPK (1987), p. 43.
118 Spence (1981), pp. 46–7, and George and Joll (1975), pp., 195–6.
119 Spence (1981), pp. 55–6.
120 Ibid., p. 56.
121 Södersten (1978), pp. 130–1, and White (1974), pp. 1013–20.
122 Jonung (1984), pp. 248–55.
123 Another advantage of a liberal trade policy as a ready-made alternative to competition policy is that is does not incur administering costs (no antitrust authorities).
124 See, for example, Spence (1981), pp. 83–4.
125 Toh (1982), pp. 284–6, and Caves (1981), pp. 203–23.

REFERENCES

Anderson, K. and Baldwin, R. (1981) *The Political Market for Protection in Industrial Countries: Empirical Evidence*, no. 492, Washington: World Bank Staff Working Paper.
Archibald, G.C. (ed.) (1971) *The Theory of the Firm*, Baltimore: Penguin Books Inc.
Arnt, H. (1976) 'Power and competition', in A. Jacquemin and H. de Jong (eds) *Markets, Corporate Behaviour and the State*, The Hague: Martinus Nijhoff.

Asch, P. (1970) *Economic Theory and the Antitrust Dilemma*, New York: John Wiley & Sons.

Bain, J. (1950) 'Workable competition in oligopoly: theoretical considerations and some empirical evidence', *American Economic Review*, 40, reprinted in J. Bain (1972) *Essays in Price Theory and Industrial Organization*, Boston: Little, Brown and Company.

Bain, J. (1951) 'Relation of profit rate to indusry concentration: American manufacturing, 1936–1940, *Quarterly Journal of Economics*, 65, reprinted in J. Bain (1972) *Essays on Price Theory and Industrial Organization*, Boston: Little, Brown and Company.

Bain, J. (1954) 'Economies of scale, concentration, and the conditions of entry in twenty manufacturing industries', *American Economic Review*, 44.

Bain, J. (1956) *Barriers to New Competition*, Cambridge, MA: Harvard University Press.

Bain, J. (1968) *Industrial Organization*, New York: John Wiley & Sons.

Baldwin, R. (1982) 'The political economy of protection', in J. Bhagwati (ed.), *Import Competition and Response*, Chicago: University of Chicago Press.

Baldwin, R. (1989) 'The political economy of trade policy', *Journal of Economic Perspectives*, 3.

Beenstock, M. and Warburton, P. (1983) 'Long-term trends in economic openness in the United Kingdom and the United States', *Oxford Economic Papers*, 35.

Bhagwati, J. (1988) *Protectionism*, Cambridge, MA: The MIT Press.

Bianchi, P. (1981) 'Price control in Italy', *Annals of Public and Co-operative Economy*, 52.

Bolin, O., Meyerson, P.M. and Ståhl, I. (1986) *The Political Economy of the Food Sector*, Stockholm: SNS förlag.

Boulding, K. (1989) *Three Faces of Power*, London: Sage.

Bourdet, Y. (1988) *International Integration, Market Structure and Prices*, London and New York: Routledge.

Brozen, Y. (1973) 'Concentration and profits: does concentration matter?', in J.F. Weston and S. Ornstein (eds) *The Impact of Large Firms on the US Economy*, Lexington: Lexington Books.

Brozen, Y. (1974) 'Entry barriers: advertising and product differentiation', in H. Goldschmid, M. Mann and F. Weston (eds), *Industrial Concentration: The New Learning*, Boston: Little, Brown and Company.

Buchanan, J. (1980) 'Rent seeking and profit seeking', in J. Buchanan, R. Tollison and G. Tullock (eds), *Toward a Theory of the Rent-Seeking Society*, College Station: Texas A & M University Press.

Buchanan, J., Tollison, R. and Tullock, G. (1980) *Towards a Theory of the Rent-Seeking Society*, College Station: Texas A & M University Press.

Cable, V. (1983) *Protectionism and Industrial Decline*, London: Hodder & Stoughton.

Cars, H.C. (1975) *Koncentration and fördelningsproblem inom marknadsekonomin*, Stockholm: Almqvist & Wiksell International.

Caves, R. (1971) 'International corporations: the industrial economics of foreign investment', *Economica*, 38.

Caves, R. (1974) 'Multinational firms, competition and productivity in host-country markets', *Economica, 41*.

Caves, R. (1979) 'International cartels and monopolies in international trade', in R. Dornbusch and J. Frenkel (eds), *International Economic Policy: Theory and Evidence*, Baltimore: Johns Hopkins University Press.

Caves, R. (1981) 'Intra-industry trade and market structure', *Oxford Economic Papers, 33*.

Caves, R. (1982) *Multinational Enterprises and Economic Analysis*, Cambridge: Cambridge University Press.

Caves, R. and Jones, R. (1985) *World Trade and Payments*, fourth edn, Boston: Little, Brown and Company.

Caves, R. and Khalilzadeh-Shirazi, J. (1977) 'International trade and industrial organization: some statistical evidence', in A. Jacquemin and H. de Jong *Welfare Aspects of Industrial Markets*, Leiden: Nijhoff.

Caves, R., Porter, M., Spence, M. and Scott, J. (1980) *Competition in the Open Economy, A Model Applied to Canada*, Cambridge, MA: Harvard University Press.

Comanor, W. and Wilson, T. (1974) *Advertising and Market Power*, Cambridge, MA: Harvard University Press.

Comanor, W. and Wilson, T. (1979) 'The effect of advertising on competition: a survey', *Journal of Economic Literature, 17*.

Cowling, K. and Mueller, D. (1978) 'The social costs of monopoly power', *Economic Journal, 88*.

Cowling, K. and Waterson, M. (1976) 'Price–cost margins and market structure', *Economica, 43*.

Cowling, K., Paul Stoneman, J., Cubbin, J., Cable, J., Hall, G., Domberger, S. and Dutton, P. (1980) *Mergers and Economic Performance*, Cambridge: Cambridge University Press.

Dalton, J. and Levin, S. (1974) *The Antitrust Dilemma*, Lexington: Lexington Books.

Deardorff, A. and Stern, R. (1983) 'Economic effects of the Tokyo Round', *Southern Economic Journal, 49*.

De Jong, H. (1976) 'Theory and evidence concerning mergers: an international comparison', in A. Jacquemin and H. de Jong *Markets, Corporate Behaviour and the State*, The Hague: Nijhoff.

De Jong, H. (1981) *The Structure of European Industry*, The Hague: Nijhoff.

Demsetz, H. (1973) 'Industry structure, market rivalry and public policy', *Journal of Law and Economics, 16*.

Demsetz, H. (1974) 'Two systems of belief about monopoly', in H. Goldschmid, Mann and Weston (eds) (1974) *Industrial Concentration: The New Learning*, Boston: Little, Brown and Company.

Demsetz, H. (1982) *Economic, Legal and Political Dimensions of Competition*, Amsterdam: North-Holland.

Dixit, A. (1980) 'The role of investment in entry-deterrence', *Economic Journal, 90*.

Encaoua, D. and Jacquemin, A. (1980) 'Degree of monopoly, indices of concentration and threat of entry', *International Economic Review, 21*.

Esposito, L. and Esposito, F. (1971) 'Foreign competition and domestic industry profitability', *Review of Economics and Statistics, 53*.

Frey, B. (1984) *International Political Economics*, Oxford: Basil Blackwell.

Frey, B. (1985) 'The political economy of protection', in D. Greenaway (ed.) *Current Issues in International Trade, Theory and Policy*, London: Macmillan.

Galbraith, J.K. (1956) *American Capitalism*, Boston: Houghton Mifflin.

George, K. and Joll, C. (1975) *Competition Policy in the UK and EEC*, Cambridge: Cambridge University Press.

George, K. and Silberston, A. (1976) 'The causes and effects of mergers', in A. Jacquemin and H. de Jong, *Mergers, Corporate Behaviour and the State*, The Hague: Nijhoff.

Geroski, P. (1982) 'Simultaneous equation models of the structure performance paradigm', *European Economic Review, 19*.

Geroski, P. and Jacquemin, A. (1982) 'Imports as a competitive discipline', *Recherches Economiques de Louvain, 47*.

Goldschmid, H., Mann, M. and Weston, F. (1974) *Industrial Concentration: The New Learning*, Boston: Little, Brown and Company.

Gorpe, P. and Hägg, I. (1983) 'Förhandlingsekonomi och blandadministration', in L. Arvedson, I. Hägg and B. Rydén (eds) *Land i olag, Samhällsorganisation under omprövning*, Stockholm: SNS.

Hedlund, S. and Lundahl, M. (1985) *Beredskap eller protektionism?*, Malmö: Liber Förlag.

Hirschmann, A. (1970) *Exit, Voice and Loyalty, Responses to Decline in Firms, Organizations, and States*, Cambridge, MA: Harvard University Press.

Hjalmarsson, L. (1976) 'On monopoly welfare gains, scale efficiency and the costs of decentralization', *Empirical Economics, 1*.

Hollingsworth, R. and Lindberg, L. (1985) 'The governance of the American economy: the role of markets, clans, hierarchies, and associate behaviour', in W. Streeck and P. Schmitter *Private Interest Government, Beyond Market and State*, London: Sage.

Hurdle, G., Johnson, R., Joskow, A., Werden, G. and Williams, M. (1989) 'Concentration, potential entry, and performance in the airline industry', *Journal of Industrial Economics, 38*.

Hutchinson, R. (1981) 'Price–cost margins and manufacturing industry structure, the case of a small economy with bilateral trade in manufactured goods', *European Economic Review, 16*.

Jacquemin, A. (1982) 'Imperfect market structure and international trade – some recent research', *Kyklos, 35*.

Jacquemin, A. (1985) *Sélection et Pouvoir dans la Nouvelle Économie Industrielle*, Paris: Economica.

Jacquemin, A. and de Jong, H. (1977) *European Industrial Organisation*, London: Macmillan.

Jacquemin, A., De Ghellinck, E. and Huveneers, C. (1980) 'Concentration and profitability in a small open economy', *Journal of Industrial Economics, 24*.

Jenny, F. and Weber, A. (1974) *Concentration et Politique des Structures Industrielles*, Préface de E. Malinvaud, Paris: La documentation française.

Jenny, F. and Weber, A. (1975) 'French antitrust legislation: an exercise in futility?', *The Antitrust Bulletin, 20*.

Jonung, L. (1984) *Prisregleringen, företagen och förhandlingsekonomi*, Stockholm: SNS.

Katzenstein, P. (1985) *Small States in World Markets, Industrial Policy in Europe*, Ithaca and London: Cornell University Press.

Katzmann, R. (1980) *Regulatory Bureaucracy: The Federal Trade Commission and Antitrust Policy*, Cambridge, MA: The MIT Press.

Leibenstein, H. (1976) *Beyond Economic Man*, Cambridge, MA: Harvard University Press.

Lerner, A.P. (1934) 'The concept of monopoly and the measurement of monopoly power', *Review of Economic Studies, 1*.

Linda, R. (1976) *Methodology of Concentration Analysis applied to the Study of Industries and Markets*, Brussels: Commission of the European Communities.

Lipsey, R. and Lancaster, K. (1956) 'The general theory of second best', *Review of Economic Studies, 24*.

Lukes, S. (1974) *Power, A Radical View*, London: Macmillan.

Lundberg, L. (1981) *Patterns of Barriers to Trade in Sweden: A Study in the Theory of Protection*, no. 494, Washington: World Bank Staff Working Paper.

Lustgarten, S. (1984) *Productivity and Prices, The Consequences of Industrial Concentration*, Washington: American Enterprise Institute for Public Policy Research.

Mann, M. (1974) 'Advertising, concentration, and profitability', in H. Goldschmid, M. Mann and F. Weston (eds) *Industrial Concentration: The New Learning*, Boston: Little, Brown and Company.

Marfels, C. (1974) 'A new look at the structure of oligopoly', *Zeitschrift für die gesamte Staatswissenschaft*, 130 Band.

Marfels, C. (1975) 'A bird's eye view to measures of concentration', *The Antitrust Bulletin, 20*.

Martin, S. 'Advertising, concentration and profitability: the simultaneity problem', *Bell Journal of Economics, 10*.

Martin, S. (1988) 'Market power and/or efficiency', *The Review of Economics and Statistics, 70*.

Marvel, H. (1980) 'Foreign trade and domestic competition', *Economic Inquiry, 18*.

Marvel, H. and Ray, E. (1983) 'The Kennedy Round: evidence on the regulation of international trade in the United States', *American Economic Review, 75*.

Messerlin, P. (1981) 'The political economy of protectionism: the bureaucratic case', *Weltwirtschaftliches Archiv, 67*.

Messerlin, P. (1982) 'Les déterminants de la demande de protection: le cas français', *Revue Économique, 33*.

Mueller, D. (1979) *Public Choice*, Cambridge: Cambridge University Press.

Mueller, D. (ed.) (1980) *The Determinants and Effects of Mergers*, Cambridge, MA: Oelgeschlager, Gunn & Hain.

Nappi, C. (1979) *Commodity Market Controls, A Historical Review*, Lexington: Lexington Books.

Neuman, M., Bebel, I. and Haid, A. (1979) 'Profitability, risk and market structure in West German industries', *Journal of Industrial Economics, 27*.

50   *Internationalization, market power and consumer welfare*

Nightingale, J. (1978) 'On the definition of "industry" and "market" ', *Journal of Industrial Economics*, 27.

NOU (Norges Offentlige Utredninger) (1978:33) *Maktutredningen*, Om konsentrasjon og marknadsmakt, Oslo: Universitetforlaget.

OECD (1979) *Concentration and Competition Policy*, Paris: OECD.

OECD (1984a) *Competition and Trade Policies, Their Interaction*, Paris: OECD.

OECD (1984b) *Merger Policies and Recent Trends in Mergers*, Paris: OECD.

Olson, M. (1965) *The Logic of Collective Action*, Cambridge, MA: Harvard University Press.

Olson, M. (1982) *The Rise and Decline of Nations*, New Haven: Yale University Press.

Olson, M. (1983) 'The political economy of comparative growth rates', in D. Mueller (ed.) *The Political Economy of Growth*, New Haven: Yale University Press.

Pagoulatos, E. and Sorensen, R. (1976a) 'Foreign trade, concentration and profitability in open economies', *European Economic Review*, 8.

Pagoulatos, E. and Sorensen, R. (1976b) 'Domestic market structure and international trade: an empirical analysis', *Quarterly Review of Economics and Business*, 16.

Pagoulatos, E. and Sorensen, R. (1980) 'Industrial policy and firm behaviour in an international context', in I. Leveson and J. Wheeler *Western Economies in Transition, Structural Change and Adjustment Policies in Industrial Countries*, London: Croom Helm.

Peltzman, S. (1977) 'The gains and losses from industrial concentration', *The Journal of Law and Economics*, 20.

Perroux, F. (1974) *Pouvoir et Économie*, Paris: Dunod.

Pincus, J.J. (1975) 'Pressure groups and the pattern of tariffs', *Journal of Political Economy*, 83.

Posner, R. (1975) 'The social costs of monopoly and regulation', *Journal of Political Economy*, 83.

Posner, R. (1976) *Antitrust Law, An Economic Perspective*, Chicago and London: The University of Chicago Press.

Pugel, T. (1980) 'Foreign trade and US market performance', *Journal of Industrial Economics*, 29.

Robson, P. (1980) *The Economics of International Integration*, London: George Allen & Unwin.

Ruffin, R. (1984) 'International factor movements', in R. Jones and P. Kenen *Handbook of International Economics*, Amsterdam: North-Holland.

Rydén, B. and Edberg, J.O. (1980) 'Large mergers in Sweden, 1962–1976', in D. Mueller (ed.) *The Determinants and Effects of Mergers*, Cambridge, MA: Oelgeschlager, Gunn & Hain.

Saving, T. (1970) 'Concentration ratios and the degree of monopoly' *International Economic Review*, 11.

Sawyer, M. (1981) *The Economics of Industries and Firms*, London: Croom Helm.

Scherer, F. (1974) 'Secrecy, the rule of reason, and European merger control policy', *Antitrust Bulletin*, 19.

Scherer, F. (1980) *Industrial Market Structure and Economic Performance*, second edn, Boston: Houghton Mifflin Company.

Scherer, F., Beckenstein, A., Kaufer, E. and Murphy, D. (1975) *The Economics of Multi-Plant Operation, An International Comparisons Study*, Cambridge, MA: Harvard University Press.

Schmalensee, R. (1977) 'Using the H-index of concentration with published data', *Review of Economics and Statistics*, 59.

Schmalensee, R. (1981) 'Economies of scale and barriers to entry', *Journal of Political Economy*, 89.

Schmalensee, R. (1982) 'The new industrial organization and the economic analysis of modern markets', in W. Hildenbrand (ed.) *Advances in Economic Theory*, Cambridge: Cambridge University Press.

Schmalensee, R. (1986) 'Advertising and market structure', in J. Stiglitz and F. Mathewson (eds) *New Developments in the Analysis of Market Structure*, London: Macmillan.

Schmalensee, R. (1989) 'Inter-industry studies of structure and performance', in R. Schmalensee and R. Willig (eds) *Handbook of Industrial Organization*, Amsterdam: North-Holland.

Schmidt, I. (1981) 'Price control in Germany', *Annals of Public and Co-Operative Economy*, 52.

Scitovsky, T. (1958) *Economic Theory and Western European Integration*, London: George Allen & Unwin.

Shepherd, W.G. (1970) *Market Power and Economic Welfare*, New York: Random House.

Shepherd, W.G. (1979) *The Economics of Industrial Organization*, Englewood Cliffs: Prentice-Hall.

Simonin, J.P. (1980) 'Indices de concentration, pouvoir de monopole et variations conjoncturales: quelques extensions', *Revue Economique*, 1.

Södersten, B. (1978) *International Economics*, London: Macmillan.

SOU (1968:5) *Industrins struktur och konkurrensförhållanden, Koncentrationsutredningen*, Stockholm: SOU.

SOU (1975:50) *Internationella koncerner i industriländer, Samhällsekonomiska aspekter*, Stockholm: SOU.

Spence, M. (1977) 'Entry, capacity, investment and oligopolistic pricing', *Bell Journal of Economics*, 8.

Spence, M. (1981) 'Competition, entry, and antitrust policy', in S. Salop (ed.) *Strategy, Predation, and Antitrust Analysis*, Washington: Federal Trade Commission.

SPK (1987) *Pris och Konkurrens*, Statens pris och kartellnämnd, no. 2, Stockholm: SPK.

Stigler, G. (1964) 'A theory of oligopoly', *Journal of Political Economy*, 72, reprinted in G. Stigler (1968) *The Organization of Industry*, Chicago: The University of Chicago Press.

Stigler, G. (1968) *The Organization of Industry*, Chicago: The University of Chicago Press.

Stigler, G. (1971) 'The theory of economic regulation', *Bell Journal of Economics and Management Science*, 2.

Stigler, G. (1974) 'Free riders and collective action: an appendix to theories of economic regulation', *Bell Journal of Economics and Management Science*, 5.

Stigler, G. (1982) 'The economists and the problem of monopoly', AEA Papers and Proceedings, *American Economic Review*, 72.

Stiglitz, J. and Mathewson, G.F. (1986) *New Developments in the Analysis of Market Structure*, London: Macmillan.

Swann, D. (1979) *Competition and Consumer Protection*, Middlesex: Penguin.

Takacs, W. (1981) 'Pressures for protectionism: an empirical analysis', *Economic Inquiry*, 19.

Toh, K. (1982) 'A cross-section analysis of intra-industry trade in US manufacturng industries', *Weltwirtschaftliches Archiv*, 118.

Tullock, G. (1967) 'The welfare costs of tariffs, monopolies and theft', *Western Economic Journal*, 5.

Turner, P. (1980) 'Import competition and the profitability of United Kingdom manufacturing industry', *Journal of Industrial Economics*, 29.

Verreydt, E. and Waelbroeck, J. (1982) 'European Community protection against manufactured imports from developing countries: a case study in the political economy of protection', in J. Bhagwati *Import Competition and Response*, Chicago: The University of Chicago Press.

Wahlroos, B. (1980) *The Economics of the Finnish Industrial Structure*, Research Reports 4, Helsingfors: Swedish School of Economics and Business Administration.

Walsh, A. and Paxton, J. (1975) *Competition Policy, European and International Trends and Practices*, London: Macmillan.

Weiss, L. (1971) 'Quantitative studies of industrial organization', in M.D. Intriligator (ed.) *Frontiers of Quantitative Economics*, Amsterdam: North-Holland.

Weiss, L. (1974) 'The concentration–profits relationship and antitrust', in H. Goldschmidt, M. Mann and F. Weston *Industrial Concentration: The New Learning*, Boston: Little, Brown and Company.

White, L. (1974) 'Industrial organization and international trade: some theoretical considerations', *American Economic Review*, 64.

Williamson, O.E. (1968) 'Economies as an antitrust defense: the welfare trade-offs', *American Economic Review*, 58.

Williamson, O.E. (1977) 'Economies as an antitrust defense revisited', in A. Jacquemin and H. de Jong (eds) *Welfare Aspects of Industrial Markets*, Leiden: Nijhoff.

Zimmermann, K. (1987) 'Trade and dynamic efficiency', *Kyklos*, 40.

Part II

Concentration, efficiency and market power

2 Concentration, prices and profitability in the Swedish manufacturing industry*

Nils-Olov Stålhammar

INTRODUCTION

The extensive use of seller concentration as a description of market structure is due to an often proposed hypothesis that the higher the level of concentration, the more likely are sellers to recognize their interdependence and to collude to lower competition and achieve a higher price. Between 1965 and 1978 the mean of the four-firm concentration ratio in the Swedish manufacturing industry (measured at the four-digit level) rose from 0.50 to 0.58 (see the appendix, pp. 80–3). Should this worry us? Does it mean that competition has been reduced? Answers to these questions depend, among other things, on the nature of the relationship between concentration and market power. The purpose of this and the next chapter is to analyse this relationship. In the present chapter, we investigate whether concentration can be related to some or all of the following effects of market power: high profits, high wages and control over prices. This is done in two empirical studies.

In the first, the relationship between concentration, profitability and wages is studied in the framework of a simultaneous analysis of the relationship between market structure and market performance. The analysis is based on the traditional structural hypothesis that has dominated empirical research in industrial economics since the 1950s. The essence of this hypothesis is caught in the so-called SCP paradigm (structure, conduct, performance), according to which the structure of the industry determines the conduct of the firms and consequently also the performance of the industry. It is the fundamental importance of structure that characterizes this approach, even if the chain of events can be reversed to some extent. The structural approach is evidently a joint hypothesis about the combined effects of different elements of structure on industry performance. The often hypothesized positive relationship between concentration and profitability is, in this context, best thought of as a partial hypothesis. Many empirical studies, often based on US data, have been performed to test this partial hypothesis. In studies using industry level data, the hypothesis has quite often been supported. There exist, however, a growing number of studies utilizing line of business data where the usual result is a negative coefficient for concentration (see e.g. Kwoka and Ravenscraft (1986)).

Another closely related partial hypothesis is that of a positive relationship between concentration and wages. It is argued – especially when no positive relationship is found between concentration and profitability – that trade unions capture the fruits of market power, i.e. that the surplus raised in highly concentrated markets is used to pay higher wages.

In the next section these two partial structural hypotheses are tested in the framework of a simultaneouis equation system. Apart from profit and wage equations, the system also contains concentration and foreign trade equations. The study is cross-sectional with 66 (in the main model) sectors at the four-digit level. The data are from the latter part of the 1970s.

In the second study, the relationship between concentration and price changes is studied. The analysis seeks to answer two questions. First, is there any relationship between changes in concentration and changes in price? According to traditional (static) economic theory, monopoly prices are higher than competitive ones. If concentration is correlated with market power there should exist a positive relationship between changes in concentration and changes in the price level. Second, is there any relationship between the level of concentration and price flexibility? According to the hypothesis of administered prices, the relationship is negative. The most often proposed explanation is that firms in highly concentrated markets use their market power to control the price. The data, which in the section covering concentration and price evolution (pp. 71–9) are used to answer these two questions, consist of yearly observations on prices, costs and quantities for 71 sectors at the four-digit level and are for the period 1975–82.

The main conclusions from both studies are presented in the last section (pp. 75–80). Since there are very few data on concentration in Swedish industry, the four-firm concentration ratios in the 71 sectors in the years 1965, 1975 and 1978 are reported in the appendix (pp. 80–3).

CONCENTRATION, PROFITABILITY, TRADE AND WAGES[1]

The model

As the positive relationship between concentration and profitability is a partial hypothesis included in the joint structural hypothesis, it is intuitively appealing to test it in the framework of a simultaneous analysis of the relationship between market structure and market performance. This can be done by formalizing the partial hypothesis in an equation which is part of a system of equations. As long as this system is simultaneous or recursive (but with correlated error terms) estimations of the equations one by one will given biased and not consistent estimates. But if some system method is used, e.g. three stage least squares (3SLS), the estimates will be consistent and asymptotically efficient. Using a simultaneous approach also allows us to test hypotheses on the relationship between concentration and other performance variables as well as hypotheses on other relationships between market structure and market performance.

Empirical studies of this kind differ, among other things, with regard to which variables are treated as endogenous. Apart from the obvious candidates, concentration and profitability, many recent studies have also integrated foreign trade into the simultaneous framework; examples are Pugel (1978), Marvel (1980) and Chou (1986). This is theoretically sound since many interrelationships between foreign trade, domestic competition and profitability have been established both in theoretical and empirical analyses (see Caves (1985)).

It is, however, sensible also to integrate wage determination into the framework. Both market structure and profitability can be assumed to influence the wage level directly. Furthermore, there are good reasons to suppose that profitability and wages are influenced by the same underlying phenomena. If these are immeasurable the error terms are likely to be correlated, which in itself motivates a simultaneous equation approach. Despite this, wages are seldom included along with trade, concentration and profitability. An exception is Caves *et al.* (1980), who include these variables as endogenous (together with several others) in a study on the Canadian economy.

The equations that are about to be estimated, with the expected sign indicated below each explanatory variable, are the following:

Seller concentration
$$CR4 = f_1(MES, KR, XP) \qquad (1)$$
$$ + \quad\ + \quad\ -$$

Foreign trade

$$NXP = f_2(FR, IOR, KL, MES, CR4, KR) \qquad (2)$$
$$ + \quad + \quad ? \quad ? \quad ? \quad ?$$

Profit

$$\left[\begin{array}{l} PCM = f_{3a}(CR4, KR, MP, PS, GROW, XP, FEM, KTS) \qquad (3) \\ \phantom{PCM = f_{3a}(} + \quad + \quad - \quad - \quad + \quad - \quad + \quad + \end{array} \right.$$

$$\left[\begin{array}{l} RRA = f_{3b}(CR4, KR, MP, PS, GROW, XP, FEM) \qquad (4) \\ \phantom{RRA = f_{3b}(} + \quad + \quad - \quad - \quad + \quad - \quad + \end{array} \right.$$

Wages

$$\left\{ \begin{array}{l} WGE \qquad\qquad\qquad\qquad\qquad\qquad\qquad\qquad\qquad (5) \\ \\ W75 = f_4(CR4, KR, MP, PCM, KL, PS, FEM, EMCH) \qquad (6) \\ + \quad + \quad - \quad + \quad + \quad + \quad - \quad + \\ \\ W78 \qquad\qquad\qquad\qquad\qquad\qquad\qquad\qquad\qquad (7) \end{array} \right.$$

The formulation and specification of each equation will now be discussed in turn.

The concentration equation (1)

The measure of concentration used is *CR4*, i.e. the four-firm concentration ratio. The traditional explanatory variables to inter-industry variation in concentration are scale economies and barriers to entry. To capture the effects of scale economies we will use an approximate measure of the minimum efficient plant size divided by the total size of the industry (*MES*). The only barrier to entry that can be included is the capital requirement for the minimum efficient plant (*KR*). For both these variables positive signs are expected.

It should be emphasized that the variables *MES* and *KR* are only approximate measures. *MES* refers to a point on the industry concentration curve, just as *CR4*, but *MES* is measured in employees and *CR4* in sales. Since the numerator of *MES* is included in *KR* (see Table 2.1, p. 65, for variable definitions), we may expect some spurious correlation between *CR4*, *MES* and *KR*. This should be kept in mind when interpreting the results.

Another variable which may be important is the export intensity. The reason being that demand is often assumed to be more elastic on the export than on the domestic market. This means that when the size of a new plant is chosen, the actual size of the market will be less of a restriction on exporting industries than on non-exporters. Thus one should expect more plants of optimal size in industries with a high share of exports. Consequently, a negative sign is expected for the variable *XP*, defined as exports divided by total sales.

The trade equation (2)

Three different preliminary trade equations were estimated: an import intensity equation (*MP*), an export intensity equation (*XP*) and a net export equation (*NXP*). The explanatory power of the import and export intensity equations turned out to be poorer than that of the net export equation. This may be due to the omission of a relevant explanatory variable in the import and export equations, namely natural barriers to trade. Some goods are simply more tradeable than others. Since these barriers affect exports and imports in the same direction they should not affect net exports (*NXP*), defined as exports divided by imports. In what follows, only the results from the net export equation are presented, results from the other two equations are commented on when appropriate.

Since Sweden is rich in forest and iron ore resources it should, according to the Heckscher–Ohlin theorem of international trade, have large exports and small imports of products produced with these resources as inputs. It is, therefore, appropriate to include measures of the use of these resources in each industry as explanatory variables to trade. The variable *FR* measures the use of forest resources, and *IOR* the use of iron ore. The capital–labour ratio (*KL*) is also included as a measure of the relative capital intensity. Though by international comparison Sweden can be considered capital intensive, this is not so obvious when compared only to the western countries, which are Sweden's most important trading partners. Therefore no prediction can be made about a negative or positive sign for *KL*.

Other structural variables are seldom thought of as explanatory variables in trade equations. The causal relationship is more often assumed to run from foreign trade to market structure, e.g. from the share of imports to the domestic level of competition, than the reverse. However, market structure can affect trade in a number of ways. In a theoretical analysis, Krugman (1979) shows that the existence of economies of scale leads to trade between countries even when they are identical. Fisher (1985) shows in a Ricardian model with two countries and two goods, where one of the goods is produced in oligopoly markets, that the country with the most competitive market for this good will export it. White (1974) shows that exports will be larger under monopoly than under perfect competition, provided that the monopolist can price-discriminate against the domestic market. White demonstrates further that if the imported and the domestically produced goods are not perfect substitutes and there is some uncertainty regarding either the price of the imported good or the level of domestic demand, imports will be larger under monopoly than under perfect competition. But it should be noted that these hypotheses concerning the relationship between the market situation on the one hand, and exports and imports, respectively, on the other, imply two opposite hypotheses concerning the relationship between the market situation and net exports. It is also unclear what sort of relation one can expect between *MES* and net exports. We shall return to this point below.

Nevertheless, the variables *MES*, *CR4* and *KR* are used to capture the influence of scale economies and the level of competition. Concentration and barriers to entry are assumed to interact (in a non-specified way) to determine the level of competition.

The profit equations (3) and (4)

Two different profit measures are used: the price–cost margin (*PCM*) and the rate of return on total assets (*RRA*). The former is based on figures from each plant in the industry and the latter on the firms' balance sheets.

The first explanatory variable is, of course, the concentration ratio. The hypothesized positive relationship between concentrations and profitability is at the very heart of our analysis. The underlying behavioural assumption is that high concentration promotes collusion among firms. Other factors that may be important to the level of competition are the conditions of entry and the competitive pressure from imports. To capture these influences on the level of competition the capital requirement for the optimal plant (*KR*) and the share of imports in the domestic market (*MP*) are brought into the model. Since a high capital requirement is a barrier to entry, a positive sign is expected for *KR*. If imports are competitive, as they usually are assumed to be, the expected sign for *MP* is negative.

The profit level will undoubtedly be affected by the degree of X-efficiency. Though the most common hypothesis is that the degree of X-efficiency is positively correlated with the competitive pressure, there are also good reasons to expect a negative relation between this degree and the absolute firm size. The main reasons are that size breeds mistakes at various levels at the same time as it weakens the management's control on cost. Size can also be supposed to weaken employees' identification with their firms and therefore to undermine their efficiency. This motivates the inclusion of the average plant size measured in number of employees (*PS*) as an explanatory variable.

Another interesting factor relates to the growth rate of industry production. It may be argued that fast growth disrupts the market and destroys the oligopolistic consensus, thus reducing profits. But usually a positive relation is hypothesized between growth and profit. The reason often given for this is that the rate of growth can be assumed to be positively correlated with deviations of actual growth from expected growth and hence positively correlated with windfall profits. Therefore, our main hypothesis is that the growth variable (*GROW*) will have a positive sign. The share of exports (*XP*) may also be an interesting variable, though there exists no obvious assumption about the sign. However, since the export market is probably more competitive than the domestic one, we expect a negative sign.

It will be argued below that the plant size (*PS*) and the share of female workers in the labour force (*FEM*) affect the strength of the local trade union, and eventually the wage level (there may also be other interrelations between these two variables and the wage level). Since this affects profitability, these variables should also be included in the profit equation. The variable *PS* has already been included with an expected negative sign. The prediction with respect to the effect of plant size on the strength of the local trade union is the same. The variable *FEM* is expected to have a positive sign since the share of female workers is assumed to be negatively correlated to the strength of the local trade union.

Finally, since the numerator of the price–cost margin includes the opportunity cost of capital, this profit measure can be expected to be positively related to the capital-to-sales ratio (*KTS*).[2]

The wage equations (5), (6) and (7)

Two different estimates of the wage level are used in the analysis. The first is calculated from data on total wage costs and total number of hours worked. This measure of wages (*WGE*) cannot be specified by sex. It also includes all kinds of wage elements. The second measure is collected from published official data on average hourly earnings. Data on the earnings of male day-time workers have been collected for two years (*W75* and *W78*).

As mentioned earlier, the relationship between the degree of market power in the product market and the wage level is closely related to the relationship between market power and profitability. It is often argued that workers will receive a share or maybe all of the surplus raised in the product market (see e.g. Garbarino (1950)). This is the most common hypothesis. But it should be noted that an opposite hypothesis can be derived from economic theory. It can be argued that increases in market power reduce production and, consequently, demand for labour. This, together with the fact that the labour market at the same time tends toward monopsony, will lead to lower wages. If the former, and more commonly hypothesized, effect dominates, the expected signs will be positive for *CR4* and *KR*, and negative for *MP*.

Since the firms' ability to pay is affected by more factors than the level of competition, it is motivated to include a measure of profit as an indicator of that ability. The expected sign for the indicator used (*PCM*) is of course positive.

The capital–labour ratio (*KL*) can be assumed to have a positive effect on the wage level for several reasons. An increase in the amount of capital per employee will increase the marginal productivity of labour and, at the same time, reduce the wage share in value added and the firms' capability of holding out during strikes.

In the literature on wage determination, it is common practice to treat the degree of union coverage as an explanatory variable. Due to the very high and rather uniform degree of union coverage throughout the whole manufacturing sector, this is probably not an appropriate variable for the case of Sweden. But since there always are local negotiations which may result in wage increases substantially above those centrally agreed upon, variations in the strength of the local trade union may be an important factor in explaining variations in the wage level. Two proposed hypotheses in this study are that this strength is positively influenced by the plant size (*PS*) and, perhaps more controversial, negatively influenced by the share of female workers in the labour force (*FEM*). The latter hypothesis is based on the fact that women, more often than men, work part-time and periodically leave the labour market to bear children or work at home. It would not be surprising if these factors were to have a negative influence on female participation in trade union activities. But it should be realized that there may also be other reasons why the plant size and the share of female workers in the labour force should have a positive and a negative effect, respectively, upon the wage level. Apart from the possibility that working in a big plant is less attractive, which motivates higher wages, both variables may also pick up differences in personal characteristics among workers in different industries. Workers in big plants may, in other words, have 'better' personal characteristics compared to those in small plants, and there may further be a female over-representation in the low-skill industries.

Finally, the wage level can also be supposed to be affected by the employment trend, especially if the industry has been declining or increasing for a long time. Therefore, a positive sign is expected for the variable *EMCH*, defined as current employment divided by employment previous year.

Functional form, estimation technique and data

Economic theory offers very little guidance when it comes to choosing functional forms for the equations. The two most often used functional forms, mainly because of ease of computation, are the linear additive form and the log–linear form. To choose between these two, a simple procedure suggested by Maddala (1977) has been applied. It turned out that for the majority of equations the log–linear form was preferred. Only in the cases of import intensity and rate of return on total assets was the linear additive form preferred.

The nine equations are estimated in three different systems. System I (the main model) includes equations (1), (2), (3) and (5), i.e. *PCM* is the profit measure and *WGE* is the wage measure. From this system the regression results for all the equations are reported. In system II, the *PCM* equation is replaced by the *RRA* equation (4) which is the only equation reported from this system. Systems IIIa and IIIb are the main model with the wage measure *W75* (6) and *W78* (7), respectively, instead of *WGE*. Only equations (6) and (7) are reported from these systems. All systems are estimated with *3SLS*. (For further details on the choices of functional form and technique of estimation see Stålhammar (1987).)

As mentioned earlier, the data are from the Swedish manufacturing industry and cover the latter part of the 1970s. The analysis is cross-sectional with (in the main model) 66 sectors at the four-digit level. Most of the variables are derived from published data from the Official Statistics of Sweden (SOS) series. Brief variable definitions and sources are given in Table 2.1. In some cases, principally where the variable can be assumed to be sensitive to the business cycle, the mean of several years has been used.

Regarding the two variables, the rate of return on total assets (*RRA*) and earnings per hour for male workers (*W75* and *W78*), the number of observations is only 37 and 39, respectively. This means that the number of observations used in the estimation of systems II and III is reduced to 37 and 39, respectively.

Empirical results

Table 2.2 (pp. 66–7) reports the estimates of all the structural equations. The R^2 figures reveal that the model's explanatory capability is relatively good for concentration, net export, rate of return on total assets and wages (at least when wages is measured by *WGE or W75*) but relatively low for the price–cost margin. A glance at the tables also reveals that the relationship which is the focus of our interest, i.e. the one between concentration and profitability, is significantly positive in one of the two profit equations but insignificant in the other. We shall now comment on the results for each equation in turn, emphasizing the profit and wage equations.

The concentration equation (1)

In the concentration equation all three variables are significant.[3] *MES* and *KR* have the expected positive signs. The export variable *XP* is significantly negative. This is consistent with the hypothesis that the actual market size is less of a restriction in exporting industries, so that the latter have relatively more plants of optimal size and consequently lower seller concentration.

On the one hand, due to the above mentioned approximate nature of the variables *MES* and *KR*, the results for these variables should be interpreted carefully. No definite conclusions should be based on these results solely. But on the other hand, all the results received for the concentration equation conform to the conventional wisdom. (See Curry and George (1983) for a survey of studies not including foreign trade. Caves *et al.* (1980) and Chou (1986), both of which include exports as an explanatory variable for concentration, receive significant negative signs for this variable.)

Table 2.1 Sources and definitions of variables

Variable (Mean, stdv)	Source[a]	Definition
CR4 (0.56, 0.25)	(2)	Four-firm concentration ratio in terms of sales, mean of 1975 and 1978
MES (0.12, 0.13)	(1)	The average size in number of employees of the largest plants accounting for 50% of industry employment, divided by total industry employment (%), 1979
KR (228.4, 365.8)	(1) & (2)	The minimum efficient plant (the numerator of *MES*) times KL 1979
KL (0.28, 0.39)	(1) & (2)	Assets divided by employment (%), mean of 1975 and 1978
MP (0.43, 0.28)	(2)	Imports divided by domestic market, i.e. total sales plus imports minus exports (%), mean of 1975–80
XP (0.38, 0.31)	(2)	Exports divided by sales (%), mean of 1975–80
NXP (1.78, 6.64)	(2)	Exports divided by imports (%), mean of 1975–80
FR (217.35, 588.29)	(3)	Total use of products from the forestry industry (SNI 12), 1975
IOR (19.8, 62.23)	(3)	Total use of products from the iron ore mining industry (SNI 2301), 1975
PCM (0.37, 0.14)	(1)	Sales minus variable costs, divided by sales (%), mean of 1975–80
RRA (0.067, 0.017)	(4)	Profits after depreciation allowances and interest income, divided by the sum of current and fixed assets (%), mean of 1977–80
KTS (1.01, 0.59)	(1) & (2)	Assets divided by sales (%), mean of 1975–79
PS (115.2, 118.6)	(1)	The average size in number of employees, mean of 1975, 1978 and 1980
GROW (0.95, 0.21)	(1)	The ratio of volume index of production in 1979 and 1974 (%)
W (23.38, 1.21) (31.04, 1.41)	(5)	Average hourly earnings for male daytime workers 1975 / 1978
WGE (30.63, 2.85)	(1)	The sum of wage costs divided by the total amount of worked hours, 1978
FEM (0.28, 0.20)	(1)	Share of female workers in the labour force (%), 1975
EMCH (1.00, 0.07) (0.97, 0.07)	(1)	Total employment divided by total employment previous year (%), 1975 / 1978

Notes: Number of observations are 66 except for *RRA* (37) and *W* (39). [a] Data sources are: (1) Manufacturing Part 1, Official Statistics of Sweden (SOS), Statistics Sweden; (2) Data ordered directly from Statistics Sweden; (3) Input–output tables for Sweden 1975, Statistical Reports, N 1980:3, table 8; (4) 'Keyfigures' published by Statistics Sweden; (5) Wages Part 2, SOS, Statistics Sweden.

Table 2.2 Three-stage least squares estimates

				Dependent variable				
		NXP						
	CR4	A	B	PCM	RRA	WGE	W75	W78
Intercept	-0.012 (-0.08)	-3.919[a] (-4.66)	-3.762[a] (-5.81)	-0.627 (-1.60)	0.025[b] (2.14)	3.102[a] (45.04)	3.040[a] (47.54)	3.301[a] (50.06)
MES	0.405[a] (15.37)	-0.210 (0.57)						
KR	0.070[a] (3.46)	0.226[b] (2.65)	0.252[a] (3.00)	0.028 (0.43)	-0.00001 (-0.66)	0.022 (1.85)	0.006 (0.56)	0.005 (0.47)
CR4		0.006 (0.01)	-0.510[b] (-2.54)	-0.57 (-0.61)	0.036[a] (2.89)	-0.034[b] (-2.17)	-0.015 (-1.14)	0.004 (0.29)
KL		0.109 (0.58)	0.136 (0.89)			0.001 (0.05)	-0.006 (-0.50)	-0.018 (-1.46)
FR		0.439[a] (5.94)	0.435[a] (6.20)					
IOR		0.231[a] (3.19)	0.229[a] (3.97)					

	(1)	(2)	(3)	(4)	(5)	(6)	(7)	(8)
MP	−0.069b (−2.39)	−0.024 (−0.73)			0.0007 (0.04)	−0.009 (−1.54)	0.003 (0.71)	−0.003 (−0.74)
XP		−0.130a (−2.81)			−0.012 (−0.56)			
PS			−0.130 (−1.15)		−0.0001b (−2.74)	0.036 (1.92)	0.029 (1.80)	0.025 (1.50)
GROW			0.215 (1.08)		0.041a (3.72)			
EMCH						0.019 (0.21)	0.218b (2.18)	0.074 (0.90)
KTS				0.266b (2.53)				
FEM				0.113b (2.52)	0.012 (0.85)	−0.047a (−6.17)	−0.023a (−3.77)	−0.023b (−3.85)
PCM						0.045 (1.34)	0.095a (2.84)	0.066 (1.79)
R^2	0.84	0.57	0.55	0.26	0.68	0.70	0.55	0.44
D.f.	62	59	60	57	29	57	30	30

Notes: The RRA equation is linear additive, the others are log-linear. T-statistics (two-tail test) are given in parentheses. Significance levels are [a] = 1% and [b] = 5%.

The trade equation (2)

In the net export equation, the resource variables FR and IOR have the expected positive signs. The third factor intensity variable, KL, is not significant. Both the importance of forest and iron ore resources intensity and the unclear role of capital intensity (KL is significantly negative in the export equation when $CR4$ is deleted), which these results seem to establish, were also found by an earlier study on the structural determinants of Swedish foreign trade, namely that of Carlsson and Ohlsson (1976).

Among the two variables included to measure the level of competition, i.e. $CR4$ and KR, only the latter is significant in the A version, having a positive sign. In version B, the variable MES has been deleted. The concentration ratio $CR4$ now has a significant negative sign. This is quite opposite to the sign of the other variable included to indicate the level of competition, i.e. the capital requirement KR. In the import as well as in the export equation, the concentration ratio is insignificant when all variables are included, but turns significantly negative when the capital–labour ratio is deleted. Thus, if we disregard the significantly positive sign of the capital requirement in the net export equation, the results concerning the concentration ratio indicate that a lower level of competition reduces exports as well as imports, but that the effect on exports is stronger. It should be noted, however, that this conclusion is based solely on results obtained in truncated versions of the trade equations. Neither Caves *et al.* (1980) nor Chou (1986) found any significant relationship between seller concentration and foreign trade. Carlsson and Ohlsson (1976) did not test this hypothesis.

Finally, while the variable used to measure economies of scale, MES, is insignificant in the net export equation, it is significantly positive in the import as well as in the export equation (at least when the capital–labour ratio is deleted. In the import equation, it is significant also when $CR4$ is deleted instead of KL.) This is not surprising since economies of scale are an important explanatory factor of the existence of intra-industry trade (see Krugman (1981)) and because this sort of trade is by definition included in the import and export variables, but not in the net export variable. This result conforms with Lundberg (1982) where a positive relationship is found between economies of scale and the extent of intra-industry trade in Swedish manufacturing industries.[4]

The profit equations (3) and (4)

In the first profit equation, the *PCM* equation, the capital-to-sales ratio, the share of female workers and the export share are significant. *KTS* is positive which, due to the construction of the price–cost margin (*PCM*), is as expected. The variable *FEM* is also positive which is consistent with the hypothesis that a high share of female workers lowers the wage level and thereby raises profits. The negative sign of *XP* may be a result of harder competition in the export markets.

In the second profit equation, the *RRA* equation, the three variables *CR4*, *PS* and *GROW* are significant. The concentration ratio and the growth variable are positive while the size variable is negative. The signs are consistent with the hypotheses proposed above.

It is rather puzzling that the two profit equations have no significant variable in common. But, on the other hand, there are no significant differences in signs either. For the growth variable it is possible to give a reasonable explanation of the difference in significance: since the value of sales is the denominator of the *PCM* variable an increase in sales will lower the price–cost margin, *ceteris paribus*. This may offset the effect of growth on the profit level and make the growth variable insignificant in the *PCM* equation.

Two variables are insignificant in both equations, namely the import intensity and capital requirement. For a small country like Sweden, competition from imported goods ought to be important. But maybe the size of imports does not have to be large to stimulate competition. A threat of an increase in imports can perhaps be just as effective in keeping prices and profitability at a competitive level. There also exists a possibility, as shown by Urata (1984), that the relationship between imports and profitability is non-negative. The commonly hypothesized negative relationship rests on the assumption that imports are competitive. If the degree of implicit collusion is greater between domestic and foreign firms than among domestic firms then the relationship between import intensity and profitability may be non-negative.

Since the capital requirement is a significant explanatory variable in the concentration equation, it exerts an indirect influence on profit through the concentration ratio (at least in the *RRA* equation). The absence of any direct influence may be due to the special character of the time period under study, i.e. the latter part of the 1970s. During this period large parts of the Swedish industry encountered severe structural problems. Some of the sectors with the greatest problems had large and capital intensive plants (e.g., the basic metal industries and the ship building industry).

The wage equations (5), (6) and (7)

The full versions of the three wage equations have only one significant variable in common: the share of female workers. The sign of *FEM* is negative in all three equations. It should be noted that female wages are not included in the wage measures *W75* and *W78*. Apart from this variable only *CR4* in the *WGE* equation and *PCM* and *EMCH* in the *W75* equation are significant. *CR4* is negative while the other two variables are positive. When the capital requirement *KR* is deleted, *PS* and *PCM* become significantly positive in all three equations and when *PS* is deleted instead, *KR* becomes significantly positive in all three equations. (These truncated versions are not reported.)

From these results it is not possible to infer any clear relationship between the level of competition in the product market and the wage level. The results are, on the other hand, consistent with the hypothesis that the strength of the local trade union is an important determinant of the wage level and that this strength is influenced by the share of female workers and perhaps by the size of the plant. It should be realized, however, that the performance of the two variables *FEM* and *PS* are consistent also with other possible hypotheses mentioned above. The positive effect of plant size may be attributed to the unattractiveness of working in a big plant or to the possibility that workers in big plants have 'better' personal characteristics compared to those in small plants. (These two explanations are the only ones cited by Caves *et al.* (1980) in the Canadian study, where a positive relationship between plant size and wage level is also found.) The negative effect of a high share of female workers upon the male wage level may be due to female over-representation in the low-skill industries. With the data available it is not possible to formally discriminate between these different hypotheses. It is interesting to note though, that Weiss (1966b), in his seminal contribution to the wage equation literature, finds a positive influence upon male wages from the share of male workers in the labour force even after having included a large number of personal characteristics as explanatory variables.

CONCENTRATION AND PRICE EVOLUTION[5]

In this section we analyse the relationship between concentration and prices. Two questions are asked. First, is there any relationship between changes in concentration and changes in prices? The answer to this question is found in the next section. Second, is there any relationship between the level of concentration and price flexibility? This question is considered in the section on concentration and price flexibility (pp. 72–5).[6]

Changes in concentration and the price level

According to traditional (static) economic theory monopoly prices are higher than competitive prices. There should, therefore, exist a relationship between changes in the degree of market power and those in the price level. Following this line of reasoning Eckard (1981) performs an analysis of the relationship between concentration, which he apparently regards as an acceptable measure of market power, and the amount of inflation which can be 'associated' with each industry. This industry inflation is defined as:

$$R_i = \frac{VA_i^1/q_i^1}{VA_i^1/q_i^0} = \frac{VA_i^1/VA_i^0}{q_i^1/q_i^0} \qquad (8)$$

where VA_i is total value added and q_i is the number of units for the ith industry. Superscripts 1 and 0 refer to current and base years, respectively. Eckard's reason for using unit value added, rather than price, is that it eliminates the effect of price changes in inputs purchased from other industries. It should, however, be noted that to the extent that the increase in unit value added corresponds to a quality increase, this index will overstate the industry inflation. It is also clear that apart from changes in market power this index will also be affected by changes in productivity as well as pure changes in prime factor input prices.

For the American industry Eckard finds no correlation between R_i and increases in concentration. He finds, however, a negative relation between R_i and the absolute value of changes in concentration. This means that the larger the change in concentration, be it positive or negative, the lower R_i will be. The explanation proposed by Eckard is that competition often takes the form of cost reductions through labour productivity increases. This will lead to reductions in unit value added, *ceteris paribus*. Depending on whether the cost reductions take place among the smallest or among the biggest firms, concentration will fall or rise, but in either case the average cost of production and the unit value added will fall.

Empirical results

With the Swedish data available in this study it is possible to perform an identical analysis for the periods 1965–75, 1965–78 and 1975–78. Tests for a relationship between R_i and the change in *CR4* are performed for (1) all 71 sectors (2) sectors with *CR4* greater than or equal to 0.50 in base year or in end year (3) sectors with a change in *CR4* of at least 0.05 (4) sectors with *CR4* $\geq$ 0.50 and $\Delta CR4 \geq 0.05$.

It turns out that in none of these cases is there a significant correlation between R_i and the actual change in *CR4* or between R_i and the absolute value of the change in *CR4*. The conclusion emerging from these results is that during the period 1965–78 changes in the price level were not caused by changes in the degree of market power.

Concentration and price flexibility: the hypothesis of administered prices

The deviation of price from its trend

The hypothesis of administered prices has been given different interpretations by different economists, but the original interpretation given by Means (1935) and based on empirical observations rather than on theoretical analysis, was that some prices, defined by Means as administered, are less flexible and less sensible to changes in demand than prices that are market-dominated. The classification of prices into administered or market-dominated was done with respect to how often they changed. But as this principle of classification almost reduces the hypothesis to a tautology, most of the later tests have used the degree of concentration as the classification principle, i.e. prices set in highly concentrated markets have been classified as administered. The main reason for this is that the degree of market power has been an important factor in many of the explanations that have been proposed.

The most common explanation is simply that firms in highly concentrated markets can use their power and choose not to change the product price when demand changes. The reason may be that they do not want to offend against price agreements with other firms, or (in the case of increasing demand) that they do not want to induce entry or governmental intervention (the latter explanation has been proposed by Galbraith (1957)).

Another explanation, which is capable of explaining not only the rigidity of administered prices, but also the sometimes observed contracyclical behaviour of these prices, is that the agreement among oligopoly firms is not that prices should be kept constant but they should be set according to an unchanged rule, for instance, that profit per unit should be constant. When demand decreases and average total cost increases this means that prices must rise. For a model of this type see Blair (1974).

In order to test the hypothesis, Means (1935) simply compares administered and market-dominated prices with respect to the deviation from their respective trends. As indicated earlier, Means finds that administered prices are relatively more inflexible. Studies using this technique and supporting the hypothesis include Blair (1972), Means (1972) and Weiss (1977). Studies not supporting the

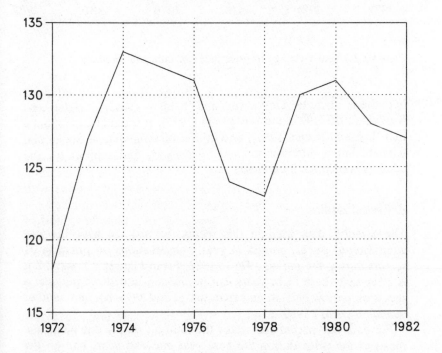

Figure 2.1 Volume index of industrial production (1968=100)

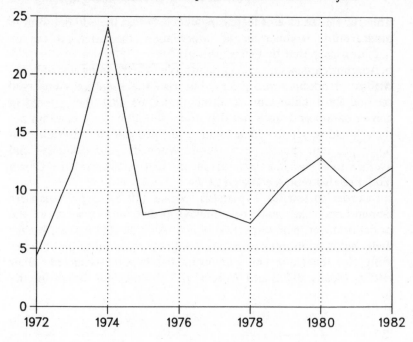

Figure 2.2   Yearly change in price index of industrial products

hypothesis include DePodwin and Selden (1963), Stigler and Kindahl (1970, 1973) and Lustgarten (1975). It should be mentioned that Ross and Krauz (1986), who utilize the same data as Stigler and Kindahl but a different method of analysis, find support for the administered price hypothesis.

Empirical results

The Swedish data used in this section to test the hypothesis of administered prices, consist of yearly observations on prices in 71 sectors during the period 1975 to 1982. From Figures 2.1 and 2.2 it is clear that these eight years can be divided into three periods; a recession period 1975–8, an expansion period 1978–80, and another recession period 1980–2.

For each sub-period and sector the ratio of, on the one hand, the mean of the price during the base year and end year, and on the other, the mean of the price during the middle years, is calculated.

This ratio is used as an approximate measure of the deviation of price from its trend.

It turns out that there are no significant differences in this ratio between sectors with high concentration ($CR4 \geq 0.50$) and those with low concentration ($CR4 < 0.50$). In other words, with this method of analysis no significant relationship is found between concentration and price rigidity.

Changes in price, demand and cost

The main drawback attached to the method of analysis utilized in the preceding section is that the only way in which differences in demand and cost conditions are brought into the picture is that the price trend is allowed to differ between sectors. A preferable method, from this point of view, is to estimate a regression function with price change as the dependent variable and changes in demand and cost as explanatory variables. Weiss (1966a) estimates the following regression equation on US data:

$$\frac{P_t}{P_0} = a_0 + a_1 \frac{Q_t}{Q_0} + a_2 \frac{(SV_t - VA_t)Q_0}{(SV_0 - VA_0)Q_t} + a_3 \frac{WC_tQ_0}{WC_0Q_t} + a_4 CR4 + u \quad (9)$$

Price change is measured as the ratio of price index in end year and price index in base year. The first explanatory variable is the change in quantity, which serves as a proxy for change in demand. The second variable is the change in unit materials cost (measured as value of sales minus value added). The third variable is the change in unit labour cost and the fourth one is the concentration ratio. If prices are market-dominated, changes in them should in principle be fully explained by cost and demand changes. If the concentration ratio turns out to be important this can be regarded as a support for the administered price hypothesis.

Weiss' basic findings (Weiss (1966a, 1977)) are a positive and statistically significant effect for concentration for 1953–9, insignificant effects for 1959–63 and 1963–8, and a significantly negative effect for 1967–9. In Weiss' view, these results support a 'lag behind and catch-up' version of the hypothesis of administered prices. According to this version administered prices shift with a lag in comparision with other prices. The positive effect for concentration for 1953–9 means that this period is a catch-up period, i.e. administered prices are raised as a temporary delayed reaction to the great inflations of the 1940s. The negative effect for concentration for 1967–9 means that this is a lag period when administered prices lag behind increases that take place in the rest of the economy.

In testing for the existence of administered prices, Lustgarten (1975) starts from the null hypothesis that the price is determined by the long-run average cost. Consequently, his regression equation includes unit capital cost. Further, each unit cost variable is weighted by its share in total cost. According to Lustgarten, the effect of concentration should change from negative during lag periods to positive during catch-up periods in order to confirm the administered price hypothesis. No such pattern is found in Lustgarten's regressions on one-year-long periods using US data covering the period 1958–70.

Garber and Klepper (1980) argue that the implicit null hypothesis is that all prices conform to the short-run predictions of the competitive model. Therefore, the regression equation should be specified in terms of changes in marginal costs instead of average costs. Further, the weights on each component of marginal cost should add up to one. Using US data for the period 1958–71, Garber and Klepper find that the concentration ratio is of importance but that the pattern of its effect is not consistent with the 'lag behind and catch-up' version of the administered price hypothesis.

Empirical results

In this section, changes in demand and cost are used together with the concentration ratio to explain price changes in the Swedish manufacturing industry. According to the 'lag behind and catch-up' version of the administered price hypothesis, the effect of concentration should shift from positive during the recession periods 1975–8 and 1980–2, which can be regarded as catch-up periods, to negative during the expansion period 1978–80, which consequently can be regarded as a lag period.

The regression results are presented in Table 2.3. Let us first concentrate on equations (1) and (2). The three periods have been pooled together, but the dummy *D1*, which is equal to one in the lag period and zero otherwise, allows concentration to have different effects in the different periods. The cost variable *AVC*, which includes unit labour and material costs, i.e. in principle unit variable cost, is in equation (1) weighted by its share in total cost, but unweighted in equation (2). Apart from the fact that capital cost is excluded, equation (1) corresponds to Lustgarten's specification, i.e.

Table 2.3 The determinants of price change

	(1)	(2)	(3)	(4)	(5)	(6)	(7)	(8)
Intercept	0.824[a] (13.79)	0.487[a] (7.93)			0.814[a] (12.39)		0.490[a] (7.57)	
Q_t/Q_0	−0.043 (−1.10)	0.011 (0.34)	0.254[a] (3.95)	0.184[a] (3.92)	−0.054 (−1.06)	0.215[a] (3.54)	0.025 (0.56)	0.177[a] (3.85)
$D_2(Q_t/Q_0)$			0.168[b] (2.20)	0.013 (0.22)	0.019 (0.34)	0.111 (1.56)	−0.023 (−0.46)	−0.001 (−0.01)
AVC_t/AVC_0	0.483[a] (11.80)	0.590[a] (16.77)	1.075[a] (15.43)	0.852[a] (22.53)	0.504[a] (7.78)	1.024[a] (15.74)	0.576[a] (12.43)	0.828[a] (22.70)
$D_2(AVC_t/AVC_0)$			−0.177[b] (−2.15)	−0.004 (−0.01)	−0.026 (−0.42)	−0.242[a] (−3.11)	0.018 (0.45)	−0.035 (−0.77)
CR4	0.061[b] (2.33)	0.053[b] (2.38)			0.070 (1.52)	0.305[a] (5.49)	0.052 (1.32)	0.147[a] (3.51)
$CR4D_1$	−0.051[b] (−2.32)	−0.055[a] (−2.98)			−0.051[b] (−2.32)	−0.090[a] (−3.12)	−0.055[a] (−2.96)	−0.073[b] (−3.52)
R^2	0.44	0.60			0.44		0.60	
D.f.	208	208	209	209	206	207	206	207

Notes: The cost variable is weighted in equations (1), (3), (5) and (7) and unweighted otherwise. T-statistics (two-tail test) are given in parentheses. Significance levels are [a] = 1% and [b] = 5%.

that the long-run average cost is decisive for the price. Equation (2), on the other hand, corresponds to Weiss' as well as to Garber and Klepper's specification. The latter correspondence, however, requires that average variable cost is constant so that marginal cost is equal to average cost.

From Table 2.3 it can be seen that the unweighted specification, i.e. equation (2) has the highest R^2. Further, quantity change, which serves as a proxy for change in demand, are insignificant while changes in cost are significantly positive in both equations. Finally, regardless of whether the cost variable is weighted or not, the concentration is significantly positive during the catch-up periods but not significantly different from zero during the lag period. Even though there is no significant negative effect from concentration during the lag period, the clear difference in the effect from concentration between the periods can be regarded as support for the 'lag behind and catch-up' version of the administered price hypothesis.

Equations (3) and (4) explore a hypothesis proposed by Phlips (1980). According to this hypothesis the higher the concentration ratio, the greater is the influence of changes in demand on the price evolution and the less is the influence of changes in cost. Phlips derives the hypothesis in an intertemporal framework using optimal control theory. But in Stålhammar (1987) it is shown that this hypothesis can also be derived in a very simple atemporal model.

In order to test this hypothesis, the changes in demand and cost are multiplied by the dummy *D2*, which is equal to one if *CR4* is greater than 0.50 and otherwise equal to zero. In equation (3) the cost variable is weighted and in equation (4) it is unweighted. None of the equations have any intercept. This is consistent with theory.

It can be seen that the specification with weighted cost variable (equation (3)) gives support to Phlips' hypothesis, i.e. the higher the concentration ratio, the greater is the influence of changes in demand on price evolution and the less is the influence of changes in costs. But this support for the hypothesis is rather weak since it is found only when the cost variable is weighted and when there is no intercept. On including the intercept, regardless of whether the cost variable is weighted or not, there is no difference between sectors with high or low concentration.

In spite of this, however, it is interesting to incorporate Phlips' hypothesis in the test of the administered price hypothesis. Equations (5) to (8) include both dummies *D1* and *D2*, i.e. the effect of concentration is allowed to be different in catch-up periods and lag periods at the same time as the effect of cost and demand changes is allowed to be different in sectors with high and low concentration. In equations (5) and (6) the cost variable is weighted and in equations (7) and (8) it is unweighted. As can be seen the regressions are done with, as well as without, intercept.

The results show that support for the 'lag behind and catch-up' version of the administered price hypothesis is maintained. Phlips' hypothesis, on the other hand, is supported in only one of the four equations. And even in this case the result supports only half of the hypothesis, namely that the higher the concentration ratio the less is the influence of changes in costs on price evolution.

To summarize, we have in this section found support for the 'lag behind and catch-up' version of the administered price hypothesis. But it should finally be noted that there may exist other explanations of the achieved results. A possible explanation may be that the concentration ratio acts as a proxy for capital. The correlation coefficient between $CR4$ and the capital–labour ratio is 0.35 (when both variables are calculated as the mean of 1975 and 1978). Decreases in demand and reduced capacity utilization during catch-up periods will result in higher unit capital cost. If the capital cost is of any importance in price determination, it may be the reason why the effect of concentration on price evolution is positive during catch-up periods.

CONCLUSIONS

The two empirical studies presented in this chapter give some, albeit weak, evidence for a positive relationship between concentration and market power in the Swedish manufacturing industry.

In the first study, we found a positive relationship between concentration and the rate of return on total capital. But this evidence of a positive relationship between concentration and profitability is somewhat weakened by the fact that no significant relationship was found between concentration and the price–cost margin. This study also revealed some other linkages, expected as well as unexpected, between market structure and market performance in the Swedish manufacturing industry. Seller concentration was found to be positively influenced by economies of scale and the capital requirement of the minimum efficient plant. The export intensity, on the other hand, was found to be a de-concentrating force via its implied relaxation of the market size restriction.

The Heckscher–Ohlin theorem of international trade was supported by the result that the use of forest resources and iron-ore resources were significant explanatory variables to net exports. But it was unclear whether the level of competition affected trade. If anything, it seemed that a lower level of competition, measured by the concentration ratio, reduces exports as well as imports, but that the influence on exports is stronger.

The clearest results from the wage equations was the negative influence of a high share of female workers upon the wage level (even when the wage measure included only male wages). Evidence was also gained for a positive relationship between plant size and the wage level. These results are consistent with the hypothesis that a high share of female workers and small-sized plants reduces the strength of the local trade union and thereby lowers the wage level. But since there also exist other possible explanations, no definitive conclusion can be reached and the issue is open for further research.

In the second study we found support for a version of the administered price hypothesis, according to which prices in highly concentrated sectors shift with a lag in comparison with other prices. The proposed explanations to this phenomenon have most often, in one way or the other, included market power. But this support for the existence of a positive relationship between concentration and market power is somewhat weakened by the fact that almost every proposed theoretical explanation can be accused of being far too *ad hoc*, i.e. most of them are not derived from a basic profit maximization principle. Yet, some evidence for a positive relationship between concentration and market power has been found. But this is only the first step in the analysis. In the next chapter, the relationship will be examined further. More precisely, an attempt will be made to estimate an explicit measure of the degree of collusion in each industry and thereafter see if it in any way is related to the degree of seller concentration.

APPENDIX: CONCENTRATION IN SWEDISH INDUSTRY

This appendix reports the four-firm concentration ratio at the four-digit level in the Swedish industry in the years 1965, 1975 and 1978. Plants belonging to the same firm have been added together before the concentration ratio has been calculated.

The mean of *CR4* has increased from 0.50 in 1965 to 0.57 in 1975 and 0.58 in 1978. During the same time the minimum value increased from 0.05 to 0.09 and 0.12.

Table 2A Concentration ratios at the four-digit level in the Swedish manufacturing industry

SNI	Industry	RRA W	CR4 1965	CR4 1975	CR4 1978
(1)	(2)	(3)[a]	(4)	(5)	(6)
3113	Canning and preserving of fruits and vegetables	R, W	0.67	0.68	0.64
3114	Canning, preserving and processing of fish, crustaceans and similar feeds	W	0.32	0.50	0.48
3115	Manufacture of vegetable and animal oils and lubricants	W	0.77	0.95	0.97
3116	Grain mill products	W	0.39	0.90	0.92
3117	Manufacture of bakery products	R, W	0.23	0.39	0.41
3118	Sugar factories and refineries		0.75	1.00	1.00
3119	Manufacture of cocoa, chocolate and sugar confectionery	W	0.64	0.67	0.70
3121	Manufacture of food products not elsewhere classified		0.37	0.56	0.57
3122	Manufacture of animal feed		0.39	0.53	0.51
3133	Malt liquors and malt		0.27	0.73	0.88
3134	Soft drinks and carbonated waters industries		0.46	0.79	0.70
3140	Tobacco manufactures		0.82	1.00	1.00
3211	Spinning, weaving and finishing textiles	R, W	0.26	0.29	0.29
3212	Manufacture of made-up textile foods except wearing apparel	W	0.29	0.25	0.26
3213	Knitting mills	R, W	0.28	0.43	0.45
3214	Manufacture of carpets	W	0.63	0.59	0.73
3215	Cordage, rope and twine industries		0.77	0.85	0.82
3219	Manufacture of textile products not elsewhere classified	W	0.51	0.57	0.69
3220	Manufacture of wearing apparel, except footwear	R	0.13	0.12	0.12
3231	Tanneries		0.54	0.80	0.87
3232	Curing of furs		0.94	0.98	0.96
3233	Manufacture of products of leather and leather substitutes, except footwear and wearing apparel		0.31	0.37	0.46
3240	Manufacture of footwear, except vulcanized or moulded rubber or plastic footwear	R	0.30	0.17	0.18
3311	Manufacture of wooden construction materials, and millwork and carpentry products	R, W	0.05	0.09	0.12
3312	Manufacture of wooden packaging material	R, W	0.22	0.39	0.51
3319	Manufacture of wood and cork products not elsewhere classified	R, W	0.27	0.25	0.31

Table 2A   continued

SNI	Industry	RRA W	CR4 1965	CR4 1975	CR4 1978
(1)	(2)	(3)ᵃ	(4)	(5)	(6)
3320	Manufacture of wood furniture	R	0.10	0.14	0.18
3411	Manufacture of pulp, paper and paper products	R, W	0.13	0.31	0.30
3412	Manufacture of paper and paperboard packaging material	R, W	0.37	0.47	0.47
3419	Manufacture of paper products not elsewhere classified	W	0.56	0.65	0.68
3420	Printing, publishing and allied industries		0.21	0.19	0.19
3513	Manufacture of artificial fibre and plastic products	R	0.49	0.46	0.47
3521	Manufacture of paints, varnishes and lacquers	R	0.59	0.60	0.66
3522	Manufacture of drugs and medicines	R	0.81	0.76	0.73
3523	Manufacture of soap and cleaning preparations, perfumes, cosmetics and other toilet preparations	R	0.60	0.57	0.56
3529	Manufactures of chemical products not elsewhere classified	R	0.37	0.41	0.54
3530	Petroleum refineries		0.97	1.00	1.00
3540	Manufacture of miscellaneous products of petroleum and coal		0.43	0.51	0.61
3551	Tyre and tube industries		0.84	0.82	0.83
3559	Manufacture of rubber products not elsewhere classified	R	0.79	0.73	0.68
3560	Manufacture of plastic products not elsewhere classified	R	0.24	0.24	0.22
3610	Manufacture of pottery, china and earthenware		0.86	0.93	0.84
3620	Manufacture of glass and glass products	R	0.45	0.61	0.66
3691	Manufacture of structural clay products	W	0.32	0.58	0.61
3692	Manufacture of cement, lime and plaster	W	0.57	0.91	0.96
3699	Manufacture of non-metallic products not elsewhere classified	R, W	0.15	0.28	0.32
3710	Iron and steel basic industries	R	0.31	0.43	0.57
3720	Non-ferrous basic industries	R	0.74	0.70	0.75
3811	Manufacture of cutlery, hand tools and general hardware	R, W	0.45	0.63	0.65
3812	Manufacture of furniture and fixtures primarily of metal	W	0.40	0.44	0.44
3813	Manufacture of structural metal products	R, W	0.14	0.17	0.13

Table 2A continued

SNI (1)	Industry (2)	RRA W (3)[a]	CR4 1965 (4)	CR4 1975 (5)	CR4 1978 (6)
3819	Manufacture of fabricated metal products except machinery and equipment not elsewhere classified	R, W	0.12	0.16	0.16
3822	Manufacture of agricultural machinery and equipment	R, W	0.73	0.72	0.71
3823	Manufacture of metal- and woodworking machinery	R, W	0.27	0.25	0.26
3824	Manufacture of special industry machinery and equipment	R, W	0.24	0.29	0.23
3825	Manufacture of computers and office machines	R, W	0.79	0.74	0.81
3831	Manufacture of electrical industrial machinery and apparatus	R, W	0.90	0.89	0.85
3832	Manufacture of telecommunications products	R, W	0.73	0.77	0.68
3833	Manufacture of household electrical apparatus	W	0.79	0.66	0.56
3839	Manufacture of electrical apparatus and supplies not elsewhere classified	R, W	0.46	0.40	0.33
3841	Shipbuilding and repairing	R, W	0.67	0.61	0.44
3842	Manufacture and repairing of rail moving equipment	W	0.48	0.95	0.94
3843	Manufacture of motor vehicles	R, W	0.87	0.84	0.83
3844	Manufacture of bicycles and motorcycles	W	0.85	0.88	0.86
3845	Manufacture of aircraft	W	0.75	0.94	0.94
3849	Manufacture of transport equipment not elsewhere classified	W	0.31	0.45	0.36
3852	Manufacture of photographic and optic products		0.65	0.62	0.64
3901	Manufacture of jewellery and related articles		0.48	0.56	0.60
3902	Manufacture of musical instruments		0.63	0.60	0.65
3903	Manufacture of sporting equipment		0.64	0.66	0.60
3909	Manufacturing industries not elsewhere classified	R	0.31	0.29	0.34

Note: [a] The letter R and/or W in column 3 indicates that values exist on rate of return on total capital and/or hourly wages for men in 1975 and 1978.

NOTES

* I would like to thank Bo Carlsson, Lennart Hjalmarsson and Stephen Martin for many valuable comments.

1 The results presented in this section are from chapter 3 of my PhD dissertation submitted at the University of Gothenburg (Stålhammar (1987)).
2 The variable missing from the profit equation, as well as from the model as a whole, is a measure of the importance of product differentiation. The usual variable, i.e. the advertising–sales ratio, cannot be calculated with the data that are available. Other *ad hoc* measures, such as the share of industry output bought by households multiplied by a dummy indicating durability, were tried but they all turned out to be non-relevant.
3 This is of course a simplifying paraphrase since it is the parameters of the variables that are significant and not the variables themselves.
4 Replacing the A version of the net export equation with the B version in the system of equations only leads to smaller modifications of the results in the rest of the equations, with one exception: the parameter of XP in the concentration equation decreases to -0.079 and becomes significant at the 1 per cent level.
5 The results presented in this section originate from an extensive revision of chapter 4 of my PhD dissertation.
6 Throughout this section seller concentration will be the only variable used to measure the degree of market power. Even though this can be partly justified by the results in the preceding section, it would be interesting in the light of later results (see the next chapter) also to include some measure of the competitive pressure coming from imports.

REFERENCES

Blair, J.M. (1972) *Economic Concentration*, New York: Harcourt B.J.
Blair, J.M. (1974) 'Market power and inflation: a short-run target return model', *Journal of Economic Issues*, 8, 453–78.
Carlsson, B. and Ohlsson, L. (1976) 'Structural determinants of Swedish foreign trade', *European Economic Review*, 7, 165–74.
Caves, R. (1985) 'International trade and industrial organization', *European Economic Review*, 28, 377–95.
Caves, R.E., Porter, M.E., Spence, A.M. and Scott, J.T. (1980) *Competition in the Open Economy: a Model Applied to Canada*, Cambridge, MA and London: Harvard University Press.
Chou, T.C. (1986) 'Concentration, profitability and trade in a simultaneous equation analysis: the case of Taiwan', *Journal of Industrial Economics*, 34, 429–43.
Curry, B. and George, K.D. (1983) 'Industrial concentration: a survey', *Journal of Industrial Economics*, 31, 203–55.
DePodwin, H.J. and Selden, R.T. (1963) 'Business pricing policies and inflation', *Journal of Political Economy*, 71, 116–27.
Eckard, E.W. (1981) 'Concentration changes and inflation: some evidence',

Journal of Political Economy, 89, 1044–51.

Fisher, E. (1985) 'Ricardo a la Cournot: why competitive industries export', Washington: Division of International Finance, Board of Governors of the Federal Reserve System, Working Paper.

Galbraith, J.K. (1957) 'Market structure and stabilization policy', *Review of Economics and Statistics*, 39, 124–33.

Garbarino, J.W. (1950) 'A theory of interindustry wage structure variation', *Quarterly Journal of Economics*, 64, 282–302.

Garber, S. and Klepper, S. (1980) ' "Administered pricing" or competition coupled with errors of measurement', *International Economic Review*, 21, 413–35.

Krugman, P.R. (1979) 'Increasing returns, monopolistic competition, and international trade', *Journal of International Economics*, 9, 469–79.

Krugman, P.R. (1981) 'Intraindustry specification and the gains from trade', *Journal of Political Economy*, 89, 959–73.

Kwoka, J.E. and Ravenscroft, D.J. (1986) 'Co-operation *v.* rivalry: price–cost margins by line of business', *Economica*, 53, 351–63.

Lundberg, L. (1982) 'Intra-industry trade: the case of Sweden', *Weltwirtschaftliches Archiv*, 18, 302–16.

Lustgarten, S. (1975) 'Administered inflation: a reappraisal', *Economic Inquiry*, 13, 191–206.

Maddala, G. (1977) *Econometrics*, New York: McGraw-Hill.

Marvel, H.P. (1980) 'Foreign trade and domestic competition', *Economic Inquiry*, 18, 103–22.

Means, G. (1935) 'Industrial prices and their relative inflexibility', Washington: US Senate Document 13, 74th Congress, 1st Session.

Means, G. (1972) 'The administered-price thesis reconfirmed', *American Economic Review*, 62, 292–306.

Phlips, L. (1980) 'Intertemporal price discrimination and sticky prices', *Quarterly Journal of Economics*, 94, 525–42.

Pugel, T.A. (1978) *International Market Linkages and US Manufacturing: Prices, Profits and Patterns*, Cambridge, MA: Ballinger Publishing.

Ross, H.N. and Krauz, J. (1986) 'Buyers' and sellers' prices and administered behaviour', *The Review of Economics and Statistics*, 68, 369–78.

Stålhammar, N.-O. (1987) *Strukturomvandling, företagsbeteende och förväntningsbildning inom den svenska tillverkningsindustrin* [Structural change, firm behaviour and expectation formation in the Swedish manufacturing industry], dissertation in economics, published by Department of Economics at School of Economics, University of Gothenburg, no. 19.

Stigler, G.J. and Kindahl, J.K. (1970) *The Behavior of Industrial Prices*, New York: National Bureau of Economic Research, General Series, 90.

Stigler, G.J. and Kindahl, J.K. (1973) 'Industrial prices, as administered by Dr Means', *American Economic Review*, 63, 717–21.

Urata, S. (1984) 'Price–cost margins and imports in an oligopolistic market', *Economics Letters*, 15, 139–44.

Weiss, L.W. (1966a) 'Business pricing policies and inflation reconsidered', *Journal of Political Economy*, 74, 177–87.

Weiss, L.W. (1966b) 'Concentration and labor earnings', *American*

Economic Review, 56, 96–117.
Weiss, L.W. (1977) 'Stigler, Kindahl and Means on administered prices', *American Economic Review*, 67, 610–19.
White, L.J. (1974) 'Industrial organization and international trade: some theoretical considerations', *American Economic Review*, 64, 1013–20.

3 Collusion and concentration in the Swedish manufacturing industry*

Nils-Olov Stålhammar

INTRODUCTION

The analysis of the preceding chapter, including most of the results, conforms very well to the mainstream of empirical work in industrial economics. It is based on the so-called SCP paradigm (structure, conduct, performance), according to which the structure of the industry determines the conduct of the firms and thereby also the performance of the industry. Furthermore, the specification of each equation is based on what might be described as a search through the relevant literature. Lately these types of studies have been criticized. It has been said, see e.g. Sawyer (1982), that since the hypotheses tested do not derive from a well-defined theoretical model, the choice of explanatory variables may be based on opposing theoretical grounds. The risk of omitting relevant explanatory variables is also fairly large. Even though this criticism is principally correct, this does not mean that empirical work should be constrained to deal only with formal theoretical models. Since it is impossible to fully capture the complexity of real world economies in a mathematical formulation, no matter how consistent it is, one is justified to study empirical models which are not derived from a formal model. (See Martin (1984) for a defence of the traditional approach.) It is, however, true that wrongly specified models may (and often do) give estimates that are biased or wrong. Further, when the model is not based on a well-defined theoretical framework the results are often hard to interpret or can be given several different explanations. A good example of this is the difficulty of interpreting the kind of positive relationship between concentration and industry profitability that was found in the preceding chapter (at least in one of the two profit equations estimated), as well as in many other empirical studies performed at the industry level. The traditional explanation is that high concentration makes co-operation between firms possible and thereby raises the profit above the competitive level. Demsetz (1974) and others have proposed the alternative explanation that efficient firms grow and become bigger as well as more profitable than less efficient ones. Industries with a few efficient big firms will have higher concentration and higher profitability than industries with many small and relatively inefficient firms.

The purpose of this chapter is to further examine the positive relationship between industry profitability and market concentration that was found in the preceding chapter. The analysis is based on a simple but very well-defined theoretical model for the behaviour of firms. The model starts from the well-known condition for profit maximization, i.e. that marginal revenue should equal marginal cost. The seminal paper on this model is Cowling and Waterson (1976). Important contributions to the development of the model are made in Dickson (1982) and Clarke and Davies (1982). An empirical application is performed in Clarke, Davies and Waterson (1984). The model implies a division of the total profit in an industry into two parts: one which depends on demand conditions and existing differences in efficiency between firms and another which depends on the degree of collusion between the firms. The strength of these two forces is an empirical matter. This means that the controversy mentioned above between the efficiency explanation and the collusion explanation is reduced to a matter of degree. It is only in the two polar cases, no collusion at all and perfect collusion (meaning that the firms are acting together as a monopolist), that one of the explanations loses relevance.

The most interesting feature of the model is, however, that it can be used to produce estimates of industry specific implicit degree of collusion. In the empirical application performed below it is found, first, that this degree is generally very low in the Swedish industry, and second, that while high seller concentration exerts a positive influence on the degree of collusion, there is a strong and counteracting competitive pressure from foreign trade.

The organization of the chapter is as follows. First, the theoretical framework is presented. The basic model is set forth in the section on pp. 89–92. The next section (pp. 92–3) presents a different interpretation of the model, given to it by Mueller (1986), which is helpful in understanding the functioning of the model. The complication of product differentiation is briefly discussed in the section on pp. 93–4. The section on imports and exports (pp. 94–6) brings foreign trade into the model, which makes it more appropriate for a small open economy like Sweden's. The empirical results are presented on pp. 96–109 and it will be seen that the data given in the section on pp. 96–7 are different from the data used in the preceding chapter. In the section on the relationship between industry profitability and concentration (pp. 97–9), regressions are perfomed to see if there is a positive relationship between industry profitability and concentration in this data as well. Thereafter the theoretical model presented in earlier sections is used to estimate the implicit degree of collusion for each industry. Such estimates are presented in the section on pp. 99–105 for a number of branches and for the two years 1965 and 1985. The section on pp. 105–9 studies the relationship between this degree of collusion, on the one hand, and the degree of seller concentration and foreign trade, on the other hand. The final section summarizes and concludes the chapter.

THE THEORETICAL FRAMEWORK

The basic model

The basic model starts from the well-known condition for profit maximization in the short run, i.e. that marginal revenue should equal marginal cost.

Suppose an industry of n firms producing a homogeneous good. Firm i's profit is:

$$\pi_i = px_i - c_i(x_i) - F_i \tag{1}$$

where x_i is output, p is price, c_i is variable cost and F_i is the total fixed cost. The price p is a function of total output in the industry $p = f(X)$ (the inverted demand function), where $X = \Sigma_i x_i$ (i = 1 . . . n). The profit maximization condition is:

$$d\pi_i/dx_i = p + x_i f'(X)(dX/dx_i) - c_i' = 0 \tag{2}$$

where

$$dX/dx_i = \Theta = 1 + d(\Sigma_{j \neq i} x_j)/dx_i = 1 + \lambda_i \tag{3}$$

and where λ_i is the i'th firm's conjecture as to its rivals' response to a change in its output. The values of λ_i can be seen as determinants (or measures) of the level of competitiion in the industry. If any λ_i is equal to -1 ($\Theta = 0$) the market result will be the same as if there were perfect competition in the market, i.e. price will be equal to marginal cost. When all λ_i equals 0 ($\Theta = 1$) there is a Cournot equilibrium in the market and when all λ_i equals $(X - x_i)/x_i$ ($\Theta = X/x_i$) there is perfect collusion in the sense that all firms believe that all other firms will react to an output change in order to keep their market shares unchanged. The latter situation can be described as:

$$dx_j/x_j = dx_i/x_i \text{ for all } j, \qquad (4)$$

which can also be formulated as:

$$\lambda_i = d\Sigma_{j\neq i}x_j/dx_i = \Sigma_{j\neq i}x_j/x_i = (X - x_i)/x_i \qquad (5)$$

This expression for λ_i inserted in (2) gives the monopoly result:

$$(p - c_i')/p = 1/\eta \qquad (6)$$

where $\eta = -(dX/dp)(p/X)$, i.e. the elasticity of demand.

Following Clarke and Davies (1982) we now define an industry parameter α that measures the degree of collusion in an industry:

$$dx_j/x_j = \alpha(dx_i/x_i) \text{ for all } j \neq i \text{ and for all } i \qquad (7)$$

This implies a negative relation between λ_i and the i'th firm's market share:

$$\lambda_i = \alpha((X/x_i) - 1) \qquad (8)$$

This modelling has been criticized by Schmalensee (1987) on the grounds that it implies that small inefficient firms should be the main restrictors of output even if the collusion is far from perfect. As Schmalensee points out, this pattern is inconsistent with most descriptions of actual behaviour of imperfect cartels. But since the great majority of markets cannot be described as imperfect cartels this should not lead us to reject generally the use of the modelling. It can for instance be noted that the modelling bears resemblance to a dominant firm model, where small firms act competitively and the dominant firm or the group of dominant firms set price to maximize profit given the supply of the competitive firms. However, the great advantage of the modelling, which will soon become apparent, is that the model becomes estimable.

Utilizing the definition of α, the profit maximization condition (2) can be written as:

$$(p - c_i')/p = \alpha/\eta + ((1 - \alpha)/\eta)(x_i/X) \qquad (9)$$

Clarke and Davies (1982) restrict α to vary between 0 and 1. Upon inserting those values for α in equation (9), the elegance of the model becomes clear. With α equal to 1 the model gives the monopoly result, i.e. the price–marginal cost margin is equal to the inverted value of the demand elasticity. With α equal to the lower bound the model gives the Cournot market result with each firm's price–marginal cost margin equal to the market share divided by the demand elasticity. With quantity setting firms the Cournot result can be thought of as the non-cooperation result corresponding to the perfect competition result, with price equal to marginal cost, in a Bertrand price setting model. The model also reveals a particular feature of the Cournot model, namely that as the number of firms increases, the market result approaches the perfect competition result, while as the number of firms decreases, the market result approaches the monopoly result.

After multiplication with x_i/X and summing over the n firms we obtain an expression for the whole industry:

$$(\Sigma_i px_i - \Sigma_i c_i' x_i)/pX = H(1 - \alpha)/\eta + \alpha/\eta \qquad (10)$$

where $H = \Sigma_i (x_i/X)^2$, i.e. the Herfindahl index of concentration. This derivation is sometimes regarded as a theoretical justification for the use of the Herfindahl index instead of other measures of concentration. But several things should be noted about this expression. First, the role of the Herfindahl index in this expression is non-causal. It is basically part of a performance measure. The left-hand side of the expression is the weighted sum of individual firm Lerner indices of monopoly power, i.e. the discrepancy between price and marginal costs. This role of the Herfindahl index should be separated from any causal role it might play, for instance in inducing collusion (see Donsimoni *et al.* (1984)). Second, in this expression the individual firm Lerner index is weighted by each firm's market share. But the choice of weights is really a normative one and there might in some circumstances be good reasons to choose other weights than the market shares (again see Donsimoni *et al.* (1984)). With other weights the expression will of course look different. Third, the Herfindahl index does not stand alone. The right-hand side of the expression also includes the demand elasticity and the implicit degree of collusion in the industry.

The equations (9) and (10) confirm Demsetz's (1974) view that efficiency differences between firms will result in a positive relationship between industry concentration and industry profitability. With α equal to 0, which is the non-collusion Cournot assumption, equation (9) shows a direct positive relationship between market share and profitability and equation (10) shows a direct positive relationship between the Herfindahl index and the industry profitability. It is also clear, however, that the positive relationship between market share and profitability will to some extent persist even when there is collusion as long as it is less than perfect, i.e. as long as α is less than 1. This implies that Demsetz's proposed methodology to view the existence of a positive relationship between firm market share and profitability as a support for the efficiency explanation in favour of the collusion explanation, is not applicable in general. As is evident from the model, both explanations will generally be relevant to some degree, despite a positive relationship between market shares and firm profitability.[1]

The degree of co-operation – another angle

The model derived in the preceding section starts from the assumption that each firm makes a conjecture about the response from other firms on a change in its own output. Mueller (1986) starts from a different set of assumptions but arrives at expressions identical to (9) and (10).

Mueller assumes that each firm maximizes an objective function, O_i, which includes not only its own profit but also a weighted sum of the profits of the other $N - 1$ firms:

$$O_i = \pi_i + \Omega\Sigma_{j\neq i}\pi_j = px_i - c_i(x_i) + \Omega\Sigma_{j\neq i}(px_j - c_i(x_j)) \quad (11)$$

Maximizing this objective function with respect to x_i, under the assumption that here dx_j/dx_i is equal to 0, one obtains:[2]

$$p + x_if'(X) - c_i' + \Omega\Sigma_{j\neq i}x_jf'(X) = 0 \quad (12)$$

Expressing firm i's profit as $\pi_i = (p - c_i)x_i$ and assuming that marginal cost is constant, and consequently equal to average cost, we can insert for $(p - c_i)$ from (12) and obtain:

$$\begin{aligned}\pi_i/x_i &= -x_if'(X) - \Omega\Sigma_{j\neq i}x_jf'(X) \\ &= -x_if'(X) - \Omega\Sigma_{j\neq i}(X - x_i)f'(X)\end{aligned} \quad (13)$$

or

$$\pi_i/x_ip = x_i/X\eta + \Omega/\eta - \Omega x_i/X\eta = \Omega/\eta + ((1 - \Omega)/\eta)x_i/X \quad (14)$$

which under the assumption of constant marginal cost is identical to equation (9).

My two main objections to this formulation of the model is, first, that the firms are not likely to possess all the information required to maximize the objective function, and second, that I find it hard to understand why any firm should put a positive weight on the profit of any other firm unless they are both members of a cartel where side payments are possible. In that case the weight should be equal to plus one. Of course, this criticism bears a strong resemblance to Schmalensee's (1987) criticism of the modelling of α in the conjectural variation model. In that context it was partly rejected, but here it is more appropriate since in Mueller's formulation of the model the firms co-operate by assumption.

But the modelling may, of course, be thought of as an *as if* modelling; as such, it is helpful in clarifying what the conjectural variation model is about. If all firms have positive conjectures about the response of other firms to an output change, the result will be the same as if they were putting a positive weight on the profit of other firms.

The complication of product differentiation

As in almost any other oligopoly model the presence of product differentiation results in theoretical as well as practical problems. Pure quality differences can be thought of as cost differences, but product differentiation in general cannot be assumed away that easily.

Clarke *et al.* (1984) allow the extent of product differentiation to be reflected in the magnitude of the parameter $\varkappa$ in:

$$dp_i/dx_j = \varkappa dp_i/dx_i \tag{15}$$

By defining market shares, s_i, in value of sales and using this in the definition of α instead of x_i and x_j, they arrive at the following counterparts to equations (9) and (10):

$$(p_i - c_i')/p_i = \frac{1}{s_i \eta_i} \{ \alpha \varkappa + (1 - \alpha \varkappa) s_i \} \tag{16}$$

$$(\Sigma_i p_i x_i - \Sigma_i c_i' x_i)/\Sigma_i p_i x_i = \Sigma_i \frac{1}{\eta_i} \{ \alpha \varkappa + (1 - \alpha \varkappa) s_i \} \tag{17}$$

where η_i is firm i's own price elasticity of demand. Clarke *et al.* (1984) note two important things about these equations. First, they need not imply a monotonic relationship between profitability and market share nor between industry profitability and concentration. Second, where the differentiation model (16) is appropriate, estimates of α calculated from regression results of equation (9) will tend to underestimate the extent of collusion.

While this effect of product differentiation upon estimates of α seems plausible, it should also be noted that there is an abnormality in this modelling since equation (16) implies a rather implausible negative relationship between market shares and the price–marginal cost margins.

The inclusion of imports and exports

When applying this model to a small open economy like Sweden's it is necessary to consider the effects of foreign trade. In doing this we will partly draw upon Urata (1984) who includes imports in a conjectural variation model.

Disregarding fixed cost, firm i's profits from sales in the domestic market and from exports may be separated in the following way:

$$\pi_i^h = p^h x_i^d - c_i(x_i^d) \tag{18}$$

$$\pi_i^e = p^w x_i^e - c_i(x_i^e) \tag{19}$$

where superscripts h and w refer to the home market and the world market respectively, and x_i^e is firm i's quantity exported while x_i^d is the quantity domestically supplied by firm i, i.e. $x_i^d = x_i - x_i^e$. The price in each market is supposed to be a function of the total quantities supplied; $p^h = f_h(X^d + X^m)$ and $p^w = f_w(X^w)$, where X^m is total quantity imported and X^w is total supply on the world market.

Maximizing the behaviour in each market, i.e. maximizing the profit functions (18) and (19) with respect to x_i^d and x_i^e respectively, and rearranging, one obtains:

$$p^h - c_i' = -x_i^d f_h'(1 + d\Sigma_{j\neq i}x_j^d/dx_i^d + dX^m/dx_i^d) \tag{20}$$

$$p^w - c_i' = -x_i^e f_w'(1 + d\Sigma_{k\neq i}x_k^w/dx_i^e) \tag{21}$$

where the subscript k refers to other suppliers in the world market than firm i. Upon dividing by p^h and p^w, respectively, this can be rewritten as:

$$(p^h - c_i')/p^h = x_i^d/X^h\eta^h(1 + \lambda_i^d + \lambda_i^m) \tag{22}$$

and

$$(p^w - c_i')/p^w = x_i^e/X^w\eta^w(1 + \lambda_i^w) \tag{23}$$

Assuming constant marginal cost the left-hand sides of the two expressions are equal to the firm's price–cost margin in each market. Allowing for the possibility of fixed cost, we now have that the firm's total profit plus fixed cost dividend by total revenue, i.e. total sales, will be equal to a weighted average of these two margins:

$$
\begin{aligned}
\frac{(\pi_i + F_i)}{R_i} &= WE_i^d \, \frac{x_i^d}{X^h \eta^h} \, (1 + \lambda_i^d + \lambda_i^m) \\
&\quad + WE_i^e \left(\frac{x_i^e}{X^w \eta^w} \right)(1 + \lambda_i^e)
\end{aligned}
\tag{24}
$$

where the weights WE are equal to sales on the respective market divided by total sales. Following Clarke and Davies' (1982) modelling of the industry collusion parameter α, presented on pp. 89–93, we make the following assumptions; $\lambda_i^d = \alpha(X^d/x_i^d - 1)$, $\lambda_i^m = \beta(X^m/x_i^d)$ and $\lambda_i^e = \gamma(X^w/x_i^e - 1)$. Inserting into (24) we end up with:

$$
\begin{aligned}
\frac{(\pi_i + F_i)}{R_i} &= WE_i^d \left(\frac{x_i^d}{X^h} \right)(1 - \alpha)/\eta^h \\
&\quad + WE_i^d \left(\frac{X^d}{X^h} \right)(\alpha - \beta)/\eta^h + WE_i^d \beta/\eta^h \\
&\quad + WE_i^e \left(\frac{x_i^e}{X^w} \right)(1 - \gamma)/\eta^w + WE_i^e \gamma/\eta^w
\end{aligned}
\tag{25}
$$

This is the analogue to equation (9) above. Upon multiplying by each firm's share of total industry sales and summing over the n firms, we obtain, after some manipulation, the following expression for the ratio of industry profit plus fixed costs to sales:

$$
\begin{aligned}
\frac{(\Pi + F)}{R} &= H^d \left(1 - \frac{S^e}{S} \right)\left(1 - \frac{S^m}{S^h} \right)\left(\frac{1 - \alpha}{\eta^h} \right) \\
&\quad + \left(1 - \frac{S^e}{S} \right)\left(1 - \frac{S^m}{S^h} \right)\left(\frac{\alpha - \beta}{\eta^h} \right) \\
&\quad + \left(1 - \frac{S^e}{S} \right)\frac{\beta}{\eta^h} \\
&\quad + H^e \left(\frac{S^e}{S^w} \right)\left(\frac{S^e}{S} \right)\left(\frac{1 - \gamma}{\eta^w} \right) \\
&\quad + \left(\frac{S^e}{S} \right)\frac{\gamma}{\eta^w}
\end{aligned}
\tag{26}
$$

where S is value of sales in the market indicated by the superscript and S without any superscript is industry total value of sales, H^d is the Herfindahl index with regard to domestically supplied quantities $\Sigma_i (x_i^d/X^d)^2$, and H^e is the Herfindahl index with regard to exports $\Sigma_i (x_i^e/X^e)^2$.

In the next section estimates of α, β, γ and η^h based on regressions of equation (25) will be presented.

EMPIRICAL RESULTS

The data

The data cover the Swedish manufacturing industry (SNI 2 and 3) during two years, 1965 and 1985. For 1965 there is one observation for each plant. For 1985, however, there are, for non-disclosure reasons, observations for groups of plants only. Each group consists of at least three plants. If a single plant is bigger in value added than the rest of the firms in the group taken together, additional plants are added to the group until this is not the case. The groups have been formed with respect to value of sales, i.e. the first group consists of the three (or more) biggest plants in value of sales, the second group of the three (or more) plants that come next and so on. These grouped data for 1985 have been disaggregated in the following way. Each plant has been assumed to have the same price–cost margin as the whole group. In groups consisting of three plants, each of them has been assigned one-third of the group's total value of sales. In groups consisting of more than three plants, one of them has been given half of the group's total value of sales and the remaining half has been divided equally between the rest of the plants. This disaggregation procedure makes the 1985 data approximative in a sense. It is therefore important to compare the results for 1985 with those for 1965, although it must be kept in mind that any differences may reflect important structural changes that have taken place.

For both years there are observations on value of sales and costs of production (excluding capital costs). For 1985 there are observations also on the industry values of exports and imports. For 1965 it was not possible to obtain actual data on foreign trade. The deflated values of exports and imports in 1969 will, however, be used as proxies for 1965.

The scheme of aggregation that was used when the 1985 data were grouped, implies the division of the manufacturing industry (SNI 2 and 3) into 102 sub-sectors at various levels of aggregation. However, the actual data set contains only 85 industries with observations on all variables. When the same scheme of aggregation is employed to the 1965 data it results in 98 industries with observations on all variables.

There is a difference between 1965 and 1985 in how plants belonging to the same firm are treated. In the 1965 data these have been brought together to one firm. In the 1985 data the sales and costs of what is called the primary plant have instead been distributed among its affiliated plants. In what follows the term 'firm' will be used instead of 'plant', though it is obvious that this term is more appropriate for the 1965 data than for the 1985 data.

The relationship between industry profitability and concentration

The main motive for the analysis of this chapter is the positive relationship between concentration and industry profitability found in one of the profit equations of the simultaneous equation system estimated in the preceding chapter. It is interesting, as a start, to see if a similar relationship can be found also in 1965 and 1985. In this estimation, however, the profit equation has to be truncated compared to the one used in the preceding chapter and, furthermore, it cannot be estimated in a system. The results from regression of industry profitability on concentration, the share of imports on the home market and the share of exports out of total sales are presented in Table 3.1.

In 1965 a non-linear relationship is found between concentration and the industry price–cost margin, while imports and exports are non-significant. The relationship between concentration and profitability is positive over a considerable part of the range of concentration found in the data. The peak value in predicted industry profitability is reached when the Herfindahl index equals 0.194. There are 26 industries with higher concentration and which consequently are in the range where there is a negative relationship between concentration and industry profitability. If the squared concentration index is deleted from the equation all variables become non-significant.

For 1985 column (3) in Table 3.1 shows a positive influence from concentration and, in addition, a positive influence from the share of exports. The share of imports, on the other hand, is non-

Table 3.1   Industry profitability and concentration, 1965 and 1985

Dependent variable: PCM	1965		1985	
	(1)	*(2)*	*(3)*	*(4)*
Intercept	0.215[b]	0.214[b]	0.181[b]	0.280[b]
	(11.2)	(9.9)	(9.4)	(8.68)
H	0.488[b]	0.496[b]	0.284[b]	
	(2.05)	(2.02)	(2.46)	
Log (H)				0.026[b]
				(2.60)
H^2	−1.276[b]	−1.305[b]		
	(−2.41)	(−2.39)		
MP		0.012	−0.074	−0.083[c]
		(0.25)	(−1.47)	(−1.66)
XP		−1.011	0.096[b]	0.102[b]
		(−0.28)	(2.00)	(2.14)
R^2	0.061	0.062	0.118	0.125
$\overline{R^2}$	0.041	0.022	0.085	0.093
D.f.	95	93	81	81

Notes: t-statistics (two-tail test) are given in parentheses. Significance levels are [a] = 1%, [b] = 5% and [c] = 10%. *PCM* = price–cost margin, H = Herfindahl index, *MP* = share of imports on the home market, *XP* = share of exports out of total sales.

significant. In column (4) we find that replacing the Herfindahl index with its logarithm, not only increases the explanatory capability as measured by R^2, but it also makes the negative sign of the import variable significant. This implies that there is a positive relationship between concentration and industry profitability, but as concentration increases the effect of an additional increase diminishes. It should finally be noted that the positive influence from the share of exports in 1985 is contradictory to the findings of the preceding chapter where it was found to have a negative influence. The results regarding the share of imports are, on the other hand, more in conformity with the former result since it was there found to be non-significant.

Estimates of the implicit degree of collusion

Estimates of industry-wide implicit degrees of collusion can be based upon regression of equation (25). However, since the data contain no observations on firm shares in the world market it is not possible to estimate the equation as it is. We have to make the assumption that each firm's share in the world market is so small that we can neglect the term containing this share. This is without a doubt a false assumption for some of the biggest Swedish firms although it is approximately true for the majority of firms participating in the world market. With this assumption and the additional assumption that marginal costs are constant, and also employing the fact that WE_i^d is equal to $1 - WE_i^e$, equation (25) can be rewritten as:

$$PCM_i = \beta/\eta^h + (1 - \alpha)/\eta^h \, WE_i^d(x_i^d/X^h)$$
$$+ (\alpha - \beta)/\eta^h \, WE_i^d(X^d/X^h) \qquad (27)$$
$$+ \{(\gamma/\eta^w) - (\beta/\eta^h)\} \, WE_i^e$$

It is clear that estimates of α, β and η^h can be calculated from regression estimates of the intercept and of the parameters adherent to the first two variables. Upon imposing the (questionable) assumption that the elasticity of demand on the world market is approximately equal to the elasticity of demand on the home market, a rough estimate also of γ can be received from the parameter adherent to the last variable. Equation (27) is estimated for the whole industry in both years 1965 and 1985. In order for α to vary between industries, dummies are employed to allow the parameter of market shares to vary between industries. This will also lead to industry differences in β, γ and η, even though the lack of observations on individual firm export shares forces us to use weights based on industry export shares, i.e. the intercept and the regression parameters adherent to the last two variables do not vary between industries.

It should be noted that using one regression equation for the whole industry, and only allowing the parameter of the market share to vary between industries, imposes the same relationship betwen α, β, γ and η across industries. The ratio between β and η^h is for instance equal across industries; it is equal to the common intercept. This is the sacrifice that we have to make in order to be able to bring foreign trade into the equation; allowing the intercept to vary between industries is not possible since it would be indistinguishable from the foreign trade variables which also vary only across industries.

As there are good reasons to believe that the influence from foreign trade upon firm profitability varies between firms, the parameters on the last two variables are allowed to vary between the largest firm in each industry and the other firms. (Note that this

Table 3.2 The implicit degree of collusion in 1965

SNI	Industry	H	N	α	η^h	γ
3140	Tobacco manufactures	0.198	7	0.125	0.62	0.100
37103	Iron and steel foundries	0.098	91	0.107	0.53	0.086
3523	Manufacture of soap and cleaning preparations, perfumes, cosmetics and other toilet preparations	0.160	57	0.086	0.42	0.069
3692	Manufacture of cement, lime and plaster	0.102	36	0.075	0.37	0.060
342011	Printing and publishing of newspapers	0.067	116	0.073	0.36	0.058
3540	Manufacture of miscellaneous products of petroleum and coal	0.074	37	0.049	0.24	0.039
34113	Manufacture of wallboard	0.079	18	0.048	0.24	0.039
36999	Manufacture of non-metallic mineral products not elsewhere classified	0.086	36	0.047	0.23	0.038
3620	Manufacture of glass and glass products	0.065	75	0.045	0.22	0.036
3117	Manufacture of bakery products	0.020	792	0.041	0.21	0.033
35111	Manufacture of inorganic chemicals	0.071	38	0.035	0.17	0.028
342102	Printing of weekly papers	0.022	831	0.033	0.17	0.027
3522	Manufacture of drugs and medicines	0.208	16	0.031	0.15	0.025
3843	Manufacture of motor vehicles	0.324	213	0.028	0.14	0.023
36991	Manufacture of stone products	0.012	729	0.027	0.13	0.022
3133	Malt liquors and malt	0.023	216	0.023	0.11	0.019
3691	Manufacture of structural clay products	0.036	134	0.023	0.11	0.018
3560	Manufacture of plastic products not elsewhere classified	0.024	170	0.022	0.11	0.018
2302	Non-ferrous ore mining and refineries	0.083	22	0.012	0.06	0.009
2901	Stone quarrying, clay and sand pits	0.031	160	0.010	0.05	0.008
35112	Manufacture of organic chemicals	0.071	75	0.007	0.03	0.006
2301	Iron ore mining	0.200	55	0.004	0.02	0.003
3419	Manufacture of paper and paper products not elsewhere classified	0.145	52	0.003	0.01	0.002
3811	Manufacture of cutlery, hand tools and general hardware	0.073	168	0.001	0.01	0.001

Table 3.3 The implicit degree of collusion in 1985

SNI	Industry	H_p	N	α	η^h	β
3845	Manufacture of aircraft	0.250	34	0.154	0.81	0.118
38411	Shipbuilding and repairing	0.155	37	0.131	0.69	0.100
3113	Canning and preserving of fruits and vegetables	0.077	40	0.118	0.62	0.090
3692	Manufacture of cement, lime and plaster	0.269	12	0.110	0.58	0.084
3133	Malt liquors and malt	0.119	28	0.091	0.48	0.069
3521	Manufacture of paints, varnishes and lacquers	0.079	34	0.080	0.42	0.061
33119	Manufacture of wood products not elsewhere classified	0.078	37	0.074	0.39	0.056
342011	Printing and publishing of newspapers	0.055	114	0.058	0.31	0.045
3114	Canning, preserving and processing of fish, crustaceans and similar feeds	0.054	57	0.055	0.29	0.042
35112	Manufacture of organic chemicals	0.154	41	0.049	0.26	0.038
3832	Manufacture of telecommunications products	0.090	89	0.045	0.24	0.035
3529	Manufacture of chemical products not elsewhere classified	0.219	56	0.045	0.23	0.034
3117	Manufacture of bakery products	0.028	274	0.043	0.23	0.033
2302	Non-ferrous ore mining and refineries	0.064	27	0.040	0.21	0.030
3523	Manufacture of soap and cleaning preparations, perfumes, cosmetics and other toilet preparations	0.114	35	0.037	0.20	0.029
36991	Manufacture of stone products	0.011	251	0.037	0.19	0.028
36999	Manufacture of other mineral products	0.056	45	0.037	0.19	0.028
3831	Manufacture of electrical industry machinery and apparatus	0.067	88	0.037	0.19	0.028
34111	Manufacture of wood pulp	0.080	20	0.035	0.18	0.026
38241	Manufacture of machinery and equipment for the pulp and paper industries	0.156	29	0.033	0.18	0.026
3813	Manufacture of structural metal products	0.013	494	0.029	0.15	0.022
38195	Manufacture of household metal products	0.064	44	0.029	0.15	0.022
34112	Manufacture of paper and paper products	0.030	54	0.028	0.15	0.021
3522	Manufacture of drugs and medicines	0.202	25	0.027	0.14	0.020

Table 3.3 continued

SNI	Industry	H_p	N	α	η^h	β
3211	Spinning, weaving and finishing textiles	0.040	93	0.026	0.14	0.020
38232	Manufacture of machinery and equipment for the wood product industry	0.257	35	0.025	0.13	0.019
35132	Manufacture of plastic raw materials	0.042	65	0.025	0.13	0.019
342012	Printing of weekly papers	0.015	755	0.024	0.13	0.018
35111	Manufacture of inorganic chemicals	0.099	25	0.015	0.08	0.011
3691	Manufacture of structural clay products	0.055	20	0.014	0.08	0.011
2301	Iron ore mining	0.277	8	0.013	0.07	0.010
3419	Manufacture of paper and paper products not elsewhere classified	0.088	51	0.011	0.06	0.008
3825	Manufacture of computers and office machines	0.255	52	0.011	0.06	0.008
3811	Manufacture of cutlery, hand tools and general hardware	0.105	139	0.010	0.05	0.008
2909	Mining and quarrying not elsewhere classified	0.118	17	0.010	0.05	0.007
3829	Machinery and equipment, except electric, not elsewhere classified	0.017	434	0.010	0.05	0.007
3903	Manufacture of sporting equipment	0.172	20	0.009	0.05	0.007
38242	Manufacture of machinery and equipment for the construction and mining and quarrying industries	0.102	49	0.008	0.04	0.006
38199	Manufacture of fabricated metal products, except machinery and equipment, not elsewhere classified	0.009	583	0.007	0.04	0.005
38393	Manufacture of incandescent and fluorescent light bulbs	0.032	108	0.006	0.03	0.004
3214	Manufacture of carpets	0.061	48	0.003	0.02	0.002
33202	Manufacture of non-upholstered wooden furniture	0.016	221	0.002	0.01	0.002
3852	Manufacture of photographic and optic products	0.146	18	0.001	0.01	0.001
38231	Manufacture of machinery and equipment for the metal products industry	0.035	110	0.000	0.00	0.000
38249	Manufacture of other industrial machinery	0.021	280	0.000	0.00	0.000
3851	Manufacture of scientific and measurement instruments (including watches and clocks)	0.038	131	0.000	0.00	0.000

does not alter the reasoning in the preceding paragraph.)

The regression results show the performance of the model as measured by R^2 to be rather poor. The overall R^2 for 1965 is only 0.022. For 1985 it is 0.061. But on the other hand, a positive and significant parameter for the market share is found in 24 out of 98 industries in 1965 and in no less than 46 out of 85 in 1985. The industries, the value of the Herfindahl index, the number of firms and the calculated values of the implicit degree of collusion, i.e. α are presented in Tables 3.2 and 3.3.[3]

The calculated values of the implicit degree of collusion for 1965 that are presented in Table 3.2, stems from the following regression equation:

$$PCM_i = 0.202^a + \ldots + 0.0004\ WE_j^d(X_j^d/X_j^h) - 0.140^b D^c WE_j^d(X_j^d/X_j^h) \quad (28)$$
$$ (15.9) \qquad\qquad (0.03) \qquad\qquad\qquad (-2.40)$$
$$-0.040^a\ WE_j^e\ (X_j^e/X_j) \qquad\qquad R^2 = 0.022$$
$$(-2.53)$$

where subscript i refers to the plant and subscript j to the industry and where the dummy D is equal to one for the largest firm in each industry and equal to zero otherwise, and where the parameters on the market shares have been left out. Of the 98 industries 26 have a significant (at the 10 per cent level) and positive parameter, while three have a negatively significant parameter and the rest have non-significant parameters. While a negative sign is clearly not in conformity with the model since it implies either a value of α exceeding one or an implausible value of the elasticity of demand, the non-significance results could at first sight be interpreted to mean that α is equal to one, i.e. that the collusion is perfect. That interpretation must, however, be regarded as false. It is too strong a conclusion to be based on a non-significant parameter in a regression. There can be many reasons why the parameter is non-significant; an inadequate aggregation scheme being one. Also, the calculated values of α based upon significant and positive parameters are very low and far from being equal to one.

The other parameters in equation (28) imply further that for the majority of firms there is no difference between α and β, i.e. they expect the same degree of collusive behaviour from foreign producers as from domestic firms. But the largest firms, on the other hand, expect more collusive behaviour from foreign producers than from other domestic firms, i.e. β exceeds α. The share of exports, finally, is found to exert a negative influence upon the profitability of all firms. With the assumption that the elasticity of demand is the same on the world market as on the domestic market (and with the additional assumption of very small world market shares for the Swedish firms that was introduced above), this implies that γ is lower than α, i.e. the degree of collusion is lower on the world market than on the domestic market. Even though this is not an implausible conclusion the results regarding the foreign trade variables should be interpreted carefully. Apart from the questionability of the assumptions just mentioned, there is also a high degree of collinearity between the two variables. If the export variable is deleted from the equation, the import share variable becomes highly signficant with a positive sign indicating that β is lower than α, i.e. that there is a competitive pressure coming from imports.

The calculate values of α, η^h and β for 1985, which are presented in Table 3.3, stem from the following regression equation:

$$PCM_i = 0.145^a + \ldots + 0.045^a \ WE_j^d \ (X_j^d/X_j^h) \quad (29)$$
$$(12.3) \qquad (3.30)$$
$$-0.107^a D^c WE_j^d \ (X_j^d/X_j^h) + 0.019 \ WE_j^e \ (X_j^e/X_j)$$
$$(-2.3) \qquad\qquad\qquad (1.31)$$
$$-0.228^a D^c WE_j^c \ (X_j^c/X_j) \qquad R^2 = 0.061$$
$$(-5.11)$$

Of the 85 industries in the data set for 1985, as many as 46 show a positive and significant parameter for the market share. The parameter is negative and significant in five industries and non-significant in the remaining 34. The parameters of the two import share variables are both significant, with a positive sign for the majority of firms and a negative sign for the largest firm. This means that a large import share reduces the profit of the majority of the firms in an industry but has no effect on the profit of the largest firm (according to the estimated parameters and their variances and covariances). Regarding the export share variables only the variable with a dummy for the largest firm is significant, with a negative sign.

The values of α presented in Tables 3.2 and 3.3 are all well below one. The majority of values are in fact very small indicating that collusion among firms is far from perfect in the sense described above. On the contrary, the majority of α-values are close to zero indicating that the behaviour of the firms in these industries are very close to being Cournot non-collusive. The three industries listed at the bottom of Table 3.3 showed very large positive and significant values for the parameter of the market share, resulting in calculated values equal to zero (at the chosen level of precision) for the structural parameters.

Even though the model's overall explanatory capability is rather low, Tables 3.2 and 3.3 reveal some sort of stability in that 16 of the 24 industries in Table 3.2 can also be found in Table 3.3. This can be interpreted to mean that the model is relevant for some, but far from all, of the industries included in the data. A possible explanation is of course that the aggregation scheme is irrelevant, bumping very different products into one market.

Determinants of the implicit degree of collusion

The central hypothesis common to almost all oligopoly models is that high concentration induces collusion. The most famous justification for this hypothesis is Stigler (1964). He shows that there is a positive relationship between Herfindahl's index and the possibility of detecting secret price-cutting by any firm participating in a formal or informal cartel. This means that the higher Herfindahl's index is, the tighter collusion will be. Hence, it is interesting to regress the values of α against the Herfindahl index. The results for 1965 are presented in Table 3.4 and the results for 1985 in Table 3.5. Apart from the Herfindahl index, imports and exports are also included as explanatory variables. (Another potentially important variable, which due to lack of data has to be omitted, is the degree of product differentiation.)

For the year 1965, the Herfindahl index alone is not a significant explanatory variable. But when imports and exports are included the Herfindahl index becomes highly significant with a positive sign, see column (1) in Table 3.4. The export variable has a negative significant sign while the import variable is non-significant. In column (2) the squared Herfindahl index is included as an explanatory variable. It becomes significant with a negative sign while the signs and significances of the other variables are unchanged. This implies that the influence from concentration upon the implicit degree of concentration becomes negative for large values of concentration. However, given the estimated values of the parameters, 23 of the 24 industries are in the range where there is a positive relationship between concentration and the implicit degree of collusion. The peak is reached where the Herfindahl index is

Table 3.4   Determinants of the degree of collusion, 1965

Dependent variable: α	(1)	(2)	(3)	(4)	(5)
Intercept	0.050[a]	0.028[a]	0.032[a]	0.025[a]	0.147[a]
	(6.07)	(4.99)	(4.91)	(5.07)	(8.56)
H	0.232[a]	0.745[a]	0.557[b]	0.747[a]	
	(2.82)	(6.10)	(2.23)	(6.16)	
H^2		−1.729[a]	−1.447[b]	−1.733[a]	
		(−5.38)	(−2.53)	(−5.51)	
$\text{Log}(H)$					0.027[a]
					(5.86)
MP	−0.019	−0.018	−0.069[a]		−0.025[c]
	(−1.22)	(−1.13)	(−2.87)		(−1.81)
XP	−0.081[a]	−0.087[a]		−0.097[a]	−0.088[a]
	(−4.34)	(−4.91)		(−7.62)	(−5.48)
R^2	0.648	0.799	0.434	0.784	0.792
$\bar{R}^2$	0.595	0.757	0.349	0.751	0.761
D.f.	20	19	20	20	20

Notes: t-statistics (two-tail test) are given in parentheses. Significance levels are [a] = 1%, [b] = 5% and [c] = 10%. α = the implicit degree of collusion, H = Herfindahl index, MP = share of imports on the home market, XP = share of exports out of total sales. See also note 4, p. 112.

Table 3.5   Determinants of the degree of collusion, 1985

Dependent variable: α	(1)	(2)	(3)	(4)
Intercept	0.055[a]	0.046[a]	0.127[a]	0.127[a]
	(8.10)	(6.60)	(7.39)	(7.36)
H	0.215[a]	0.456[a]		
	(3.65)	(2.96)		
H^2		−0.903[a]		
		(−1.46)		
$\text{Log}(H)$			0.019[a]	0.019[a]
			(4.57)	(4.59)
MP	0.011	0.004	0.002	
	(0.57)	(0.23)	(0.17)	
XP	−0.080[a]	−0.076[a]	−0.075[a]	−0.073[a]
	(−3.88)	(−3.97)	(−4.31)	(−6.95)
R^2	0.603	0.622	0.623	0.623
$\bar{R}^2$	0.574	0.585	0.596	0.606
D.f.	42	41	42	43

Notes: t-statistics (two-tail test) are given in parentheses. Significance levels are [a] = 1%, [b] = 5% and [c] = 10%. α = the implicit degree of collusion, H = Herfindahl index, MP = share of imports on the home market, XP = share of exports out of total sales. See also note 4, p. 112.

equal to 0.208. There is only one industry with higher concentration and which consequently is in the range where there is a negative influence from concentration upon the implicit degree of collusion. This of course implies that the relationship between concentration and the implicit degree of collusion has a logarithmic form rather than an inverted U-form. This is also confirmed in column (5), where the logarithm of the Herfindahl index is the sole concentration variable. The R^2 is slightly lower than in column (2), but the adjusted R^2 is higher. The performance of the foreign trade variables can also be regarded as better in this column since not only the export share but also the share of imports are now significant, both having a negative sign. The non-significance of the import share in column (2) as well as its rather low t-ratio in column (5) may be due to the high degree of correlation that exists between this variable and the share of exports. The correlation coefficient between them is 0.60 in these 26 industries. Upon deleting the export variable from column (2) we find that the import variable becomes highly significant with a negative sign (column (3)). Another indication that the import variable is not unimportant is that when this variable is deleted (column (4)) adjusted R^2 becomes slightly lower compared to column (2). Qualitatively the same results are reached when the import variable and the export variable are deleted, one by one, from column (5).

For 1985 the Herfindahl index is found to have a positive influence on the implicit degree of collusion even if it is the sole explanatory variable. As column (1) in Table 3.5 shows, this positive influence from concentration is also present when the import and export shares are included as explanatory variables. The export variable is significantly negative while the import variable is non-significant. In column (2) the squared Herfindahl index has been included. Even though this variable fails to be significant the R^2 as well as the adjusted R^2 become higher than in column (1). This means that the possibility of a non-linear relationship between concentration and the implicit degree of collusion cannot be ruled out. The results in column (3) imply that this relationship has a logarithmic form, since the logarithmic value of the Herfindahl index is strongly significant with a positive sign. Regarding the foreign trade variables the same results are achieved in all three equations, i.e. the import variable is non-significant and the export variable is strongly significant with a negative sign. Upon deleting the export variable from columns (1), (2) or (3) the same result as in Table 3.4 is received, i.e. the import variable becomes highly significant with a negative sign. But, when the import variable is deleted the adjusted R^2 becomes, in contradiction to the former results, higher than when it is included. The result received when the share of imports is deleted from column (3) is shown in column (4), but the results are qualitatively the same whether the starting column is column (1), (2) or (3). These results indicate, in contradiction to what was the case for 1965, that the import variable is an unimportant variable.[4]

To summarize, while the results presented in Tables 3.4 and 3.5 show a positive relationship, but with a decreasing slope, between the implicit degree of collusion and the degree of seller concentration, the extent of foreign trade seems to be of even greater importance. Not only does its inclusion result in a considerable increase in explanatory power, especially in 1965, the absolute value of the elasticity of collusion is also larger with respect to foreign trade than with respect to seller concentration; this is especially pronounced in 1985. In 1965 the elasticities with respect to concentration, exports and imports are 0.67, −0.69 and −0.21, respectively (based on the values in column (5) in Table 3.4 and calculated at the mean values of respective variables). In 1985 the elasticities with regard to concentration and exports are 0.53 and −1.15 respectively (based on the values in column (4), Table 3.5).

The strongly negative influence from exports upon the implicit degree of collusion may at first sight be surprising. But apart from the above mentioned high correlation between imports and exports, which may result in the export variable picking up some of the effect of the competitive pressure from the world market which usually is assumed to be manifested in the import share variable, it may also be the case that the export variable in itself is a measure of this pressure. If a product can be exported then it can also be imported. No matter how high the actual import share is, there will always be a competitive pressure from potential imports. The market can in this respect be regarded as contestable. It should be mentioned that efforts were made to measure the degree of tradeability of the produced product, and thereby also the degree of openness to the world market, by a variable defined as imports plus exports divided by total sales by domestic firms. But even though it was significant in both years (with a negative sign), it resulted in a substantial fall in both R^2 and adjusted R^2 compared to when the import and the export shares were included separately as well as to when only the export share was included.

It should also be realized that exports *per se* may well have a negative influence on the implicit degree of collusion on the domestic market. The reason is that exporting firms have to work with a relatively large excess capacity in order to be able to satisfy the market throughout the whole business cycle. It is not unreasonable to assume that the need to have excess capacity is more severe the more export-oriented an industry is. The fluctuations in demand are probably stronger and the risk as well as the cost of losing customers because of temporary shortages in supply can also be assumed to be higher. Large excess capacity is of course an obstacle to any output restricting policy on the home market. When the demand on the world market is low, it will be tempting for the firms to increase output on the home market.

The fact that the relative importance of the home market decreases as the export share increases may also be relevant in this context. Less effort will probably be put into analysing the market, and this is likely to reduce the probability of a collusive behaviour.

CONCLUSIONS

The study presented in this chapter draws several interesting conclusions, not only about the extent of market power in Swedish industry and how to stimulate competition, but also about the benefit of using individual plant data and a proper model specification.

The theoretical model presented in the study lends support to Demsetz's view that a positive relationship between industry profitability and concentration can be the outcome of efficiency differences between firms as well as of the presence of market power. But the method proposed by Demsetz for discriminating between these explanations, i.e. to look for differences in profitability between firms of different size, is shown not to be generally applicable. The existence of profitability differences between firms of different size does not mean that there is no collusion among the firms. It only rules out the possibility of perfect collusion.

After the model was extended to include foreign trade it was applied to Swedish data in order to get direct estimates of the implicit degree of collusion. The main impression from this empirical exercise was that the degree of implicit collusion is rather low. All values are far below one. The mean for 1965 is 0.040 and the highest value is 0.125. By 1985 the mean had decreased slightly to 0.036, but the highest value had risen to 0.154. Thus, the conclusion from this is that the implicit degree of collusion is far from perfect. On the contrary, it is very close to zero in the majority of industries indicating that a Cournot-like non-collusive behaviour is predominant. However, as was noted above, the existence of product differentiation may give a downward bias to the estimates of the implicit degree of collusion. Results in this part of the empirical analysis also indicated that imports exert a competitive pressure, resulting in reduce profitability for all domestic firms other than the largest ones. Further it was found that exports had a negative influence upon firm's profitability in 1965. In 1985 this was the case only for the largest firms in each industry. The effect upon the profitability of other firms was positive but non-significant.

When looking at possible explanatory variables to industry differences in the implicit degree of collusion it was found that the Herfindahl index exerts a positive influence, which is in conformity with for instance Stigler's oligopoly theory. It was found, however, that the relationship was more likely to be logarithmic than linear. But it was also found that variations in the degree of foreign trade, exports in particular, were of even greater importance in explaining industry differences in the implicit degree of collusion. The results show that the higher the share of exports the lower the implicit degree of collusion among domestic firms with regard to their behaviour on the home market. No clear conclusion could, however, be reached on whether it is exports *per se* that have this influence or if it functions as a measure of the competitive pressure from the world market.

It is interesting from the standpoint of methodology to compare these results with the ones found in the preceding chapter where only industry data were used, and also with the regressions based on industry data performed in this chapter. In the preceding chapter a negative influence from exports was found in one of the profit equations, but no significant influence at all from imports. Using aggregated data for 1965 and 1985, the export share as well as the import share were found to be non-significant in 1965, while in 1985 the export share was found to exert a positive influence and the import share was just significant with a negative sign. However, when individual plant data are used to estimate a properly specified model, it is found, first, that there is a competitive pressure from imports, and second, that exports also exert a competitive pressure in both years, despite the positive influence on industry profitability found in 1985.

It is finally time to try to answer the questions set out at the beginning of the preceding chapter, i.e. should the increase in *CR4* between 1965 and 1978 worry us? Does it mean that competition has been reduced?[5] The answer is that seller concentration is not unimportant. There is a negative relationship between seller concentration and competitive behaviour. But since we have also found that foreign trade, imports as well as exports, exert a strong competitive pressure on the domestic market, and since the share of imports on the home market has risen from 0.39 in 1965 to 0.44 in 1985, and the share of exports from 0.37 to 0.47, there is no reason to believe that competition in general has been reduced during the last twenty years. The generally very low degrees of implicit collusion estimated in this chapter, together with the fact that the Swedish economy is internationalized to a very high degree, lead to the conclusion that seller concentration in general is not a severe problem for the Swedish economy in the sense of giving market power to some firms. This should not, on the other hand, lead anyone to jump to the conclusion that seller concentration does not matter at all. There may well be individual markets where seller concentration is high and where the positive effect of this upon the degree of implicit collusion is not neutralized by foreign trade. The results above show, however, that the most efficient way to stimulate competition in such markets is, whenever this is possible, to stimulate foreign trade and increase the openness to the world market rather than trying to reduce seller concentration. It will not only be more efficient in terms of the effect upon the implicit degree of collusion, but it may also – at least if the policy leads to larger exports – result in achievements of economies of scale. Furthermore, according to the result in the preceding chapter there does not need to be any fear that increases in export will give rise to increases in seller concentration, since exports were found to have a negative influence upon the degree of seller concentration.

NOTES

* I would like to thank Bo Carlsson, Jurgen Franke, Lennart Hjalmarsson, Stephen Martin and Dennis Mueller for many valuable comments.

1 This is also in conformity with recently reported empirical results by Martin (1988) who employs a different methodology.

2 Though this is Mueller's assumption, one could, in principle, omit this assumption and consequently combine the degree of co-operation and conjectural variations approaches.

3 Due to limitations in the software, the number of estimated parameters of the market share variable had to be restricted to 85. The results presented in Tables 3.2 and 3.3 are calculatd from regressions where a sufficient number of industries were included without any market share variable. Those industries were chosen among the ones that in a sequence of regressions showed up to have a very low t-ratio for the parameter on the market share variable.

4 According to the Goldfeld–Quandt test, the null hypothesis of homoskedasticity can be rejected on the 0.05 level of significance for all columns in Tables 3.4 and 3.5. In order to avoid, at least asymptotically, the problem of biased estimation of the variances, the following estimator of the variances was used (see Kmenta (1986: 292): Est $Var(\beta)$ = $(X'X)^{-1}X'EEX(X'X)^{-1}$ where E is a matrix with the values of the least squares residuals in the diagonal and zeros elsewhere. The reported t-ratios stem from the estimates of the variances given by this estimator. It should be noted that the use of the OLS parameter estimator, which in the presence of heteroskedasticity gives unbiased but inefficient estimates, together with this estimator of the variances, may result in 'unnecessarily' wide confidence intervals and may consequently increase the risk of type II error.

5 It should be mentioned that the mean of Herfindahl index has in fact fallen between 1965 and 1985, from 0.129 to 0.097 (the mean in 1965 among the 85 industries that are in the 1985 year data was 0.116). But it must be remembered that the figure for 1985 is only approximate since it is based upon the initially grouped data.

REFERENCES

Cowling, K. and Waterson, M. (1976) 'Price–cost margins and market structure', *Economica*, *43*, 267–74.

Clarke, R. and Davies, S.W. (1982) 'Market structure and price–cost margins', *Economica*, *49*, 277–87.

Clarke, R., Davies, S.W. and Waterson, M. (1984) 'The profitability–concentration relation: market power or efficiency', *The Journal of Industrial Economics*, *32*, 435–50.

Demsetz, H. (1974) 'Two systems of belief about monopoly', in H.S. Goldschmid, H.M. Mann and J.F. Weston (eds) *Industrial Concentration: the New Learning*, Boston: Little, Brown & Co.

Dickson, V.A. (1982) 'Collusion and price–cost margins', *Economica*, *49*, 39–42.

Donsimoni, M.-P., Geroski, P. and Jacquemin, A. (1984) 'Concentration indices and market power: two views', *The Journal of Industrial Economics*, *32*, 419–34.

Kmenta, J. (1986) *Elements of Econometrics*, New York: Macmillan.

Martin, S. (1984) 'Comment on the specification of structure–performance relationships', *European Economic Review*, *24*, 197–201.

Martin, S. (1988) 'Market power and/or efficiency', *The Review of Economics and Statistics*, *70*, 331–5.

Mueller, D. (1986) *Profits in the Long Run*, Cambridge: Cambridge University Press.

Sawyer, M.C. (1982) 'On the specification of structure–performance relationships', *European Economic Review*, *17*, 295–306.

Schmalensee, R. (1987) 'Collusion versus differential efficiency: testing alternative hypotheses', *The Journal of Industrial Economics*, *35*, 399–425.

Stigler, G. (1964) 'A theory of oligopoly', *Journal of Political Economy*, *72*, 44–61.

Stålhammar, N.-O. (1987) *Strukturomvandling, företagsbeteende och förväntningsbildning inom den svenska tillverkningsindustrin*, [Structural change, firm behaviour and expectation formation in the Swedish manufacturing industry], dissertation in economics published by Department of Economics at School of Economics, University of Gothenburg, no. 19.

Urata, S. (1984) 'Price–cost margins and imports in an oligopolistic market', *Economics Letters*, *15*, 139–44.

Part III

International integration and multinational competition

4   The white goods industry

Örjan Sölvell

INTRODUCTION

In this article market power and consumer welfare are discussed in relation to the white goods industry.[1] Short-run welfare losses carried by domestic consumers, following from a highly concentrated industry structure, are put into a more dynamic and long-run context. National concentration ratios give very limited information in industries where competition is becoming increasingly international, or even global, in character. Swedish consumers gain by having perhaps the most efficient producer in the world – Electrolux – based in Sweden. However, two issues emerge regarding consumer welfare: the vertical structure in Sweden is dominated by Electrolux, and Electrolux does not face domestic rivals.

The white goods industry has been transformed into a mature and highly international industry during the last few decades, dominated by a few large multinational corporations, among them the Swedish firm Electrolux.[2] The process has been characterized by rapid concentration and internationalization. Domestic and more recently international mergers and acquisitions, have been motivated by a drive to lower manufacturing costs, and to gain market power to improve profitability. While some firms have moved aggressively into international markets, others retaliated to defend home market positions.

As the pace of change continues, new strategies have emerged within the industry. International co-ordination of manufacturing plants, sourcing arrangements with foreign competitors, multi-brand strategies, component and product standardization across national markets, are some of the key strategies pursued by the leading multinational firms today.[3] On the other hand, distribution channels, brand images, marketing and purchasing decisions are still local phenomena – typical for a nation, or smaller region within a nation.

With increasing internationalization, components and assembled appliances are shipped across and between continents in complex patterns. Today's consumers face a number of different brands: a domestic or a foreign manufacturer's brand, and sometimes a wholesaler's, or retailer's brand. An appliance with a domestic manufacturer's brand might be assembled by a competing foreign manufacturer, which in turn is using components from yet another competing manufacturer. For example, the microwave oven sold in Sweden, under a Swedish brand, might be imported from the United States, using mostly Japanese components. Another oven with a German brand, might originate in Korea, using the same Japanese components as the oven imported from the United States. Yet another Swedish consumer might buy a microwave oven with a Dutch brand (partly owned by a US manufacturer), manufactured in Sweden. Again, many components probably originate in Japan.

Consumers care about prices, service, quality, brand images, retail outlets and so on, but they know nothing about the competitive struggle behind the scenes – a struggle which is becoming increasingly global.

Setting the new stage

During the last two decades, the white goods industry has been characterized by rapid concentration in major national markets, such as in the United States, and in most European markets. In Japan, the industry has been dominated by six firms throughout the post-war period. Before the 1970s competition was largely confined to nations, i.e. competition in each national market was *independent* of competition in other national markets, with each national market being dominated by indigenous firms. International trade was limited to nearby markets, and few manufacturers had established foreign manufacturing operations. In Europe, a few Italian firms were the leading exporters, mostly selling unbranded, low-end products to other manufacturers (so called OEM sales) and larger retailers (so called private label sales), who would sell them under their own domestic brands.

In the last fifteen years, the international scene has changed dramatically. Competition has become increasingly international. Major European markets, such as Great Britain, France, West

Germany and Italy, have been penetrated by foreign firms, and the US market is no longer dominated by indigenous firms. Electrolux have restructured the European arena acquiring Zanussi, the number one producer in Italy, and one of the leading European manufacturers; the appliance division of Thorn-EMI in Great Britain; Zanker in West Germany; and a number of smaller manufacturers. All in all, Electrolux have acquired some twenty-five white goods manufacturers since the mid-1960s (see the Appendix, p. 143). With the acquisition of White Consolidated Industries, WCI, in the United States, a first major transatlantic step was taken by a European firm. Whirlpool, one of the three leading US manufacturers (together with General Electric and WCI), and Philips (the number two European manufacturer) followed suit by joining forces in mid-1988.[4] The large Japanese manufacturers Matsushita (National and Panasonic brands), Sharp, Toshiba, Hitachi, Mitsubishi and Sanyo have slowly built up positions in the United States, and throughout Europe, focusing upon microwave ovens and compact appliances. More recently, Goldstar and Samsung of Korea have become global suppliers of microwave ovens.

Today, competition in any national white goods market is increasingly *interdependent* with competition in all other national white goods markets. Thus, competition is no longer nationally bound, it has become highly international. One product stands out as a truly global product – the microwave oven. The microwave oven quickly became a global product, with homogenous product standards and consumer preferences. On the other hand, technical standards and consumer preferences regarding cooker (ranges) vary considerably across markets. Overall the white goods industry is moving towards a state of global competition.

Product characteristics

The parallel emergence of white goods industries in a large number of countries, led to the development of a wide variety of technical configurations, designs, features, etc. Technical standards differed, and clearly consumer preferences differed across national markets. This is still true for many appliances such as cookers and washing machines. Microwave ovens, refrigerators and freezers (especially low-end, stand-alone units) and dishwashers, have become highly homogenous products. The larger multinational firms can standard-ize both components and assembled products to an increasing extent. The national touch can be added with minor product adjustments, and local marketing and distribution activities. With increasing homogenization, the larger European manufacturers have rationalized their plant networks. Thus, each plant becomes responsible for one product line for the whole European market. Where national technical standards and preferences have prevailed, such as for cookers, the multinational manufacturers are still forced to operate many national plants.

Each national market is segmented in various ways. Product segments range from high-end, colour co-ordinated, built-in appliances (including all possible features), to low-end, stand-alone units devoid of any frills. Apart from differences in capacity (compact, standard and large size appliances), quality, technical sophistication, appearance, etc. appliances are offered in an almost unlimited number of combinations (refrigerator–freezer combinations, microwave ovens with built-in convection ovens, steamer, bakery and browner, washer–spinner–dryer combinations, etc.).

Continuous development efforts have led to better featured and more energy-efficiency appliances. Product standardization, the use of new materials, electronics, etc., have led to products which are more efficient to manufacture and use. Metal has been substituted for plastics, fibreglass insulation for foam, flat steel for coiled steel, etc. New features have been constantly added in order to speed up replacement demand, to beat competitors, and to reduce price elasticity among consumers. Cost reductions in production, together with product differentiation (adding features in order to differentiate a product from standard products offered in the market), have become key strategies as markets have matured. Many of the leading manufacturers pursue multi-brand strategies to cover a range of market segments. Furthermore, new brands are constantly added through acquisitions.

Most brands are still only used within one national market. However, a few brands like Electrolux,[5] Panasonic and Philips are highly international brands. As economies of scale has become increasingly important, many manufacturers have chosen to reduce the range of products in production, but kept or expanded the number of brands and models sold by sourcing from competing firms. This practice has been much more developed in the United States than in Europe or Japan. It is most pronounced in microwave ovens. Japanese and Korean manufacturers account for some 75 per cent of total world production, and at least half of that is sold through brands belonging to foreign appliance manufacturers and retailers.

MARKET STRUCTURE – CONCENTRATION AND INTERNATIONALIZATION

In this section we will describe major changes in market structure throughout Europe, in the United States and in Japan.

Europe

In the 1960s, markets began to open up with the formation of EFTA and the EEC, and an increasing export activity could be noticed. However, national structural characteristics, such as existing distribution networks, established brands and old customer ties in combination with high transportation costs, made export strategies less successful. Thus, entry barriers effectively kept out foreign intruders, even when trade barriers had largely disappeared. Given the underlying economies of scale, some firms continued to strive for a larger market than their home market, in spite of these export problems. This led to a wave of foreign direct investment, often in the form of acquisitions. The national consolidation phase moved into a European consolidation phase in the 1970s. Six firms moved into a leading position, followed by some 300 smaller manufacturers. The smaller manufacturers are typically family-owned companies, running a single plant (specializing, for example, in 'wet' products like washing machines, 'cold' products like refrigerators and freezers, or 'hot' products like cookers and ovens), and marketing the products on the national market. Components are sourced from local suppliers, and from the larger appliance manufacturers such as Zanussi. Moreover, sales are often limited to the home market or neighbouring countries. A few niche firms have opted for the high end of the market, such as Miele in West Germany.

The leading six firms in Europe include Electrolux (Sweden), Philips-Whirlpool (Italy), Bosch–Siemens (West-Germany), AEG (West Germany), Thomson (France) and Indesit (Italy). In 1985, the number of firms, each manufacturing equal to or more than 0.1 per cent of total production in western Europe amounted to 30 firms in freezers, 28 in refrigerators, 26 in washing machines, 22 in dryers and 15 in dishwashers. The four-firm concentration ratios reached 59.9 per cent in dishwashers, 53.6 per cent in refrigerators, 42.0 per cent in dryers and 39.5 per cent in freezers. The number of cooker manufacturers exceeded 100. In Italy alone there were 30 firms with 0.1 per cent or more of the Italian production in 1985.[6]

Two firms, Philips–Whirlpool and Electrolux, have built up truly international operations, with plants, design functions, sales and service organizations throughout Europe. Philips has an old 'multinational' tradition with plants in a large number of countries throughout the world. These were set up in a world of significant trade barriers and thus local production was the only feasible way of building up international sales. Electrolux, on the other hand, has grown through acquisitions, first in the Nordic markets, then throughout Europe and the United States. Electrolux was a rather small player until the mid-1970s. Faced with a growing number of plants, reduced trade barriers and reduced transportation costs, Electrolux embarked upon a programme of European-wide integration. The goal was to have one plant per product in Europe (except cookers where demand and technical standards differ from country to country). Today, most of Electrolux plants are specialized in one product line, and have sole responsibility for the European market.

Philips was also forced to rationalize its international production network (in total Philips has closed 80 plants since 1972),[7] and move in the direction of 'focused factories'. With its diversified operations in consumer electronics, telecommunications, lighting, white goods, etc., Philips now pursue a strategy of joining forces with other companies.

United States

The major manufacturers of home appliances in the United States include GE, Whirlpool, WCI (acquired by Electrolux in 1986) and Maytag–Magic Chef. In addition, the large retail chain Sears holds a very strong position in the market, selling both branded goods as well as its in-house brand Kenmore. The industry has gone through a significant concentration process, starting from a base of some 230 manufacturers in the late 1940s. Today, only less than ten firms have any significant manufacturing operations of white goods. Except for the 'big four', a few niche players have managed to survive.[8]

In 1970, there were four leading brands – GE, Whirlpool, Frigidaire (later acquired by White Consolidated, WCI, in 1979) and Kenmore (Sears). Excluding the cooker market which was highly fragmented, these four firms accounted for some 60 to 70 per cent of the market (40 per cent for cookers). During the 1970s, WCI expanded rapidly through acquisitions, broadening its range of brands and products. WCI also produced significant amounts of unbranded products (OEM and private label) and became a second source to Sears, after Whirlpool. The most volatile market has been the microwave oven market, where old established brands and new ones have competed for positions. For other products, market shares of leading brands have not changed significantly in the last decades. Instead, firms have grown by acquiring brands, the most active ones including WCI, Magic Chef, Raytheon and Maytag. In 1985, Whirlpool acquired Kitchen Aid. The antitrust climate changed, and the leading manufacturers now met increasing competition from WCI. In 1986, Electrolux acquired WCI, and Maytag acquired Magic Chef.

In this process of concentration, both smaller manufacturers and larger diversified firms left the industry. The surviving firms built up a competitive advantage around a few strategic dimensions. Scale economies in production at the plant level aided the larger manufacturers, which consolidated production into only a few plants per product line. To lower costs, production was rationalized (requiring continuous investment), but whole product lines were also phased out, replaced by externally sourced appliances (inter-firm sourcing), or by other in-house brands (manufacturing plants belonging to one brand producing for other in-house brands as well). Some narrow line manufacturers also used the strategy to source from competing firms, in order to grow into new product areas, such as dishwashers, disposers and microwave ovens. Thus, a specialization could be seen in manufacturing, while each brand broadened its range of products. Design & Manufacturing (D&M) (acquired by Electrolux in 1987) became a major supplier of dishwashers, while microwave ovens were purchased from Japan and Korea.

The broad line manufacturers have gained economies of scale in manufacturing (both on a product line basis and a plant basis), and economies of scope through the co-ordination of purchases across product lines and in-house manufacturing of components shared among several product lines. However, the main differences in competitive advantage relate to product differentiation. Brand proliferation has developed into a cornerstone of competitive advantage, based on a combination of brand loyalty and a large installed base built up over the years.

As products have become more of a commodity, successful manufacturers invested heavily in brand proliferation. Such differentiation strategies minimized the loss of bargaining power *vis-à-vis* retailers (and price sensitivity of consumers), and lessened rivalry within the industry. Without a strong brand image, the threat of backward integration (or contracting out to manufacturers with weak brands) by retailers, would have grown considerably as the products matured.

In 1970, there were many firms with highly differing strategic configurations. The main discriminating dimensions were width of product lines, quality brand image, number of product lines, degree of vertical integration, degree of diversification, geographical scope and distribution channels. The leading US firms today are characterized by:

- Broad coverage from low-end to high-end of the market, through a number of brands.
- Brands covering all types of products (with partial inter-firm sourcing and intra-firm sourcing).
- Low levels of component production.
- Sales of both private label and branded products.
- Sales both to the retail market and the construction market.
- In-house service organizations covering the whole US market.
- Low degree of diversification (excluding GE and Raytheon).
- A focus on the domestic market. This focus changed somewhat in the late 1980s, with Whirlpool joining Philips, GE forming a joint venture with GEC in the UK and Maytag acquiring Hoover (with white goods operations in the UK).

The non-survivors were diversified firms with full product lines and single-business firms with a narrow line of appliances. Even GE, the industry leader, considered leaving the business in the late 1970s.

Japan

With a population of some 120 million people, Japan is second only to the United States in terms of size of the market for consumer products. Rapid economic growth has fostered a very large and diversified industrial sector for electrical consumer products. Matsushita is the leader in most of these industries. Other leading firms include Toshiba, Hitachi, Sharp, Mitsubishi Electric and Sanyo.[9] These six firms have dominated the industry in the post-war period. The industry was domestic-oriented until exports of microwave ovens took off in the 1970s. With the strengthened international positions in microwave ovens and compact appliances, the Japanese manufacturers established plants, first in the United States, and later in Europe and some Third World countries (see discussion on microwave ovens, pp. 127–33).

While the Japanese firms have successfully penetrated the major national market, almost no counter-measures have been taken by European or American firms in Japan. Domestic producers have managed to keep a firm grip on the market. Almost no white goods are imported. Most important, the Japanese manufacturers control the distribution chain tightly. Control covers in-house sales companies, various layers of wholesalers and retail chains. Out of some 70,000–80,000 retail shops in Japan, over 30,000 are controlled by Matsushita, 12,000 by Toshiba, 11,000 by Hitachi, 4,500 by Sanyo and 3,800 by Sharp.[10] Structural changes in the distribution sector, where supermarkets, large speciality stores (superstores) and discount stores have been on the increase, forced manufacturers to consolidate their sales company systems in the early 1980s. Korean microwave ovens out-compete Japanese ovens, especially in the smaller segments, in many markets around the world. However, they are virtually non-existent in the Japanese market. The independent retail chains (which are most likely 'gate openers')[11] have not had the power to open up the Japanese markets to imports (potential openings would be minimal).

We have now seen how national white goods industries throughout the world have become highly concentrated over the last few decades. This concentration process has been especially pronounced in the major manufacturing countries, such as the United States, Japan and some European countries (including Sweden). In Japan, the top six firms control 90 to 95 per cent of the market. In the United States, only four firms control roughly the same share. In Sweden, Electrolux alone controls some 70 per cent share of the market. While the concentration process in the United States has in part been driven by powerful retailers, this has not been the case in most European markets or in Japan.

Towards a state of global competition

Competition in Europe has slowly integrated into a larger whole, with Electrolux and Philips building up European-wide networks of plants, distribution channels, brands, etc., while some other manufacturers have become leading exporters (mainly Italian and German firms). In order to lower costs (through larger component volumes, standardization of product designs across national markets, etc.) and to increase market power, several routes were used to grow internationally. Philips moved into various joint venture agreements (the most significant ones in West Germany, Italy and later with a US firm). The German and Italian joint venture partners were later acquired. Electrolux, as we have already discussed, expanded largely through acquisitions.

While intra-European trade has increased rapidly during the last decades, inter-regional trade between Europe, the United States and Japan has not. Large differences in standards and tastes, combined with substantial transportation costs, have kept trade at low levels. There have been small pockets of demand for large US appliances in Japan and other countries, for high-end European style appliances in the United States, and for Japanese compact appliances in Europe and the United States. With the growth of the microwave oven market, this pattern began to change, as we will discuss later.

The Japanese firms used various penetration routes. They formed alliances with strong local retailers (private label sales), and sold unbranded products to local manufacturers (OEM sales). In addition they built up local distribution of branded appliances (microwave ovens and compact appliances), and continued penetration led to greenfield investments in new plants. It is important to note that the Japanese firms began to build up world supremacy (limited to microwave ovens) in a market, characterized by very high barriers to new competition. These barriers were composed of well-established brands, design skills, long manufacturing experience (with large-scale, cost efficient operations), and tight control over distribution. The leading local brand names they had to fight sometimes had a history dating back to the turn of the century (such as the GE brand in the United States).

High barriers to entry had tended to isolate competition to 'islands', i.e. to individual nations. To break this pattern of national competition, long-term dedication was needed. Penetration of these 'fortresses' was the result of a long process of investment and innovation in design, manufacturing technologies, world-wide distribution networks and in an effort to build up brand recognition around the world, including markets with the most well-established brand names.

In the white goods industry overall, Electrolux stands out as the premier international change agent, first throughout the scattered European markets, and more recently across the Atlantic. In the microwave segment, a few Japanese firms, and more recently a few Korean firms, stand out as the key players on the global scene. Electrolux has yet to show that it can become a dominant player in

Japan, before it can reach the status of a global leader. In 1989, Electrolux announced an alliance with Sharp in Japan.

MARKET CONDUCT IN ONE SEGMENT: THE CASE OF THE MICROWAVE OVEN MARKET

Innovation in the United States

As for many other post-Second World War products, initial development of the microwave oven technology took place in the United States. The microwave oven was invented by Raytheon in the mid-1940s. The first applications were in restaurants and hotels. Raytheon, a high technology firm and defence contractor, had no previous experience in consumer markets, and did not put much emphasis on the new technology, licensing it freely to other firms. Therefore, Tappan, a smaller range manufacturer, introduced a microwave oven in 1955 (GE's Hotpoint division followed within a year). However, the first microwave oven using standard household circuits was introduced by Raytheon's Amana division in 1967. The leading appliance manufacturers were slow in entering the microwave segment, giving room for smaller manufacturers to gain positions (including Amana, Caloric and Tappan). It also opened up the way for entry into the market by new firms. Two domestic newcomers diversified into microwave ovens in the 1970s: Corning (a glass manufacturer that introduced the glass surface range); and Litton (a diversified company and also defence oriented). In 1977, Litton dominated the microwave oven market with a 25 per cent share. However, as the leading brands decided to invest in microwave capacity, Litton's position was slowly eroded and in 1984 their share had dropped to around 10 per cent. Litton tried to fight back increased competition by being the leading innovator. In 1984, they introduced the first sub-compact microwave. However, increased competition from Japanese manufacturers in the late 1970s, and from Korean firms in the early 1980s, almost forced Litton out of business. In the mid-1980s, Litton's microwave division was taken over in a management buy-out.

With increasing Japanese competitiveness, even the leading US manufacturers of microwave ovens decided to source from Japan and later Korea, including Amana (Raytheon) in 1983, GE (from Matsushita and Samsung) in 1984 and Tappan (from Toshiba) in 1985. Sourcing strategies had begun much earlier with magnetrons, the key component in the oven. Already in 1977, the last magnetron was produced in the United States. Three leading Japanese manufacturers were slowly taking over total world demand for this strategic component. US manufacturers (with domestic origin) reached a peak production of 3.5 million microwave oven in 1984. In the next four years production was halved and taken over by imports and local production by Japanese and Korean firms.

Penetration by the Japanese manufacturers was facilitated by a number of factors. First, the microwave oven was a new product with a high-technology image. Thus, brand loyalty in home appliances like refrigerators and washing machines did not work as a significant entry barrier. The domestic entrant, Litton, could also utilize the high-technology image. Second, as demand for microwave ovens was not related to replacement demand, or new housing demand, there was room for new consumer brands. Third, the major Japanese manufacturers had already built up efficient distribution networks throughout the North American continent (for consumer electronics) and they were, of course, used when introducing their microwave ovens. Fourth, Japanese brands had gained a high reputation in consumer electronics, such as Hi-Fi equipment and TV sets. This brand recognition could easily be brought over to microwave ovens, which had an electronics image, and were often sold together with stereo equipment and other consumer electronics. Thus, microwave ovens are found both in the department for major appliances and the stereo and TV department in a US department store. Fifth, entry was facilitated by the fact that microwave ovens are a rather homogenous product, and thus the Japanese manufacturers could begin exporting without costly adoptions to US standards and tastes. Finally, Sears and other large retailers played a major role in opening up the US market. They acted as 'gate openers', as did the US manufacturers in a later stage (design know-how, customer know-how, etc. was actively transferred to the Japanese and Korean manufacturers).

Sears have played a key role, not only in the retailing of major home appliances, but also in shaping the structure of the manufacturing industry. In the early days, it had mastered the merger of two companies into Whirlpool, it had induced entry by new entrepreneurs (such as Roper in ranges, and Design & Manufacturing in dishwashers) and finally it invited foreign competition. As early as in 1976, Sears had negotiated a deal where Sanyo was to acquire Warwick's main plant for TV sets. Sears was not satisfied with Warwick's performance, and looked abroad for someone who could compete with RCA and Zenith on cost (the two leading TV set manufacturers at the time). Warwick, manufacturing TV sets and electronic organs, was jointly owned by Whirlpool (75 per cent) and Sears (25 per cent), and sold almost all its output through Sears. In 1977, the line of colour TV sets was discontinued and the plant sold off to Sanyo. Two years later, Sanyo began the manufacturing of microwave ovens in that plant and later, also, refrigerators. Thus, Sears acted as a 'gate opener' for Sanyo into the US market. Other large retailers also induced imports of Japanese- and Korean-made microwave ovens. Furthermore, US manu- facturers began to source their microwave ovens from Japan and Korea, as they were falling behind in the race for volumes and technical innovation; this race quickly turned into a global race.

With the advent of the microwave oven, the first new brands were established in the US major home appliance market since the Second World War.

A fragmented Europe

The European microwave oven market experienced a slow take-off in the early 1980s – the penetration rate reaching 4 per cent in 1984, as compared to 42.5 per cent in the United States. However, with a bright growth potential (a rarity in this mature industry), all leading European manufacturers had entered the industry by the late 1970s. Philips, who pioneered the European market, decided to centralize production to its plant in Sweden. Electrolux, which became the leading force in Europe in the mid-1980s, brought in the larger sized microwave ovens from its American subsidiary, Tappan, and began sourcing from Japanese manufacturers (Imanishi and others) and later, from Korean manufacturers for the smaller ovens.

The German market is dominated by the domestic firms Bosch–Siemens, AEG and Miele. The two French manufacturers, Moulinex and Thomson, are only strong in their home market. Electrolux and Philips have positions throughout Europe (weakest in West Germany). Electrolux made a major inroad into the British market when it acquired Thorn–EMI's white goods division in 1987. Through this acquisition, Electrolux got hold of the Tricity brand (a strong microwave oven brand in the UK) and a distribution network, as well as a plant manufacturing microwave ovens (in addition to distribution and plant capacity for other white goods).

Japanese firms building up production capacity

The Japanese manufacturers of white goods put an early focus on microwave ovens. In 1961, Sharp entered the production of microwave ovens as the first Japanese company to do so. Soon after, the other major electrical firms followed suit, and in 1965 all the major producers had entered the industry. Technology was licensed from US manufacturers. Most importantly, technology to build the key component – the magnetron – was licensed from US companies including Advanced Transformer. For example, in 1968 Hitachi started production of magnetrons with a licence from that company. The smaller Japanese microwave oven manufacturers typically sourced their magnetrons from their larger domestic competitors. Sanyo, for example, sourced from Hitachi until they managed to build their own magnetrons.

From the beginning, Sharp established itself as the leading firm, but Matsushita worked hard to take over this position. Since the 1970s, Sharp and Matsushita have controlled roughly 30 per cent each of the market. Hitachi and Toshiba control around 10 per cent to 15 per cent. See details in Table 4.1.

Table 4.1 Market shares in the Japanese microwave oven market, 1978 and 1984

Firms	1984 (%)	1978 (%)
Sharp	31.9	28.8
Matsushita	28.5	28.5
Hitachi	13.2	12.7
Toshiba	10.9	13.8
Mitsubishi	4.4	5.3
Sanyo	2.9	5.0
Others	8.2	5.9

Source: Yano Research Institute, Tokyo, 'Market share in Japan', 1979 and 1985.

Production of microwave ovens took off rather slowly. In 1970, only some 400,000 units were produced in Japan. The same slowness was also true for household penetration, which had reached only 8 per cent in 1972. However, in the late 1970s a surge in exports and in domestic demand led to large investments in new plant capacity, and production rose from less than 2 million units (annual output) in the late 1970s to over 6 million in 1984. In 1986 a peak was reached at almost 8.5 million units. Household penetration reached 57 per cent in 1988.

The use of microwave ovens did not grow as quickly in Japan as in the United States. The Japanese market reached 1.22 million units in 1984 (with exports reaching 4.83 million units), up from 0.9 million units in 1979. Cooker–oven combinations comprised 65 per cent and single-purpose ovens 35 per cent, reflecting the fact that Japanese households often lack an oven and thus two appliances can be added to an already crammed kitchen in a single unit.

Global strategies

Until microwave ovens were shipped around the world, there had been limited trade of white goods between the three leading regions: the United States, Japan and Europe. Typically, markets with an indigenous industry have been largely untouched by foreign competition. The largest multinational players have concentrated their efforts on markets with weak competition, i.e. markets characterized by low barriers to competition (in Third World markets and smaller industrialized markets). For example, Electrolux did not threaten any of the largest manufacturers until the mid-1980s, when it moved into Italy and later into the United States. Before that, Electrolux had concentrated its efforts to its 'home' Nordic market, Third World markets and European markets without strong indigenous competitors (Electrolux is still weak in West Germany despite its leading position in Europe). In a similar fashion, US firms did not make any major inroads into Europe. Japanese firms were until recently largely absent in Europe and held only minor positions in the US market. Neither European nor US firms have made any major efforts to penetrate the Japanese market.

With the growth of the microwave oven market, this pattern began to change. With homogenous demand across countries, and with negligible differences in national technical standards, there was a clear export potential to be developed. In addition, the product could be transported over long distances at minimal cost.

Japanese penetration of European markets

Except for Great Britain, the European markets were slow to take-off. The Japanese manufacturers, which were rapidly becoming the most efficient producers in the world, captured a dominant share of the European market early in the take-off stage. In 1983, the Japanese share amounted to 50 per cent of a market of less than 1 million units. In Great Britain, penetration reached over 70 per cent. Again, large volumes were shipped under private label arrangements to British retailers, which acted as 'gate openers' into the British market. Again, the Japanese firms began to substitute exports for local production. The Japanese manufacturers had by now become leaders in new technology and licences were sold to a number of European manufacturers wishing to enter the booming microwave oven market. In Great Britain, Hitachi set up a joint venture with Creda (now owned by British GEC). Toshiba formed an alliance with Thomson in France, and Matsushita did likewise with Bosch–Siemens, the largest German manufacturers. Later, all major Japanese manufacturers established their own plants in the UK (only to be followed by the Korean firms a few years later).

Japanese exporters turn into global manufacturers

A large percentage of the Japanese microwave oven production has been exported. The export share of total production accounted for 52 per cent in 1979, 81 per cent in 1985 and 63 per cent in 1987. Thus, in spite of a growing home market, the export share rose during the early 1980s. Exports have been geared to the US market (60 per cent in 1985) and the European market (28 per cent in 1985). The heavy focus on the US market is the result of several factors. First, the US market was the first to take-off and thus the sheer size was attractive. Second, Matsushita, Sharp, Hitachi, Toshiba, Mitsubishi and Sanyo had already established strong positions in the US market (in TV sets, Hi-Fi equipment and, to a lesser extent, smaller sized major home appliances). Third, the US market was one homogenous market, far easier to penetrate than the fragmented European markets. And fourth, large US retailers (and later manufacturers) pulled the Japanese manufacturers into the US market (acting as 'gate openers') by offering attractive private label sales (and later OEM sales).

Both in the United States and Europe, a large part of sales have been made under private label (vertical sales) and OEM arrangements (horizontal sales). Private label sales include US retail chains like Sears (supplied by Sanyo and later Goldstar), Montgomery Ward (supplied by Sharp), and Penney's (supplied by Samsung). OEM sales (from manufacturer to manufacturer) have included virtually every major producer of home appliances in the United States and throughout Europe.

In the late 1970s, Sanyo, Matsushita and Sharp had become major exporters, and to expand further, exporting alone was not sufficient. Matsushita and Sharp were the two leaders in Japan and they decided that they would capture a larger share of the global 'pie', which in turn necessitated foreign production. Sanyo was partly pulled by Sears into the US market. Given its small share of the home market, sales in foreign markets was obviously the most feasible alternative if growth was to be achieved. Sanyo and Matsushita both started local manufacturing of microwaves in the United States, in 1979. In 1980 Sharp followed suit. Penetration of the US market proved to be successful and, in 1984, 60 per cent of the US market was supplied by Japanese and Korean producers – through imports and local production.

On a global scale, manufacturers are now connected in a complex web involving sourcing arrangements, alliances, mergers and acquisitions, and technical licensing arrangements. Intra-firm sourcing is common within the multinational manufacturers. Sharp, for example, export microwaves made in their US plant to its European subsidiaries. Electrolux bring in US-made ovens to its subsidiaries throughout Europe. Similarly Electrolux distribute ovens made in the United Kingdom throughout its network of subsidiaries. Philips–Whirlpool uses its Swedish subsidiary as a basis for Europe.

Technical tie-ups are common. We have already touched upon a few Japanese joint ventures in Europe. For components, all US and European manufacturers source magnetrons from Japan, mainly from Matsushita, Hitachi and Toshiba. Mitsubishi and Sharp do not produce magnetrons, but source them from the other Japanese firms. Hitachi supplies Goldstar in Korea with magnetrons.

As the Japanese and Korean manufacturers have become low-cost producers of microwave ovens, with significant market power both in components and assembled ovens, the question is whether the time is ripe for them to move into other segments of the white goods industry – on a global scale! In a fierce competitive climate at home, these firms try to differentiate themselves by offering a constant flow of new product features including microprocessor controlled functions, compactness, improved energy efficiency and so on. The technological know-how is there,[12] the distribution channels are in place, and the brands have become familiar to American and European consumers.

MARKET PERFORMANCE AS SEEN BY THE SWEDISH CONSUMER

Welfare among Swedish consumers is based on a wide variety of products offered at competitive prices. Open borders and an efficient retail sector are important prerequisites. If such conditions exist, there is no particular reason why there should be a Swedish white goods industry in place. The fact is, however, that there is a white goods industry in Sweden. The important question then becomes: is the structure of the Swedish white goods industry such that it creates welfare to consumers, or are consumers paying too high a price for a too low quality product? The answer is dependent upon several factors. First, we have to consider the performance of the Swedish white goods industry – or more specifically, the performance of Electrolux. Second, the vertical structure in Sweden has to be taken into account. The bargaining positions between manufacturers–wholesalers–retailers–consumers means that responsibility for 'welfare' is unevenly spread. Third, since competition is becoming global in nature, we have to put the Swedish white goods industry, Electrolux, and the Swedish consumer into a global perspective.

National industry structure in the Swedish white goods industry

The Swedish white goods industry once consisted of several firms, most of them specializing in either 'wet', 'cold' or 'hot' appliances. As mentioned above, Electrolux became the change agent in the industry. Starting in Sweden and nearby Nordic markets, they later moved on to restructure Europe. In Sweden, Electrolux became the dominant actor in the 1970s (especially with the acquisition of Husqvarna in 1978). Market shares reached some 70 per cent. The rest of the market was accounted for by imports (especially from German and Italian manufacturers) and a few smaller manufacturers. Given the dominance of Electrolux, our discussion regarding the Swedish white goods industry will focus on that company.

The Swedish consumer is better off having a domestic, highly efficient industry, or no industry at all (under the assumption that borders are open and distribution is efficient), rather than having a domestic, poorly performing industry. Thus, as a first step, we have to consider the 'health' of Electrolux, where health should be interpreted as the ability to maintain international competitiveness.

If Electrolux is to survive and prosper in the long run, it must be able to meet the world's leading manufacturers, both at home and in international markets.

Electrolux has grown from a very weak company in the mid-1960s (lacking financial resources and up-to-date technology) to a world leader in the late 1980s. This growth has been a result of a continuous drive to improve manufacturing costs and to differentiate its wide range of products and brands at minimal cost. Acquisitions has been the key. By acquiring competitors, production rationalizations (first between plants in Sweden and the Nordic countries, and later between plants in various countries in Europe) were possible. Increased scale and financial strength created a base for larger investments in product development (not compared to many other industries, but in comparison with the smaller manufacturers in the industry) and new manufacturing technology (automating plants with state-of-the-art technologies). Thus, by actively concentrating the industry, Electrolux improved its cost position considerably. It also led to enhanced market power. Lowered costs add to consumer welfare on the one hand, while increased market power (if translated into monopoly rents) lowers welfare on the other. Consumers want a highly cost-efficient industry, implying large-scale operations, in combination with fierce competition, implying a limitation on market power. In Sweden, however, Electrolux became a highly efficient manufacturer, but it took almost full control over the Swedish white goods industry.

High concentration in itself does not necessarily imply that the industry is 'sleepy'. The Japanese microwave oven market is also highly concentrated (where two firms control roughly 60 per cent, with 30 per cent each), the industry is characterized by fierce rivalry and the firms being highly innovative. Equality among oligopolistic firms (as opposed to industries with a dominant firm) tends to enhance dynamism. Another example would be the Swedish heavy truck industry, which is highly concentrated and totally dominated by the two domestic producers: Scania and Volvo (controlling roughly 95 per cent of the Swedish market). They have equal shares of the home market and competition is characterized by intense rivalry.

By having an open market, domestic producers are continuously tested against foreign competition. Clearly, Electrolux has managed not only to meet this test, but has gradually built up international competitiveness over the last three decades. It is now one of the leading, if not to say the leading, manufacturer of white goods in the world. Hence, it would be easy to imagine that having such a competitive firm would be advantageous to Swedish consumers. However, the question about consumer welfare is more complex than that. Having a domestic competitive industry (or firm) does not automatically equate with improved consumer welfare. The vertical traits of market structure might imply reduced consumer welfare.

The Swedish vertical structure

Market power must be put in perspective. Bargaining positions between manufacturers–wholesalers–retailers–consumers differ significantly across national markets. Strong retailers can offset market power among manufacturers. The strength of retailers is related to concentration in the retail industry, whether the retailers have their own brands, design departments, etc. Strong retailers in the United States and the United Kingdom have actively created cost-efficient producers of standard appliances, i.e. they have actively affected industry structure in the manufacturing industry (encouraging entry, mergers, etc.). Furthermore, by importing large volumes of microwave ovens from Japan and Korea, they have fostered foreign industries (where Japanese and Korean manufacturers get the volumes rather than the domestic suppliers). In Japan and Sweden, on the other hand, distribution is tightly controlled by the manufacturers, which translates into rather high prices.

Manufacturers have built up market power in the vertical chain through various ties into wholesaling and retailing. Most importantly, they own part of the retail and wholesale industries and they use exclusive dealerships. Strong brands is another source of market power in the vertical chain. With a few manufacturers controlling a large number of brands, the power position among retailers *vis-à-vis* the manufacturers is limited. The vertical power balance is always threatened by entry of new retailers. Various types of retail chains, superstores, discount stores and the like have emerged in many of the industrialized markets. These retailers are sometimes strong enough to bring in new competition (they act as 'gate openers' to foreign firms) to stir up local competition.

Entry by foreign firms does not necessarily lower the national concentration ratio (when a local firm is acquired), but most often it upsets well-established structures. Dynamism is enhanced. In order to counter foreign penetration, a number of counter-moves are likely to follow.[13] A typical counter-measure is to upgrade products (include new features, improve service, etc.), or to lower cost through rationalizations.

The most powerful retailers have developed in-house brands and design departments. They sell both leading brands (sometimes even those brands that otherwise are only sold through exclusive dealers) and low-end products with less well-known brands, sometimes including in-house brands. This tendency has not been so pronounced in Sweden as in many other markets. Rather, Electrolux has managed to keep its power position in the vertical chain. This is detrimental to consumer welfare. With stronger retailers in Sweden (for example, with in-house brands like the wholesaler ABB–Skandia), a better test of the competitiveness of Electrolux would be available. By comparison, the Japanese manufacturers of microwave ovens are highly competitive. However, emerging competition from Korean firms has not been felt in the Japanese market, since the Japanese manufacturers have far-reaching control over distribution. The Japanese manufacturers would face an even tougher test, if there were retailers strong enough to bring in Korean microwave ovens.

Global competition and consumer welfare

The structural evolution towards a global industry will sooner or later force all appliance manufacturers to re-orient their strategies. Until the 1970s most manufacturers were largely domestic oriented. The large structural changes that followed have forced firms either to retreat to local niches, or to increase their international presence (through green-field investments, various alliances and through mergers and acquisitions).

The Swedish white goods industry was faced with two basic options: either the Swedish manufacturers could choose to develop international competitiveness, and become key players in the international market, or they could try to survive by staying local, i.e. selling to the Swedish or nearby markets and limiting manufacturing to Sweden.[14] Electrolux chose the first route, while a few other manufacturers followed the second route and remained niche players. As we have seen in this industry, it has been possible to play the 'national game' over extended periods, even if competition is globalizing. There are always niches to develop. Strong local brands and distribution channels might keep out more efficient multinational producers over long periods. However, many smaller players have been forced out of business in major industrialized markets. In the 1960s, Electrolux was one of over 400 smaller manufacturers in Europe with a limited product range. Many of these companies have not changed much since those days, but Electrolux has. Electrolux is now a very strong company, built on global competitive advantages, created out of a global network of plants (component and assembly plants), distribution systems, design centres and brands. Many of the smaller manufacturers are on the verge of bankruptcy, and the remaining competitive advantage is very thin – usually confined to a local brand and a local distribution network. They are forced to source all components, assembly operations are not up-to-date, and investments in R&D and design are lagging behind. The viable way to stay healthy in the long run in a globalizing industry, both as as company overall and in the home market, is to become one of the world leaders. If Electrolux had not managed to become an international leader, it is most likely that Swedish consumers would have suffered under an inefficient and slowly contracting industry.

An evolving international, or global, industry structure has implications for all consumers over the world: both to those which have a domestic industry (competitive or uncompetitive) and to those that do not. All consumers are, in one way of another, affected by the race for cost leadership and technological superiority among leading multinational manufacturers (both in components and assembled products). The emergence of global competitors has stirred up industry structure throughout the industrialized world. As companies move towards homogenizing components and assembled products around the world (such as in microwave ovens), consumers in various countries are now facing almost identical products (differentiation is often limited to colours, knobs, handles and so on). But something else has happened. Innovation activity has become a key factor in the race for global leadership. Thus, consumers are faced with a steady stream of new features. The force behind this renewed interest in product development (and not only process innovation, but also product improvements made in order to increase manufacturing efficiency) is fierce competition – or what could be labelled technological rivalry. The Japanese firms are especially active in turning out new products and features on a continuous basis. As we discussed earlier, most United States and European firms could not keep pace with the Japanese firms in the microwave oven market. Instead, they gave up manufacturing, and started to source from Japan and Korea (components as well as assembled ovens).

International strategies, or even global strategies, have on the one hand led to product homogenization (or at least component homogenization), but on the other hand, the nature of competition is changing as leading manufacturers from Europe, United States, Japan and Korea are becoming close rivals. New emphasis is put on product innovation, such as new features (with the help of advanced electronics including microprocessors and sensors), and more flexible manufacturing technologies permit increased product differentiation to fit local tastes.

To summarize this section, we emphasized that performance in the Swedish market has to be put into a global context. The survival of Electrolux as an efficient producer is dependent upon its global performance in the race of product and process innovation. Furthermore, consumers are affected by the local structural setting (horizontally and vertically). There are structural characteristics which are national in character, at the same time as there are structural characteristics which are international, or in the extreme case global, in character.[15] The welfare of the Swedish consumer is therefore affected both by the structural setting in Sweden, as well as the international structural setting.

CONCLUSION: MARKET POWER AND CONSUMER WELFARE

The traditional way of estimating consumer welfare is to judge how far from the case of perfect competition the industry structure is (limited to the domestic industry). A concentrated industry implies reduced consumer welfare. In this chapter we have developed a more dynamic perspective on consumer welfare. Consumers suffering in the short run, can turn out to be winners in the long run. National concentration ratios tell a very limited story. A highly concentrated industry can be very 'sleepy', but on the other hand, highly concentrated industries are sometimes the most competitive in the world. World leaders in white goods all have their home bases in concentrated national industries, and several countries with fragmented white goods industries face ailing firms. Today, Electrolux is a highly efficient company with considerable market power. Swedish consumers benefit in various ways by having a domestic world leader. On the other hand, we believe two issues are unresolved. First, we discussed the vertical structure in Sweden. Here Electrolux enjoys a market power position which is translated into monopoly rents. The Swedish consumer pays a higher price for their microwave ovens than the US consumer. Again, in a static sense, the consumer is a loser, but in a more dynamic sense, monopoly rents are clearly invested in new technologies, and are used to build up positions in international markets,[16] which in turn enhances the competitive advantage of Electrolux. In a strict economic sense, however, the consumer is a loser if he or she is paying a price that yields monopoly rents to the manufacturer (above the level that would prevail if the market was perfectly competitive). Second, Electrolux is a world leader facing weak competition in its home base, Sweden.

The importance of domestic rivals: a future issue?

Electrolux is clearly a healthy firm today, and has managed to become one of the most efficient white goods manufacturers in the world. However, there is always the risk that Electrolux becomes overly self-confident, lacking any real threats in its most proximate environment. When you are confident that you will win every match at home, it gets more and more difficult to motivate the team, which in this case consist of some 30,000 employees in Sweden.

Many will argue that proximity between rivals is not an issue. As already noted, competition is rapidly becoming global in nature, with Electrolux as a leading actor – why bother about the competitive climate in Sweden? The Swedish market is an open one, without trade barriers, and Electrolux with its strong foreign involvement, has proximate rivals in foreign markets. Some would argue that the 'home' market of Electrolux is Europe, or even the world, not Sweden. There is some truth in these statements, and those circumstances clearly help to make sure that Electrolux continues to be innovative and efficient, rather than a sleepy monopolist. But there are good reasons to suspect that very close rivals (often translated into rivals of the same nationality) play a different role than the more distant rivals.

Overall, Electrolux is a global company. It can fill the world map with flags, symbolizing various activities such as sales, service, manufacturing, design, finance, etc. But on the other hand Electrolux, like any other multinational firm, is home biased. This is especially true for top management and research and development functions (the core strategic functions). A large proportion of the workforce is employed in Sweden (21 per cent of the total workforce in Electrolux in 1987). Sweden accounted for 16 per cent of total group sales in 1987. Electrolux is highly dependent on the Swedish labour markets for top managers and skilled engineers. All of these biases get less pronounced as Electrolux builds up its global network, including large acquisitions. For example, Zanussi is playing an increasingly important role as component centre for Europe. The White subsidiary in the United States plays a major strategic role in the North American market. However, key decisions are made in the centre of Stockholm, by people who are essentially thinking in 'Swedish' terms. If there was another Swedish world leader in white goods (as there are two Swedish world leaders in heavy trucks, two in rock drills, and so on),[17] the self-confidence of Electrolux would be reduced, and probably the whole organization, not only the top management, would better understand the competitive race – a race that works as an insurance against 'sleepiness'.

There are many reasons as to why proximate rivals do play an important role as drivers of innovation, and international competitiveness:[18]

- Domestic rivalry goes beyond economic rivalry, and becomes emotional and personal, with elements of pride. If the firm can be compared with other domestic rivals (well known to the public), success and failure become more visible. Domestic comparisons are frequent in the business press, while international comparisons are rare.
- Visibility of pressures. Success of one firm proves that it is possible to make new breakthroughs, e.g. in new products.
- Quick responses (imitation) are facilitated, built on a better understanding of competitors' moves. It is easier to understand domestic competitors than foreign ones.
- Success of foreign rivals are often attributed to unfair advantages (low labour costs, government subsidies, etc.). With domestic competitors there are no excuses.
- Domestic competition push out firms into international markets, in order to grow. This is 'the second tier firm' argument, where diversification or internationalization are the only feasible alternatives for a second-tier firm wishing to grow.
- Diffusion of technology is likely to move faster within the nation if there are rivals closely monitoring each other. This creates an extra spur to build an innovational lead (the temporary monopoly power is shortened).

The competitive climates in the home markets (where key strategic decisions are made) of, for example, Electrolux and Matsushita are thus very different. Even if Matsushita is a highly efficient manufacturer with enormous market power, domestic rivals make sure that they always 'stay awake'.

Obviously, Electrolux has developed into a world leader without strong rivals in the home market (as almost all of them were acquired). Other forces (demanding customers, linkages to firms in related technologies, advanced factors of production, etc.), both in the Swedish and the international environment, in combination with the management of the company, have been strong enough to offset the lack of domestic rivalry. In the long run the welfare of Swedish consumers, and Electrolux, is dependent on one important circumstance: the market power of Electrolux must always be under attack. Strong market power tends to ingrain a sense of supremacy and overconfidence, which is detrimental to innovation and openness to signals of change in the competitive environment. The international competitiveness of Electrolux will be ensured if the whole organization 'is kept on its toes'. Rivalry close to core activities, such as headquarters, R&D centres and key manufacturing plants, is the best insurance policy there is to keep up pressure for innovation in a market economy.

NOTES

1 Including appliances like refrigerators and freezers; dishwashers, washing machines and dryers; cookers (ranges) and microwave ovens. Appliances are divided between gas and electrical appliances. Sometimes white goods are referred to as major home appliances.
2 Electrolux Major Appliance.
3 The 'globalization' of competition is partly driven by the multinational firms themselves – they act as international change agents.
4 Whirlpool is expected to take over the venture.
5 The Electrolux brand is used globally, except in the United States. This is due to the fact that Electrolux sold off its US subsidiary in the 1960s, and the right to use the brand was transferred to the new owner, a small manufacturer of vacuum cleaners. Instead, Electrolux sells under a number of acquired US brands like Tappan, Frigidaire, White–Westinghouse, Gibson, Kelvinator and Philco.
6 Sölvell (1987).
7 *Electronic Business* (November 1, 1988).
8 In addition, Japanese and Korean manufacturers have entered with local production.
9 Sony is the second largest consumer electronics firm in Japan, but is not active in the white goods industry.
10 *Daily Yomiuri* (January 8, 1989).
11 'Gate openers' are local firms with strength to open up a market to foreign firms, which are otherwise kept out due to high entry barriers (see Sölvell (1987)).

12 The Japanese manufacturers are now in the process of upgrading appliances like refrigerators (larger size, attractive designs), while in other products, such as dishwashers and washing machines, they are lagging behind.

13 For a taxonomy, see Sölvell (1987), ch. 3.

14 Cylinda (owned by ASEA) specialized in wet products and did not develop international markets to any large extent. In 1988, Finnish UPO acquired Cylinda in its own efforts to internationalize.

15 The notion of parallel industry structures, national and international, is developed in Sölvell (1987).

16 It is not uncommon among multinational companies that penetration of foreign markets surrounded by high entry barriers are subsidized by profits made in the home market (see Hamel and Prahalad (1985)).

17 An important implication that can be drawn from these highly

APPENDIX

Table 4A Acquisitions made by Electrolux in the white goods industry, 1964–89

Acquired company	Country	Year
Electrohelios	Sweden	1962
Electra	Norway	1967
Scan-Atlas	Denmark	1967
Ankarsrums Bruk	Sweden	1968
Oy Slev	Finland	1969
Håkansons Industrier	Sweden	1971
Kreft Sarl	Luxembourg	1972
A/S Vestfrost	Denmark	1972
Wilhelm Loh	Germany	1973
Arthur Martin[a]	France	1976
Menalux	Switzerland	1976
Bono	Switzerland	1976
Therma AG	Switzerland	1977
Prometheus	Switzerland	1977
Husqvarna	Sweden	1978
Tappan	United States	1979
Zanussi[b]	Italy	1984/86
Zanker	West Germany	1985
White Consolidated (WCI)	United States	1986
Thorn-EMI[c]	United Kingdom	1987
Design & Manufacturing (D&M)	United States	1987
Corbero'/Domar[d]	Spain	1988
Buderus[e]	West Germany	1989

Source: Compiled by the author.
Notes: [a] Including Neston Martin in Belgium; [b] Acquired a 49% share in 1984, including Ibelsa in Spain; [c] The white goods division (Tricity brand); [d] Acquired 56% of the shares. The remaining shares must be acquired before the end of 1991; [e] The white goods division.

competitive industries is that the small size of the home market does not mean that Sweden can only hold one world leader. If domestic growth is substituted for international growth, two or more Swedish firms can grow into highly efficient world leaders. Scale economies are not nationally bound! (See Sölvell, Zander and Porter (1990)).

18 See Porter (1990).

REFERENCES

Hamel, G. and Prahalad, C.K. (1985) 'Do you really have a global strategy?', *Harvard Business Review*, July–August, no. 4, pp. 139–48.

Porter, M.E. (1990) *The Competitive Advantage of Nations*, New York: Free Press.

Sölvell, Ö (1987) *Entry Barriers and Foreign Penetration – Emerging Patterns of International Competition in Two Electrical Engineering Industries*, Stockholm School of Economics, Institute of International Business.

Sölvell, Ö., Zander, I. and Porter M.E. (1990) *Advantage Sweden*, Stockholm: Norstedt.

5 The pharmaceutical market*

Bengt Jönsson

INTRODUCTION

The pharmaceutical industry is a young industry. The majority of the drugs used today have been introduced during the last fifty years. In Sweden, 75 per cent of sales are referable to drugs (specialities) that are 15 years old or less (see Berlin and Jönsson, 1985). It is also a heavily regulated industry. Pharmaceuticals have been regulated since the seventeenth century in Sweden. From the beginning, it was the pharmacies that were regulated, but since the 1930s the industry has been the focus of regulation. During the last three decades, the regulation of safety and efficacy has become increasingly stringent. In Sweden, the prices of pharmaceuticals have also been regulated since 1934.

The pharmaceutical industry is a controversial industry. The report by the 1983 Drugs Commission (SOU 1987:20) is only one in a long line of public investigations of the pharmaceutical industry and the pharmaceutical market.[1] At the heart of the controversy has been the profits gained by multinational pharmaceutical firms from the introduction of successful new drugs. Are these profits a reasonable return on risky investments in R&D or unjustified profits extracted from a market with low (virtually no) price elasticity?

The standard model of economics textbooks with many small firms producing homogeneous products and each firm unable to affect prices is clearly not representative of the pharmaceutical market. The pharmaceutical market is on the contrary characterized by large firms depending on product innovation and product differentiation and spending significant resources to influence the use of their products. It is a typical example of an oligopolistic market. A firm with a patented drug can be said to have a monopoly until the patent expires. But the strength of this monopoly depends on the existence of substitute drugs that can be used for the same indication. A profitable monopoly is also continuously challenged by competitors trying to invent new products that can be introduced on the market. The pharmaceutical market is thus a typical example of a contestable market.[2]

When assessing the competitive situation in the Swedish pharmaceutical market, it is necessary to take into account both the international development of the pharmaceutical industry and the specific national institutional framework. At the global level there is a trend towards forming strategic alliances among the research-based companies. The purpose of these alliances is to improve market power and R&D productivity. We can also see an increasing number of mergers and acquisitions, particularly in the United States. With the establishment of the internal market among the EEC countries in 1992, this process will be intensified in Europe. Part of what is happening in the pharmaceutical market cannot therefore be influenced by domestic policy-making.

The single most powerful actor on the Swedish pharmacies market is Apoteksbolaget [The National Corporation of Swedish Pharmacies] which has a monopoly on retail pharmacy and, therefore, a monopsony position in relation to the pharmaceutical industry. Apoteksbolaget also plays a key role in the regulation of pharmaceutical prices.

Another important national institution is the drug reimbursement scheme. This reduces the incentives for consumers, patients and doctors to take price into account when making prescription decisions and therefore the incentives for firms to be competitive with their prices.

MARKET SIZE AND CONCENTRATION

The total sales in the Swedish drug market were 5,922 million SEK in wholesale prices and 8,280 million SEK in retail prices (VAT excluded) in 1988 (Apoteksbolaget, 1989a). In total there were 174 firms represented on the Swedish drug market in 1988, of which 31 were domestic (Apoteksbolaget, 1989a). The market is dominated by a few major firms as can be seen from Table 5.1.[3] The five largest firms accounted for 50 per cent of the market in 1988 and the ten largest for nearly 65 per cent of the market. Of these ten, three are domestic and seven are foreign.

Table 5.1   Sales in Sweden by the ten largest pharmaceutical firms, 1988 and 1978

	1988 sales			1978 sales	
Firm	SEK (m.)	%	Firm	SEK (m.)	%
1 Astra	1,028	17.4	1 Astra	401	19.4
2 Kabi	829	14.0	2 Kabi	269	13.0
3 Pharmacia	574	9.7	3 Leo	133	6.4
4 Glaxo	297	5.0	4 Pharmacia	104	5.0
5 MSD	231	3.9	5 ICI	77	3.7
6 ICI	199	3.4	6 Ciba-Geigy	77	3.7
7 Novo	192	3.2	7 Ferrosan	74	3.6
8 Sandoz	158	2.7	8 MSD	72	3.5
9 Ciba-Geigy	139	2.3	9 Sandoz	60	2.9
10 Hoechst	101	1.7	10 Hoechst	48	2.3
All	3,747	63.3		1,315	63.5
Total sales	5,922	100.0		2,072	100.0

Source: SDM (1978, 1988) Läkemedelsstatistik AB, Swedish Drug Market.

The seller concentration in Sweden is higher than in other countries. De Wolf (1988) reports an average market share of 8 per cent in the United States, 5 per cent in Japan and 3 per cent for total EEC for the largest seller (top seven) and 30, 24 and 15 per cent respectively for the five biggest (top five). However, we have to admit the limited utility of these macro-concentration measures for reaching conclusions about the real competition in the pharmaceutical market in the different countries.

Between 1978 and 1988 we have seen a significant change in the structure of the Swedish pharmaceutical industry through the acquisition by Pharmacia of Leo and Ferrosan. This has moved Pharmacia from seventh to third place in terms of sales on the Swedish market. However, this has not significantly changed the structure of the market. The four-firm concentration ratio has actually declined from 0.39 to 0.36. Since 1988 there has been a merger between Kabi and Pharmacia, thus further reducing the number of Swedish firms (a concern and its subsidiaries are treated as one economic unit) and increasing the seller concentration.

Table 5.2 shows the fifteen leading products in 1978 and 1988. The leading product accounts for just over 2 per cent of sales and the five leading products for under 10 per cent of the total market. Only three out of the fifteen leading products on the drug market in 1988 were among the fifteen leading products in 1978. This illustrates the rapid changes in the drug market and that leading products are continuously being challenged by new drugs. The market is also rapidly expanding, a three-fold increase in ten years, which makes it difficult for firms to collude. It is not easy to predict who the winners in the future will be.

Table 5.2 Fifteen leading products, 1988 and 1978

	1988 sales			1978 sales	
Product	SEK (m.)	%	Product	SEK (m.)	%
Seloken	130	2.2	Inderal	49	2.4
Tenormin	123	2.1	Aptin	35	1.7
Octonativ	116	2.0	Novalucol	32	1.5
Zantac	95	1.6	Lasix	29	1.4
Bricanyl	81	1.4	Naprosyn	28	1.4
Naprosyn	78	1.3	Seloken	28	1.4
Adalat	60	1.0	Insulin, novo	26	1.2
Alvedon	58	1.0	Aldactone	26	1.2
Becotide	57	1.0	Treo	22	1.1
Genotropin	56	0.9	Moduretic	21	1.0
Ventoline	55	0.9	Vibramycin	21	1.0
Nezeril	54	0.9	Bisolvon	20	1.0
Treo	51	0.9	Indomee	20	1.0
Kåvepenin	50	0.8	Estracyt	19	0.9
Blocadren, eyedrops	49	0.8	Natriumklorid	19	0.9
Total	1,113	18.8	Total	395	19.1
Total sales	5,922	100	Total sales	2,072	100

Source: As for Table 5.1.

Another way of illustrating the dynamics of the market is to study the total sales over time for a group of leading products. Figure 5.1 shows the total sales for 1972–88 for the twenty leading products in 1980. The relative sales of these products are lower before and after 1980, when they were the leading products. The figure can be interpreted as a product cycle. In 1972 the share of total sales for these products was about 12 per cent, it increased to nearly 22 per cent in 1980, and was down again to 13 per cent in 1988. This is an indication of the rapid changes in the market.

The turnover variability for products over time can be measured by the so-called index of market instability. This index is defined as the difference between the largest and smallest market share of a product in a sequence of years divided by the average market share in the observed period. This instability index gives an indication of

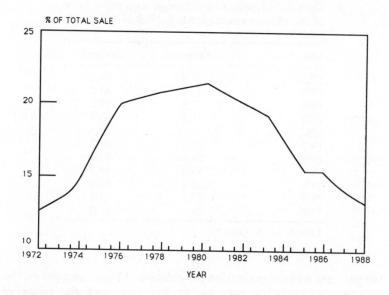

Figure 5.1 Share of total drug sales 1972–88 for the twenty leading products in 1980
Source: As for Table 5.1.

the degree of exposure to competitive products. For the top twenty selling products in 1980, this index was 0.53 for the period 1972–88.

The pharmaceutical market is highly and increasingly international. As can be seen from Table 5.3, the foreign companies' share of the Swedish market has increased over time, from about 51 per cent of the market in 1978 to nearly 60 per cent in 1988.[4]

The domestic market share in the hands of national producers is between 50 and 60 per cent in France and Germany and in the United Kingdom, 33 per cent. In the smaller countries in the EEC it is no more than 10–15 per cent (see De Jong, 1981). The high share for domestic firms in Sweden has historical reasons, and we can see that it is significantly declining over time.

The internationalization of the drug market can only partly be accounted for by the foreign companies' increasing share of the market. The domestic companies are also increasingly dependent on the export of their products. As is shown in Table 5.4 both exports and imports grew rapidly between 1978 and 1988. The growth of imports was about 175 per cent and the growth of exports was about

Table 5.3   Domestic and foreign companies' share of the pharmaceutical market, 1978–88 (wholesale prices)

Year	Foreign	Domestic
1978	50.8	49.2
1979	50.8	49.2
1980	52.8	47.2
1981	51.1	48.9
1982	53.2	46.8
1983	55.3	44.7
1984	56.6	43.4
1985	56.0	44.0
1986	58.1	41.9
1987	58.8	41.2
1988	58.7	41.3

Source: As for Table 5.1.

340 per cent without correction for inflation. In the same period the consumer price index rose by 92 per cent and the index of pharmaceutical prices rose by 62 per cent (Apoteksbolaget, 1989a). The trade balance went from a deficit of 80 million SEK to a surplus of 1,972 million SEK between 1978 and 1988. The relatively higher increase in exports compared with imports is an indication that Swedish firms are competitive on the international pharmaceutical market. About 80 per cent of the total sales of the Swedish pharmaceutical industry comes from exports.

Table 5.4   Import and export of pharmaceuticals between 1978 and 1988

Year	Export SEK (m.)	Import SEK (m.)	Trade balance SEK (m.)
1978	881	941	−60
1979	979	943	36
1980	1,074	1,110	−36
1981	1,224	1,220	4
1982	1,550	1,432	118
1983	2,007	1,753	254
1984	2,161	2,298	−137
1985	2,611	2,161	450
1986	3,439	2,332	1,107
1987	3,804	2,587	1,217
1988	4,767	2,795	1,972

Source: Fakta 89, p. 13.

It is important to note that the market for pharmaceuticals is not one homogeneous market where products are perfect substitutes, as in the idealized market in the classical theory of the firm. The market can instead be characterized as a number of sub-markets with a high degree of product differentiation. The data needed to analyse these sub-markets would be sales according to different indications, since drugs used for the same indication can be considered as substitutes. Unfortunately it is impossible to arrange Swedish drug market statistics in this way at the moment. The closest we can come to these ideal sub-markets is sales according to 'classification group' in SDM (Läkemedelsstatistik AB).[5] This classification is based on the pharmacological properties (the anatomical therapeutic chemical classification system) of the different drugs.

The concentration ratios of two of these classsification groups have been calculated for illustrative reasons and are presented in Table 5.5. In the classification group antipeptic ulcerants (A2B), the four largest companies' sales account for 91 per cent of the total sales in the group. Note the significant change in the market from a monopolist with 99 per cent of the market in 1980 to an oligopolistic market structure in 1988. This is a consequence of the introduction of new drugs (Ranitidine from Glaxo and Omeprazole from Astra) as well as generic competition (Orion) for the first H2 receptor blocker Cimetidine (SK&F). The concentration ratio is likewise high in the classification group beta-blockers (C7). Here the four major components have a market share of 98 per cent.

According to this example, the concentration ratios seem to be considerably higher in different sub-markets than in the market as a whole. This is in accordance with earlier studies, for example, De Jong (1981).[6] But when interpreting these figures it is important to bear in mind that 'classification group' is not the correct definition of a market for pharmaceuticals. The bulk of beta-blockers for instance is used as therapy for hypertension (high blood pressure), but beta-blockers is not the only drug available for hypertension. Anti-hypertensives (C2), diuretics (C3), calcium antagonists (C8) and ACE inhibitors (C9) are drugs that are also used in the treatment of hypertension. They have therefore been added to beta-blockers in Table 5.6 to see if the concentration ratio is affected. The concentration ratio now becomes considerably lower (61 per cent).

The broader definition of market used in Table 5.6 is unfortunately far from perfect, since these drugs are not only used as

Table 5.5 Concentration ratios in 1988 and 1980 in two selected classification groups (wholesale prices)

Classification group A2B, antipeptic ulcerants

Firm	% market 1988	% market 1980
Glaxo	50	0
SKF	22	99
Orion	13	0
Hässle (Astra)	6	0
Total	91	99
Market size	191 SEK (m.)	17 SEK (m.)

Classification group C7, beta-blockers

Firm	% market 1988	% market 1980
ICI	44	40
Hässle (Astra)	42	50
Sandoz	8	8
Bristol	4	1
Total	98	99
Market size	349 SEK (m.)	178 SEK (m.)

Source: As for Table 5.1.

Table 5.6 Concentration ratios in 1988 and 1980, classification groups C2, C3, C7–C9 (wholesale prices)

Firm	% market 1988	% market 1980
Hässle (Astra)	21	25
ICI	20	20
MSD	13	10
Ferrosan	7	6
Total	61	61
Market size	756 SEK (m.)	355 SEK (m.)

Source: As for Table 5.1.

hypertensive therapy. However, the example shows that conclusions about concentration ratios and competition in different sub-markets depends on the market definition used.

THREE DIFFERENT MARKETS

Figure 5.2 describes the Swedish pharmaceutical market. The figure is adapted from Gerdtham (1989). It can be divided into five sections: production, wholesale, retail pharmacy, consumption and

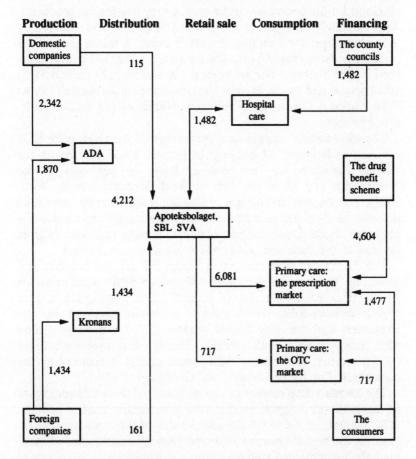

Figure 5.2 The Swedish pharmaceutical market (million SEK 1988)[a]
Source: Adapted from Gerdtham (1989).[7]
Note: [a] Production and distribution figures in wholesale prices. Retail sale, consumption and financing in retail prices (VAT excluded).

financing. The production is divided between domestic and foreign producers. A minor part of the drugs are distributed directly to the retail sellers (276 million SEK, wholesale prices), while the bulk (5,646 million SEK, wholesale prices) is distributed by the two distribution companies ADA and Kronans. ADA is owned by Apoteksbolaget and Kronans is owned by a consortium of foreign producers. Approximately 4.9 per cent of the wholesale prices is paid to ADA and Kronans for the distribution (Gerdtham, 1989).

Almost all of the retailing in Sweden is done by Apoteksbolaget (8,194 million SEK, retail prices) which produces a monopoly situation for the consumers and a monopsony one for the producers. Approximately 28.5 per cent of retail prices 1988 was retained by Apoteksbolaget for handling the retail sales. A minor part of the retailing is also managed by the Statens Bakteriologiska Laboratorium (SBL) [The National Bacteriological Laboratory] (73 million SEK, retail prices) and by the Statens Veterinärmedicinska Anstalt (SVA) [The National Centre for Veterinary Medicine] (13 million SEK, retail prices).

The pharmacists' margin as a percentage of the retail price is 31 per cent in Belgium, 33 per cent in France, 25–33 per cent in the United Kingdom, 25 per cent in Italy, 36 per cent in the Netherlands and 23–40 per cent in West Germany (see de Wolf, 1988). The wholesalers' margin in Sweden is significantly lower than the average 7–13 per cent of the retail price margin reported in the countries above. Using margins as outcome measure obviously gives an idea of the successful government regulation in Sweden.

The fourth and fifth sections in Figure 5.2 are consumption and financing. The hospital market (1,482 million SEK, retail prices) is wholly financed by the county councils. The prescription market (6,081 million SEK, retail prices) is jointly financed by the consumers and the drug benefit scheme (1,477 and 4,604 million SEK respectively, retail prices). Finally, the over-the-counter (OTC) market, (717 million SEK, retail prices) is financed by the consumers. For further details, see Gerdtham (1989).

The Swedish drug market can be divided into three different types of markets: the hospital market, the prescription market and the OTC market. In Table 5.7 the relative size of these markets can be seen. In the period between 1978 and 1988 the relative size of these markets has remained stable.

The distinction between these three markets is very important. They differ from each other primarily with respect to the demand side of the market and we will therefore initially focus on the

Table 5.7 The size of the three different markets in 1978 and 1988 (retail prices, VAT excluded)[a]

| | 1988 sales | | 1978 sales | |
| | SEK | | SEK | |
Market	(m.)	%	(m.)	%
The hospital market	1,482	18	523	17
The prescription market	6,081	73	2,357	74
The OTC market	717	9	294	9
Total	8,280	100	3,174	100

Source: Apoteksbolaget, 1989a.
Notes: [a] The sales by SBL (National Bacteriological Laboratory) (0.9 per cent of total sales 1988) are assumed to be divided between the three markets according to the size of each market in the sales of the National Corporation of Swedish Pharmacies. The sales of SVA (National Centre for Veterinary Medicine) (0.2 per cent of total sales 1988) are assumed to be divided between the OTC and the prescription market according to the size of these markets in the sales by the National Corporation of Swedish Pharmacies.

demand in these markets. The hospital market accounted for 18 per cent of the total sales in 1988 and this market is financed by the county councils who own the hospitals. Hospitals purchase drugs as an input factor to hospital production and each hospital has a drug formula committee that makes recommendations on drug purchases within a restricted hospital budget.

The budget restriction means that hospitals are likely to be cost-conscious in drug decisions. The resources used for drug purchases have an opportunity cost. However, physicians using the drugs within the hospitals may not always be aware of the opportunity costs. The market can be assumed to be more efficient when individual hospital departments are responsible for the costs of drugs. When the hospital has one global drugs budget and no incentives for individual clinics and departments to contain drug costs (the 'free-rider' problem), the price consciousness of the buyer is lower. But still, since each hospital must finance drug purchases, price becomes a relevant factor in purchase decisions and this is likely to affect competition in this sub-market in a positive way.[8]

The smallest market of the three is the OTC market with a market share of 9 per cent in 1988. The OTC market is characterized by well-known, low-price drugs that have been on the market for a relatively long time. This market can be assumed to be the one that functions the best of the three. Since the consumers of the OTC drugs pay out of their own pockets, they will be cost-conscious and price will enter into the purchase decision. This market can therefore be assumed to function well on the demand side and this gives incentives for price competition among producers.

The third market is the prescription drug market. Total sales in the prescription market were 6,081 million SEK in 1988 (VAT excluded) which is 73 per cent of the total market. In this market the incentives for consumers to be price-conscious are weak. The Swedish reimbursement system, the drug benefit scheme, is valid for all prescription drugs with a few exceptions. The basic rule is that the drug benefit scheme covers all the costs above 65 SEK for all drugs prescribed at the same time for at most 90 days use that are purchased on that occasion.[9]

Since consumers in Sweden only pay at most 65 SEK at every drug purchase for prescription drugs they will only be cost-conscious up to this point. The physicians who prescribe the drugs have no incentives at all to consider the price of the drugs. This means that the physicians will have no opportunity cost for drugs and the price elasticity of demand will be zero.

This demand side deficiency is probably the most important factor for efficiency in the Swedish pharmaceutical market. Since the finance and purchase decisions are taken separately it could lead to substantial allocation inefficiency and welfare losses. However, we also have to take into account the fact that other factors in the production of health are subsidized as well. A high co-payment for drugs, but not for physician visits of hospital admissions can give false incentives for the choice of cost-effective treatment alternatives.

PRICE COMPETITION

The price elasticity of demand in the largest market, the prescription market, is likely to be zero for most prescriptions. This makes the consumers (the tax-payers) vulnerable to exploitation from high prices and constitutes the major argument for the regulation of pharmaceutical prices in Sweden.[10] The prices of drugs are decided in a negotiation process between Apoteksbolaget and the producer. The position as monopoly seller, monopsony purchaser and price regulator gives Apoteksbolaget a considerable amount of market power in Sweden. A difficult question to answer

---

though, is how Apoteksbolaget uses this market power. According to Table 5.8 price increases for pharmaceuticals were considerably lower between 1978 and 1988 compared with price increases for all consumer goods. We have to bear in mind, however, the problems connected with constructing a relevant price index for the drug market with its many new product introductions.

Table 5.8 Price index of pharmaceuticals (retail prices, VAT excluded) and consumer price index (VAT excluded) (December 1978 = 100)

| Year | Pharmaceuticals | | Consumer goods | |
	Price index	Yearly change (%)	Price index	Yearly change (%)
1978	100	5.1	100	9.8
1979	103	2.9	110	10.0
1980	112	8.6	122	11.0
1981	123	10.5	135	10.8
1982	133	7.9	148	9.6
1983	140	4.7	157	5.7
1984	145	4.2	170	8.2
1985	153	5.0	180	6.1
1986	157	3.1	186	3.0
1987	162	2.8	192	3.4
1988	166	2.5	206	7.1

Source: Apoteksbolaget, 1989a.

It is also interesting to note in Table 5.9 that prices increased at a slower rate for pharmaceutical specialities by foreign firms between 1978 and 1988 compared with prices for pharmaceutical specialities by domestic firms. As we showed earlier in Table 5.3, the foreign firms also increased their market share in the same time period. One explanation for this could be that price competition is higher among foreign firms. But the major explanation is probably found in differences in products marketed by domestic and foreign firms respectively. The foreign firms have more new drug introductions, which have lower annual price increases than older products marketed by domestic firms.

The change in total drug costs between 1978 and 1988 and their share of total health care expenditure and the GNP can be seen from Table 5.10. The share of drug costs in total health care expenditure, 8.8 per cent in 1988, and of the gross national product (GNP), 0.76 per cent in 1988, remained relatively constant between 1978 and 1988. Over a longer time period the share for drugs in

Table 5.9 Price indices (wholesale prices) of domestic and foreign pharmaceutical specialities (December 1978 = 100)

Year	Domestic specialities	Foreign specialities	Total
1978	100	100	100
1979	105	104	104
1980	115	108	111
1981	128	118	123
1982	132	135	134
1983	150	144	147
1984	159	148	153
1985	166	152	158
1986	172	156	163
1987	178	159	168
1988	184	163	172

Source: Apoteksbolaget, 1989a.

Table 5.10 Drug costs in relation to total health care costs and GNP in Sweden, 1978–88

Year	GNP SEK (m.)	Health care costs SEK (m.)	Drug costs SEK (m.)	Share of health care costs (%)	Share of GNP (%)
1978	412,450	35,303	3,174	9.0	0.77
1979	462,307	39,023	3,408	8.7	0.74
1980	525,099	46,413	3,765	8.1	0.72
1981	573,040	51,041	4,100	8.0	0.72
1982	627,678	56,507	4,696	8.3	0.75
1983	705,365	62,838	5,277	8.4	0.75
1984	789,583	69,047	5,567	8.1	0.71
1985	860,884	75,241	6,087	8.1	0.71
1986	931,784	79,186	6,570	8.3	0.71
1987	1,005,226[a]	86,900[a]	7,335	8.4	0.73
1988	1,093,764[a]	94,113[a]	8,280	8.8	0.76

Source: National Accounts and Apoteksbolaget, 1989a.
Note: [a] = Preliminary figures only.

health care expenditures have decreased. The major reason for this is the previous fast increase in hospital expenditures.

In Table 5.11 we have separated changes into price and volume. The share of drug costs in the GNP increased from 0.77 to 0.94 in fixed prices between 1978 and 1988. An important question is what the increase in volume, 57 per cent between 1978 and 1988, consists

of. In the same period the increase in the number of prescriptions
was only 4.1 per cent (Apoteksbolaget AB, 1989a). The most
probable explanation is that there has been a switch from cheaper to
more expensive pharmaceuticals. One typical example is drugs for
treatment of hypertension where diuretics, costing 500 SEK per
annum, have successively been replaced by beta-blocking agents
costing 1,000 SEK per annum. In recent years ACE-inhibitors and
calcium-antagonists costing 2,000 SEK or more per annum have
taken an increased share of the hypertension market.

Another example is drugs for treatment of ulcer disease where
antacids was replaced by cimetidine, which later lost market share
to the more expensive ranitidine. The last years omeprazel (Losec,
Astra) have taken a significant share of the ulcer market, despite a
higher cost per day for treatment. However, we must remember
that higher prices are often payed for better effectiveness or for
fewer side effects. Increased costs must therefore be balanced by
improvements in quality. The construction of the price index for
pharmaceuticals does not take this into account.

Table 5.11 Index on drug costs in current and fixed prices (volume) (1978
= 100)[a]

Year	Index, current prices	Index, fixed prices	Yearly change in fixed prices (%)	Share of GNP, fixed prices
1978	100	100	–	0.77
1979	107	104	4.3	0.79
1980	119	106	1.8	0.78
1981	130	105	1.4	0.78
1982	148	111	6.4	0.84
1983	166	119	7.0	0.84
1984	175	121	1.3	0.82
1985	192	126	4.2	0.84
1986	207	132	4.6	0.83
1987	231	143	8.6	0.87
1988	261	157	10.1	0.94

Source: Apoteksbolaget, 1989a.
Notes: [a] GNP has been deflated by index on consumer goods, VAT excluded.

The increase in volume has been significantly higher during the last
two years. This explains the rebound in the share of drugs in total
health care costs and the GNP after a decline during the first half of
the 1980s. It is still too early to say if this is a new trend or just a
temporary rebound in the long-term trend of a decreasing share of

drugs in total health care expenditures. The strong expenditure restraint in hospital care and the emphasis on out-patient and home care makes it fairly reasonable to assume that the share for drug expenditures can increase in the future.

Table 5.12 International price comparison of 559 selected pharmaceutical specialities, Swedish volume, 1 July 1987–30 June 1988, for compared drugs

Country	Number of specialities	In Swedish prices SEK (m.)	In each country's prices SEK (m.)	Index (Sweden = 100)
Denmark	357	2,513	3,367	134
Norway	362	2,540	2,741	108
Belgium	203	1,604	1,439	90
England	279	2,106	1,944	92
Finland	355	2,663	3,341	126
France	142	1,109	765	69
Holland	282	2,061	3,412	166
Italy	145	1,161	877	76
Switzerland	246	1,763	3,118	177
West Germany	178	1,420	2,199	155
Austria	206	1,604	2,006	125

Source: Apoteksbolaget, 1989b.

In Table 5.12 a price comparison of 559 pharmaceutical specialities is made between Sweden and eleven European countries. The table shows actual sales value in Sweden in 1988, compared with the hypothetical sales value if the retail price ruling in other countries had been charged in Sweden. According to Table 5.12 drug prices in Sweden are relatively low compared to other European countries: only Belgium, England, France and Italy have lower drug prices out of these eleven countries. This confirms the results from other studies that prices are lower in Sweden than in those European countries where pricing is free; for example, West Germany, Switzerland, the Netherlands and Denmark.

Firms are normally protected from parallel import through various non-tariff barriers related to authorization and certification of products. Differences in the price level of drugs between countries are explained by different reimbursement systems, different rules for governmental price control, economic variables like the GNP per capita and the presence of a domestic research-based pharmaceutical industry. Higher drug prices on the home market make it easier for domestic firms to attain higher prices abroad. The higher costs for the health service have to be weighed against the benefits from increased export revenues. The internal market in 1992 will probably significantly reduce differences in pharmaceutical prices between countries in the European Community. The prices established in the European Community will basically determine the price level in Sweden as well.[11]

DYNAMIC COMPETITION

The pharmaceutical market is characterized by uncertainty, change and complexity. Product competition and innovation play a central role in the market. A description and analysis of the performance of the pharmaceutical industry must therefore employ a dynamic framework. In this section we will look at new product introductions, patent protection and generic competition on the market. We will also review a case study illustrating economies of scale, monopoly and contestable markets.

New product introductions

From Table 5.13 we can see the number of new drug registrations with new chemical entities (NCEs) and without NCEs in Sweden 1960–88. A new chemical entity is a drug that contains an active ingredient with a new chemical structure, that has not before been introduced on the market. Most important new drugs include an NCE.[12]

Table 5.13 Introduction of pharmaceutical specialities with and without NCEs in Sweden between 1960 and 1988 in five-year groups

Registration year	Pharmaceutical specialities without NCE	Pharmaceutical specialities with NCE	Total
1960–4	1,264 (86)	211 (14)	1,475 (100)
1965–9	819 (87)	124 (13)	943 (100)
1970–4	552 (88)	74 (12)	626 (100)
1975–9	398 (85)	73 (15)	471 (100)
1980–4	651 (91)	67 (9)	718 (100)
1985–8	693 (89)	84 (11)	777 (100)
1960–88	4,377 (87)	633 (13)	5,010 (100)

Source: Berlin, H. and Jönsson, B. (1989).
Note: Figures in parentheses are percentages.

The annual number of new drug introductions decreased from 1960 to 1980. After 1980 we can see a rebound in the total number of new drugs. The decline in registrations was most pronounced for pharmaceutical specialities with new chemical entities. However, since 1970 the annual number of NCEs has been fairly constant with a small increase over the last few years. This could be a sign of decreased innovation, but another quite natural explanation may be that it becomes more difficult and more expensive to discover and develop new chemical entities over time. Foreign companies' share of new registrations increased from about 60 per cent in the period 1960–4 to about 70 per cent in the period 1985–8 (Berlin and Jönsson, 1989).

The total number of pharmaceutical specialities at the beginning of each year between 1978–89 can be seen from Table 5.14.

Table 5.14 The total number of domestic and foreign pharmaceutical specialities in Sweden at the beginning of each year

Year	Domestic	Foreign	Total
1978	959	1,529	2,488
1979	926	1,535	2,461
1980	920	1,512	2,432
1981	914	1,545	2,459
1982	884	1,560	2,444
1983	916	1,630	2,546
1984	910	1,645	2,555
1985	904	1,663	2,567
1986	900	1,727	2,627
1987	906	1,792	2,698
1988	878	1,893	2,771
1989	898	1,945	2,844

Source: Apoteksbolaget, 1989a.

According to Table 5.14 the number of pharmaceutical specialities was 2,844 at the beginning of 1989, which is an increase of nearly 15 per cent since the beginning of 1978. In the same time period the number of pharmaceutical specialities from foreign companies increased by 27 per cent to 1945 and the number of pharmaceutical specialities from domestic companies decreased by 6 per cent to 898. This is in accordance with our earlier results indicating an increasing market share for the foreign companies.

If the total number of registered pharmaceutical specialities remains constant at the same time as the number of new registrations decrease, we would expect an increase in the average life-time of pharmaceutical specialities over time. As can be seen from Table 5.15 this is also the case for the period between 1960 and 1979.

Table 5.15 Data on life-time of pharmaceutical specialities registered between 1960 and 1979

Registration year	More than 30 months (%)	More than 60 months (%)	More than 90 months (%)	Lower quartile months	Median months
1960–4	91	80	59	72	155
1965–9	95	80	61	73	171
1970–4	96	87	73	111	–
1975–9	94	87	–	–	–

Source: Berlin and Jönsson (1989).

Of those 311 NCEs that were registered 1960–9, 162 (52 per cent) were still on the market in 1990. Of those 127 NCEs registered 1970–9, 111 (87 per cent) were on the market in 1990. There is a strong tendency towards increased life-time for pharmaceutical specialities. This will make patent protection even more important in the future.

Patents

Probably the most important factor for market power is patent protection. Patent protection means a monopoly position for the producer and it can be seen as an incentive and a compensation for investments in the research and development necessary to produce a new drug (NCE). A trade-off has to be made between patent life and generic synonym competition (see next section). An increase in patent life can be expected to lead to increased innovation, while a decrease in patent life can be expected to lead to increased synonym competition and lower prices. This means that there is a conflict between static efficiency (low prices in the short run) and dynamic efficiency (better drugs in the long run).

The nominal patent term is decided by state regulation and is twenty years at the moment in Sweden. Most important though is effective patent life. Effective patent life is the time left of the nominal patent term when a new chemical entity is passed by the registration authorities. In Table 5.16 effective patent life is shown for new chemical entities registered between 1965 and 1987

(Andersson, 1989). Note that the rules for the nominal patent term changed on 1 June 1978. At that date the nominal patent term increased from seventeen to twenty years. New chemical entities, the applications for patents of which were sent in between 1 June 1966 and 1 June 1978 were granted an extention of seventeen to twenty years to the nominal patent term. Therefore we have two columns in Table 5.16, one based on the actual nominal patent term (seventeen years for some and twenty years for others), and one based on a hypothetical twenty-year nominal patent term for all new chemical entities.

Table 5.16   Effective patent life for NCEs registered between 1965 and 1987 (NCEs for animal health excluded)

Year	Number of obs.	Actual nominal patent term mean years	20-year nominal patent term for all NCEs (hypothetical) mean years
1965–9	43	11.5	14.5
1970–4	40	9.6	11.7
1975–9	50	9.4	10.3
1980–4	43	9.0	9.3
1985–7	35	8.3	8.3
Total	211	9.6	10.8

Source: Andersson, F. (1989).
Note: Obs. = Observations, the number of NCEs for which there is patent information.

As can be seen from Table 5.16 there has been a continuous decrease in effective patent life between 1965 and 1987. The decrease is more pronounced if we adjust for the difference in the nominal patent term, but even with no adjustment there is a sizeable decrease.

Only four out of the fifteen best-selling products in 1988 were protected by patent. For the two best-sellers, Seloken and Tenormin, the patents will expire in 1990. For Blocadren the patent expired in 1989 which means that unless new products are coming onto the list, which they will, only one product out of the fifteen best-selling products in 1988 will be protected by patent after 1990.

Generic (synonym) competition

An increase in the market life of new drugs and a reduction in the effective patent life will increase the opportunities for synonym competition. Synonym competition means that a pharmaceutical speciality with the same chemical entity is available from different producers. Obviously synonym competition can only be present after the expiration of patent for the original product. The share of new chemical entities affected by synonym competition and the percentage of drug sales covered by synonym competition for NCEs registered between 1960 and 1985 are illustrated in Table 5.17.

Table 5.17 Synonym competition among NCEs registered between 1960 and 1985 and not withdrawn from the market in 1986 (NCEs for animal health excluded)

Registration year	% of NCEs with synonym competition (no. in parentheses)	% of drug sales covered by synonym competition
1960–9	23 (40)	63
1970–9	22 (25)	32
1980–5	8 (6)	10
1960–85	19 (71)	42

Source: Berlin and Jönsson (1989).

The percentage of drug sales covered by synonym competition is more than twice as high as the percentage of NCEs with synonym competition for NCEs registered between 1960 and 1985. This is what could be expected since new chemical entities with large sales are more likely to attract competition than new chemical entities with minor markets. For the market as a whole, about 50 per cent of the turnover is subject to generic competition. In practice, the market share for generics is even smaller. With an average market share of 15 per cent for generic products, the total sales of generics are probably in the area of 5 per cent of the total turnover on the market.[13]

Since the share for generics is small, there have been several estimates of the potential savings from a greater use of low-priced generic drugs. The most realistic estimates are in the area of 300–400 million SEK. However, the registration of generic drugs is rapidly increasing. In 1989, more than fifty synonyms were introduced. Therefore, it is reasonable to assume a greater market share for generics in the future. The consequences for total drug expenditures is difficult to estimate since we have to expect adjustments in terms of higher prices for patented drugs and increased margins in the distribution.

Many of the generic drugs will also become obsolete through the introduction of new drugs. One example of this is diuretics and beta-blockers for treatment of hypertension that are replaced by ACE-inhibitors and calcium antagonists.

The dynamics of generic competition can be illustrated with an example. In 1965, the diuretic Lasix was introduced by Hoechst. Although the patent did not expire until 1978, a generic competitor was introduced in 1972.[14] The sales for this firm were small and the price only slightly lower than the original. At the beginning of the 1980s, several firms introduced a generic competitor at a price 35–40 per cent lower than the original. Figure 5.3 shows the development of the total market and market shares for the competing firms.

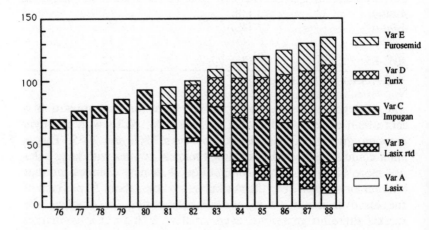

Figure 5.3 Millions of defined daily dosages (DDD) for Furosemide, distributed on different products, 1976–88

The market share for the original, Lasix, has been reduced significantly in terms of DDD. But due to a higher price and the introduction of a new slow release form (Lasic retard) the originator has been able to keep about 40 per cent of the sales in the market. For most other generic markets the share of the originator is higher. In many cases, however, the originator has been forced to reduce the price. The importance of generic competition can therefore not be judged only on the basis of the market share of generic products.

Generic competition is no new element on the Swedish pharmaceutical market, but the nature of generic competition has changed during the 1980s. Earlier generic products were introduced at a price 10–15 per cent below the price of the original product. The price was not a significant factor in the competition and sales were modest. Today the pricing strategy is more aggressive with prices 30–50 per cent below the originator's, and price is the major sales argument. The explanation for the change in strategy is probably due to changes in demand, with a more cost-conscious health service. This shows the importance of the demand side for competition in the pharmaceutical market.

Economies of scale and contestable markets – a case study

The market for sterile solutions (nutrition solutions, sugar/salt solutions and blood substitutes) is a pure hospital market with a total turnover of about 200 million SEK. The market was, until the late 1970s, dominated by three domestic firms: ACO Läkemedel AB, Kabi Vitrum AB and Pharmacia. At that time, in 1977, a US-owned competitor, Baxter Travenol AB, established production in Norway and started to compete on the market. In 1983, Pharmacia and ACO had 25 per cent each of the market, Kabi Vitrum 20 per cent and Travenol 30 per cent. In 1984, an agreement was made between Pharmacia and ACO where ACO withdrew from the market for infusion solutions and concentrates. At the same time ACO took over the rights for flushing fluids (spolvätskor) and injection solutions from Pharmacia. This agreement was reached because of losses due to price competition from Travenol, which had a more efficient technology.

In 1987, Kabi Vitrum AB took over the rights and know-how for infusion solutions and concentrates from Pharmacia and simul-taneously sold parts of these rights to Travenol. Travenol and Kabi also established a joint venture, Kabi–Travenol Infusion AB, for the marketing and distribution of all nutrition and infusion solutions produced by the two firms. In practice this meant a monopoly situation in the Swedish market. Pharmacia's withdrawal from the market was brought about because of losses in production. There are significant economies of scale in the production and distribution of these products.

The Swedish Antitrust Ombudsman (NO) found no reason to object to this monopoly. There were two main reasons for this. First, the price control on drugs will limit the possibilities for the monopolist to increase his price. Second, there is potential (contestable) competition from firms in other countries, mainly West Germany. This will restrict the behaviour of the monopolist. This case illustrates the importance of international trade for competition in the Swedish pharmaceutical market. It also shows that a monopoly does not necessarily have to be a problem. With significant economies of scale there are cost advantages from having only one producer. Since this market is also a typical example of a contestable market, with low costs for entry for a foreign firm, the behaviour of the monopolist is constrained by potential entrants.

CONCLUSIONS

The Swedish pharmaceutical market is highly international. Foreign companies are increasing their market shares in Sweden and companies are selling an increasing share of their production as export. These tendencies can be expected to continue. The degree of market power on the pharmaceutical market depends on how markets are defined. If we take the market as a whole, no individual company can be expected to have a significant degree of market power. For specific products the market power is very strong for the producer. But in these cases monopoly and market power are often connected with the patent protection granted to secure future innovation. A trade-off has to be made between price competition resulting in cheaper drugs in the short run and patent protection resulting in better drugs in the long run.

The effective patent time and the number of new chemical entities introduced on the market declines over time. This increases the opportunities for generic manufacturers to enter the markets. The market share for generic drugs is low in Sweden compared with, for example, the United States, but it can be expected to increase significantly in the 1990s. Political and economic factors will support this development. The number of drugs sold over-the-counter (OTC) will also increase for the same reasons. The barriers to entry are significant for firms aiming at developing new patented drugs. But the international nature of the market makes it possible for multinational companies to enter the Swedish market at low cost. Therefore, the dynamic competition is working well in the Swedish market.

The most important problem with the Swedish drug market is not market power or limited competition on the supply side, but the deficiencies on the demand side. With the present system there is a lack of incentives in the prescription market to take price into account in the selection of drugs. Since more than 70 per cent of the market consists of prescription drugs this could be a serious source of economic inefficiency and loss in consumer welfare. However, this loss has to be balanced against the distributional benefits of a general drug reimbursement scheme. We also have to keep in mind that hospital admissions and physician visits, complements to and substitutes for drugs, are subsidized even more. Changes in the drug reimbursement system must be valued in relation to the total financing of health care in Sweden.

The price regulation scheme has managed to keep Swedish drug prices at a reasonable level, judged by international price comparisons. The changes over time in drug prices have also been significantly smaller than the changes in the general price level. However, price regulation contributes to increased market power for existing firms and makes it more difficult for new producers to enter the market. A system of administrative prices also reduces the transaction costs for collusion among producers. Generic competition is limited compared with markets with free pricing, but it is not obvious that free pricing and more generic competition should be preferred from a social point of view.

NOTES

* I am grateful to Ulf Edstedt, RUFI and Läkemedelsstatistik AB for help with data and to Magnus Johannesson for research assistance. The usual disclaimer applies.

1 See SOU (1969:36) Läkemedelsindustrin [The Pharmaceutical Industry] for a thorough review of the structure and competition in the pharmaceutical industry. The conclusion was that there were some areas where the social and private returns diverged, for example in R&D and marketing, but that the arguments for public intervention were weak. The report did not result in any regulatory or other interventions from the government.

2 Contestable markets are those in which competitive pressures from potential entrants exercise strong constraints on the behaviour of incumbent suppliers.

3 The definition of 'firm' in Table 5.1 assumes that firms that are controlled through share majority by another firm belong to the controlling firm. This means for instance that Hässle, Draco and Tika are counted as part of Astra, and Vitrum and ACO as part of Kabi in Table 5.1.

4 In 1952, the share of imported drugs was 11 per cent and increased to 40 per cent in 1967, see SOU (1969:36) Läkemedelsindustrin, p. 8.

5 However, combining information from Medical Index Sweden (MIS)

and Swedish Drug Market (SDM) (Läkemedelsstatistik AB) can give some further evidence.

6 De Jong (1981) reports concentration ratios for beta-blockers from 40 per cent share held by the top five brands in France up to 85 per cent in the United Kingdom. Also in sub-markets, seller concentration in Sweden seems to be higher than in other countries.

7 The model was originally developed by Gerdtham to cover sales of pharmaceutical specialities (96.5 per cent of total drug sales, 1988), but there is no reason to believe that including extempore sales and pharmaceuticals sold on licence (the remaining 3.5 per cent of total sales) will significantly change the model.

8 Drugs account for less than 3 per cent of hospital costs in Sweden. In relation to other factors of production, for example, staff and buildings, drug costs are more variable and it is reasonable to assume that hospitals are more alert to the opportunities to contain drugs costs.

9 One exception to the standard rule is that some drugs for selected chronic diseases are totally free of charge. There is also a special rule that maximizes the total costs for drugs, physician visits and nurse visits to 15 × 65 = 975 SEK. Fifteen visits or prescriptions at a maximum estimated payment of 65 SEK for a twelve-month period.

10 A problem usually referred to as moral hazard.

11 The model for price negotiations used by Apoteksbolaget is based on international price comparisons. The 'median' international price will in most cases be the price for the countries in the European Community.

12 New drugs that do not include an NCE are combinations of existing products, new dosage forms and new brands (copies) of existing drugs.

13 Estimates by Apoteksbolaget indicates an even smaller share, 2–3 per cent in value for 'real' generics.

14 In 1972, only a process patent was available which did not provide adequate protection from competitors claiming a different process of production.

REFERENCES

Andersson, F. (1989) 'Effektiv patenttid för nya läkemedelssubstanser registrerade i Sverige 1965–1987', Center for Medical Technology Assessment, Discussion paper 1989:3, Linköping: Linköping University.

Apoteksbolaget AB [the National Corporation of Swedish pharmacies] (1989a) *Svensk Läkemedelsstatistik 1988* [Swedish drug sales statistics], Stockholm.

Apoteksbolaget AB (1989b) *Verksamhetsberättelse 1988* [Annual report], Stockholm.

Berlin, H. and Jönsson, B. (1985) 'Market life, age structure and renewal – an analysis of pharmaceutical specialities and substances in Sweden 1960–1982', *Managerial and Decision Economics*, 6, 246–56.

Berlin, H. and Jönsson, B. (1989) 'Svensk läkemedelsmarknad: Utveckling- och förnyelse under tre decennier', *Svensk farmaceutisk tidskrift*, 93, 10–16.

De Jong, H.W. (1981) 'Competition and economic power in the

pharmaceutical industry', in H.W. De Jong (1981) (ed.) *The Structure of European Industry*, The Hague: Martinus Nijhoff.

De Wolf, P. (1988) 'The pharmaceutidal industry: structure, intervention and competitive strength', in H.W. De Jong (ed.) *The Structure of European Industry* (2nd edn), Boston, Dordrecht, London: Kluwer Academic Publishers.

Fakta 89 (1989) Läkemedelsmarknaden och hälso- och sjukvården [Pharmaceutical market and health care], LIF/RUFI.

Gerdtham, U. (1989) 'Läkemedelsförsörjningen i Sverige', Center for Medical Technology Assessment, Discussion paper 1989:2, Linköping: Linköping University.

SDM (1978, 1988) Läkemedelsstatistik AB, Swedish drug market (SDM).

SOU (1969:36) Koncentrationsutredningen, Läkemedelsindustrin, Stockholm: SOU.

SOU (1987:20) Läkemedelsutredningen, Läkemedel och hälsa, Betänkande av 1983 års läkemedelsutredning, Stockholm: SOU.

6   Competition and prices in the passenger car market*

Yves Bourdet

INTRODUCTION

The passenger car market is one of the most important in Sweden as far as household budgets are concerned. In 1988, purchases of passenger cars, repair work included, accounted for 9 per cent of total private income consumption.[1] A new car is, after a house, the most expensive item that most families purchase. The state of competition in such a market is therefore critical for consumer welfare, mainly because of its possible effect on prices. Furthermore, the large place of the Swedish passenger car industry in terms of its contribution to GNP and employment illustrates the importance of this issue for the Swedish economy as a whole.

The main purpose of this chapter is to analyse competition and prices in the Swedish passenger car market. It should be stressed that the focus of attention is on the Swedish passenger car *market* and not the *industry*. This distinction is important because of the high degree of import penetration of the Swedish passenger car market and the high degree of export involvement of the Swedish industry. Factors that concern the passenger car industry, such as economies of scale, are touched upon only as far as they have some influence on competition and prices in the Swedish market.

The organization of the chapter is as follows. The first part examines the structural aspects of the Swedish passenger car market and their evolution over time. It concerns itself principally with aspects like buyer demand, market concentration and obstacles to entry. A reason for this focus of attention is that these aspects have some influence, the extent of which remains to be determined, on the behaviour of firms. In the second part we discuss market conduct, in particular price policy, and make an attempt to see how it is influenced by the structural features of the passenger car market. Another issue that is analysed is the impact of exchange rate variation and trade policy on pricing behaviour. Market conduct in turn determines the quality of the market's performance. In a final section, we concentrate on various dimensions of market performance. Here particular emphasis is placed on allocative efficiency.

As to method, we use a cross-country comparative approach as far as available statistics permit. It is our belief that the dynamic interaction between market structure, conduct and performance is better assessed in a comparative framework. For example, departures from competitive prices in a national market are easier to detect in a cross-country framework. By the same token, comparison of a market's performance with that of its counterparts in comparable countries yields valuable guidelines for public policy.

MARKET STRUCTURE

A passenger car is a durable and differentiated product. The market for passenger cars can, however, be considered a uniform market, in spite of product differentiation. The outer boundaries of the market are defined by the low cross-elasticity of demand between passenger cars and any other good. Passenger cars are highly differentiated products. Differentiation derives from the quasi unlimited combinations of features rather than from advertising. Although they belong to the same market, passenger cars are imperfect substitutes for one another.

Market structure consists of several elements that vary from market to market and that evolve over time. These elements constitute the setting that surrounds firms. They act as constraints on market conduct. The causation goes principally from structure to conduct. However, conduct can react back on structure. At first glance, the focus of attention on *national* market structures can be questioned because of the high level of international integration of west European markets that derives from the existence of a free trade area in western Europe. However, because of the large price differences for tradeable goods that are observed between tariff-integrated west European markets,[2] the analysis of national market structures as possible determinants of firm behaviour is not yet out of date. There still do exist national markets in the sense that, other things being equal, a price increase in only one west European market only leads to a very limited move by consumers from this market to the other ones. This argument applies to the passenger

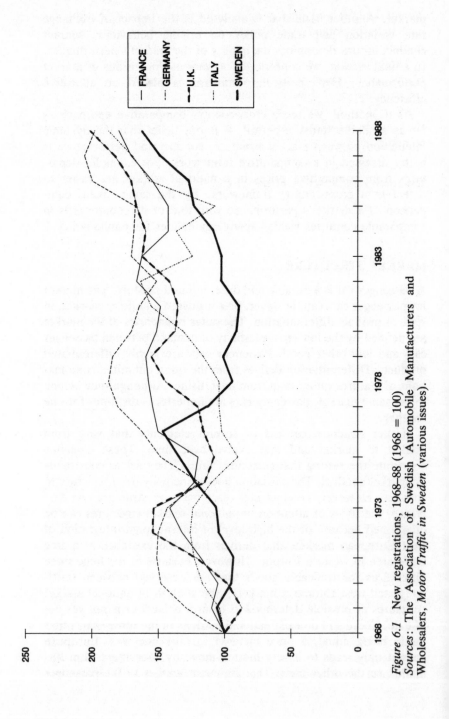

Figure 6.1 New registrations, 1968–88 (1968 = 100)
Sources: The Association of Swedish Automobile Manufacturers and Wholesalers, *Motor Traffic in Sweden* (various issues).

car markets as well since they exhibit large price differentials that cannot be explained by the costs of research and ignorance of the market.[3]

Three elements of market structure are most likely to shape the competitive conditions in the Swedish passenger car market: first, the evolution and structure of buyer demand; second, the degree of market concentration and the scope of foreign competition; third, the various obstacles that act as barriers to the entry of new competitors.

Evolution and structure of demand

The rate of growth of demand is one of the main determinants of competitive conditions in a market. A high rate of growth of demand fosters competition and technical change. It plays a destabilizing role in existing collusive business agreements. In such a market it is difficult for dominant firms to inhibit smaller firms and to exclude new entrants, in particular, foreign firms that are already well-established abroad. On the other hand, a slow-growing or stagnating market makes firms more aware of their interdependency, since every small price cut by one firm encroaches upon the sales of competitors in absolute terms. This kind of market creates an incentive for firms to restrict competition.

Table 6.1 Estimated income and price elasticities for new passenger cars

$$\log R = 5.269 + 0.462 \log Y + 1.078 \log(P_a/P_{cpi}) - 0.267 \log Un \quad (1)$$
$$(1.693) \quad (1.948) \qquad (1.585) \qquad\qquad (2.176)$$

$$R^2 = 0.603 \qquad\qquad F = 10.896 \qquad\qquad \text{Obs:1962–88}$$

Sources: New passenger car price index and consumer price index: The Association of Swedish Automobile Manufacturers and Wholesalers, *Motor Traffic in Sweden* (1989), pp. 26, 35; GNP and unemployment rate: Statistics Sweden (SCB).
Notes: The equation is estimated with the OLS method and corrected for serial correlation with the Cochrane–Orcutt procedure. The critical value of the t-statistic (within parentheses) at the 5 per cent level with a one-tailed test is t(23) = 1.714.
Variables: R, new registration of passenger cars; Y, income variable (GNP at constant prices); P_a/P_{cpi}, price index for passenger cars divided by the total consumer price index; Un, unemployment rate (variable representing general cyclical movements).

The demand for passenger cars in Sweden has fluctuated over the last two decades, but a marked and relatively long upward turn can be observed since 1981 (see Figure 6.1).[4] In other west European countries, demand for new cars has increased faster than in Sweden, if the past two decades are considered. Two main factors explain this difference between Sweden and the other west European countries. First, in Sweden there has been a relatively low income elasticity for new cars due to the fact that the demand for new cars has been predominantly a replacement demand over the major part of the period examined. This is illustrated by the low income elasticity in Table 6.1 (+0.5). In other west European countries, the income elasticity for new passenger cars has been significantly larger (around +1).[5] Second, the rate of economic growth in Sweden has been less rapid than in most other European countries over the past two decades.

Two related aspects of the demand for cars are worth examining: first, the change in the mix of cars between large, intermediate and small cars; second, the large role of business demand. Table 6.2 shows that a shift in the composition of new car demand has taken place, in favour of intermediate and large cars and away from small cars. The shift is particularly significant over the past five years. The share of small cars halved between the mid-1970s and 1987–8, while both the shares of intermediate and large cars increased substantially. Note, however, that these results should be interpreted with some care since they depend upon where we put the boundary between size-classes. For example, no clear-cut changes occur in the small size-class if we take 900 kg instead of 1,000 kg as the upper bound of this size-class (see the figures within parentheses in Table 6.2). Compared to other west European car producing countries, Sweden has a larger large-size segment and a smaller small-size segment, the intermediate segment being by and large of the same order of magnitude.[6] Presumably, this difference between Sweden and other car producing countries is mostly due to the larger place of business demand in total demand in Sweden, which in turn can be explained by the tax system applied to business cars.[7]

Table 6.2   Distribution of new car sales by size-class (%), 1974–88

Year	Small[a]	Intermediate[b]	Large[c]
1974–5	31.6 (8.6)	23.1	44.3 (29.3)
1977–8	27.9 (9.9)	23.8	48.3 (32.5)
1981–2	27.0 (7.2)	24.7	48.3 (33.3)
1984–5	21.3 (8.2)	29.0	49.7 (33.9)
1987–8	15.2 (9.0)	32.5	52.3 (39.4)

Sources: The Association of Swedish Automobile Manufacturers and Wholesalers, *Motor Traffic in Sweden* (1981), p. 11; (1989), p. 13.
Notes: [a] service weight <1000 kg (<900 kg); [b] 1000 < service weight <1200 kg; [c] service weight >1200 kg (>1300 kg).

Demand for passenger cars emerges from two different groups, private individuals and fleet buyers (mainly business firms and governments). The first group is the more important. However, the percentage of cars purchased by firms has increased sharply since the 1960s. Since the mid–1970s, business firms have accounted for some 40 per cent of the total number of new car registrations.[8] This large share is very important for the pricing policy of car producers since this kind of buyer is presumably less responsive to changes in prices. Conceivably, this is one of the factors behind the absence of price responsiveness among Swedish consumers for all new cars considered together.

The estimate presented in Table 6.1 shows a positive but non-significant price elasticity for all new passenger cars. But the price elasticity of demand for any particular make of passenger car is probably much higher because of the availability of close substitutes. Admittedly, individual models have many more substitutes than do passenger cars as a whole. It has been estimated that the cross-elasticities of demand between car models of adjacent size-classes are relatively large, but diminish the more the car models differ in size.[9] The differentiated nature of passenger cars thus implies that a price increase for a particular model only leads to a limited exit of purchasers of this model. Note further that exit can be expected to decrease with size-class since the price elasticity for large-size and luxury passenger cars is likely to be smaller than for small-size cars.[10]

Table 6.3 Market shares and prices, 1988–9

All cars (65 obs)	Msh = 4.024 − 1.118 Pri (0.460) (1.264)	$R^2 = 0.025$	(2)
Small cars (<1000 kg) (18 obs)	Msh = 23.808 − 3.464 Pri (1.337) (1.822)	$R^2 = 0.172$	(3)
Intermediate cars (1000 < · < 1200) (14 obs)	Msh = −0.162 − 2.110 Pri (0.010) (0.754)	$R^2 = 0.045$	(4)
Large cars (>1200 kg) (33 obs)	Msh = 1.341 − 0.218 Pri (0.147) (0.198)	$R^2 = 0.001$	(5)

Sources: Computed from The Association of Swedish Automobile Manufacturers and Wholesalers, AB Bilstatistik; Market shares: *Nyregistreringsstatistik* (March 1989); Model prices: *Nybilpriser* (January 1988 and 1989).
Notes: Variables: Msh, changes (%) in the market shares of individual models between the first three months of 1988 and 1989; Pri, changes (%) in the prices of individual models between January 1988 and 1989.

Statistical evidence tends to confirm that this is also the case for the Swedish market. Table 6.3 is concerned with the impact of changes in prices on the distribution of market shares between the first three months of 1988 and the corresponding months of 1989. The whole sample is composed of 65 models and covers approximately 90 per cent of the Swedish passenger car market. As expected, equations (2), (3), (4) and (5) in Table 6.3 all exhibit a negative sign for the price variable. They show further that the price coefficient is larger for small-size cars than for intermediate and large cars. However, it is only in equation (3), which is concerned with the small-size market, that the price coefficient is statistically significant (at the 5 per cent level with a one-tailed test). In other words, the results of Table 6.3 suggest that it is only in the small-car segment that changes in prices affect the distribution of market shares.[11]

Concentration and foreign competition

The degree of concentration in a market provides an indication of the interdependency among the firms of this market. The higher the degree of concentration, the fewer the number of firms[12] and the more likely that firms will attempt to co-operate to limit competition. The reason for this is that the higher the degree of concentration the lower the cost of organizing firms and the more likely that this cost is lower than the gains from collusion. Conceivably, this outcome can be either counteracted or amplified by other elements of market structure, such as the price elasticity of demand, the nature of the product, etc. On the other hand, the lower the degree of concentration, the larger the number of incumbent firms and the more difficult collusion between them will be, the cost of organizing firms being probably too high compared with the return from collusion. Here, too, other aspects of market structure may exert an influence on the behaviour of firms.[13]

The degree of concentration in the Swedish passenger car *industry* is high because of the existence of only two producers, Volvo and Saab. The degree of concentration in the Swedish passenger car *market* is much lower because of the large extent of foreign competition in Sweden. Since we are concerned with prices on the Swedish market, the degree of market concentration is more relevant than the degree of industry concentration. As shown by Table 6.4, the degree of market concentration is high, even if it has decreased over time. Today, the four largest firms still account for

Table 6.4 Market concentration and import penetration, 1960–88

Year (average)	C_2	C_4	C_5	M/R	CM	JM
1960–5	42.4	71.1	81.2	67.3	–	0.0
1966–70	42.0	68.5	76.9	60.0	–	0.5
1971–5	41.0	65.0	73.0	65.9	–	5.9
1976–80	38.5	60.4	70.0	73.2	6.8	14.4
1981–5	40.4	62.4	72.1	75.5	6.5	19.9
1986–8	34.9	55.3	64.1	82.0	4.4	27.7

Sources: Computed from The Association of Swedish Automobile Manufacturers and Wholesalers, *Motor Traffic in Sweden* (1961–89 issues).
Notes: C_2, C_4, C_5 – two-, four- and five-firm seller concentration ratios; M/R – share of the passenger car market captured by imports; CM – share of captive imports (imports by Volvo and Saab) in total imports; JM – share of imports from Japan in total imports.

more than 50 per cent of the market. By European standards, however, the degree of concentration in Sweden is low. Concentration is higher in the other west European car-producing countries.[14] In 1983, for example, the four-firm concentration ratio in France, Germany, Italy and the United Kingdom amounted to 80.2, 68.9, 78.5 and 68.2 respectively, while it amounted to 62.2 in Sweden. On the other hand, the level of concentration is lower in other European countries, such as Belgium and Holland, which do not have a national passenger car industry.

The changes in market concentration in Sweden have been small over the past two decades. The same five firms (Volvo, Saab, Opel, Ford and Volkswagen) have dominated the market over the past three decades, forming a kind of oligopolistic core. Their share of the Swedish market has, however, declined over time, albeit very slowly. The five firms accounted on average for some 81 per cent of the whole passenger car market during the first half of the 1960s, 73 per cent during the first half of the 1970s and 72 per cent during the first half of the 1980s. This means that the five largest firms lost only 10 per cent of the market over two decades of trade liberalization. After the mid-1980s, the decline accelerated. In 1987 and 1988, the same five firms captured only 65 and 61 per cent, respectively, of the market. Table 6.4 shows that the first two firms, Volvo and Saab or Volkswagen alternatively, maintained their cumulated share of the market up to the mid-1980s, indicating that it is the share of the three other members of the oligopolistic core that contracted. Thereafter, the two-firm concentration ratio decreased rapidly, amounting to some 35 per cent over the 1986–88 period. In other west European markets, the decline in concentration was more pronounced over the past two-and-a-half decades. In some countries, however, market concentration increased as a result of merger activity.[15]

Increased foreign competition is the main reason behind the decrease in market concentration over the past two decades. The same pattern can be observed in other west European countries. Table 6.4 shows that imports account for some 80 per cent of the Swedish passenger car market today, while it only accounted for some 60 per cent during the second half of the 1960s and some 70 per cent during the 1970s. Import competition has increased rapidly over the past three years, causing a sharp decrease in market concentration. As shown by Table 6.4, it is imports from Japan that account for this sharp increase. In other car-producing countries in western Europe, import penetration is less important than in Sweden, although it has increased faster over time. In the early 1960s, imports captured less than 10 per cent of the domestic market in west European car-producing countries. Nearly three decades later, in 1988, imports accounted for 45, 53, 46 and 61 per cent of the German, French, Italian and British passenger car markets respectively. Note that all imports do not exert a competitive effect on market structure. Imports made by domestic manufacturers, so-called captive imports, have come to play a growing role in passenger car trade in western Europe over the past decade. However, as indicated by Table 6.4, this form of imports is rather limited in Sweden and has even declined somewhat since the early 1980s.

Conditions of entry

The main reason behind the persistence of high levels of concentration is the existence of barriers to entry. By stopping entry or making it difficult, barriers to entry limit the number of firms in the marketplace and allow established firms to charge prices in excess of unit costs. The kinds of barriers faced by new entrants vary from market to market, even if some kinds are to be found in almost all markets. Some of the restrictions on competitive activities are provided by the government. Others are determined by the nature of the product, the technical conditions of the industry and the policy of incumbent firms. The traditional approach in industrial economics – the Bain approach – has focused on three main barriers to entry: product differentiation, absolute cost advantages for incumbents and economies of scale.[16]

Product differentiation can be considered a barrier to entry because it provides an absolute cost advantage for incumbent firms. Product differentiation is in part the result of advertising, the cost of which is sunk. The effect of advertising on consumers lasts over time. Advertising creates brand loyalty. This implies that new entrants, who want to break the existing brand loyalty and create goodwill for their products, will have to spend more on advertising than established firms per unit of sales. The high degree of brand loyalty in the passenger car industry,[17] which derives from either advertising or uncertainty about the quality of new products, means that this barrier plays a far from negligible role in preventing new entry. Another absolute cost advantage for incumbents is provided by the higher costs that a new entrant seeking funds is very likely to face because of the higher risks that are borne by its lenders. The larger these funds are, the greater the risks borne by lenders and the unit cost disadvantage of new entrants will be. An implication of this is that the more capital intensive the production technique is, the more important the barrier to entry and the unit cost advantage of incumbents will be. This being so, it is likely that the high capital intensity of motor vehicle production and the large volume of the funds required to start car production play a deterrent effect on new entry.

According to the Bainsian tradition,[18] large-scale economies relative to the size of the market means that entry at the least-cost scale will increase market supply significantly and depress price, if the established firms do not reduce their output by an amount equal to the output of the newcomer. If, on the other hand, incumbent firms do not reduce their production, the price may fall below the unit cost of the newcomer, making entry unprofitable.[19] Assuming that new entrants anticipate the price fall, incumbents can charge prices above minimal average costs without inducing entry.[20] The larger the scope for economies of scale relative to the market, the higher the economies of scale barrier will be. The extent of economies of scale in the passenger car industry is very large. Annual production of 500,000 units is necessary to reach the minimum average cost in the production of engines, which is the process that gives rise to the largest economies of scale in passenger car production.[21] The size of the minimum efficient scale is still larger if account is taken of multi-plant activities, such as marketing and R&D,[22] the costs of which are largely sunk.[23] Conceivably, these substantial economies of scale combined with the relatively small size of the Swedish passenger car market (on average some 250,000 units per year over the 1975–88 period) constitute a very important barrier to fresh entry.

Barriers to entry in the Swedish passenger car market are directed towards potential rivals that intend to start passenger car production and towards foreign firms that are already established abroad. As suggested above, new production has been deterred by barriers to entry. The quasi absence of fresh entry over the past two decades in west European, American and Japanese passenger car industries confirms *ex post* that barriers to entry have been effective against potential entrants. This being so, in the passenger car market, potential competition is not as powerful as the Theory of Contestable Markets implies in limiting the exercise of market power by incumbents. A major reason behind this result is the existence of sizeable sunk costs that make hit and run entry very risky. Admittedly in the Swedish passenger car market, actual competition in the form of foreign competition is much more important as a mechanism to erode market shares and control market power. Foreign firms do not face the capital requirement and scale economies barriers to entry. Further, they already benefit from a well-established image abroad that makes it easier for them to break domestic firm brand loyalty. The various obstacles met by foreign firms are thus decisive for the state of competition on the Swedish market. What are these barriers to foreign entry?

Obstacles to foreign entry

The first kind of obstacle is raised by trade policy in the wide sense of the word to include tariffs as well as non-tariff barriers.[24] Tariff policy has changed substantially over the past two decades. The creation of an enlarged free trade area that comprises the EEC and EFTA countries has led to the suppression of tariffs among members of the so-called European Economic Space. The suppression was first achieved in mid-1977. There remain, however, tariffs towards non-member countries, in particular Japan. As a result of the Tokyo Round of trade negotiations, the outer tariff was gradually reduced during the first half of the 1980s. Today, in Sweden, it amounts to only 6.2 per cent of the import price (cif) of passenger cars. In other west European car-producing countries the tariff level is somewhat higher: namely 10 per cent of the import price.

Tariffs play a minor role in trade policy nowadays. They have been replaced by non-tariff barriers that have become the favourite instrument of trade policy over the past one-and-a-half decades. Before the spring of 1988, no quantitative restrictions were imposed on passenger car imports in Sweden. In many west European countries, in particular car-producing countries, severe restrictions have been imposed on passenger car imports. In Italy, a quota limits imports of passenger cars from Japan to 1,700 passenger cars per year. Italy is also protected by quantitative restrictions directed towards exports from east European countries. In France, a 'voluntary' export restraint limits to 3 per cent the share of the domestic market to be captured by Japanese firms. In the United Kingdom, the 'voluntary' export restraint towards Japanese exporters amounts to 11 per cent of the domestic market. As for West Germany, in 1981 the Japanese car manufacturers were 'persuaded' not to expand their exports too quickly. The absence of quantitative restrictions in Sweden explains the rapid increase of passenger car imports from Japan (see Table 6.4, last column). To stop this rapid increase, an informal restraint agreement was concluded between the Swedish and the Japanese governments in April 1988.[25] The agreement, enforced by the Japanese Ministry of International Trade and Industry (MITI) through administrative guidance, determines the quantities that each Japanese car manufacturer is allowed to export to Sweden.[26] Preliminary registration figures for 1989 show that the 'voluntary' export restraint has acted as an effective barrier to the progression of Japanese exports to Sweden.[27]

In respect to tariffs and quantitative restrictions, the Swedish market is less protected than markets in other producing countries. However, this is not the whole story. There are non-tariff barriers that are higher in Sweden than in other west European countries, in particular, EEC countries. An example is administrative barriers. In most European countries, the inspection procedure by the national authorities applies to *basic* passenger car models. In Sweden, it applies also to the various versions of the basic models. In addition, every new model-year version is inspected in Sweden, even if it has nothing new. The inspection fees to be paid by car manufacturers being a fixed cost, this procedure affects principally those producers who sell small volumes on the Swedish market, namely some foreign producers.

Another example of non-tariff barriers is technical regulations. Differing regulations oblige firms that want to export to Sweden to adapt their products. These adaptation costs act as barriers to foreign entry. Swedish regulations for passenger cars are more

Table 6.5 Comparison of EEC directives and Swedish regulations for passenger cars with the regulations of the Economic Commission for Europe

	EEC directives	Swedish regulations
Whole vehicle type approval	b	b
Exhaust emission	b	c
Exhaust smoke by diesel engines	a	c
Exhaust tailpipe-routing requirements	a	b
CO in passenger compartment	a	c
Measuring of fuel consumption	b	c
Measuring of engine power	b	a
Prevention of fire risks	c	a
Tyres	b	a
Total weight	a	c
Compressed air tanks for braking systems	a	c
Steering system	c	a
Body; external projections	b	c
Body; interior fittings	a	c
Protection shield for taxicab driver	a	c
Child-restraining devices	a	c
Communication system; direction indicators	b	a
Parking lamp	b	a
Driver's field of vision	b	c
Windshield wipers	b	c
Defrosting and demisting devices	b	c
Control symbols	b	c
Tachograph	a	c
Kilometre counter	a	c
Vehicle identification	a	c
Cadmium ban	a	c
Asbestos ban	a	c

Source: Based on The Association of Swedish Automobile Manufacturers and Wholesalers, *Sweden Out of Step*, (1983), Stockholm.
Notes: a – requirements agree with the regulations of the Economic Commission for Europe; b – certain deviations; c – distinctly deviating requirements or other scope of requirements.

stringent than the regulations designed by the United Nations Economic Commission for Europe which laid down international technical standards. As illustrated by Table 6.5, they are also more stringent than the regulations designed by the European Community. (Only deviating regulations are considered in Table 6.5.) Technical barriers principally affect foreign firms that export to Sweden, in particular EEC producers that account for the major part of Swedish imports. They result in an adaptation cost that amounts to the difference between the average unit cost of the production for the home market (or a combined production for the home and most export markets) and of production intended to be sold on the Swedish market. Note, however, that this adaptation cost is likely to be relatively small since the deviating regulations are concerned with the non-central parts of passenger cars (see Table 6.5). Furthermore, recent changes within the EEC and Sweden, regarding, for example, exhaust emission, tend to bring regulations closer to each other. As with administrative barriers, technical barriers principally affect firms having small shares of the Swedish market.

Another barrier to entry is the cost of penetrating the market. The minimum fixed cost of building up a distribution and service network in Sweden is very high. This cost is largely sunk. Foreign firms that intend to enter the Swedish passenger car market thus suffer from a unit cost disadvantage, which can be regarded as an entry barrier. An alternative to building up its own marketing system is to rely on established dealers that already sell different makes, or on domestic producers. This is the policy of several foreign firms.[28] Undoubtedly, this facilitates access to the Swedish passenger car market. On the other hand, such a system is inimical to vigorous price competition and can in some way be regarded as a barrier to expansion. Actually, a dealer selling two different makes may not want to favour one of them at the expense of the other, that is increase its sales, even if such an increase can be justified by changes in production costs, exchange rates or car manufacturer pricing policy.

PRICING BEHAVIOUR

Market structure makes up the economic environment of firms. Its elements affect the behaviour patterns which firms exhibit. These patterns are termed market conduct. In this section, we will concentrate on one aspect of market conduct that is of prime importance for the quality of market performance, namely pricing behaviour.

As stated above, the high degree of product differentiation in the passenger car market is one of the main structural characteristics of this market. Differentiation derives from the intrinsic heterogeneity of the product in question and the quasi unlimited combinations of attributes of passenger cars, rather than from advertising and sales promotion. This high degree of product variety means that passenger car firms face a downward sloping demand curve and, as a result, that firms have some degree of discretion over their prices. In other words, product differentiation provides firms with some market power. Another consequence of product differentiation is that firms can use product policy instead of pricing policy to capture more market shares.

Another structural element that can be expected to strongly affect pricing behaviour is the small number of sellers. If one considers the passenger car market in segments instead of the whole market taken together, the number of firms on the supply side is still fewer and, thus, more likely to shape market conduct. On theoretical grounds, because of this small number and the limited role of potential competition, we may expect the pricing behaviour of passenger car firms to be one of oligopolistic interdependence. Interdependence may be further strengthened by the widespread inter-firm co-operation in the industry[29] and the slow growth experienced by the Swedish market over the last two decades, with the exception of the past few years. The form taken by oligopolistic interdependence may, however, vary from national market to national market because of, among other things, differences in structural conditions. Interdependence may result in some form of oligopolistic co-operation, which by nature is unstable, with periods of intense competition alternating with attempts to collude. The reason behind this is that an individual firm has an incentive to break the collusive agreement when others conform to it. The differentiated nature of the car product may further accentuate the instability of oligopolistic price agreements by having a destabilising effect on market share distribution.[30] (It is reasonably assumed that the agreement does not cover non-price dimensions of the product.) Actually price-constrained firms can increase their market shares by successful changes in product design or advertising campaigns. In the remainder of this section, we will concentrate on two aspects of pricing behaviour, price leadership and price discrimination, and see how they are influenced by changes in exchange rates and by the imposition of an export restraint.

Price leadership

Over the past few years, pricing behaviour in west European passenger car markets has been scrutinized in several studies.[31] By and large, these studies confirm the interdependency hypothesis, even if deviations from the pattern can be observed from time to time and from country to country. The most common form of interdependency in the passenger car markets is price leadership. Prices are announced by the leader, the other firms making price changes of the same order of magnitude with little time lag. The leading firm is usually a domestic firm but it can also be an importing firm which holds a substantial share of the market. Admittedly, price leadership practices do not rest on formal agreements. They reflect an underlying agreement among the market's sellers to let one of them make the decision. They do guarantee adherence. As other forms of oligopolistic interdependence, however, they are by nature unstable. Changing demand or cost conditions, entry of new competitors, changes in the product policy of incumbent firms and public policy affect their sustainability over time.

Volvo and Saab act as the price leaders in the Swedish passenger car market. In most cases, they initiate changes in *list prices*. However, patterns of the way prices are followed vary from market segment to market segment. In the large-car segment, which accounts for more than 50 per cent of total passenger car sales in Sweden (see Table 6.2, p. 176), it is generally admitted that importing firms take into account the timing and extent of price adjustments by Volvo and Saab when they fix their own local prices.[32] The largest price changes usually take place with the introduction of new year models at the very end of the summer.[33] In addition, minor price changes take place during the course of the year, once or twice. It thus happens that prices stay stable for nearly half a year, free from adjustments due to changes in competitive conditions or in exchange rates. Price leadership practices seem sufficiently robust to permit price increases in times of both booming and stagnating demand. Completely absent from the market are the kinds of secret price cuts that characterize competitive markets. In the intermediate- and small-car segments, the role of price leaders is played by importing firms, even if the price changes are initiated by the two Swedish firms. Presumably German firms, which hold a substantial share of the market, decide on the magnitude of price changes and can be regarded as the price leaders. Their position seems, however, to have been challenged by Japanese producers over the past decade.

An implication of the widespread use of price leadership practices is of course that firms charge different prices in different markets. In other words, passenger car firms discriminate. They discriminate because of different price leaders or different competitive conditions rather than, as in the textbook case, because of different perceived price elasticities in the various national markets. It should be stressed that, in order to persist, these practices require trade barriers that impede profitable arbitrage-induced trade flows by dealers outside the official distribution network and consumers dissatisfied with the level of price prevailing in their home market. In short, market power needs extra-market power to persist. Empirical evidence supports the view that the introduction of barriers to parallel trade flows is often the result of the lobbying activities of motor vehicle producers and official distributors.[34]

Price discrimination

A result of price leadership practices is price discrimination between different markets for *similar* car models. This is illustrated in Table 6.6, which reports wide and changing price differences among some west European countries that belong to the same tariff-integrated area. The most sold car models on the Swedish market have been selected (20–25 models) and their list prices compared with the list prices of corresponding models in France. Other studies concerned with price differences within the EEC have been used to provide an idea of price differences between Sweden and the other EEC countries.[35]

Table 6.6 shows that prices *net of taxes* among tariff-integrated markets differ widely, refuting the law of one price for internation-

Table 6.6 Comparison of prices (net of taxes) of similar passenger car models

Year	Sweden	Benelux	Britain	Denmark	France	Germany	Italy
1970	100	70	n.a.	n.a.	68	72	72
1975	100	73	80	69	81	78	83
1980	100	77	106	68	85	85	92
1981	100	73	112	60	81	81	n.a.
1982	100	70	107	59	77	80	82
1984	100	n.a.	n.a.	n.a.	87	n.a.	n.a.
1985	100	84	109	n.a.	93	92	104
1986	100	86	107	71	92	91	102
1987	100	90	107	74	95	95	96
1988	100	n.a.	n.a.	n.a.	92	n.a.	n.a.

Sources: 1970–84: Bourdet (1988a), p. 164. 1985–88 (Swedish and French prices): computed from *L'argus de l'automobile et des locomotions*, October–September 1985, 1986, 1987, 1988 and *Nybilpriser*, July 1985, 1986, 1987, 1988; Comparion with other countries: BEUC (1988) and Sachwald (1989), p. 197.

ally traded products. For the whole period examined, prices have been lower in non-producing than in producing countries. Table 6.6 also shows that prices in Sweden have been higher than in other countries over most of the period considered, with the exception of prices in Britain since the beginning of the 1980s and in Italy in the mid-1980s. The price difference between Sweden and the EEC countries has, nevertheless, contracted substantially since the beginning of the 1970s, when it was at its maximum. Today, the Swedish prices net of taxes are on average between 5 and 10 per cent higher than the corresponding prices in the EEC countries.

Conceivably, the removal of tariffs between the EEC and Sweden is the main reason behind the narrowing price deviations between the beginning and end of the 1970s. Thereafter the price difference has continued to contract, although no marked changes in trade policy between Sweden and the EEC have taken place. Part of the explanation can be found in the fact that the samples of passenger cars considered between 1985 and 1988 contain a larger proportion of medium and large models, which exhibit less pronounced price deviations than the small and light models.[36] However, there remain large price differences that are a priori difficult to explain for several reasons. First, the Swedish passenger car market is protected by a tariff that is lower than in the EEC (6.2 per cent as opposed to 10 per cent of import price). Second, Sweden, unlike most other west European countries, was not protected by any quantitative restrictions towards Japanese exports prior to 1988. The question which arises is therefore what are the factors behind the emergence and persistence of these price differences?

Exchange rates and prices

One of the reasons put forward to explain the large and changing price differences among west European markets is the combination of exchange rate variations and price leadership practices. Prices of imported cars are essentially fixed in local currency and maintain a fixed relationship to the prices set by the price leaders, regardless of exchange rate variations. This means that exchange rate variations are absorbed in profit margins. A large body of literature has grown up in the last few years on the relationship between exchange rate changes and local currency import prices.[37] Most of them confirm that exchange rate changes are very imperfectly transmitted into import prices, but that the pass-through coefficients vary from market to market and within markets from exporter to exporter.

For example, studies of the US car market show that exchange rate variations are to a larger extent transmitted into import prices by Japanese than by German exporters.[38] There also exist a few studies concerned with the impact of exchange rate volatility on price differentials among the passenger car markets of the EEC.[39] Their conclusion is that there is little evidence of changes in exchange rates being passed on in import prices, either directly or with a time lag.[40]

The exchange rate issue is particularly interesting in the Swedish case since the Swedish currency has exhibited larger fluctuations than the EMS currencies, mainly because Sweden has chose to remain outside the process of monetary integration in western Europe since 1977. Another reason is that on several occasions the Swedish currency has been subject to huge exchange rate adjustments, which are particularly suitable when it comes to the analysis of pricing behaviour in conjunction with exchange rate changes.

Table 6.7 concentrates on the pricing policy of domestic and foreign firms in the Swedish passenger car market. The price data concern the twenty to twenty-five most sold passenger car models. Our purpose is to find out whether there is a simple pass-through of exchange rate changes into import prices or whether other factors, such as price followership practices, characterize importers' behaviour. Because of the short length of the sub-periods examined, we can consider other factors of importance for the formation of prices, in particular costs, to be constant or to affect equally all firms in the market. The sub-periods examined have been selected for three main reasons. First, three of the sub-periods examined were subject to significant changes in exchange rates. In September 1981 and October 1982, the Swedish krona was devalued by 10 and 16 per cent, respectively. In spring 1986, the Japanese currency appreciated substantially in relation to the Swedish krona. Second, in five of the sub-periods analysed, opposite changes took place in the exchange rates of the German and Japanese currencies in relation to the Swedish currency. In the last period analysed, both the yen and the DM depreciated in relation to the Swedish currency. Finally, an important change in trade policy (imposition of a VER) occurred during the next to last sub-period considered.

Price changes vary from model to model and manufacturer to manufacturer, even within the same size class. However, some empirical regularities emerge that yield valuable insights into pricing behaviour in the Swedish market. The most conspicuous finding within Table 6.7 is that market power matters, since exchange rate

Table 6.7 Pricing and exchange rate changes

	Price changes[a] (%)	Exchange rate changes (%)
(1) January 1980–July 1980		
Swedish cars (4 models)	+0.9	
German cars (11 models)	+2.0	−1.8
Japanese cars (7 models)	−0.8	+7.1
(2) September 1981–January 1982		
Swedish cars (4 models)	+0.5	
German cars (11 models)	+8.0	+15.5[b]
Japanese cars (8 models)	+6.0	+10.0[b]
(3) September 1982–January 1983		
Swedish cars (5 models)	+7.5	
German cars (12 models)	+12.1	+23.2
Japanese cars (6 models)	+9.3	+32.6
(4) January 1983–July 1983		
Swedish cars (5 models)	+4.0	
German cars (13 models)	+4.3	−3.0
Japanese cars (5 models)	+3.3	+1.6
(5) January 1985–July 1985		
Swedish cars (5 models)	+2.8	
German cars (12 models)	+3.0	+1.7
Japanese cars (8 models)	+2.6	−1.5
(6) January 1986–July 1986		
Swedish cars (5 models)	+2.4	
German cars (12 models)	+5.6	+5.4
Japanese cars (6 models)	+4.7	+17.3
(7) January 1987–July 1987		
Swedish cars (5 models)	+2.3	
German cars (12 models)	+3.4	−2.1
Japanese cars (7 models)	+4.5	+2.6
(8) March 1988–November 1988		
Swedish cars (5 models)	−0.2	
German cars (10 models)	+0.1	−1.8
Japanese cars (6 models)	+3.4	+5.6
(9) November 1988–July 1989		
Swedish cars (5 models)	+5.0	
German cars (10 models)	+6.7	−1.9
Japanese cars (7 models)	+8.2	−7.0

Sources: Car prices: computed from The Association of Swedish Automobile Manufacturers and Wholesalers, *Nybilpriser*, various issues, 1980–89; Exchange rates: computed from *Statistical Yearbook* (Sveriges Riksbank), various issues 1980–88 and data provided by the Swedish Central Bank for 1989.
Note: [a] Unweighted average price changes for the most sold car models in the Swedish market.
[b] August 1981–January 1982.

changes are *very imperfectly* passed on in the prices of imported vehicles. Simple pass-through of exchange rate changes to the import prices, which is the rule in competitive markets, does not characterize German and Japanese exporter's price behaviour on the Swedish market. None of the three sub-periods subject to very large exchange rate adjustments (sub-periods 2, 3 and 6) shows a close relationship between changes in the exchange rates and changes in import prices. Note that a smaller part of exchange rate changes were passed on in local prices by Japanese exporters than by German exporters during these three sub-periods.[41] In other words, Japanese firms, more than German firms, allowed export profits to absorb the effects of the large exchange rate adjustments.

Table 6.7 provides only limited support for the price leadership hypothesis. When exchange rates vary within a limited range (sub-periods 4, 5 and 7), prices of domestic and foreign firms on the Swedish market move by the same order of magnitude. On the other hand, price changes differ substantially in response to large variations in exchange rates, invalidating a strong version of the price followership hypothesis. What Table 6.7 seems to show is a weak version of the price followership hypothesis. When setting their local prices, importing car firms take into account the extent of price adjustments by other firms under 'normal circumstances', i.e. with small variations in exchange rates. On the other hand, under large variations in exchange rates, importers are mostly influenced by the changes in exchange rates, without transmitting them automatically, even if account is taken of the prices charged by the other firms.

Another striking result of Table 6.7 concerns the pricing behaviour of Japanese exporters. With the exception of the three last sub-periods examined, the increase in the prices of Japanese cars in the Swedish market have been smaller than the increase in the prices of German cars, regardless of the relative changes in exchange rates. For example, between January and July 1986, the prices of Japanese and German cars in the Swedish market increased by 4.7 and 5.6 per cent respectively, though the yen appreciated much more than the DM. No doubt this pricing policy of Japanese firms has contributed to the in-roads they have made into the intermediate-car segment, a segment which had been dominated by German manufacturers over the past three decades.

Non-tariff barriers to trade and prices

As illustrated earlier, technical and administrative barriers to trade are somewhat higher in Sweden than in the EEC countries. Non-tariff barriers result in fixed costs. They affect principally those firms which sell small quantities on the Swedish market. Because of the relatively small size of the small-car segment in Sweden, these firms are mainly foreign firms having a large proportion of small cars in their export mix to Sweden. Presumably, non-tariff barriers account for part of the price differential between Sweden and the EEC countries. This applies particularly to the price differential for small cars, which is larger than that for larger cars.[42]

Another trade policy related measure that may have an upward effect on the prices of passenger cars is the 'voluntary' export restraint imposed on Japanese car makers since spring 1988. On theoretical grounds, we expect this VER to affect car prices in different ways. By suppressing the incentive of Japanese exporters to use prices as a way to gain market shares, it encourages them to increase their mark-up over costs and thus their prices. The way the VER is administered[43] (by the MITI) reduces competition among Japanese exporters, inducing further price increases. Note, however, that the existence of alternative imports may temper price increases by Japanese firms. The VER is also likely to raise the prices of the domestically produced cars and of the non-restrained car exports (principally west European exports) that are close substitutes for the restrained imports, with their costs being pushed up by their expanded supply. In differentiated markets, a third price effect of quantitative restrictions works through quality upgrading. Actually, the export restraint incites firms to shift the composition of restrained exports towards passenger cars of higher quality, higher mark-ups and higher prices, while staying within the quantity restraint.

The effects of quantitative restrictions have been scrutinized in various studies concerned with the United States and west European passenger car markets.[44] These studies confirm that restraints have had an upward effect on the prices of imported cars and domestically produced cars. Most of the rise in import prices in the US market was ascribed to the quality upgrading of individual models.[45] Somewhat conflicting evidence is provided by Daniel Jones.[46] He shows that quality upgrading in the United Kingdom was rather the result of a long-term change in the product policy of the Japanese firms (caused in part by the US restrictions) than a direct effect of the VER. The British market being relatively small for Japanese firms, they had very little incentive to develop new models and change their product mix just for this market. Another striking result of these studies is that the export restraint has altered significantly the pass-through of exchange rate changes into import prices, exchange rates and import prices following two different paths after the imposition of the VER.[47]

As regards Sweden, the introduction of the VER is too recent to use the kind of methods that have been utilized in these studies. For example, quality upgrading can hardly be measured yet, since it is likely to stretch out over several years. So far, only tentative reasoning can therefore be used. Pieces of empirical evidence seem, nevertheless, to confirm the existence of the above price effects on the Swedish market. Focusing first on Table 6.6 (p. 188), it is likely that at least part of the increase in the price differential between Sweden and France (and probably other EEC countries) in 1988 can be ascribed to the introduction of the VER. Table 6.7 (p. 191) provides some further indication of such a price effect. It shows that during the last three sub-periods examined, the prices of Japanese cars have increased more than the prices of German cars, removing the pressures put on non-Japanese firms to keep prices down. This pattern, which began in 1987, has probably been reinforced by the imposition of the export restraint.

In addition, Table 6.7 highlights a switch in pricing behaviour in the Swedish passenger car market as a result of the VER. The imposition of the VER has altered significantly the mechanism of transmission of exchange rate fluctuations into prices, in the way described by other studies concerned with the British and US car markets.[48] The large depreciation of the Japanese currency over the last sub-period examined does not seem to have had any effect whatsoever on the pricing behaviour of Japanese exporters. Thus an effect of the VER has been to prevent the large depreciation in the yen exchange rate from being passed on in import prices.

MARKET PERFORMANCE

The Swedish passenger car market is largely open to international trade. Tariffs and quantitative restrictions on intra-European trade have been removed and tariffs towards non-European countries reduced substantially. The remaining tariffs levied on passenger car imports from non-European countries are very low. In spite of this, the Swedish market still constitutes an independent entity. Prices there do not take the same level as international prices, with ease and rapidity. The exclusive dealer arrangements permit firms to effectively separate the national markets and to discriminate between them. In short, it gives them opportunities to exert market power. The question that arises is what the end results for consumers and society are of this exercise of market and extra-market power? In other words, what is the performance of the Swedish passenger car market? A precise quantitative assessment of the different dimensions of market performance is hardly possible. This being so, we will tentatively discuss various dimensions of the performance of the Swedish passenger car market.

As illustrated above, over a three-decade period we could observe a high degree of market share stability and a stable leadership structure with the same top five firms in the Swedish passenger car market. This 'stickiness' of the leaders' market shares is surprising because of, *inter alia*, the substantial changes in trade policy that took place over the period examined. Market share stability is consistent in principle with either collusion or competition, while we may expect market share instability to be inconsistent with collusion. Most would argue, however, that the longer the period that the leaders' market shares persist, the most attenuated the competitive process at work must be and the less satisfactory the market performance is likely to be from the consumer point of view.[49] *Per se* the persistence of the leaders' market shares in the Swedish passenger car market over the past three decades thus suggests that the working of the market does not correspond to the competitive ideal. On a priori grounds, the absence of vigorous competition in the Swedish market may be one of the reasons behind this high degree of stability of market share distribution. Yet our study of pricing behaviour shows that price competition is not totally absent from the Swedish market, even if price leadership practices and other forms of tacit collusive behaviour seem to prevail from time to time. Furthermore, non-price competition in the form of styling and model changes has increased over time and is likely to continue to increase in the near future,[50] exerting a destabilizing effect on market share distribution. Presumably, a reason behind the relative high degree of stability in the Swedish market is the presence of a high degree of brand loyalty in Sweden. Another reason is the importance of business demand, some 40 per cent of total demand, the price responsiveness of which is considered very low.

The misallocation effect of non-competitive markets gives a basis for judging whether the problem of market power is a serious one. Compared to its counterparts in western Europe, the Swedish passenger car market has not performed very well. For most of the period analysed, prices have been higher in Sweden than in the EEC countries, the United Kingdom excepted. Swedish consumers have thus suffered a loss that can be regarded as the *cost of non-Europe*. This cost has two components. The first corresponds to the sum of the additional money paid in higher prices by the consumers who actually bought a car. The second corresponds to the consumer triangle (the deadweight loss) that expresses the gain that would have been earned by consumers induced to buy a new car, had prices been at their EEC level. In 1987-8, Swedish car prices were between 5 and 9 per cent higher than prices in Germany and France (see Table 6.6, p. 188). Taking 5 per cent as the price deviation and assuming that foreign as well as domestic producers benefit equally from higher prices, a rough estimate of this 'cost of non-Europe' for Swedish car buyers can be calculated.[51] For 1988, this cost amounted to some SKr 1.4 milliards, the major part (some SKr 1.1 milliards) representing a transfer of income from Swedish consumers to foreign exporters. The rest is divided between the domestic producers (some SKr 0.2 milliards) and the net welfare cost to society (i.e. the sum of the consumer and producer triangles).

This estimate is best regarded as a lower bound of the consumer burden for several reasons. First, the price deviation has been larger during most of the period under examination and the cost to consumers is likely to be greater. If, as was actually the case for some years, the average price deviation is in the 10 per cent range, the above estimate of the consumer cost will be doubled. Second, prices in the EEC are probably affected by the various quantitative restrictions that exist towards Japanese exports and by the higher tariff. This being so, the EEC prices can hardly be regarded as competitive, implying that the consumer burden in Sweden is much larger than the above estimate. Third, the costs of strategic efforts (like lobbying costs) to obtain protection towards foreign competitors and prevent exit by consumers dissatisfied with the relatively high Swedish prices are not captured by our estimate.

To conclude, it should also be noted that the cost burden is unequally distributed among consumers of different income classes. That the price differential is larger for small cars means that low income groups bear a larger share of the consumer losses. In addition, the quality upgrading that may result from the imposition of an import restriction towards Japanese exports harms low income consumers, who are denied inexpensive passenger cars, but benefits high income consumers, who now have more car models to choose from.

NOTES

* An earlier draft of the paper benefited from constructive comments by Göte Hansson, Inga Persson and Nils-Olov Stålhammar.

1 SPK (1989), p. 6.
2 See e.g. Wieser (1989) and Emerson *et al.* (1988), pp. 147–50.
3 See e.g. BEUC (1986) and BEUC (1988).
4 This upward turn did, however, stop in 1989.
5 See e.g. Bourdet (1988a), p. 183.
6 Altshuler *et al.* (1984), p. 130.
7 A new business tax system less favourable to large cars was introduced in 1990, in spite of the opposition of Volvo and Saab (Schwartz 1989, p. 13). However, a drop in the market shares of the Swedish firms in early 1990 and further pressures from the two domestic producers led the government to again change the tax system in favour of large business cars.
8 *Motor Traffic in Sweden* (1982), p. 9; *Motor Traffic in Sweden* (1985), p. 11 and *Motor Traffic in Sweden* (1989), p. 11.
9 Irvine (1983), pp. 774–9.
10 This was illustrated by Blomqvist and Haessel in a study of the Canadian market. See Blomqvist and Haessel (1978), p. 485.
11 Note, however, that even in this size-class only a modest part (17 per cent) of market share variation is explained by changes in prices.
12 Since concentration reflects both the distribution of market shares and the number of firms, it can happen that an increase in concentration only reflects a change in the distribution of market shares, the number of firms remaining unchanged.
13 On the relation between the degree of concentration in a market and the degree of market power, see e.g. Stigler (1968), pp. 39–63 and Martin (1988), ch. 5. There exists also in the industrial organization literature a large number of models that relate the departure from competitive prices (i.e. the Lerner index of monopoly) to the degree of concentration, the price elasticity of demand and the conjectural variations (which reflect the way each firm expects the others to react to what it does). See e.g. Donsimoni, Geroski and Jacquemin (1984). It should be stressed, however, that these models do not derive a *causal* relationship between concentration and performance.
14 See Bourdet (1988a), pp. 119–22.
15 See Bourdet (1988a), Tables 5.1 and 5.2, pp. 120–1.
16 For a survey, see e.g. Martin (1988), ch. 8 and Gilbert (1989).
17 See e.g. Adams and Brock (1986), p. 137.
18 See e.g. Bourdet (1988b), pp. 20–1.

19 The way the structure–conduct–performance tradition views the role of economies of scale as an entry barrier has been challenged by the Chicago tradition. According to Stigler, for example, barriers to entry are only those costs that are borne by firms that attempt to enter the market but are not borne by incumbents (Stigler 1968, p. 67). According to this definition, economies of scale cannot be regarded as a barrier to entry since it is borne by established firms as well.

20 Incumbents can further deter entry by building enough capacity to produce the competitive output (or excess capacity) and by threatening to use it if entry occurs.

21 Altshuler *et al.* (1984), p. 182.

22 Bourdet (1988a), pp. 87–8.

23 The Theory of Contestable Markets considers the existence of sunk costs, i.e. irrecoverable investments, to be the major impediment to the establishment of new firms in an industry (Baumol and Willig 1981, pp. 418–19).

24 The following discussion of barriers to trade is mainly based on Bourdet (1988a), ch. 2.

25 Hamilton (1988). The Swedish government denies the existence of a quantitative restriction on Japanese exports (see e.g. SPK 1989, p. 78). However, newspaper information (*Dagens Nyheter* 1988) suggests that Japanese producers have limited their exports to the Swedish market since April 1988. In a survey by the Competition Commissioner (NO 1989a) it is indicated that only two Japanese car makers were affected by the restrictions.

26 For the details of the restriction by producer, see *Dagens Nyheter* (1988), p. 14.

27 For the January–September 1989 period, Japanese manufacturers captured 24.5 per cent of the Swedish market, 1 per cent less than their market share in 1988.

28 For example, BMW, Honda, Daihatsu and Subaru are marketed by the Söderström group, Mercedes–Benz and Nissan by Philipson Bil AB and Renault by Volvo.

29 For a list of the various joint ventures and other co-operative arrangements in the motor industry, see Sölvell (1989), pp. 202–7.

30 On the relation between product differentiation and oligopolistic instability, see e.g. Caves and Porter (1978), pp. 292–3.

31 See e.g. Mertens and Ginsburg (1985), Bourdet (1988a), Kirman and Schueller (1989) and Le Cacheux and Reichlin (1989).

32 See e.g. SOU (1981), p. 566.

33 SPK (1989), p. 13.

34 For a recent illustration of the way official distributors and car makers hamper parallel imports in Sweden, see NO (1989b). The activities of the passenger car producers and dealers to separate the west European national markets have been illustrated in various publications of the BEUC (*Bureau Européen des Unions des Consommateurs*) and in the EEC yearly Reports on Competition Policy. See also Bourdet (1988a), pp. 192–9.

35 The results provide an indication of price differentials among west European national markets. They should be interpreted with some care

since the models considered may not be totally identical. However, these small differences are unlikely to explain large and changing price deviations between Sweden and other west European countries.

36 In 1988, for example, out of the twenty-five most sold car models, six could be considered to belong to the small-car segment with a service weight of less than 1000 kg and ten to the large-car segment with a service weight of more than 1200 kg. On average, prices (net of taxes) in Sweden were 12 per cent higher than in France in the small-car segment while they were only 7 per cent higher in the large-car segment.

37 See e.g. Krugman (1986), Froot and Klemperer (1988), Knetter (1989) and Feenstra (1989).

38 Feenstra (1989) and Knetter (1989).

39 See e.g. Kirman and Schueller (1989), pp. 27–38, and Le Cacheux and Reichlin (1989), pp. 144–52.

40 Due to statistical problems it has, however, proved hard to econometrically provide non-refutable evidence on the impact of exchange rate changes on import prices.

41 The results of Feenstra (1989) and Knetter (1989) put together point to the opposite being the case in the US car market, with Japanese exporters passing through a larger part of exchange rate variations than German exporters prior to the introduction of an export restraint towards Japanese producers.

42 See note 36.

43 *Dagens Nyheter* (1988), p. 14.

44 See e.g. Feenstra (1985) and (1988), Willig and Dutz (1987), Messerlin and Becuwe (1987), Jones (1987) and Melo and Messerlin (1988).

45 Feenstra (1985), pp. 55–6.

46 Jones (1987), pp. 157–60.

47 Feenstra (1985), Willig and Dutz (1987), pp. 55–7 and Jones (1987), pp. 152–4.

48 Ibid.

49 On these aspects, see Mueller (1986), ch. 3.

50 Car manufacturers, in particular Japanese ones, are showing a tendency to shorten the design cycle, from four to two years, in order to introduce new models more quickly.

51 We used a price elasticity of demand for new cars of −1 to calculate the cost to consumers. This is the lower range of the price elasticity that is estimated to prevail in western Europe (see EC Commission 1988, p. 29).

REFERENCES

Adams, W. and Brock, J.W. (1986) 'The automobile industry' in Walter Adams (ed.) *The Structure of American Industry*, New York and London: Macmillan.

Altshuler, A., Anderson, M., Jones, D., Roos, D. and Womark, J. (1984) *The Future of the Automobile, The Report of MIT's International Automobile Program*, London and Sydney: George Allen & Unwin.

Baumol, W. and Willig, R. (1981) 'Fixed costs, sunk costs, entry barriers, and sustainability of monopoly' *Quaterly Journal of Economics*, 96.

BEUC (Bureau Européen des Unions de Consommateurs) (1986) *Car Price Differences in the EEC*, BEUC/121/86.

BEUC (Bureau Européen des Unions de Consommateurs) (1988) *Car Report 1987*, BEUC/200/87.

Blomqvist, Å, and Haessel, W. (1978) 'Small cars, large cars, and the price of gasoline', *Canadian Journal of Economics, 11.*

Bourdet, Y. (1988a) *International Integration, Market Structure and Prices*, London and New York: Routledge.

Bourdet, Y. (1988b) *Market Power and Consumer Welfare in Open Economies*, ch. 1 of this book.

Caves, R. and Porter, M. (1978) 'Market structure, oligopoly and stability of market shares', *Journal of Industrial Economics, 26.*

Dagens Nyheter (1988) 'Kvoter hindrar inte Japans bilexport', 6 October.

Donsimoni, M.-P., Geroski, P. and Jacquemin, A. (1984) 'Concentration indices and market power: two views', *Journal of Industrial Economics, 32.*

EC Commission (1988) 'The EC92 Automobile Sector', in *Research on the 'Cost of Non-Europe'*, Luxembourg: EC Commission.

Emerson, M., Aujean, M., Catinat, M., Goybet, P. and Jacquemin, A. (1988) *The Economics of 1992, The E.C. Commission's Assessment of the Economic Effects of Completing the Internal Market*, Oxford: Oxford University Press.

Feenstra, R. (1985) 'Automobile price and protection: The US–Japan trade restraint', *Journal of Policy Modeling, 7(1).*

Feenstra, R. (1988) 'Quality change under trade restraints in Japanese autos', *Quarterly Journal of Economics, 103.*

Feenstra, R. (1989) 'Symmetric pass-through of tariffs and exchange rates under imperfect competition: an empirical test', *Journal of International Economics, 27.*

Froot, K. and Klemperer, P. (1988) 'Exchange rate pass-through when market share matters', *National Bureau of Economic Research*, working paper no. 2542.

Gilbert, R. (1989) 'The role of potential competition in industrial organization', *Journal of Economic Perspectives, 3(3).*

Hamilton, C.B. (1988) 'Grova lagbrott av regeringen', *Dagens Nyheter*, 12 August.

Irvine, F.O. (1983) 'Demand equations for individual new car models estimated using transaction prices with implications for regulatory issues', *Southern Economic Journal, 49.*

Jones, D. (1987) 'Prudent marketing and price differentials in the United Kingdom car market: a case study', in OECD (1987) *The Costs of Restraining Imports, The Automobile Industry*, Paris: OECD.

Kirman, A. and Schueller, N. (1989) 'Price leadership and discrimination in European car markets', mimeo, European University Institute, Florence.

Knetter, M. (1989) 'Price discrimination by US and German exporters', *American Economic Review, 79 (1).*

Krugman, P. (1986) 'Pricing to market when the exchange rate changes', *National Bureau of Economic Research*, working paper no. 1926.

Le Cacheux, J. and Reichlin, L. (1989) 'Taux de change et prix des importations: le cas des automobiles en Europe' in *Observations et diagnostics économiques*, no. 27, April 1989.

Martin, S. (1988) *Industrial Economics, Economic Analysis and Public Policy*, New York and London: Macmillan.

Melo, de J. and Messerlin, P. (1988) 'Price, quality and welfare effects of European VERs on Japanese auto', *European Economic Review, 32.*

Mertens, Y. and Ginsburg, V. (1985) 'Product differentiation and price discrimination in the European Community, the case of automobiles', *Journal of Industrial Economics, 34.*

Messerlin, P. and Becuwe, S. (1987) 'French trade and competition policies in the car industry' in OECD (1987) *The Costs of Restraining Imports, The Automobile Industry*, Paris: OECD.

Motor Traffic in Sweden (1961–89 issues) Stockholm.

Mueller, D. (1986) *Profits in the Long Run*, Cambridge: Cambridge University Press.

NO (Näringsfrihetsombudsmannen: Competition Commissioner) (1989a) *Begränsningar av den japanska bilimporten*, Dnr 350/88.

NO (1989b) *Direktimport-motorfordon*, Dnr 117/89.

Sachwald, F. (1989) *Ajustement sectoriel et adaptation des entreprises, le cas de l'industrie automobile*, Centre d'Etudes Prospectives et d'Informations Internationales, Paris.

Schwartz, B. (1989) 'Företaget som medborgare', Reseach Report EFI, *Ekonomiska Forskningsinstitutet vid Handelshögskolan i Stockholm.*

Sölvell, Ö. (1988) 'Is the global automobile industry really global?' in N. Hood and J.-E. Vahlne (eds) *Strategies in Global Competition*, London: Croom Helm.

SOU (Statens offentliga utredningar) (1981: 42) *Prisreglering mot inflation?*, Stockholm.

SPK (Statens pris- och konkurrensverk) (1989) *Varor och tjänster på bilområdet*, Stockholm.

Stigler, G. (1968) *The Organization of Industry*, Chicago: The University of Chicago Press.

Wieser, T. (1989) 'Price differentials in the European economic space', *European Free Trade Association*, Occasional Paper 29, Geneva.

Willig, R. and Dutz, M. (1987) 'US–Japanese VER: a case study from a competition policy perspective' in OECD (1987) *The Costs of Restraining Imports, The Automobile Industry*, Paris: OECD.

Part IV

Producer behaviour, public policy and the market

7 Agricultural policy: old wine in new bottles

Ewa Rabinowicz

INTRODUCTION

Agriculture is an extensively regulated sector. Agricultural policy results in high domestic food prices taxing the consumers and subsidizing the producers. In the first part of the chapter this issue is examined in detail, providing estimates of the degree of taxation. In the second part, the question is asked why the consumers are taxed while producers are subsidized or why the policy is what it is. Two different explanatory models are examined in the process of pursuing the issue. The first approach is viewing the policy as an outcome of supply and demand forces on the political market. The second approach views policy as a sequential process which exhibits a great degree of inertia and which is influenced by long run economic forces.

AGRICULTURAL POLICY IN SWEDEN

Unlike other sectors in the economy, there exists a special policy for agriculture. The Swedish agricultural policy has its roots in the international crisis of the 1930s. The policy which is still in place is based on the agricultural policy decision of 1985. A new policy decision has, however, been taken which will be implemented starting in mid-1991. Furthermore, negotiations about agricultural policy and trade liberalization within the framework of GATT, which were supposed to be completed by 1990 but which are still going on, will certainly have implications for the policy. Describing Swedish agricultural policy in these circumstances is a somewhat difficult. The main feature of the new policy is a partial deregulation of agriculture. Many of the regulations which have been decided to be removed will, however, still be in place in a somewhat simplified form during a transition period (until 1993–4). Furthermore, the analysis of the impact of the policy, presented in the following sections, concerns the 'old' policy, because it is not yet possible to fully evaluate the impact of the 'new' one. Not least because many issues remain unresolved. It seems, therefore, appropriate to start with the old policy and indicate where changes are taking place. A more detailed analysis of the new policy will be given in the section on the evolution of agricultural policy.

The main official objective of the 'old' policy was to safeguard the provision of food during times of peace, blockade and war. Other objectives were: good food quality at reasonable prices to consumers, a farm income equivalent to that of comparable groups, efficient resource utilization, protection of the environment and a balanced regional development. In the new policy the farm income objective is treated as a precondition of achievement of the other objectives, not as an objective *per se*.

The main instrument used to pursue the agricultural policy was the price policy implemented by the National Agricultural Market Board (NAMB). The policy consisted of price regulations, domestic market regulations and border protection in the form of import levies – variable or fixed within price limits. This type of protection insulates the domestic market almost completely from the price movements on the international market. In the new policy, both the level and the form of border protection have been left unchanged awaiting the outcome of GATT negotiations for possible further changes.

While the border protection restricted external competition, the internal market regulations eliminated competition on the domestic market in order to maintain the prices established by the price regulations. The measures used included mainly the removal of surplus quantities from the domestic market through export or storage. The internal market regulations were carried out by seven Market Regulation Associations (MRA). Price regulations and domestic market regulations have been decided to be removed by the new policy and will gradually disappear. MRAs will disappear as well, as their duties expire.

The MRA for milk products was performing additional duties by administering a revenue equalization scheme between dairies, which enabled milk farmers to act as a price discriminating monopoly, pricing products in relation to the demand elasticities (high on milk, low on butter). A simplified version of this scheme will stay in place until 1994.

Export subsidies were used to facilitate the removal of the surplus commodities from the domestic market. Since domestic market regulations are going to cease, the export subsidies will disappear as well. Exports will, however, still be subsidized during a transition period (until 1992–3 for livestock products and 1993–4 for grains and oilseeds). Government budgetary funds were used until 1991 to finance low-income initiatives and to support agriculture in northern Sweden where production costs are higher and remoteness from markets leads to high transport costs.

Growing surpluses during the 1980s have brought about increased use of supply management measures such as ban on building investments for livestock production, production quotas in milk,[1] fallow land compensation schemes, etc. A number of other policy instruments are used as well: rationalization, restrictions on the acquisition of farm land, legislation of animal protection, etc.

The institutional structure surrounding agriculture is extensive for a sector contributing only 1.6 per cent to GDP and in comparison with other sectors of the economy. It consists of a department of agriculture, a parliamentary agricultural committee, an agricultural university and two civil service departments – The National Agricultural Market Board and The National Board of Agriculture, which supervises 24 County Boards of Agriculture.

IMPACT OF THE POLICY ON CONSUMER WELFARE

Welfare losses and transfers

As a result of the agricultural policy the prices of agricultural products in Sweden are considerably higher than in the world market. The impact of the higher prices on consumers can be calculated in various ways. One possibility is to ask how much the present level of consumption would cost in an unregulated market. The resulting concept is the Consumer Subsidy Equivalent (CSE). This concept is illustrated in Figure 7.1. Since agricultural products are tradable and Sweden is a small country (i.e. a price taker on the world market) the present level of prices on the world market would prevail in Sweden in the absence of domestic regulations.

As can be seen from Table 7.1, consumers are heavily taxed. Almost 13 billion SEK are spent on food in excess of the cheapest source. This represents 56 per cent of the consumption valued at the farm gate price level.[2] Since the budget share of food is higher at a low income level the impact of the taxation on the income

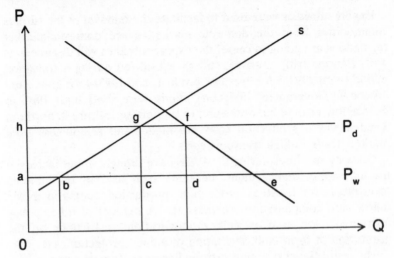

Figure 7.1   Illustration of the consumer subsidy equivalent
Source: The consumer subsidy equivalents were estimated by the OECD
(OECD, 1988). Results are presented in Table 7.1.
Notes: Total CSE = $-C (P_D - P_W) + G$ = a d f h; percentage CSE = 100
(Total CSE/(C×P_D)); C = Level of consumption, P_D = Domestic
consumer price at farm gate level; G = Budget payments to consumers, not
shown in figure.

distribution is regressive. The taxation of consumers varies across
products. We can ask if the structure of taxation is biased towards
any particular income category? Meat products are taxed above the
average, while milk is taxed below because of a consumer price
subsidy on fluid milk. Since low income consumers eat relatively less
meat, the tax structure has an equalizing effect on income. This
effect is, however, small since differences in consumption structure
between different income classes in Sweden are not large.

CSE simply measures money transfers at the existing consumption
level. Had the prices been lower, the consumption would be higher.
The correct measures of welfare losses are the compensating or
equivalent variations (CV or EV respectively). However, most
empirical studies are, for reasons of simplicity, based on the concept
of consumer surplus.[3] The consumer surplus is the area behind the
demand curve and above the price line. It is equal to a e f h of CSE
plus net loss in consumption – e d f in Figure 7.1.

The loss of consumer surplus due to the present policy was
previously estimated by Bolin *et al.* (1986). Deregulation of

Table 7.1 Consumer subsidy equivalents, CSE

Product	CSE total (SEK b.)	CSE 1986 (%)	CSE 1982–6 (%)
Wheat	−1,025.2	−70.7	−59.7
Coarse grains	−1,247.3	−35.9	−27.0
Oil seeds	1,004.0	−77.1	−45.5
Sugar	−551.0	−34.0	−29.1
Milk	−4,273.2	−48.5	−34.6
Beef	−1,703.3	−65.9	−51.5
Pork	−2,359.5	−70.2	−50.5
Poultry	−252.6	−67.2	−65.9
Sheep meat	−7.0	−7.0	−4.3
Eggs	−404.0	−51.3	−39.5
Total	−12,828.9	−56.0	−40.2

Source: OECD (1988).

agriculture in 1982 (elimination of border protection and consumer subsidies)[4] would have increased consumer welfare by 2.7 billion SEK. Average world market prices from the 1970s were used as reference prices. Fahlbeck (1989) estimated losses to consumers to 20.0 billion SEK using OECD's reference prices and keeping subsidies unchanged.[5] The losses are calculated at the retail level by estimating the impact of changing farm prices on retail prices of processed food commodities by assuming constant (commodity specific) processing costs and proportional trade margins. The results are shown in Table 7.2.

Table 7.2 Welfare loss to consumers

Product	Loss of consumer surplus, 1986 price level (SEK m.)	Share of consumption at retail level (%)
Wheat	418	6.3
Rye	73	4.7
Oats/barley	13	7.9
Sugar	762	31.0
Milk	9,567	46.4
Beef	2,129	28.0
Pork/poultry	3,273	25.6
Total	20,040	31.0

Source: Fahlbeck (1989).

Examining the assumptions

The calculations in the first section were based *inter alia* on the following assumptions: tradability and constant world prices (the small country assumption). Both are, to some extent, open to criticism. Using constant reference prices tends to overstate the losses. Since reference prices are considerably lower than the present domestic prices, induced changes in consumption and production would be quite substantial resulting in imports probably too large to be bought at constant prices. The balance of trade for the products in Fahlbeck's study is estimated to change from +20 million SEK to −1,360 million SEK, valued at reference price level. Imports of that size purchased regularly over a long time would certainly induce higher purchasing prices, particularly for fluid milk products, which must be delivered on a daily basis.

The preceding point relates to the issue of tradability which can be questioned for fluid milk products. Consumption of fluid milk products in Sweden is among the highest in the world (165 kg per person/year). High loss of welfare on milk products in Table 7.2 is due both to the high level of consumption and the very low reference price used. The OECD's reference price of milk is calculated implicitly assuming that the milk is 'recreated' from skimmed milk powder and milk fat both valued at New Zealand prices. It is doubtful if this price really represents an opportunity cost of producing domestic consumer milk. Using an alternative evaluation of milk, for instance the import price of fluid milk from Denmark, reduces total losses to the consumer in Fahlbeck's calculations by 6 billion SEK.

Furthermore, since Sweden is a net exporter, export prices which are lower than import prices are used as the reference. However, if the prices are as low as assumed, Sweden would change status to a net importer and import prices would be more appropriate – resulting in a reduction of the loss to the consumers by approximately 10 to 15 per cent.

Correcting for externalities

Buying expensive products from domestic producers instead of cheap imports reduces consumer welfare as stated above. At the same time, domestic production of food may result in positive externalities or collective goods that increase consumer welfare and negative externalities working in opposite direction. The total impact on consumer welfare consists, therefore, of a food component and a net externality component. The issue is to identify externalities and then to evaluate them if possible.

Food security

Due to low probability of wars or other major disturbances, there is no guarantee that unregulated markets will secure food supply would the need arise. The question one can ask is how much production would be reduced at the reference price level as used by Fahlbeck and how this reduction translates to loss of food security? Food security is usually defined as 'access by all people (at all time) to enough food for an active, healthy life'.[6] If one really stresses 'all time' in the definition above, it is doubtful if food security can be achieved in any country at a reasonable cost. Food security will here be defined as the ability of assuring a diet of 2,900 calories per person per day during a period[7] when Sweden is isolated from trade (presumably during a military conflict in which the country, being neutral, is not involved). This very particular definition is motivated· by the fact that the Swedish defence/agricultural planning is based on it.

In Fahlbeck (1989), production is estimated to be reduced as follows: wheat −17 per cent, coarse grains −27 per cent, sugar beet −35 per cent, milk −32 per cent, beef −19 per cent, pork and eggs −11 per cent.[8] What complicates the analysis is that all commodities are not covered, most notably the oil seeds which are very important for the supply of dietary energy and where the level of self-sufficiency is much lower. However, it can be argued that we can limit our analysis to the commodities included in Fahlbeck's study, since the aim is to calculate how much the welfare loss of 20 billion SEK should be reduced because of lower food security. Reductions for commodities not contributing to this loss can hardly be made. Furthermore, even if a food security policy for oil seeds is very expensive, the cost cannot exceed the (uncounted) loss due to present policy for that commodity.

Arable land is the key factor. Using simple supply elasticities does not reveal the decomposition of the production response into acreage and yield changes. Since arable land by and large lacks alternative value,[9] one could assume that fertilizer input would be reduced first and that the impact on acreage would be less than on production – leaving not less than 2.2 million hectares (out of 2.9). It would be necessary to store fertilizers/pesticides to avoid further production decreases or even to increase production more. Storing of fertilizer and pesticides are, however, already a part of present policy. Additional storage would thus not be required for fertilizer. On the other hand, storage of protein feed has to be increased considerably since the switch to higher milk consumption which is assumed in the official crisis-diet will not be possible to the same extent, due to fewer number of cows. The cost could be estimated at 200 million SEK.[10]

The main problem is, however, uncertainty in estimating the impact of lower producer prices on production. The price reduction is far more substantial than any variation historically observed. The impact of a deregulation of the agricultural sector was previously analysed by Bolin *et al.* (1986) who predicted only a marginal impact on production. The reference/world market prices used in his study, however, were considerably higher than the 1986 prices used in Fahlbeck's study. The loss of consumer welfare was accordingly much lower.

The food security problem is analysed in depth by Molander (1988). He examines a rather severe isolation scenario of three years, but reduces the crisis-diet to 2,700 calories. The food security issue boils down to 'storing arable' land versus storing fertilizer, or rather storing additional acreage above the free trade level. Assuming this level to be only 1 million hectares – a very pessimistic view – the optimal level would be 2.04 million and the total cost of providing food security would be at most about 500 million SEK per year. Molander limits his analysis to plant production claiming that sufficient quantities of milk will always be produced domestically due to natural barriers to trade. However, if milk is partly non-tradable the losses to consumers are accordingly lower.

In the discussion above we have been taking the official defence scenario seriously. But the relevance of the defence scenario which looks very much like a shorter version of the Second World War can be questioned in view of today's military situation. The present policy can be characterized as identifying one possible scenario – believed to be the most probable one – and planning for it (in detail!) accordingly. An alternative approach would be to formulate a policy that is robust under several possible scenarios.

Scenic values of agriculture

Preventing the arable land from afforestation is a fiercely argued issue in the public debate on agriculture. Forest already covers a substantial portion of the Swedish land area. Cultivated land, it is argued, preserves variability of the landscape. Drake (1987) estimates, using an interview method, a willingness to pay for preserving arable land of up to 1,000 SEK per hectare. Estimation of willingness to pay by surveys, however, has serious drawbacks. The questions are hypothetical and the respondents' behaviour is not restricted by a limited budget forcing them to choose between different ways of using their income. The resulting estimates are, therefore, unreliable. However, the estimated value is high enough to indicate that such willingness exists.

If farmers, under free trade conditions, wished to use 2.2 million ha of arable land, 0.7 billion ha would have to be preserved from afforestation to achieve the same benefit. The cost of preserving 1 ha of arable land is estimated to be 100–150 SEK a year (Molander, 1989) giving a total cost of 70–105 million SEK. The estimate by Molander covers only the cost of preventing trees from invading arable land. If scenic value of agriculture includes diversity of biological life, etc., the cost would be higher.

National preferences

Given the opportunity to freely buy cheap imported products it is possible that some consumers would prefer more expensive, domestic ones. Farmers' representatives frequently claim that protecting agriculture does not harm consumers since they would prefer buying domestic products anyhow. However, if farmers really believed in this argument themselves they would not demand protection for agriculture as they do. 'Buy domestic' campaigns in other industries (like textiles) do not seem to save inefficient producers. Food production is, to some extent, different. Domestic products may be perceived as safer, of a higher quality, etc. It is, however, difficult to determine how much domestic food would be sold at higher prices if free imports were possible. Swedish tomatoes, which are sold at considerably higher prices than imported ones, show a market share of 23 per cent. It is doubtful, however, if this figure can be used to estimate the willingness to pay for all domestic food.

Conclusions

A closer examination of the impact of the present agricultural policy on consumer welfare reveals that the loss of consumer surplus due to higher prices, as estimated by Fahlbeck to 20.0 billion, is overstated and has to be reduced (Fahlbeck, 1989). The reduction would at most amount to 8.4 billion SEK (non-tradability of fluid milk: 6.0; import prices on remaining production: 2.1; food security and scenic value of agriculture: 0.3), still leaving a welfare loss of 11.6 billion, implying considerable taxation of consumers. Furthermore, it should be remembered that the analysis does not cover all commodities thereby underestimating the loss to consumers. The additional source of error is the omission of processing industries. The estimated losses are due to higher prices at the farm gate level only. It is reasonable to believe that the present policy impairs efficiency in the processing industry. This is due to the fact that variable levels are, as a rule, calculated for tradable processed commodities instead of for non-tradable primary farm products, for instance, for processed milk and not for raw milk. There are several indications of low efficiency in agricultural processing industries, but no reliable estimates. Productivity growth in dairies and slaughter-houses has also been considerably lower than for the whole processing industry.[11] Comparison of processing costs in Swedish and Danish dairies shows 20 per cent higher Swedish costs (Albertson, 1985). If this figure is representative for the whole protected agricultural processing industry, the additional loss to consumers would be 3.5 billion SEK.[12]

WHY IS THERE AN AGRICULTURAL POLICY?

Explaining high prices by referring to the present agricultural policy is, of course, correct but, in a way, trivial. The real issue is why we have a *special* policy for agriculture. Similar policies do not exist for other sectors of the economy. On the other hand, similar policies exist for agriculture in other industrialized countries – all of them support agriculture using similar types of arguments (Winters, 1987). On what grounds can agricultural policy be justified? Two possible candidates are equity and efficiency. Let us examine them as explanations for the policy.

Fair agricultural policy?

Equity considerations have played an important role in the formulation and the implementation of the present policy. Prices were determined in relation to calculated historical costs of production, often above market clearing levels and prevented by internal market regulations from falling. In other words, the idea is to find a 'fair price' for agricultural products. The underlying assumption has been that production factors in agriculture are unable to command a fair return in an unregulated market because of the specificity of agriculture. Beliefs about the specificity of agriculture were widely held by agricultural economists in the 1950s and 1960s with the Cochrane technology treadmill theory as a foremost example.[13] Specificity was supposed to include such factors as (Gardner, 1981):

- monopsony power of middlemen;
- the tendency for a smaller share of income to be spent on food as an economy grows;
- more rapid technological advance in agriculture than in non-agricultural production;
- over-optimistic investment in fixed capital by farmers;
- inflexibility in adjustment of the farm labour supply;
- lack of schooling and skills among farmers and their families.

It was argued that one or a combination of these results were in a state of constant disequilibrium with too many resources in agriculture. This type of analysis is hardly relevant to Swedish agriculture of today. It is, of course, true that production volume is limited – GDP in agriculture has not changed much during the last forty years but the agricultural labour has responded by leaving the sector. Between 1950 and 1987 the labour force in agriculture was reduced by 84 per cent. Two-thirds of the income of farm households emanates from sources outside farming. Furthermore, the total income per farm is roughly the same regardless of the farm size! (See *Yearbook of Agricultural Statistics*, 1987). What differs is income composition. Neither do farmers lack schooling and skills. The level of education (number of years) is almost the same for farmers and industrial workers. Agricultural labour is demonstrably mobile and equally educated and should not be expected to earn a lower return in agriculture than in other sectors.

The apparent low profitability of farming is another argument for interventions in the market subscribing to the idea of specificity of agriculture (in this case, agricultural capital as opposed to agricultural labour as discussed above). According to an analysis by Sandberg (Riksrevisionsverket, 1988a): 'there is a true low profitability of agriculture'. Sandberg has examined seven different types of profitability estimates commonly used in Swedish agriculture. The estimates ranged between −12 per cent and +0.3 per cent for total capital in real terms, 1977–88. Sandberg's analysis has, however, been criticized on several points (Andersson and Bolin, 1990), in particular, it appears to rest on an inconsistent set of assumptions.

Furthermore, even if there was a farm income problem – this has, perhaps, been the case during the long history of agricultural policy – price support would never be the right solution to it. Adjustment in that case, should be in the factor markets, by increasing mobility, and not in product markets. Increased prices will only retain more resources in agriculture and raise land values. Direct income support to disadvantaged farmers is another possible way of easing the problem. This type of policy has been used to some extent (a retirement subsidy in the 1960s and a low income initiative which is part of the present policy). These measures have, however, been overshadowed by price support. Furthermore, the impact of price policy on the income distribution is regressive since larger producers (or more precisely larger landowners) benefit more. To conclude, it is doubtful if there is a farm income problem today, and if it ever existed, it was not handled in the most appropriate way.

Efficient agricultural policy?

Moving to efficiency considerations, agricultural policy could be motivated by market failures such as externalities, public goods, etc. The issue has been partly covered by the discussion on pp. 210–13, while estimating the impact of externalities on consumer welfare. The food security argument which belongs to this category has been critically evaluated in the previous discussion. One may add that a scepticism about the argument as justification of the present policy has been expressed by other authors as well. Hedlund and Lundahl (1985) rejected the argument with references to standard trade theory (optimal intervention in the presence of a domestic distortion). Bolin *et al.* (1986) argue along two lines: first, liberalizing agricultural policy would not produce a substantial impact on agricultural production; second, a total embargo in case of war would furthermore change all relative prices and the resource availability. In this situation, agriculture as a vital industry would compete easily for resources and adjust. Winters (1988b) emphasizes the flexibility of consumption, the dependence of the present agriculture on imported inputs and the low probability of trade embargoes (for England, as a case study). Similar types of arguments can be found in the World Development Report (1986).

Can agricultural policy be justified as generating positive externalities in the field of environmental protection? In some respects, the answer is certainly no! High prices provide a stimulus to high inputs of fertilizer and pesticides with potentially harmful effects on the environment. In other respects, the answer may be positive – agricultural policy probably keeps marginal agricultural land in production which, in some cases, can be beneficial for the environment. Preserving agricultural land for its scenic value has been discussed on p. 213. If this produces positive externalities it can be attained more cheaply by subsidizing only marginal land. A related issue is the idea of preserving the rural way of life or vital rural communities. It is open to debate whether an empty countryside is a 'market failure'; this issue, as well as similar ones, is often presented as a 'non-economic' objective of agricultural policy. However, as Winter (1988a) points out, the critical dimension of each objective is economic because its achievement requires the absorption of resources having alternative uses and because the degree of achievement may be monitored in economic terms. Present agricultural policy generates higher agricultural and hence rural employment than the unregulated market. However, the policy has not prevented farm employment from declining. Nor is such a policy a real possibility. Keeping employment, i.e. productivity, unchanged would result in either ever increasing food prices or ever increasing government spending.

Agricultural markets are often claimed to be chronically unstable because of the low elasticity of demand, weather-dependent production and biologically determined lags in production. The lack of a complete set of insurance markets for sharing risk is another problem. Since there is a gain to be had from stabilization, a case is frequently made for governmental intervention to achieve stability. There exist, however, market institutions which at least partly can cope with instability such as contract deliveries, futures markets, crop insurance schemes, etc.

The discussion above boils down to a conclusion that, albeit some intervention in agricultural markets can be justified, it is not possible to view the present agricultural policy as an efficient way of responding to the issue. Self-sufficiency is not an effective way of providing food security; policy contributes to negative externalities and does not cope with positive externalities in the cheapest way; and the market could handle some of the instability.

Efficient achievements of policy objectives?

In the discussion above, the economic theory has been used to evaluate the policy. One could, however, claim that the agricultural policy should rather be evaluated in relation to its stated objectives. Nevertheless, it does not change the conditions very much. There is some overlap between the analysis in welfare economic terms and in terms of achievements of the objectives. Several analyses of the achievements have been made, the most recent by Wetterberg (Ds 1988: 54) for Sweden and for all Nordic countries in 'Jordbruks-politiken i nordiska länder' (Nord, 1989). Several critical evaluations of the Common Agricultural Policy (see, for instance, Hill, 1984), which is similar to Swedish policy, have also been made. Critical analysis of agricultural policy in industrialized countries made by OECD should also be mentioned. The common conclusion from all these studies is that the policy either does not fulfil its objective or does so in a very costly way.

Agricultural policy is, indeed, costly. For all OECD countries jointly the loss is estimated to be US$51.5 billion.[14] Fahlbeck (1989) estimates the net welfare loss due to agricultural policy to be 2 billion SEK, not including all commodities.[15] OECD's country study of Sweden (1988) estimates the total transfer to Swedish farmers in terms of income equivalents (Producer Subsidy Equivalent)[16] to be 14 billion SEK in 1986. This figure is a transfer not a cost, but it constitutes more than 50 per cent of the value of production in the sector and exceeds the value added.

Other explanatory models

The above discussion can be viewed as an attempt to explain the present agricultural policy in terms of principled behaviour on the part of politicians. Since this obviously has failed, the opposite model has to be tried: namely, viewing the policy as an opportunistic response to political influence. What makes this approach attractive is the fact that the present policy constitutes a substantial transfer to the farmers – a welfare gain of 10.1 billion SEK (Fahlbeck, 1989) at the expense of the consumers and taxpayers, suggesting a different ability of exerting political pressure. A political market model – supply of and demand for support – operates along those lines. The model will be described and evaluated against Swedish data. A political market approach, however, is based on an equilibrium assumption which can be questioned. The present agricultural policy is still heavily influenced by its original setting. Viewing the policy as a dynamic process of adjustment to changing conditions, political and economic, will be tested as an alternative explanation.

The political marketplace theory

Different conceptualizations of the political market exist: the pure interest group model (Becker) or a model of interaction of pressure groups with politicians (Peltzman, Niskanen). Politicians are viewed as suppliers of protection or support for the sake of re-election. Groups who expect to gain from a policy invest in lobbying or propagandizing for adoption of the policy up to the point where marginal benefit (MB) is zero. The offering of support has some costs because of opposition from consumers and others who are adversely affected – the marginal cost of offering protection can be expected to increase. The equilibrium level of protection is then determined by the intersection of MC and MB (see Figure 7.1, p. 208).

Models of the political marketplace, as outlined above or similar, have frequently been applied in the field of trade theory to analyse levels of tariffs, changes of tariff levels, trade policy decisions at various levels, etc. (see Lavergne, 1983; Baldwin, 1985; Finger *et al.*, 1982; Goldstein, 1986). Agricultural policy analysts have been attracted by the model as well, in particular to explain the striking difference between agricultural policy in developing and developed countries (Anderson and Hayami, 1986; Anderson and Tyers, 1989). Developing countries tax agriculture, particularly export crops, while developed countries tend to subsidize it. According to Anderson and Tyers, the cost of protecting agricultural producers in developing countries is high because of high sensitivity of consumers to food prices when a sizeable share of the budget is spent on food. Demand for protection is low because of the high cost of collective action by farmers relative to potential benefits from lobbying. Anderson and Tyers rely heavily on Olson's (1965, 1985) theory of collective action. Factors such as large numbers, dispersion and heterogeneity are claimed to play a decisive role for the ability, or rather inability, or farmers to control free riders and organize themselves. In addition, there is a strong demand for industrial protection and willingness to support growing industries for various reasons. This explains why agriculture is not only directly taxed but indirectly taxed as well. As an economy grows, subsistence farmers become more commercialized, the share of agriculture in GDP and employment declines as well as the share of food in the consumer budget. Resistance to protection of agriculture thus becomes much weaker while demand for protection grows stronger, since farmers become better organized and supported by allies (input suppliers, etc.). Furthermore, there is a tendency for growing economies, especially densely populated ones, to lose their comparative advantages in agriculture and become food importers. This makes it still easier to protect agriculture. The last point is of particular relevance for fast growing economies in east Asia and the model is influenced by development there. Anderson and Tyers (1989), however, claim that there is 'a general tendency for governments of industrialized countries to gradually change from taxing to increasingly assisting agriculture relative to other tradable sectors' and that the post-war growth of agricultural protectionism in the industrialized countries is a part of that pattern.

The political market model is difficult to test econometrically. By its very nature, the process is non-quantifiable, secret and often not issue-specific (Lavergne, 1983). Since the process, as such, cannot be observed, all kinds of proxies indicating the stake, the strength or ability are used. Hayami and Honna (in Anderson and Hayami, 1986) use the share of agriculture in GDP (or employment). The problem is that this indicator is so vague that the result (higher level of support at lower share) may validate several different hypotheses. Gardner (1987) uses the number of producers, index of geographical concentration and the size of an average production unit as indicators of the cost to producers in generating political pressure and finds these variables, as well as social costs (deadweight losses) of redistribution, significant for explaining inter-industry patterns of protection within agriculture. The inter-industry pattern of protection of industrial activity has been examined by Lavergne (1983) with discouraging results for politial market variables (similar to those used by Gardner). The tariff structure in the United States is mainly explained by its historical heritage (Smot–Hawley tariff). Baldwin's (1985) and Goldstein's (1986) results are not entirely encouraging for the political market hypothesis either.

Agricultural policy as a sequential process

In an equilibrium model as presented above, the level of protection would adjust relatively quickly to the underlying level of structural determinants. In reality, there is a lot of inertia in the system preventing frequent changes of policy. Furthermore, if a policy has been in place for some time it can easily be perceived as some kind of 'right' or a 'status quo privilege' (Lavergne, 1983). Reversing the policy means as a rule a decapitalization of asset values – particularly in agriculture where support raises land prices – imposing serious adjustment problems on those involved. Injuring one party (producers) for the benefit of others violates the 'conservative welfare function' as Corden formulates it – the principle that a significant reduction of the income of any major group should be avoided.

Variable import levies, frequently used in agricultural policy, create another problem with the equilibrium interpretation. The tariff equivalent of Swedish levy on wheat, for instance, was 1978–9: 39 per cent, 1980–1: 12 per cent, 1982–3: 40 per cent. At the same time the underlyng commodity regime for wheat remained unchanged. Do these very different levels of protection represent three different equilibrium points on the political market of wheat protection in spite of the fact that the policy rules remain unchanged?

An alternative way of pursuing the issue of why agricultural policies are what they are would be to recognize that the making of the policy is a sequential process which seldom starts from scratch. Petit (1985) uses that kind of approach in analysing and comparing the evolution of commodity programmes in France and the United States. Petit bases his framework on two general hypotheses:

> In the short run, the process is driven by conflicts of interest, mainly economic. These interests are organized to influence public authorities, and the conflicts are regulated through political institutions. In the long run, economic forces affect the interests at stake and their relative weight. (p. 7)

A similar type of analysis is used in Rabinowicz *et al.* (1986).

The rest of the chapter aims to examine the two explanatory models, viewing policy as an outcome of supply and demand forces on the political market or as a result of a sequential process, in the light of empirical evidence from Sweden. A formal econometric type of examination is difficult here due to the difficulty of measurement of all relevant variables. The approach used should be seen as a way of organizing the discussion.

TESTING THE EXPLANATORY MODELS

Issues to examine

This leaves us with several issues to examine. How has Swedish agricultural policy developed? Has it become increasingly more protectionist as Anderson claims, or can we observe cycles in the domestic willingness to support agriculture in response to long-run economic forces in line with Petit's analysis? The analysis of agricultural policy development cannot be done in one dimension only. There are at least three aspects which have to be distinguished. The level of protection is an obvious candidate. However, as pointed out before, variable levies automatically adjust the level of protection without changing policy rules. The direction in which rules (market regulations or other support) are changing – in favour or against agricultural interests – shows the political will and recognizes the sequential nature of decision-making. An analysis of major policy reforms is thus necessary as well. Comparing domestic with international prices provides an external point of reference. The Swedish agricultural policy is, however, very much oriented to the domestic market. Thus an evaluation in terms of internal references is also justified. This could include the comparison of producer prices, with a production cost index and general price index or an analysis of trends in production, investment and land values as indicators of profitability in agriculture. The underlying issue is whether the policy is aiming at speeding up or at slowing down the movement of resources out of agriculture.

The second issue concerns farmers' influence, strength and ability to exert pressure. In what ways may Swedish farmers influence the present policy? Through which channels is the influence passed? Have those channels evolved in such a way as to give farmers more formal possibilities to influence the policy over time? How has the farmers' ability to exert pressure changed? Have they become stronger since they are fewer, as claimed by Anderson, Olson and others? Are they better organized, or do they have better ability to control 'free-riders'? A particular issue is whether there is a difference in strength between different groups of producers and if such a difference is visible in different levels of protection. Similar questions can be asked for consumers. Have the consumers any influence on setting and implementing agricultural policy? Are the affluent consumers more tolerant to high prices?

If the influence of 'long-run economic forces' is to be analysed one needs to define the concept further. Petit (1985) mentions: agricultural prices, farmer income, government budget, food prices and balance of trade. The present author would emphasize the cost of the policy, in particular the cost of surplus production, as especially embarrassing. A still better indicator is the opportunity cost of resources, labour and capital, used in agriculture – the growth rate of GDP and an indicator of the shortage of labour. This last point is of special interest since the two theories discussed here generate different testable hypotheses as far as the impact of economic growth on agricultural policy is concerned: Anderson and Hayami (1986) predict increased protectionism when the growth rate of GDP is high. However, too many resources in agriculture at such a time, on the other hand, is expensive in terms of opportunity costs and policy should adjust by pushing labour, etc. out of the sector if the second theory is the correct one.

Ideology and the value systems are other important factors, particularly in understanding the success of pressure groups in influencing policy. Appealing to the general public for support is perhaps the main channel of lobbying. An analysis of the changing ideological climate will therefore be provided as well.

Development of agricultural policy: major policy decisions

During its more than half century-long history, the modern agricultural policy has been subject to several investigations by Governmental Committees on Agriculture, preceding agricultural policy decisions in the parliament. A brief examination of the decisions will be given below. A question should be asked, however, concerning how much, if any, importance should be attached to the officially stated objectives of the agricultural policy. After all, we have previously argued that the existing policy is not the most efficient response to the stated objectives. Winters (1987) claims that policy statements should be seen as excuses rather than real objectives – if they really mattered the policy would have been different. On the other hand, one could argue that the objectives do matter. Once an objective is stated it serves as a justification and legitimization of the policy. The objectives cannot be openly disregarded, so they thereby create a restriction on future policy changes. Furthermore, changes in the priority ordering of objectives are highly significant.

The birth of the present agricultural policy in Sweden is

surrounded by circumstances similar to those in other countries (Petit, 1985) – the severe economic crisis of the 1930s and the arrival in office of a new government, a coalition of the labour party and the farmer party. The labour party dropped its free trade orientation in agriculture in exchange for the farmer party's acceptance of a Keynesian type of general stabilization policy.

The interventions in agricultural markets were not a result of a carefully prepared strategy, the regulations were introduced in an *ad hoc* manner when different commodities were hit by the crisis. 'The only systematics which could be observed was that the interest of the producers were put in the first place' (Hedlund and Lundahl, 1985). All major agricultural commodities were covered. The external competition was restricted by border protection. A main type of internal regulations used were (involuntary) fees (slaughter fees, oil cake fees, etc.) collected from producers for the purpose of financing the exports. In the case of butter, a competing product, margarine, was exposed to a tax. For grains, a proportional quota (milling regulation) was used. The introduction of each new regulation was accompanied by the formation of new organizations, forerunners of the MRAs of today, for the sake of the administration. At the same time, the MRAs were supervised by various government boards. In 1937, the National Agricultural Market Board was formed, replacing several sectoral boards.

The policy was originally conceived to be temporary. The aim was to restore the pre-crisis level of domestic prices while waiting for world market prices to improve. The policy of insulating the domestic market was, however, very much the same in other European countries; as a result the world market was thrown into still greater chaos perpetuating both the crisis and the need for the protection (Tracy, 1982).

In the late 1930s, the policy was criticized by G. Myrdal and others. The outbreak of the war changed the situation dramatically. Food security, which was never the issue in the surplus crisis of the preceding period, became a key priority, strongly affecting the work of the Public Committee on Agriculture (1942–7). The agricultural policy decision of 1947 (based on the work of the committee) confirmed and prolonged the agricultural policy of the 1930s. Income parity for farmers[17] and a high degree of self-sufficiency and efficiency in food production were highlighted as the main goals. The main instruments of agricultural policy introduced in the previous period, the border protection (variable levies) and internal market regulations, were prolonged. Additional instruments were added, aimed at promoting efficiency in farming (rationalization policy) through intervention in the land market, subsidized credit, extension services, etc. The policy decision of 1947 not only made the previous *ad hoc* policy permanent but also legitimated it through officially stated objectives. The principal reason for the continuation of the policy was the concern for food security – a natural reaction to the war experiences, shared by all members of the committee. The lack of surpluses and a relatively high level of (war-inflated) world market prices at that time probably contributed to the policy not being perceived as costly to society.

Agricultural policy was re-examined by a 1960 Committee on Agriculture. Agriculture was producing surpluses[18] sold at low world market prices (see the next section). At the same time the rapidly growing economy (4.5 per cent per year, 1960–5) experienced acute shortages of labour. Workers were imported from abroad. In spite of a rapid structural change, agriculture at the beginning of the 1960s still employed 10 per cent of the labour force (man-hours) and was perceived as a labour reserve. The food security argument had begun to lose some of its appeal as memories of the war faded away. The agricultural policy decision of 1967, based on the work of the Committee, emphasized the goal of efficiency in agriculture and in society as a whole. The aim was to reduce self-sufficiency in agriculture to 80 per cent. Agricultural prices were to increase more slowly ('price-pressure') to discourage the expansion in agriculture. The mobility of agricultural labour was encouraged by pre-pension schemes and resettlement subsidies.

The policy continued along these lines until 1971: real prices to farmers decreased by 15 per cent, surpluses were reduced, milk production fell to the lowest level since the Second World War. The policy was then reversed. Prices, in particular the milk price, were allowed to increase (in real terms) again. The official reason for the policy reversal was the threat of a supply deficit in the milk market. But this was what the policy was supposed to be about – to reduce the level of self-sufficiency. In any case, all surpluses had not been eliminated. The real reason for the policy reversal was probably that structural change was pushed too fast. Between 1966 and 1971, agricultural labour was reduced (in man hours) by 30 per cent. The number of milk producers went down by 41 per cent. This induced not only sectoral but also geographical mobility, emptying vast parts of the already sparsely populated regions.

Increased food prices (as a result of increased farm prices) led to consumers' protests ('Skarholmen-wifes'). In response, food subsidies were introduced in 1973, probably due to unwillingness to bring the agricultural policy issue into the general election held the same year. The new committee on agricultural policy started its work in 1972. At the time of the 1977 policy decision, several conditions had changed. Food subsidies and high wage increases (1974–5) resulted in higher demand replacing surpluses with imports. High world market prices had recently (1973–4) been experienced and expected by many in the future. National economic growth slowed, with a recession in 1976–7. Demand for labour decreased. Food security at the global level, particularly after the Food Conference of Rome in 1974, had become an issue. The ideological climate favoured a 'green' attitude. Last, but not least, the government consisted of a coalition of non-socialist parties with both the prime minister and minister of agriculture being active farmers! Not surprisingly, the policy decision emphasized income distribution rather than efficiency and growth, making farm income a prime objective. The efficiency objective had been reformulated, taking into account the family farm and regional considerations. Arable land in Sweden was to be kept in production. The resulting surpluses were to be exported in the form of grains rather than livestock products.

The agricultural policy decision of 1977 proved to be unsustainable. Production grew fast while consumption (in particular, meat) fell. As the government budget deteriorated, caused by slow economic growth, the new food subsidy ceased and eventually old ones were removed.[19] The result was a serious surplus situation.[20]

A new agricultural committee was appointed in 1983 by the labour party government and a new agricultural policy decision was taken in 1985 after a short period of investigation. It did not make substantial changes. Food security was reinstated as the prime objective of agricultural policy. The 'consumer objective' (which already had been added by the preceding committee) was given equal status to the farm income objective. Farm prices were no longer to be raised automatically as costs increased. The objective of keeping all arable land in use was forgone and it was stated that farmers should assume full responsibility for export subsidies on grains after a transition period (five years). In the meantime, the cost would be divided 40/60 between the government and the farmers.

The cost of export subsidies escalated enormously (2.4 billion SEK in 1986–7) following the sharp decline in world market prices. In response, a temporary land retirement scheme was introduced in an attempt to manage supply by a quantitative restriction. Quantitative restrictions (quotas) were also applied in the milk sector (1985). However, for other animal products the price mechanism (slaughter levies) was used, reducing prices to farmers.[21]

A new public investigation of agricultural policy started in 1988, not as a committee but in a less formal way as a 'parliamentary working group' (called LAG). Proposals for agricultural policy reform as put forward by the government in April 1990 were based on the work of LAG. Several modifications have, however, been made. The most visible sign of the modifications is the total budgetary cost of the reform which has increased from 5.5 billion SEK to 13.6 billion, mainly due to more generous (longer and higher) transitory direct income support. The removal of internal regulations – the main idea of LAG heavily attacked by farmers – has been preserved, but a transition period has been added. A revenue equalization scheme in the milk market is to be removed, again after a transition period. Biological diversity of rural landscape is to be supported directly on a contract basis. Production of bioenergy is to be supported (including research activities) to the cost of 0.5 billion SEK per annum to be paid during the transition, officially called 'adaptation' period. During the same period, substantial subsidies, differentiated according to geographical location and the kind of activity, will be paid to farmers for switching to 'alternative' uses of agricultural resources (forest plantation, short rotation forestry, extensive pasture, etc.).

Some interesting features of these reforms can be observed:

1 The reform can hardly be described as efficient according to standard textbook prescriptions. In such a case, domestic prices of the heaviest protected commodities would be reduced most. The present reform proposal puts the hardest burden of adjustment on the most oversupplied commodities. Grains belong to this category since they had been favoured by past policy as being less inefficient than livestock.

2 Compared with previous agricultural policy reforms in Sweden and with reforms in other countries (EC countries and the United States), a very different reform strategy has been chosen. The initiative aims at major institutional change with far reaching long-term implications rather than an attempt to reform the policy within its present framework.

3 The policy decision appears somewhat inconsistent, emphasizing market orientation of agriculture on the one hand and

providing lots of detailed regulations during the 'adaptation' period on the other.

Development of agricultural policy: external and internal indicators

The level of protection in Swedish agriculture was estimated by Gulbrandsen (Gulbrandsen and Lindbeck, 1969) to increase from 34 per cent in 1948 to 63 per cent in 1960, measured at the wholesale level. An update by Hamilton (1986) shows increased protection between 1970 and 1980. Protection was, however, negative for some products in 1973–4. Figure 7.2 shows the development of the producer price index and the world market price index since 1960. The relation between the two indexes does not show the level of protection as such but indicates the development of protection since 1960. Domestic prices were increasing faster than world market prices in the 1960s. The picture was more mixed in the 1970s followed by the collapse of world market prices in the 1980s, while domestic prices were increasing. The level of support, measured as the total percentage PSE, has changed between 47.9 per cent in 1979 to 38.7 per cent in 1984 and 54.4 per cent in 1986.

Figure 7.3 shows the development of the producer price index, the production cost index and the general consumer price index. The slow development of producer prices in recent years is due to surpluses in livestock products which have been exported with aid of producer financed export subsidies lowering producer prices.

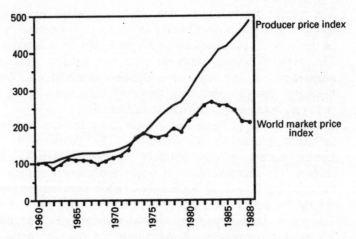

Figure 7.2　Producer prices and world market prices

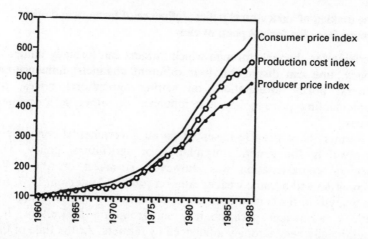

Figure 7.3 General price level, production costs, producer prices

Looking for other indicators, one can analyse development of production (Figure 7.4 shows production of milk – the main product in Swedish agriculture), investments (Figure 7.5), employment (Figure 7.6) and land values (Figure 7.7). Using these indicators one can recognize different periods in the development of Swedish agriculture: from the mid-1960s to 1971–2, from 1971–2 to the mid-1980s and the period after 1985. The first period can be distinguished by falling production (milk 17 per cent, meat 2 per cent), falling investments (machinery), rapidly falling employment (−30.4 per cent) and stable real land values. In the second period, production was rising, employment decreased more slowly (−40 per cent in 14 years), investments in machinery and buildings increased sharply in the beginning of the period and land values increased in real terms. The situation after 1985 shows some similarities to the late 1960s.

If external and internal indicators are compared, two different pictures emerge. In the late 1960s, protection increased while agriculture was rapidly contracting. The opposite occurred in the early 1970s. This highlights the danger of limiting the analysis to the rate of protection only.

The making of agricultural policy: influence of farmers and other groups from the formal point of view

Looking for channels through which farmers can formally influence policy, one can distinguish four different channels: influence on general policy formulation, on setting agricultural prices, on implementing price policy and influence on other sector-related issues.

Farmers have been represented on all governmental committees involved in the general formulation of agricultural policy. The farmers' representation was, however, strongest on the 1940s committee and became weaker later on (see Å. Anderson, 1987, for an analysis of the composition of the committees). 'Jordbruksutskottet', a permanent parliamentary sub-group on agriculture, has traditionally been strongly influenced by farmers. At the time of the 1977 agricultural policy decision almost half of its members were farmers or others related to the farming sector.

Farmers' influence on pricing of agricultural commodities depends on the pricing formula used. Different formulas have been used, starting with the price parity formula which, in 1940, was replaced by a production cost formula. This was first based on a total account for the farm sector and later (1956) on a concept of the representative farm. In 1967, the principle of automatic cost compensation was eliminated. A return to this principle occurred in the 1970s, tying prices to the production cost index. Since 1984, prices which were not formally bound to the cost development have been set in free 'negotiations'. In the new policy, price negotiations of the previous type will disappear. At first, farmers negotiated with the government. In 1963, a Consumer Delegation was created. Agricultural price negotiations are, however, not true 'negotiations' but rather a deliberation between one delegation representing farmers and one representing consumers. The process is supervised by the National Agricultural Market Board and the outcome submitted to parliament which makes the final decision.

The question one can ask is if prices were intended to follow cost, what was there to negotiate about? However, the issue was not that trivial. For example, production costs included an income parity component implying a comparison between farmers and non-farmers which always raises a lot of problems. Some other technical issues were the subject of negotiations as well. However, only a minor part of the total compensation amount was negotiable.[22] The switch to free negotiations has undoubtedly given the consumers an

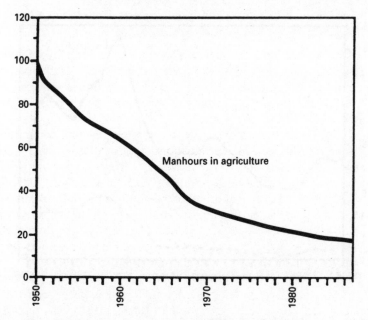

Figure 7.4 Employment in agriculture (million man hours)

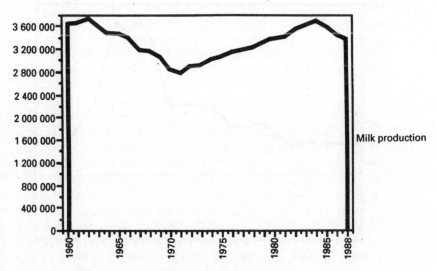

Figure 7.5 Milk production (thousand tonnes)

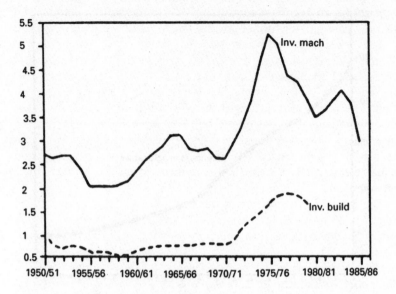

Figure 7.6   Investment in agriculture

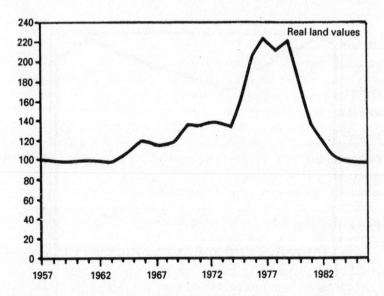

Figure 7.7   Land values

opportunity to negotiate about the whole compensation amount and thereby gain greater formal possibilities to influence the price level.

The price policy decisions were implemented by seven Market Regulation Associations. From the legal point of view, a MRA consisted of an unusual mixture of a public authority responsible for the collection of involuntary fees and a private economic association. The board of directors of the MRAs included representatives of government and consumers, but they were dominated by farm interests.[23] This was reinforced by the sheer complexity of the regulatory system, making it difficult for 'outsiders' to participate on equal terms. MRAs have had a similar construction since their introduction.

The issue of price setting in the new policy is very unclear. The removal of internal regulations will immediately push down the prices of commodities produced in surplus at *existing levels of border protection*. The key issue for the future level of prices is how the level of border protection will be decided in the years to come. In the policy decision of 1990 this issue is left to GATT. The question is which, if any, price or rather 'protection formula' would be used if GATT negotiations fail.

Farmers influence several other sector related issues, most notably agricultural research (by membership on the board of directors of the Swedish University of Agricultural Sciences (SLU) and the Research Foundation for Agricultural Research). In a recent evaluation of SLU by the Riksrevisionsverket (1988b), the issue of farmers' influence on research was raised. The bureau concluded that although farmers' representatives do not have any formal control over the research, the issue is more complicated than that. There is undoubtedly a tendency at the university to perceive problems from the viewpoint of the agricultural sector rather than from the whole society perspective. It should be noted that SLU, Sweden's only agricultural university, is financed by the Department of Agriculture not by the Department of Education as other universities. This situation creates interdependence between the agricultural sector and agricultural research.

Exerting a political pressure is, as stated before, a complicated often invisible process. In the discussion above the formal, visible aspects of the policy influence have been emphasized. It can be concluded that farmers have strong formal possibilities to influence agricultural policy and agricultural sector related matters. Farmers' representatives are involved both in the setting and in the implementation of the policy as well as in agricultural research. It

234 Internationalization, market power and consumer welfare

can, however, hardly be claimed that farmers' influence has increased during the post-war period. The evidence given above shows rather a decreased influence, particularly as far as setting prices is concerned.

In the new policy, MRAs are going to disappear as public authorities. There exists, however, a considerable danger that MRAs or similar organizations may re-emerge as private monopolies, since farmer-owned co-operatives dominate the market (compare next section). There are some signs of such developments, for instance, Arla, the biggest milk co-operative, is now trying to introduce a production quota among its members.

The strength of the farmer

Formal influence of farmers and consumers is only one side of the coin. One could argue that what really matters is the strength of both groups. In discussing strength of the farmers, Anderson and Tyers rely heavily on Olson's (1965, 1985) theory of collective action. Olson claims that smaller groups are more easily organized than large ones, the main reasons being the size of the stake (the motive) and the ability to control free-riders. The claim is easily confirmed by comparing well-organized producers with badly-organized consumers. This static observation has in Anderson's or Olson's work been transformed to a dynamic hypothesis: it is easier for a group to organize itself as it becomes smaller or more concretely that farmers are nowadays better organized, partly because they are fewer.

The size, and sometimes the stake, is used here as a proxy for strength without examining the organizational achievements of farmers as such. Let us examine the issue closely, starting with the stake. Are farmers more eager to push for protection today than in say the 1950s, since the stake – the income per farmer – now is much higher? This argument is used by Anderson. It is doubtful that this is the case. In fact, the opposite can be argued, taking into account the changes in the farm sector. Farm income has increased but the farmers as a group are much less dependent on it (it now equals only one-third of total income of farm households). The income of other groups in society has increased as well. Furthermore, finding additional or alternative employment to farming is easier when farm labour only accounts for 3 per cent of the total labour force in society. On the other hand, the growth of part-time farming might encourage farmers to be more militant about the price level. If they are risk averse, the lower dependence on agricultural income means that they are more ready to gamble on losing it.[24] Needless to say, the stake is still very important, especially when comparing producer's and consumer's willingness to oppose agricultural policy changes. Bolin *et al.* (1986) estimates that an average farmer's wealth would be reduced by 500,000 SEK (immediately) while an average consumer would gain 2,000 SEK (annually) by the total deregulation of agriculture.

Moving to the issue of organization of farm interests, most Swedish farmers are organized in the Federation of Swedish Farmers (LRF). The federation was created in 1971 by an amalgamation of the Federation of Swedish Farmers' Associations (SAL) and the National Swedish Farmers' Union (RLF), thereby creating a strong organization uniting both the co-operative movement (SAL) and farmers' trade union organization (RLF). The union branch is constructed on three levels. The base consists of 144,996 members (including 23,680 non-farm members) collected in 1,650 local departments and 26 county unions. The extent of affiliation is about 72 per cent.[25] The co-operative branch has around 1,050,000 members – each farmer belongs, on average, to five societies. There are around 700 societies, divided into 16 branches of business organizations. The co-operatives have high market shares (see Table 7.3).

Table 7.3 Market shares of farmer co-operatives in different sectors (%)

Fertilizers	80
Feed	86
Farmer insurances	85
Farmer loans	86
Machinery	40
Milk processing	100
Slaughterhouses	78
Grains	80

Source: Bolin *et al.* (1986).

Bolin *et al.* (1986) argue that the affiliation between co-operatives and trade unions greatly enhances LRF's capacity to control free-riders, since producers who are not entirely loyal in delivering to LRF associations are labelled as 'unsolidaristic' in propaganda at both the central and the local level. Producers who wish to stop supplying to one co-operative can immediately lose the right to trade with other farmer–co-operatives or lose financial credit in the input co-operatives. Nor is the capital share automatically refunded.

Farmers are obviously well organized and LRF is a strong organization. The issue is whether the strength of farmers has increased as their numbers have decreased. To answer the question we have to go back to the early agricultural and co-operative movement in Sweden. The history of co-operatives dates back to the nineteenth century. These early stages of development can perhaps be best understood in terms of Wiliamson's transactions cost theory. The first co-operatives were local mutual insurance associations, farm credit associations or input purchasing associations (the first one was created in 1850 near Uppsala). Through small-scale local co-operation, transaction costs (including risk) could be reduced. The development of co-operative slaughterhouses and dairies followed. In 1917, the Federation of Swedish Farmers' Associations (SAL) was founded. In the meantime, farmers started to organize themselves into trade-union type organizations with labour unions serving as models. RLF was formed in 1929. The collaboration between RLF and SAL was at that time an open question. Many farmers were of the opinion that the co-operatives should be favoured only if they offered better terms than private firms. The issue was formally set in 1932 when a decision about compulsory membership of members in RLF in the co-operative movement was taken. However, differences in strategy between RLF and SAL were still very much present during the 1930s. In the beginning of the 1940s the process was completed, resulting in a united agricultural movement (see Hedlund and Lundahl, 1985, ch. 4; Thullberg, 1977). Formal unity occurred in 1971.

The development of agricultural policy played a decisive role in strengthening farmers as a pressure group and enhancing the collaboration between RLF and SAL. Each new regulation gave birth to a new organization to participate in its administration. As a consequence, the market share of the farmer co-operatives rapidly grew during the 1930s, e.g. from 77 per cent of the milk market in 1933 to 93 per cent in 1939. Supporting farmers by border protection created a common interest between processing co-operatives and farmers. Finally, moving from a price parity formula to a production cost formula for setting agricultural prices further increased the participation of farmers in the regulatory process.

Analysing the history of the farm/co-operative movement one can therefore conclude that farmers gained enormously in strength between the 1920s and the 1950s. However, farm organizations probably reached their full strength by that time. It is difficult to understand why a group who already had managed to organize itself and become officially recognized as the legitimate representative of farmers in negotiations, policy formulation, etc., would gain any additional strength as its size diminished. The collaboration between farmers is not based on a direct interaction – the number of farmers is too large – the farm organizations consist of three levels and fewer farmers just means fewer members on each level. One could rather claim that a declining number of farmers would eventually make them weaker. Rabinowicz and Bolin (1988) put several arguments in favour of that claim:

1 Farming is the only sector for which an official income objective is stated. This unique position *vis-à-vis* other small groups of self-employed managers will be difficult to defend when farmers themselves become a small group.
2 Farmers are an increasingly heterogeneous group due to such factors as part-time farming and involvement in production of 'niche' commodities (including traditional commodities produced in non-traditional ways).
3 Small-scale processing, which is now a real possibility on larger farms, has already created a situation of competition between farmers and the farmer-owned processing industry.
4 Last, but not least, fewer farmers represent fewer votes.

Strength and ability of non-farmer groups

As has been demonstrated before, the consumers, as represented by the Consumer Delegation (CD), are given the formal ability to influence agricultural policy, etc. But what is the real strength of consumers? CD was created with the clear intention of changing the balance of power between consumers and producers.[26] The issue is, however, whether any administrative decision can do much about it. All groups are not equally well organized, consumers probably being the least able to organize themselves. Accordingly, CD is an artificial consumer representation appointed by the government. It is not accountable to consumers. Many of them are not even aware of its existence. CD consists, for example, of representatives from the agricultural processing industry and the labour unions, which have at least a partial vested interest in the continuation of the present policy. Furthermore, as often happens in a small country, consumer representatives more easily become a part of the system itself, or of the 'iron triangle'. The members of the 'iron triangle' consist of bureaucrats, pressure groups and politicians who tend to develop the same attitudes about what the problems are and how they should be handled (Hernes, 1975). It is even conceivable that CD, in the long run, might have a negative impact on consumer interests by contributing to the process of legitimization of the policy, in particular, as far as prices are concerned. As an outcome of a negotiation, prices can accordingly be presented as fair. The impact of the CD on prices is difficult to analyse, as it pre-supposes a comparison with a contra-factual situation without the CD. However, comparing the development of real food prices in the Scandinavian countries 1970–85 shows that the fastest price increase (+12 per cent) to be in Sweden. The switch to freer negotiations after 1984 has not produced any substantial deviation from the past trend either.

Another interesting issue is the attitude of consumers towards farm prices. Anderson and Hayami argue that increasing affluence (decreasing share of food in the consumer budget) makes consumers more tolerant of high food prices. Share of food (excluding beverages) has decreased between 1950 and 1987 from 25 per cent to 17 per cent. But this does not necessarily make the consumers less concerned. In 1973, when reversal of the farm policy of the previous decade resulted in higher real food prices, housewives in Stockholm suburbs protested vigorously. The government responded by introducing food subsidies. When the subsidies were removed the real food prices increased considerably (see Figure 7.8) and consumption of meat fell (see Figure 7.9). Discontent with food prices at that time was widespread according to several public opinion polls.

The role of the bureaucracy is often emphasized. Some authors (Messerlin, 1983) claim that the bureaucracy is more keen on protection than the politicians. A clientele relationship can easily develop between the bureaucracy and the sector which it administrates. People knowledgeable about a complicated, highly specialized regulatory system will lose their unique competence if the system is abolished or simplified. It is obviously not a coincidence that the task of investigation of past policy and drafting of the reform proposal for the present reform initiative, aimed at simplifying the policy has been entrusted to the investigators outside the agricultural bureaucracy. Without going into depth on this question, it can be pointed out that the Swedish ministry of agriculture tends to be more understanding towards problems of agriculture and that the reform initiatives in Sweden today have come from the ministry of finance.

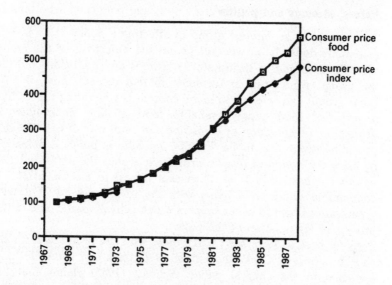

Figure 7.8 General price level and food prices

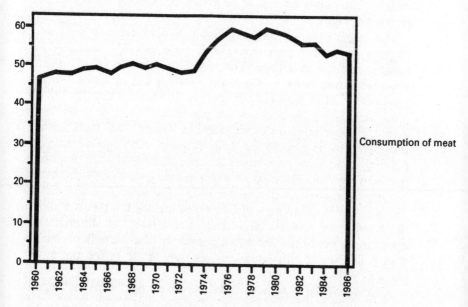

Figure 7.9 Consumption of meat in kg per person (per annum)

Values, ideology and politics

The success of an interest group in affecting a policy in its favour essentially depends on whether or not the objectives of the group are acknowledged as legitimate by citizens and politicians outside the group. Agriculture is fortunate in that respect. Few, if any, other groups can refer to so many consensus generating causes like security of food supply, reliable food quality, environmental protection, preservation of landscape and rural way of life. Besides providing these nice public benefits, agricultural policy is defended by using the notion of justice: protection against the unfair practice of other countries (low world market prices) to ensure farmers a comparable standard of living with the rest of society. Farmers' organizations own four newspapers which actively participate in the process of legitimation of the policy.

As far back as Jefferson (1781) 'those who labour in the earth are chosen people of God', the virtues of farmers and rural life have appealed to the general public. Schmitt (1985) claims that the present agricultural policy in Germany is supported by many groups in society, not only those dependent on agriculture or on farmers' votes. 'Agricultural fundamentalism' as the phenomenon is often named is widespread in other countries as well. According to Tweeten (1989) 80 per cent of Americans agree with statements such as 'The family farm must be preserved because it is a vital part of our heritage'.

The importance of public opinion is demonstrated by recent changes in animal protection laws, most notably reducing the number of hens in a cage. The reduction, introduced in spite of opposition from farmers, will cause a serious loss of income for egg producers.[27] Most hens (78 per cent) in Sweden are kept by 192 big producers. Being big and few has proven not to be an asset but a liability. Those large-scale producers in 'factory-like' units are not considered to be 'proper' or 'true' farmers. An opposite example pointing in the same direction is the case of regional price support in northern Sweden. Ths support which mainly goes to milk producers has increased strongly during the 1980s. The increase is not due to the organizational strength of farmers in the north – they are small, dispersed over a very large area and belong to different co-operatives – but to the enormous popularity of small milk producers with politicians of all persuasions not only in the region but in big cities as well.

Attitudes towards farming have, however, not been unchanged.

During the Second World War, the farmers (and the agricultural policy) enjoyed strong sympathy. In the 1950s and 1960s, growth-oriented attitudes did not favour agricultural interests. This situation changed in the 1970s. The first report to the Club of Rome (Meadows *et al.*, 1972) blamed industry for pollution, depletion of resources, etc. The wide impact of the book induced a zero-growth, anti-industrial ideology favouring agriculture. Furthermore, agriculture was favoured by emphasizing distribution and regional balance objectives rather than growth. These attitudes shifted in the 1980s. The simple zero-growth prescription has been replaced by a much more informed debate on different environmental problems. Farming is no longer synonymous with natural resource conservation. Modern farming is increasingly blamed for negative externalities such as environmental damage and causing stress and manipulating animals in factory-like production plants. Agriculture as a highly regulated sector is also sensitive to public attitudes towards regulation versus free market in general. Sceptical attitudes towards market regulations as such and deregulation efforts in other sectors (for instance, money markets) which occurred in the 1980s diminished confidence in agricultural policy.

Critical evaluations of agricultural policy have an important role to play since the policy is credited with merits it does not possess, particularly by farmers. Critical evaluation of agricultural policy by Gulbrandsen, who was involved as an expert in the work of the committee, affected the agricultural policy decision of 1967. During the 1970s and at the beginning of the 1980s, the agricultural policy was practically unchallenged. This situation changed with the publication of *The Political Economy of the Food Sector* (Bolin *et al.*, 1986). Unlike previous attempts to criticize agricultural policy, this book was directed at the general public and it strongly questioned the validity of the consensus generating arguments in favour of the policy. An intense debate followed (see Palmgren, 1985). Several other critical evaluations have been published since that time.

The political aspect is worth mentioning as well. The former farmer party (Centerpartiet) is a non-socialist party, but there are income similarities between small farmers and industrial workers which create common interests between the labour and farmer parties on many issues. Accordingly, the 'farmers' party' can become an attractive coalition partner both for socialist and non-socialist parties. Both wings have consequently tended to approach agricultural policy in a way that does not spoil coalition possibilities with the farmer party (von Ehrenheim, 1984).

The internal legitimacy of the policy, as opposed to the external legitimacy discussed above, is very important to the organizational stability of an interest group, especially farmers, since ideological factors such as the idea of co-operation played a decisive role in unifying farmers. 'The Swedish farmer was thinking in a different way in 1945 than in 1926. It was obvious in 1945 to think in terms of collective' (Thullberg, 1977). Unequal treatment of different commodities would be detrimental to the stability of the farm organization. Analysing differences in support (in terms of PSE) one can conclude that they can, to a great extent, be explained by variations in cost of production, i.e. in terms of comparative disadvantages.[28]

CONCLUSIONS

Let us return to the previously presented models and re-examine them in the light of the evidence given in the preceding section. In the political marketplace theory the level of protection is determined as an equilibrium between supply and demand. As farmers became fewer, they managed to organize themselves better, demanding more protection. At the same time, badly organized and increasingly affluent consumers offered diminishing resistance. As a result, both supply and demand schedules shifted to the right, reaching equilibrium at an increasingly higher level of protection. The model seems attractive taking into consideration well-organized farmers and poorly organized consumers. The level of protection has increased in Sweden and in other industrialized countries. Agriculture is protected in rich countries and taxed in poor ones. The question is, however, whether political market models can explain the genesis and the evolution of agricultural policy? It is doubtful if it is the case. It has been shown that agricultural policy was hastily introduced as a result of a political compromise in response to an acute economic crisis. The present policy was introduced when farmers still constituted a large part of the society (40 per cent), much larger than in some developing countries today which heavily tax agriculture. Similar protectionist agricultural policies were introduced in several countries at a different stage of economic development at the same time. The large size of the farm population was rather a source of strength than of weakness in a democratic country – farmers represented many votes and had a political representation. Furthermore, the severe economic crises which hit so large a part of the population could not be politically disregarded. However, farmers were not that well organized. Roughly speaking, it was not a well-organized interest group which created the agricultural policy, but rather the policy that created a strong, organized interest group. The strength of the farmers increased tremendously in the 1930s and 1940s, probably reaching its full potential in the early 1950s. The same can be said about the farmers' formal possibilities to influence policy. Farmers had been given the chance to influence both the setting and the implementation of agricultural policy in the 1940s or even earlier. We can conclude that the increase in protectionism is not correlated to the increase in farmers' strength and formal influence. Neither can the increase in protectionism be explained by weaker resistance from consumers or the lower cost of supplying policy. As it has been previously demonstrated, consumers have been mostly confronted with stable real food prices. On the occasions when the prices increased in real terms the result has been demonstrations, falling consumption and discontent with the policy, in spite of food share in the budget being lower today than in the 1950s.

The most devastating argument against the political marketplace model, however, is the fact that, roughly speaking, the agricultural policy once introduced has remained unchanged for over half a century; not the level of protection though, but the set of rules and instruments. But is the level of protection an interesting variable? With domestic prices formally tied to various concepts of cost of production for most of the period and with variable levies adjusting automatically to world market prices it is not valid to interpret a changed level of protection, with unchanged policy rules, as a response to the pressures of the political market. Regressing domestic prices on world market prices in such a case would simply show the difference between the domestic rate of inflation and the price development on world markets. The central issue is not why protection has increased but why the rules have remained unchanged.

This points to the second model viewing policy as a sequential process which exhibits a great degree of inertia and a strong bias towards status quo, with status quo privileges playing a major role. Policy changes do not materialize unless a major crisis forces the system to adjust to new circumstances. Viewing policy as a process is not denying the influence of the pressure groups. The strength of the farmers is the most probable explanation as to why agricultural policy has not been revised, especially as the policy contributed to the increase of this strength. The farmers didn't have to push for increased protection, the policy by its construction generates the increase when needed, only to ensure that the policy (i.e. the rules) remain unchanged. Thereby, the farmers have benefited tremendously by agricultural policy becoming a status quo privilege. Had the government decided to abolish the policy the result would have been serious hardship to farmers, in particular, a decapitalization of their asset values. An increased level of protection due to falling world market prices (on the other hand) prevented the hardship to farmers at no visible cost to consumers. This kind of transfer is quite different from increasing prices to farmers at the expense of consumers. Though the two transfers may be identical from a welfare economic point of view, they are quite different if evaluated in terms of the conservative social welfare function. Reducing protection (or even keeping it unchanged) would imply an active decision by the government, visibly hurting one group and benefiting the other. Increasing protection was done without making any explicit decisions, merely by inducing invisible transfers.

Furthermore, it can be argued that the policy has perpetuated itself by the lack of efficiency – rather than solving the problems at hand the policy has exacerbated them due to an inappropriateness of the instrument chosen (price policy for solving an income problem).

The high degree of inertia in agricultural policy can further be illustrated by the following exmple. In response to a temporary glut in the potato market a regulation was passed in 1934 forcing domestic producers of alcohol to use potatoes and not grain as an input. This regulation was in place for fifty-five years, governing the production of alcohol in spite of the considerably higher cost.[29]

Society's attachment to its past choices or collective conservatism is by no means specific to agricultural policy. Policy continuity over time can be observed in many areas. In the discussion above, the collective conservatism in agricultural policy is explained by social phenomena. Kuran (1987) provides an individual choice-based model of conservatism.

However, the policy rules have not been totally unchanged. Analysing the policy in terms of the internal indicators demonstrates cycles of willingness to support (rather than protect) agriculture. The influence of long-term economic forces, the opportunity costs of agricultural policy, can be clearly observed in the agricultural policy of the late 1960s. High growth, shortage of labour, surplus production and low world market prices contributed clearly to the agricultural policy decision of 1967. This situation is in part similar to the present state of affairs (low world market prices, shortage of labour, commodity surpluses) and the new reform decision. The strongly pro farm policy of the 1970s is perhaps more easily explained by a changed coalition situation in parliament, which vastly increased the ability of the 'farmer party' to influence policy. However, the long-term forces favoured, or at least did not prevent this policy by lack of surpluses, higher world market prices[30] and a low demand for agricultural labour.

Contrary to Anderson and Hayami's hypotheses, high rates of national economic growth in the 1960s induced the policy of pushing resources out of agriculture rather than increasing farm support, while slow growth in the 1970s coincided with greater willingness to support agriculture.

NOTES

1 Quotas were introduced in 1985 and have been removed in 1989.
2 Comparable figures for EC countries are −51 per cent, and for the United States −26 per cent.
3 If several prices are changing at the same time and income changes substantially the consumer surplus does not give a correct picture of welfare losses to consumers. The error involved can, however, be calculated (see Just *et al.*, 1982 for a discussion).
4 Consumer price subsidies were at that time applied to several commodities and amounted to 3,315 million crowns.
5 The Fahlbeck study was part of a study of the agricultural policy in the Nordic countries conducted on behalf of the ministers of finance in these countries. The work of the committee is presented in 'Jordbrukspolitiken i de nordiska länderna', Nord (1989:15). The secretary of the group was the author of this chapter.
6 *Poverty and Hunger*, World Bank (1986).
7 An exact length of the period is not specified, but half a year is commonly used.
8 Estimates are based on long-term production elasticities as estimated by Tyers and Anderson (1986) for EFTA countries.
9 Afforestation of the land, which is the nearest alternative, is as a rule not profitable for farmers due to a very long period of rotation.
10 This calculation aims at estimating the order of magnitude rather than giving a precise figure. This is due to uncertainty of the impact on arable land and on products not covered by the analysis. Storage of 1 ton protein feed is assumed to cost 300 SEK. How much protein feed and fertilizer is stored during the present policy is classified information. Average import of protein feed during the 1980s was 320,000 tons. Storing twice as much would cost 200 million SEK.
11 17–18 per cent as compared with 50 per cent for all processing industry for the period 1970–80.

12 Processing costs and trade margins account for 44 per cent of the value of consumption of protected agricultural products at retail level or for 23.3 billion SEK. Processing costs are assumed to account for 75 per cent of this figure.

13 All the benefits of technical progress are passed over to the consumers because of the inelasticity of the demand. Farmers are unable to grasp the fruits of their hard work because of falling prices.

14 If OECD countries had liberalized their agriculture in 1980–2 the welfare gain in 1995 would have been US$51.5 billion (Anderson and Tyers, 1990).

15 The new welfare loss consists of net social loss in consumption: area f d e and net social loss in production: area b c g in Figure 7.1, p. 208.

16 Producer Subsidy Equivalent (PSE) is defined as the payment that would be required to compensate farmers for the loss of income resulting from the removal of a given policy measure. The measures are classified into: market price support, direct payments, reduction of input costs and general services. A market price support component is given by the area a c g h in Figure 7.1, p. 208.

17 Farms between 10 and 20 ha have been taken as a norm.

18 Surplus for meat products was 14 per cent.

19 Subsidies on beef, pork and cheese, amounting to 850 million SEK, were eliminated in the autumn of 1983.

20 In the beginning of the 1980s: wheat 76 per cent, barley 10 per cent, red meat 15 per cent, pig meat 19 per cent, milk on aggregate 11 per cent.

21 The reduction was highest for pork. In 1984–5 a slaughter levy of 3.2 kg/SEK was collected, the net price to farmers being 12.6 kg/SEK.

22 The negotiations had the form of a two-step procedure. In the first step, a total compensation amount was decided. In the second step, the amount was divided between different commodities.

23 The number of directors was different in different MRA, from 9 to 12. Government and consumers had together three to four representatives (Indevo report, 1989).

24 This argument is due to A. Winters (personal communication).

25 Measured as a percentage of the farms, LRF (personal communication).

26 See Åke Anderson (1987) (interview with E. Holmqvist, minister of agriculture, in the 1960s). See also Callert (1988).

27 A producer with 10,000 hens in four-hen cages will lose 17,750 SEK annually if he cuts production (to 7,500 hens) or he will have to invest to keep the same net income. Calculations based on Rowinski and Johnsson (1988).

28 As an indicator of the comparative disadvantages in agriculture a share of total per unit cost not covered by world market price is taken. The total per unit cost used refers to the southern parts of Sweden according to standard calculations made by Agricultural University (Områdeskalkyler, 1985–6). The figures are used as indicators of cost rather than true cost (the calculated figures often show a persistent tendency to exceed domestic price).

Product	1 − P_w/ATC	Gross PSE
Wheat	7	46
Coarse grains	27	39
Oils	20	44
Sugar	34	67
Milk	73	76
Beef	59	54
Pork	46	43
Poultry	62	68
Egg	57	54
Sheep meat	72	16

29 According to an estimate by NAMB (December 1987) the production and storage cost would be reduced by 52 million SEK by switching to grains.
30 But at that time and even later on, several authorities did believe in rising food prices in the future (see Johnson, 1984 for the discussion).

REFERENCES

Albertson, J. (1985) 'En studie av effektiviteten inom svensk mejerinäring – en jämförelse med Danmark', Examensarbete 115, Lantbrukets marknadslära, Institutionen för ekonomi och statistik.

Anderson, Å. (1987) 'Vårt jordbrukspolitiska system', report 284 from the Department of Economics, Uppsala, Sweden: Swedish University of Agricultural Sciences.

Anderson, K. and Hayami, Y. (1986) *The Political Economy of Agricultural Protection*, London: Allen & Unwin.

Anderson, K. and Tyers, R. (1989) in A. Maunder and A. Valdés (eds) 'Agriculture and governments in an interdependent world', *Proceedings of the Twentieth International Conference of Agricultural Economists*, Buenos Aires, Argentina, 1988, IAAE, University of Oxford, Dartmouth.

Anderson, K. and Tyers, R. (1990) 'How developing countries could gain from agricultural trade liberalization in the Uruguay Round', in *Agricultural Trade Liberalization. Implications for Developing Countries*, T. Goldin and O. Knutson (eds), Paris: OECD.

Andersson, Y. and Bolin, O. (1990) *Myten om jordbrukets låga lönsamhet.*

Baldwin, R.E. (1985) *The Politial Economy of US Import Policy*, Cambridge, MA.: MIT Press.

Bolin, O., Meyerson, P.-M. and Ståhl, I. (1986) *The Political Economy of the Food Sector*, Stockholm: SNS.

Callert, L. (1988) 'Konsumentrepresentant på statens villkor. Statsvetenskapliga institutionen', Skytteanum, unpublished thesis, University of Uppsala, Sweden: Department of Public Science.

Drake, L. (1987) 'Värdet av bevarat jordbrukslandskap', report 289 from the Department of Economics, Uppsala, Sweden: Swedish University of Agricultural Sciences.

Ds (1988) Alternativ i jordbrukspolitiken Rapport till ESO.

Fahlbeck, E. (1989) 'Välfärdseffekter av dagens jordbrukspolitik – en jämförande studie för de nordiska länderna', Department of Economics, Uppsala, Sweden: Swedish University of Agricultural Sciences.

Finger, J.M., Hall, K. and Nelson, D.R. (1982) 'The political economy of administered protection', *American Economic Review*, 72, 452–66.

Gardner, B. (1981) *The Governing of Agriculture*, Lawrens, Kansas: Kansas University Press.

Gardner, B.L. (1987) 'Causes of US farm commodity programs', *Journal of Political Economy*, 95(2), 290–310.

Goldstein, J. (1986) 'The political economy of trade: institutions of protection', *American Political Science Review*, 80, 161–84.

Gulbrandsen, O. and Lindbeck, A. (1969) *Jordbruksnäringens ekonomi*, Stockholm: Almqvist & Wicksell.

Hamilton, C. (1986) 'Agricultural protection in Sweden 1970–80', *European Journal of Agricultural Economics*, 13(1).

Hedlund, S. and Lundahl, M. (1985) *Beredskap eller Protektionism*, Stockholm: Liber.

Hernes, G. (1975) *Makt og avmakt*, Oslo: Universitetsförlaget.

Hill, B.E. (1984) *The Common Agricultural Policy: Past, Present and Future*, Cambridge: Heinemann.

Indevo (1981) 'Översyn av Jordbrukets Regleringsföreningar', unpublished report on behalf of the ministry of agriculture, Indevo Svenska AB.

Johnson, G. (1984) 'Agriculture and global food system in resourceful earth', in *A Resourceful Earth: A Response to Global 2000*, J.L. Simon and M. Kahn (eds), Oxford: Basil Blackwell.

Jordbruksekonomiska Meddelanden (journal), Jorbruksnämnden, various issues.

Just, R., Darrell, H. and Schmitz, A.(1982) *Applied Welfare Economics and Public Policy*, Englewood Cliffs, NJ: Prentice-Hall.

Kuran, T. (1987) 'Preference falsification, policy continuity and collective conservatism', *The Economic Journal*, 97, Sept.

Lavergne, R.P. (1983) *The Political Economy of US Tariffs: an Empirical Analysis*, London: Academic Press.

Meadows, D.H., Meadows, D.L., Randers, J. and Behrens, W. (1972) *Limits to Growth*, New York: Universe Books.

Messerlin, P.A. (1983) 'Bureaucracies and the political economy of protection, reflections of a continental European', Staff Working Paper no. 568, The World Bank, Washington DC, also *Weltwirtschaftliches Archiv* (1981) 117, 461–96.

Molander, P. (1988) 'Säkerhetspolitiska aspekter på livsmedelsförsörjningen', FOA-rapport C 10311–1.2.

Molander, P. (1989) *Jordbrukets miljövärden*, unpublished paper.

Nord (1989) Jordbrukspolitiken i nordiska länder – målen, medlen och konsekvenserna. Nord: 15.

OECD (1988) *National Politics and Agricultural Trade. Country Study – Sweden*, Paris: OECD.

Olson, M. (1965) *Logic of Collective Action*, Harvard: Harvard University Press.

Olson, M. (1985) 'The exploitation and subsidization of agriculture in developing and developed countries', paper given at XIX Conference of

Agricultural Economists, Malaga, Spain.
Palmgren, A. (1985) 'Debatten kring makten över maten', *Företag och Samhälle*, 4, SNS Orientering, Stockholm: SNS.
Peltzman, S. (1976) 'Towards a more general theory of regulation', *Journal of Law and Economics*, 19, 211–40.
Petit, M. (1985) 'Determinants of agricultural policies in the United States and the European Community', research report for the International Food Policy Research Institute, November, New York: IFPRI.
Rabinowicz, E. and Bolin, O. (1988) *Towards Deregulation of Agricultural Markets in Sweden*, unpublished.
Rabinowicz, E., Haraldsson, I. and Bolin, O. (1986) 'The evolution of a regulation system in agriculture: the Swedish case', *Food Policy*, 11(4), 323–33.
Riksrevisionsverket (National Audit Bureau) (1988a) *Lönsamhetskalkyler inom jordbruket*, DNR, 1989:33.
Riksrevisionsverket (National Audit Bureau) (1988b) *Går det att förändra forskning? Exemplet Sveriges lantbruksuniversitet*, DNR, 1986:991.
Rowinski, T. and Johnsson, B. (1988) 'Economic analysis of a few systems for laying hens', Report 6 from the Department of Economics, Uppsala: Swedish University of Agricultural Sciences.
Statens jordbruksnämnd (National Agricultural Marketing Board) (1987) 'Socker, andra sötmedel, stärkelse, sprit', internal report.
Schmitt, G. (1985) 'The role of institutions in formulation of agricultural policy', paper given at XIX Conference of Agricultural Economists, Malaga, Spain.
Swedish University of Agricultural Sciences, Research Information Centre (1986) *Områdeskalkyler för GSS*, Uppsala, Swedish University of Agricultural Sciences.
Thullberg, P. (1977) *Bönder Går Samman. En studie i Riksförbundet Landsbygdens Folk under Världskrisen 1929–1933*, Thullberg: L.T.'s forlag.
Tracy, M. (1982) *Agriculture in Western Europe – Crisis and Adaptation since 1880*, London: Granada Publishing.
Tweeten, L. (1989) *Farm Policy Analysis*, Boulder, CA: Westview Press.
Tyers, R. and Anderson, K. (1986) 'Distortions in world food markets: a quantitative assessment', World Development Background Paper, Washington DC: World Bank.
von Ehrenheim, J. (1984) *Public Choice – En ny syn på svensk jordbrukspolitik*, Report no. 242 from the Department of Economics and Statistics, Swedish University of Agricultural Sciences, Uppsala.
Winters, L.A. (1987) 'The political economy of the agricultural policy of industrial countries', *European Review of Agricultural Economics*, 14, 285–304.
Winters, A. (1988a) *The So-called 'Non-economic' Objectives of Agricultural Policy*, Paris: OECD.
Winters, A. (1988b) *The National Security Argument for Agricultural Protection*, London: Centre for Economic Policy Research.
World Bank (1986) *Poverty and Hunger*, Washington DC: World Bank.
World Development Report (1986) Washington DC: World Bank.
Yearbook of Agricultural Statistics (1987) Stockholm: Official Statistics of Sweden.

8 The textile and clothing market: towards a liberalization?

Eva Lindström

INTRODUCTION

The Swedish textile and clothing market has been subject to regulation for a long time. The goals of Sweden's policy in matters concerning textiles and clothing[1] have been numerous and, in many cases, contradictory. Sweden's textile policy has been implemented in part through significant trade barriers, including tariffs and quantitative restrictions, and in part through an entire spectrum of state support mechanisms. Many interest groups within the market have undoubtedly used various lobbying techniques in their efforts to influence the choice of means in the arsenal of textile policy.

In recent years, Swedish textile policy has been under reconsideration. At the close of 1988, Sweden's parliament, the Riksdagen, decided that bilateral treaties concluded with various low-cost producing countries under the auspices of the Multi-Fibre Arrangement (MFA) would be allowed to lapse after 31 July 1991. In the spring of 1989, the parliament also partially reassessed the primary objectives of textile policy. The changes in policy ought to lead to a better utilization of resources within the Swedish economy. Moreover, deregulation will lead to decreased transfers of income from Swedish consumers to domestic and foreign producers alike.

The purpose of this chapter is to identify the goals of Swedish textile policy and to analyse the effects of the methods used to achieve these goals. Attention will be focused on two fundamental questions. First, what influences textile policy? Second, what costs does the regulation of textile and clothing markets impose on Swedish consumers?

It is obviously difficult to provide a comprehensive answer to the first question. From the perspective of pure economic efficiency, textile policy – if such a thing exists – should have been formulated quite differently than has been the case in recent decades. The government and the parliament have formulated other, often inscrutable and unworkable objectives. In the choice and adjustment of the various means comprising textile policy, non-economic motives have certainly played a role. Moreover, the strength and interrelationships of various interest groups have undoubtedly had an impact on the formulation of ends and selection of means.

It is also difficult to give an exact answer to the second question. I will primarily examine the costs of trade barriers erected against clothing and textile imports. The analysis of the effects of these obstacles proceeds from traditional tariff theory. A limited number of studies have sought to quantify these effects in recent years. Proceeding from various assumptions, these studies have attempted to estimate the costs of restrictions on the textiles trade. I shall briefly summarize these results.

The structure of this chapter is as follows: the next section provides a short description of the framework of the international rules which have regulated the global textile trade for more than a quarter of a century. An account of the goals and tools of Swedish textile policy is provided in the section starting on p. 255. The next section (p. 260) describes the general effects of tariffs and quantitative restrictions. Its aim is to refresh the reader's recollection of some well-known conclusions drawn from trade and tariff theory.

To enhance the reader's understanding of the development of trade restrictions in the textile and clothing industry, the section beginning on p. 266 introduces the various actors and interest groups operating in the market. Drawing on general conclusions reached in previous sections, it will identify the winners and losers of the current policy, as well as the interests which abolition of quantitative restrictions will favour and harm respectively. The final part (p. 269) estimates the costs of trade restrictions for Swedish consumers.

INTERNATIONAL BACKGROUND

The volume of international trade in clothing and textiles has risen steeply in recent decades. Global exports of these products have increased at a markedly higher rate than world production. This development indicates that production of clothing and textiles has been the subject of an increasingly international specialization.

At the same time, global trade in textiles and clothing has grown more slowly than total global trade in manufactured goods. Changes in relative prices account for this result. The price of textiles and clothing has risen slower in recent decades than the price of many other goods. This trend can be explained by the redistribution of exports across various countries. Certain developing and newly-industrialized countries especially have increased their share of global exports in clothing.

The increase in textile and clothing imports in the industrialized countries has led to louder demands from their domestic firms for trade restrictions. Today most industrial countries have a comprehensive system of trade barriers directed at textiles and clothing imports from countries with low production costs. The protective network for domestic firms has consisted partly of tariffs and partly of quantitative restrictions. Amongst EC and EFTA countries, however, free trade agreements have allowed unrestricted trade in clothing and manufactured textile products. Trade barriers have thus been directed against countries outside western Europe, mainly developing and newly-industrialized countries.

Table 8.1 shows the tariff levels in certain industrialized countries for various textiles and clothing products and for industrial goods generally. The figures provided represent the so-called MFN-tariffs, that is, the general tariff levels that apply to countries which do not receive tariff preferences.[2]

As Table 8.1 clearly demonstrates, tariff reductions carried out in the 1960s and 1970s concerned trade in clothing and textiles to a much lesser extent than industrial goods in general. Above all,

Table 8.1   Tariffs on textile products and industrial products (%)

Countries	All textile products[a]	All industrial products
United States	18.2	4.3
Japan	5.4	2.7
EC	8.5	4.6
Austria	20.2	7.7
Finland	22.1	5.5
Norway	17.9	3.1
Sweden	12.1	4.0
Switzerland	5.7	2.2

Source: OECD (1983).
Notes: [a] Including fibres, yarns, fabrics, made-up articles and clothing; the table shows the post-Tokyo Round tariffs. Weighting is according to imports of MFN-origin.

tariffs on manufactured textile and clothing products are considerable. Without exception, industrialized countries' tariffs on such goods are significantly higher than their average tariffs on industrial goods.

The most important components in the industrialized nations' arsenal of trade protections are the quantitative restrictions which, for more than a quarter of a century, have limited imports from low-cost producing countries. As early as July 1961, an agreement on global trade in cotton goods was reached within the GATT framework. This agreement, the Short-Term Arrangement (STA), was superceded the following year by the Long-Term Arrangement (LTA). Originally intended to last four years, the LTA continued until the beginning of 1974 as the result of a series of extensions. It was strictly limited to cotton goods. Permissible forms of trade restrictions under the LTA included bilateral agreements on export restrictions and unilateral import restrictions.

The long-term agreement on cotton permitted different treatment for imports from different countries, and thus ran contrary to a fundamental GATT precept: the principle of non-discrimination. Under GATT all imports are to be accorded equal treatment regardless of their country-of-origin. That the agreement none the less received GATT's institutional approval has been explained as the result of a choice between two evils: an agreement regulating trade under the auspices of GATT was deemed preferable to an uncontrolled development of import restrictions and compulsory 'voluntary' agreements.

During the 1960s and 1970s, clothing and textile products in various synthetic and mixed fibres experienced a marked increase in trade. Imports from developing countries rose steeply for clothing of various forms and fibres. This development led producers in industrialized nations to press for a more comprehensive system of rules. At the end of 1973 a new agreement, the Multi-Fibre Arrangement (MFA), was reached.

The MFA I took effect at the beginning of 1974 and had forty-two members, with the EC considered a single signatory. This agreement included products of cotton as well as wool and synthetics. Under the MFA, import restrictions may be introduced upon disruption of the market or threat of the same. 'Market disruption' is defined as serious harm or risk of harm for domestic industries due to a substantial increase of imports at prices considerably below domestic production costs. If an importing country suffers from market-disrupting imports, negotiations are to commence between it and the exporting nation(s). Negotiations may result in bilateral agreements regarding the size of quotas, rates of growth, etc. In the event that no agreement is reached, the importing country may introduce unilateral import restrictions; however, where there is only a potential disruption of the market, the parties must reach bilateral agreement.

The expressed objective of the MFA I was to liberalize trade in clothing and textiles without significantly disturbing import markets. In exchange for the expanded range of products the MFA encompassed relative to prior textile agreements, the traditional industrial countries were committed to accelerating the restructuring of domestic sectors to allow increased imports of textiles and clothing from developing countries. Quotas were not permitted to grow at an annual rate below 6 per cent.

The concept of 'minimum viable production' was written into the original agreement. This addition is often dubbed 'the Nordic clause', and it seeks to provide special protection for countries with small markets, exceptionally high import levels and low domestic production of clothing and textiles. Signatories to whom the clause applies may allow import quotas to grow at larger rates than the agreement permits other countries. The clause also makes it possible to limit the transfer of unutilized quotas between different product categories. The name 'Nordic clause' derives from the fact that it is regarded as being primarily applicable to the Nordic countries.

The MFA I was in effect from the beginning of 1974 to the end of 1977. The successor, MFA II, took effect during a period of weak economic recovery and higher unemployment in industrialized countries than had existed during the negotiations leading to MFA I. Several industrial nations therefore sought a tightening of import restrictions. The overall trend was towards a considerable increase in restrictions on clothing and textiles imports into industrialized nations, with special emphasis on clothing imports. The system created was fully extended for many countries, with respect to export countries as well as products. The rates at which quotas were allowed to grow were for many products less than 6 per cent and, in several cases, quotas shrunk to lower levels than had existed in the previous period.

A new series of negotiations began in 1981 with a view to extending the Multi-Fibre Arrangement. MFA III went into effect at the beginning of 1982 and remained in force until the end of July 1986. It was later agreed that a further extension, MFA IV, would last until 31 July 1991. The most important change that MFA IV brought about was a considerable expansion in the range of products covered. MFA IV makes no reference to the MFA's termination date.

To summarize, for a quarter of a century the clothes and textile trade has been regulated by means of quantitative restrictions. The extent of these restrictions has continually increased, in terms of both the degree of restrictiveness and the number of products and countries covered. Quantitative restrictions, as well as tariffs, have been directed primarily at clothing and textile imports from countries with low production costs. Generally, import restrictions in the industrialized countries have been primarily directed against imports from those countries which have had the largest and most rapidly growing export potential.

THE ENDS AND MEANS OF SWEDEN'S TEXTILE POLICY

At the end of 1988, Sweden's parliament decided that restrictive bilateral agreements concluded under the auspices of the MFA would be allowed to run out after 31 July 1991. This decision signified the end of a quarter of a century of substantial quantitative regulations. The goal of textile policy has also been re-evaluated. In order to explain the growth of restrictions on clothing and textiles, a summary of recent official objectives will be provided.

The objectives

The overarching goals of the Swedish textile policy have been based partly on consideration of industry and employment, partly on Sweden's support ability in times of war and crises. In the fiscal year 1982–3, the government proposed two long-term objectives. The first of these goals arose from considerations of industrial policy (the industrial policy goal), while the second revolved around the market share for the Swedish industry (the output goal). Two additional objectives were also put forward, which may be roughly characterized as a support goal and a production goal. According to the government proposal, these latter goals should serve as guideposts.[3]

Consideration of support ability in times of war and crises has been the traditional argument for political measures adopted in Sweden on behalf of the clothing and textiles industry. This support goal was previously based on a scenario with a three-year crisis period in which foreign trade is severely limited. In 1987, the parliament approved a new defence policy resolution, which incorporated, among other things, a considerably shortened crisis period. The resolution has weakened the argument of support to sustain a certain level of production. Undoubtedly, the 1987 resolution paved the way for the decision not to extend the bilateral restrictions agreements.

The industrial policy goal has been generally described as the need for textile and clothing industries to strengthen their position within the domestic market and for the clothing industry to put an end to its decline in production and export market share. The output goal and the production goal may be viewed as refinements of the industrial policy goal. According to the output goal, domestic industry was to strive to produce 30 per cent of the output of clothing and textiles in the Swedish market. The rationale behind specifying a certain market share and an explanation of the desirability of 30 per cent were not provided.[4] The production goal dictated that the volume of production achieved in 1978 should essentially be maintained. Also for this goal an explanation was lacking as to why a certain volume of production should be pursued. The output goal and the production goal have lacked sufficient precision to be immediately operational. For example, it has not been specified whether an aggregate goal or goals for each individual product should be targeted. With regard to the output goal, it was not made clear whether market share should be measured in terms of value or volume.

In addition to the foregoing objectives, there has also been a labour market goal. This goal has not been stated explicitly; rather, it has mainly been expressed through state support measures directed at the Swedish clothing and textiles industry.

There has been no clear definition of the order of priority in which these different objectives stand. To some extent there are conflicts amongst the various goals. For example, support given to maintain the production of one sector diverts resources from more efficient sectors with greater potential for achieving the industrial policy goal. Furthermore, there is no necessary correlation between achieving the production goal and attaining the output goal. For instance, an increase in production volume might go hand-in-hand with a reduction in market share (e.g. as a result of increased exports).

Along with changes in the scenario upon which the defence policy is based, the decision to scrap most quantitative restrictions certainly altered the assumptions under which textile policy operates. The government proposed in the budget for 1988–9 that the textile and clothing industry would have to function under largely the same conditions as other industries. It was also suggested that the government authorities would not establish production levels or target market share goals for various industries. This seemed to spell out the end to goals of 30 per cent market share for domestic producers and the maintenance of 1978 production volumes. The parliament later approved the proposals.

The means

A combination of various measures is used in Sweden to support domestic textile and clothing industries. Firms have been the subject of various government support schemes financed by the national budget. However, the most important means to protect the Swedish industry have been the considerable trade barriers in the form of tariffs and quantitative restrictions.

Government aid

Sweden has traditionally provided fairly comprehensive support to domestic textile and clothing firms. Direct supports expanded substantially during the 1970s and eventually developed into an entire system of various subsidies. Between fiscal years 1975–6 and 1980–1, the total amount of subsidies for Swedish textile and clothing industries increased from 40 million SEK to 500 million SEK. This figure reflects only direct financial support.

The most important component in the state support scheme has been an employment subsidy intended to boost industries with a high percentage of older workers (the so-called 'äldre-stödet'). The textile and clothing sectors have also enjoyed government subsidies based on consideration of industry and support ability. Examples of subsidies to industry include support of marketing, financial guarantees and favourable loans for efficiency-promoting investments. Since 1982, the government also pays for certain services with the purpose of maintaining production capacity and developing import substitutes in case of war and crises.

During the 1980s, government subsidies for Sweden's textile and clothing industries tapered off significantly. Direct financial support for the clothing and textile sector amounted to 85 million SEK in the fiscal year 1989–90. The parliament has decided to continue a policy benefiting the textile and clothing industry, including providing government support to export promotion and rationalization. The perpetuation of these measures was motivated in part by an expected increase of competition, due to the removal of the quantitative restrictions.

Tariffs

Sweden, like the rest of Europe, imposes different tariffs on the same product depending on the country from which it originates. This implies a discrimination amongst different countries-of-origin which is a deviation from one of GATT's most fundamental principles, the 'most-favoured-nation' concept. This deviation has, however, received recognition under GATT. The countries amongst which Sweden discriminates may be divided into three main groups. The first group consists of countries with which Sweden has concluded free trade agreements, that is, the members of the EC and EFTA. These countries enjoy tariff-free access to the Swedish market for virtually all finished goods, including clothing and textile products. The second group is comprised of those countries which receive tariff preferences from Sweden pursuant to the General System of Preferences (GSP).[5] This group generally encompasses all developing countries outside of Europe, along with Yugoslavia, Cyprus, Malta and Turkey. In addition, there is more modest special treatment for imports from Bulgaria, Romania and China. However, when it comes to imports of textiles and clothing, the most important product groups are excepted from the system. The third group consists of all other countries. It includes industrial countries outside of the EC and EFTA and East European countries other than Romania and Bulgaria. General MFN tariffs apply to these remaining countries. For most finished textile and clothing products, GSP countries by and large do not receive tariff preferences, and the same tariff rates therefore apply to these remaining countries and GSP countries alike.[6]

As discussed in the previous section, tariffs on finished textile and clothing goods are high in every industrialized nation. Sweden is no exception. The average tariff rate on clothing and garment items reaches 13–14 per cent. Of course, tariff rates vary among different products and go as high as 20 per cent for certain goods. Tariffs for textile goods are generally lower: average tariff rates for these producs are estimated to be 6–7 per cent. Even within this category there is variation for different goods ranging from 0–16 per cent. These tariff rates for clothing and textiles may be compared to the average tariff in Sweden on industrial products, which is around 4 per cent. In short, tariff protection in Sweden is characterized by discrimination amongst different countries as well as different products.

Quantitative restrictions

To date, Sweden has concluded bilateral restrictions agreements under the MFA with fourteen countries (the Philippines, Hong Kong, India, Indonesia, Yugoslavia, the People's Republic of China, the Republic of Korea, Macao, Malaysia, Pakistan, Singapore, Sri Lanka, Thailand and Turkey). A similar agreement has been reached with Malta outside the MFA. There are also restrictions on imports from Taiwan and from eastern European countries. Up to 1989, Sweden has had an oversight arrangement with the EC covering exports of clothing and textiles from Portugal.

Agreements on export restrictions have generally been quite comprehensive in terms of the total amount of textile and clothing experts covered. By 1985 there were regulations on approximately 96 per cent of all textile and clothing exports from MFA countries to Sweden. In conjunction with extensions of the 1986 MFA, the countries covered by the Nordic clause undertook to liberalize their imports. In connection with the re-negotiation of Sweden's agreements, the Swedish government announced that this would be carried through by a gradual increase in imports from MFA countries. Those goods assumed to need little protection, and thus not necessary to include within the agreement, were estimated to comprise around 20 per cent of the previous MFA imports.

As mentioned previously, the parliament has decided not to extend the bilateral restrictions agreements when MFA IV expires on 31 July 1991. The lapsing of these agreements will undoubtedly lead to a significant decrease in the total level of trade barriers. On the other hand, government authorities have expressed no intention of reducing Swedish tariff levels unilaterally. This means that even after the abolition of quantitative restrictions, levels of protection for clothing and manufactured textile products are still going to be around 13–14 per cent.

To summarize, a number of different objectives have driven Swedish textile policy. The various goals have often been hazily defined. Also lacking has been a clear articulation of the rationale behind these goals and guidelines for reaching them. There has also been a certain inconsistency amongst the various goals. Sweden's textile policy has traditionally been carried out through a series of government support mechanisms as well as through considerable trade barriers in the form of tariffs and quantitative restrictions. In the next section, the general effects of these measures will be analysed. Attention will be focused on trade barriers.

THE EFFECTS OF TRADE BARRIERS

Trade barriers can be defined as public measures, the primary purposes of which are to affect the flow of trade amongst countries and the distribution of industry. Tariffs and quantitative restrictions naturally belong to this category, as well as such state support mechanisms as subsidies, credits and public procurement. Also important in this context are technical barriers to trade of various sorts, including tariff procedures which deliberately make imports more troublesome and expensive, campaigns like 'Buy Swedish', etc.[7] Further discussion will, however, be limited chiefly to tariffs and quantitative restrictions.

The direct effect of trade barriers is a rise in the price of the regulated goods. This increase leads to a reduction in consumers' purchasing power. Moreover, consumers are likely to decrease consumption of the regulated good relative to other goods and services. Trade restrictions also often lead to a reduction in product variety. But trade barriers also have more long-term effects on household economies. Trade barriers lead to shifts in overall demand for various factors of production and thus to changes in factor prices. The owners of the factors used intensively in the protected sector experience income gains at the expense of other groups in society.

In the long term, it is quite probable that the most serious effect of trade restrictions is their impact on structural readjustments in the economy. Society's resources are channeled from sectors that can compete without protection to less productive sectors. The market's price signals are distorted, creating uncertainty and complicating assessment of long-term market developments and investment needs. In time, this dampens growth in productivity and output and leads to a lower standard of living for members of the community than they would enjoy under free trade.

The direct short-term effects of trade barriers will be discussed on pp. 261–5. The analysis proceeds from a simple model built on assumptions of homogeneous products in one sector, perfect competition and determination of prices on the world market. A further assumption is that domestic producers cannot influence prices. This assumption is reasonable for a small country like Sweden. Figure 8.1 illustrates the demand and supply curves for an importing country. The international market price is depicted by p_0. The supply of import goods is assumed to be completely elastic and coincides with the price line. If the government introduces a tariff of amount t, prices rises to p_1 and domestic production rises from q_0 to q_1. Consumption drops from q_3 to q_2. The cost to consumers in the import country is represented by the sum of areas a, b, c and d. Areas b and d indicate so-called deadweight losses. Area a constitutes a pure income transfer to the country's producers. Area c represents the government's tariff revenue, which, of course, can be redistributed to consumers.

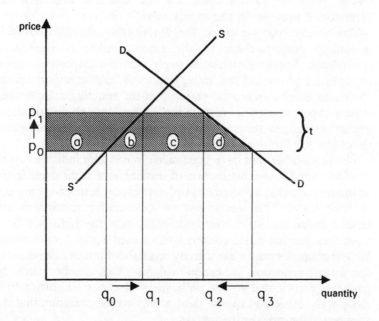

Figure 8.1 The costs of a tariff for households: the shaded areas $a + b + c + d$

In principle, a quantitative restriction has the same effect on consumers as a tariff. If the government chooses to restrict imports to a certain volume, corresponding to $q_2 - q_1$ in Figure 8.1, price rises from p_0 to p_1 as a consequence of the resulting shortage. The difference from the prior scenario is that the amount collected by the government as tariff revenue, area *c*, now goes to importers and/or exporters in the form of scarcity rents. Who collects these rents is not altogether certain. They may be captured completely by either importers or exporters, or be divided between the two groups. Both groups may be expected to try to maximize their share of these rents.

The division of scarcity rents may be viewed from two vantage points. The first concerns the market situation and the power relationship between importers and exporters. If there is high concentration on the supply side (i.e. among exporters) such that there are only a few large producers, while the demand side is characterized by numerous small importers, exporters are likely to collect the larger portion of scarcity rents. The opposite result holds where there is concentration on the demand side and free competition prevails on the supply side.

The second starting point for illuminating the distribution of monopoly profits relates to the administration of quantitative restrictions. Import restrictions imply that the importing country administer and control the trade. Importers holding import licences should be able to secure the majority of the resulting scarcity rents. Where export countries organize the market through distribution of export licences, on the other hand, exporters holding export licences should be able to seize the rents.[8]

The few studies that have been made in this area indicate that the decisive factor in the distribution of scarcity rents is the organization of the market, that is, whether import or export restrictions are used to limit trade. The agreements on quantitative restrictions concluded under the MFA therefore imply that the rents will go to exporters. For importing countries this means a pure economic loss. Export countries may view scarcity rents as a form of compensation for forced reduction in export volume. This compensation has probably contributed to the willingness of export countries to go along with restricted exports, though only on the condition that they administer the market themselves.

Both tariffs and quantitative restrictions will have effects on different consumer groups that vary with the product selected for protection. If a tariff or import surcharge is imposed on goods of special importance to low-income households, such as basic foodstuffs and clothing, low-income groups will bear a relatively large share of the costs of tariff protection. Within the textile and clothing sector, tariffs and quantitative restrictions are primarily directed against low-price imports which are likely to play a relatively large role in lower income strata. Price increases for clothing in consequence of trade restrictions have thus probably had a regressive effect on income distribution.

Despite the similarities between quantitative restrictions and tariffs, there are certain differences that should be emphasized. As previously mentioned, quantitative restrictions generate scarcity rents for importers and/or exporters, while tariffs create government revenue. Second, a tariff will shrink in absolute terms if the price of the restricted good drops, since tariffs are usually geared to a certain percentage of the import's value. This should operate to restrain prices. A quantitative restriction, on the other hand, creates no such incentive for holding down prices. Third, constant tariff rates do not lead to supply constraints when demand increases. Quantitative restrictions, on the other hand, set import volume at a certain level and may lead to greater supply constraints, and thus further price hikes, if demand rises. In comparison to tariffs, quantitative restrictions may thus be said to be more disruptive of market mechanisms, in so far as they reduce the market's ability to adjust to changes in the structure of costs and demand.

Finally, the protection offered by quantitative restrictions may often be eroded through so-called 'upgrading'. Since quantitative restrictions are most often expressed in terms of volume rather than value, export countries faced with quantitative restrictions tend to seek increased profits by switching over to more expensive product varieties. Such restrictions can result in the displacement of low-price imports by more expensive, higher quality products – properties often characteristic of the domestic product selected for protection.[9] A decreased supply of products can then force households to consume goods that are more expensive than those they actually want.

The imports of textiles and clothing which are regulated through quantitative restrictions, are at the same time subjected to significant tariffs. The effect of quantitative restrictions has been described above. If a tariff is introduced as well, scarcity rents going to importers/exporters will be wholly or partially taxed. The remainder represents actual or *realized* scarcity rents.

The simple model presented is built on the assumption that trade policy measures are not applied in a discriminate manner; that is, that all imports are affected equally. In reality, however, import countries discriminate amongst different suppliers. As described in the previous section (p. 255) Sweden's restrictions on clothing and textile imports provide a quite clear example of this. In the following, the effects of discrimination in trade policy will be analysed. The example provided shows the consequences of restricting imports from certain countries while allowing imports from other countries to enter freely. The discussion is based on previous assumptions concerning homogeneous products and price-taking suppliers in the importing country.

Price formation depends in large part on the suppliers' supply elasticity. One can imagine two extreme cases. If imports from the free trade area are characterized by perfect supply elasticity, trade barriers imposed on imports from the remaining countries will have no effect on prices. In this event, trade barriers will naturally have no effect on domestic production or employment. In the second case, supply of the restricted imports is assumed to be completely elastic, while the supply curve for unregulated imports is assumed to have a positive slope. This situation is illustrated in Figure 8.2.

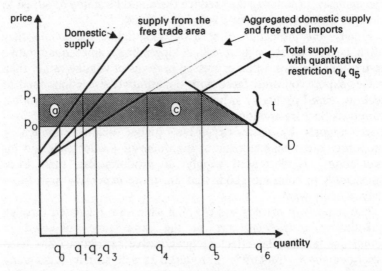

Figure 8.2 The effects of a trade policy discriminating amongst supplying countries

Initial price is depicted by p_0. Domestic production is q_0. Imports from the free trade area amount to q_1 and the remaining imports, $q_6 - q_3$, come from other countries. If a trade barrier is imposed on imports from countries outside the free trade zone, price increases to p_1. The dotted curve in the graph depicts the aggregate supply curve. Total consumption decreases to q_5. At the same time, total supply is redistributed amongst different countries-of-origin at the market. Domestic production rises to q_2. Imports from the free trade area also increase. Regulated imports fall from $q_6 - q_3$ to $q_5 - q_4$.

Two reasons explain the ultimate drop in imports from countries outside the free trade area: first, total consumption is forced down; second, domestic production and unrestricted imports are substituted for restricted imports. It is interesting to note that, assuming that the free trade area's supply elasticity exceeds domestic supply elasticity (an assumption that is quite reasonable for Sweden), free trade area exporters will increase their market share to a greater extent than domestic producers. Summing up, the not particularly surprising conclusion is that trade barriers protect not only domestic production, but also producers in the free trade area. As before, consumers in the import country bear the costs of trade barriers.

In the foregoing reasoning, it has been assumed that products are homogeneous and consumers are indifferent to goods of different origins. This assumption may hold for basic standardized products. For manufactured goods (e.g. items of clothing) it is natural to assume that products are differentiated and that domestic and imported goods are more or less near substitutes for one another. The total effects of trade barriers are largely dependent on the substitutability of products of different origins.

Normally, a rise in import prices caused by trade barriers will give rise to a proportionately smaller price increase for the corresponding domestically produced good. As a general matter, the higher the degree of substitutability between imported and domestic products, the greater the trade barrier's price impact on domestic production. The costs of protection, both for consumers and society as a whole, will also be correspondingly higher.

In two cases, the costs of protection against imports will not lead to increased prices for domestically produced goods. The first case occurs when domestic supply is perfectly elastic – an assumption which is not very reasonable in Sweden's case. The second case is when imported goods and domestic products are not substitutes in the least. If the aim of the trade restriction is to protect domestic production and employment, protective measures in such instances will be pointless.[10]

INTEREST GROUPS IN THE MARKET

The section on the internatioal background (pp. 251–5) described how production of textile and clothing products in industrialized countries met with increased competition in the 1960s and 1970s, especially from certain rapidly growing developing countries. Sweden was no exception in this regard. At the same time, general increases in productivity within the textile and clothing sector heightened the risk of structurally-based unemployment. In Sweden, as in several other industrialized countries, the textiles industry has been highly concentrated in certain geographical areas. The group of employees most affected by plant closures has by and large been female labour with low levels of education, and as such, limited opportunities for alternative employment. These developments have led to increased demand for various supports for Sweden's clothing and textile industry and protectionist measures. Calls for trade restrictions have come from industry leaders and employees alike.

The demand for trade restrictions was largely met. However, a counter-reaction has gradually been building. Economists have pointed out the costs of barriers to trade. The opponents of trade barriers have, naturally enough, included importers and wholesale dealers. Motions to liberalize the Swedish textiles trade have been put forth in the parliament in recent years. Yet more organized pressure from consumer groups has not arisen because, quite simply, Sweden lacks a strong, independent consumer organization.

The government and parliament determine the overall direction of textile policy. The ministry of foreign trade and the ministry of industry have been at the centre of the textile policy arena and have been the main architects of support measures in Swedish trade politics. The ministry of finance has through its overall responsibility for economic policy to some extent represented a counterbalance, and has increasingly emphasized the importance of reducing Sweden's relatively high rate of inflation. The textile and clothing industry has been singled out as a clear example of a sector whose regulation has spurred inflation.

The administration of direct state supports is handled by the National Industrial Board. The Swedish Board of Trade administers the trade restrictions. In alliance with the labour union, the industry represented by the Textile Council has largely succeeded in lobbying officials and politicians to maintain and even increase protection of the Swedish textiles industry. These interrelationships furnish a clear example of the so-called 'iron triangle' joining government authorities, industry and labour unions. The authority responsible for overseeing the interests of consumers, the National Swedish Board for Consumer Policies, has scarcely been involved in the textiles trade debate. Moreover, the National Price and Competition Board, the authority charged with monitoring prices has, by and large, lingered on the debate's periphery during the past two decades.

Exporters comprise a heterogeneous group in the arena of textile policy, and include firms that have been winners as well as losers in the current regulatory scheme. The winners have been exporters who can freely send goods to Sweden. Significant income transfers from Swedish consumers to producers in the EC and EFTA have, no doubt, occurred. The export countries benefiting most are likely to be those belonging to the 'low price stratum' within EFTA and the EC; that is, countries whose textile and clothing exports are relatively close substitutes for restricted imports from low-cost producers outside those organizations.[11] Countries within these organizations have a clear collective interest in other countries maintaining their regulations on trade from nations outside EFTA and the EC. As the previous section illustrated, exporters in free trade areas are favoured by the regulations in the same way as Swedish high-cost producers. This mutual interest recently manifested itself when the Swedish organization, the Textile Council, turned to the EC Commission for support in its efforts to prevent Sweden's MFA agreements from lapsing.[12] The Commission has also expressed its dissatisfaction with deregulation. Its official explanation is that low-cost imports might enter the EC via Sweden. A strong motive, however, is certainly that textile exporters within the EC stand to lose some of their preferential treatment in the Swedish market.

The unfavoured group under this system of regulations has been exporters in low-cost countries with which Sweden has concluded bilateral restriction agreements. As the previous section stressed, the administration of the regulations, which allows transfers of scarcity rents to export countries, may be viewed as remuneration for those countries' agreement to reduce volumes of exports. It should also be pointed out that these restriction agreements have had dissimilar effects on different countries. The hardest hit exporters have probably been the low-cost countries with large, expansive economies and considerable export potential (e.g. Hong Kong and South Korea). These countries are also the ones that have the most to gain from deregulation.

Swedish importers are also likely to gain from deregulation, at least in the short term. With the combination of current Swedish price levels and unfettered supply of low-cost imports, Swedish importers and wholesale merchants stand a good chance of reaping increased profits. Textiles importers have also conducted a very active campaign in the 1980s for deregulation of the textile and clothing trade. They have often done this 'on the consumer's behalf'. The major winners of deregulation are indeed consumers. Assuming the functioning of competition in wholesale and retail markets, the price of clothing will fall and the purchasing power of Swedish households will rise. The final section discusses the magnitude of costs that restrictions create for consumers and the gains that deregulation yields.

Two important concluding questions can now be posed. Why did deregulation of textile policy take so long? Why did it occur just at this moment? In the past few decades a number of economists within and outside Sweden have reiterated their message about the costs of textile policy. It obviously takes time for such a message to seep into the political process. Politically-inspired decisions concerning support measures appear to be largely irreversible, at least in the short term. The effects of trade policy, and thus its costs, are often difficult to quantify. This fact has probably facilitated the ease with which interest groups seeking protective measures may advance their claims. It is obvious that government authorities have sometimes regarded trade barriers as costless support for sectors displaced by competition.

Lastly, and perhaps most important, is the fact that those who have to pay for the policies, consumers, are clearly less organized than other interest groups. No strong and independent consumer organization currently exists in Sweden. Instead, government authorities are supposed to attend to consumers' interests. Relative to an independent consumer organization, a government body can probably lend greater weight to consumers' interests in conflicts with private producers. But when it comes to looking after households' concerns about public production and state interference, it has obviously been more difficult for these government authorities to take action. Moreover, restrictive measures have essentially pre-empted the field of competition legislation in so far as textiles and basic necessities are concerned.[13]

The reason for the current reconsideration of textile policy can probably be partly traced to shifts in the main focus of economic politics in recent years. In part, this is the natural consequence of changes in the nature of national economic problems over the past ten years. The significance of reducing inflation has been strongly underscored. Such regulated sectors as transportation, agricultural products and clothing have been pointed to as sources of inflation. Simultaneously, there seems to have been a toning down of arguments for society-wide responsibility for full employment at any price and demand-side measures to generate jobs. Also important in this regard is the very low rate of unemployment that prevails in Sweden today. But in Swedish politics, and the economic debate in particular, there has also been a conscious shift from demand-side to supply-side policies. By Swedish standards, such concepts as competition and market solution have taken on a more positive hue. The coming liberalization of the textile and clothing trade may be regarded in a broader context where deregulation is the current lodestar of several important fields in Sweden's economy: agriculture, the credit market and the currency exchange market.

THE COSTS OF TEXTILE POLICY FOR CONSUMERS

In recent years, a number of reports and investigations have sought to quantify the costs of restrictions on textiles and clothing imports for Swedish consumers.[14] The starting point for these studies has been an effort to determine the size of the realized scarcity rents.

When exports are limited by quantitative restrictions, the right to export itself becomes valuable. The highest price that an exporter is willing to pay for an export licence is in principle the extra profit that the quantitative restrictions bring, that is, the realized scarcity rent. In several of the larger developing countries whose exports are regulated under the MFA, there exists a trade in export licences. The price of export licences may be used as an approximation of the price-increasing effect of restrictions. To this must be added the effect of tariffs. A study by Hamilton (1984) calculated various industrial countries' degrees of protection for imports of clothing. The calculations were based in part on quoted prices for export licences in Hong Kong in 1981-2. Of the countries included within the study, Sweden had the highest degree of protection. Sweden's total degree of protection for clothes in 1982-3 was calculated to be almost 50 per cent of the value of imports.

Prices of export licences vary greatly across different goods, seasons and trends. In some cases the costs of licences have been up to 100 per cent of the market price. A study by Hagström (1984) concluded that a reasonable estimate of the value of monopoly rents would be between 20 and 50 per cent of the price of regulated textile products. In addition to this, there are tariffs. The total cost of trade protections depends mainly on two factors. First, the degree to which different products serve as substitutes for one another is decisive in this regard. Generally speaking, the higher the degree of substitutability amongst regulated products, domestic products and unrestricted imports, the larger the impact on price.

The National Price and Competition Board (SPK 1988) has in a study calculated that the degree of substitutability between goods from restricted countries and products originating elsewhere falls somewhere between 40 and 70 per cent; that is, between 40 and 70 per cent of the goods from countries on which quotas had been imposed were assumed to be good substitutes for products from other sources. The liberalization of the textile and clothing trade carried out in 1987 was mainly directed at goods considered to be poor substitutes for domestic goods. According to the Board, this means that substitutability today probably lies in the upper part of the 40 to 70 per cent range.

The second basic question in the determination of the costs of trade barriers for consumers is how changes in the import prices and producer prices affect consumer prices. The answer is largely dependent on the market situation and the criteria by which different actors in the distribution chain set their profit margins, and by that, their prices. In practice, there are several different methods for making this determination within different sectors. To prevent profits from declining, distributors try to compensate for increased import prices with price hikes of their own. Price increases may match the initial rise in import costs in terms of absolute value or as a percentage of it. It is also common for retailers to use different kinds of rules of thumb, or simply adopt prices suggested by suppliers. The composite price structure makes it difficult to ascertain how a price increase at the import level affects prices farther down the distribution chain.

According to the National Price and Competition Board, retailers in the garment trade set profit margins as a percentage of cost. Smaller retail firms often use fairly uniform percentages across the board, without regard for different price classes or origins. Larger firms, on the other hand, use a system of differentiated percentages. In practice, setting consumer prices on a percentage profit basis brings about a proportionate price increase. This may seem to be a strong assumption. There are also grounds to assume that, where competition prevails in the market, the price effect at the consumer level will be proportionately lower than initial increases in import and production prices. In addition, there is likely to be a certain asymmetry in price formation to the extent that the retailer reacts differently to cost increases and decreases.

From the above-mentioned studies, one can reasonably assume that abolition of quantitative restrictions would lead to a 20 to 30 per cent fall in the import prices of clothing from low-cost countries. To determine the total costs of trade restrictions, tariffs must also be taken into account. Abolition of tariff protections should lead to further price reductions of around 12 per cent. It has been calculated that approximately 40 per cent of the volume of all Swedish clothing imports comes from sources on which restrictions have been imposed. Swedish production is responsible for around 22 per cent of the supply in the market. Given a degree of substitutability between 40 and 70 per cent for products of different countries-of-origin, average prices at the import and production levels should drop between 19 and 33 per cent if trade barriers are abolished.

Provided that retailers determine their prices on the basis of percentage profit margins, consumer prices should drop at the same rate upon removal of trade restrictions. A significantly more cautious estimate of retail profit margins is based on compensation for costs in absolute terms. The cost of clothing to consumers, excluding value-added tax, consists of cost price faced by retailers and the distribution costs of the retail trade in roughly equal parts. Where there is compensation for costs in absolute terms, price reductions of 19 to 33 per cent of import and producer prices lead to approximately an 8 to 13 per cent drop in consumer prices.

The value of total clothing consumption in 1988 was nearly 33 billion SEK. According to calculations referred to above, the cost of trade barriers amounted to between at least 2.6 to 4.3 billion SEK per year. If one merely looks at the costs of quantitative restrictions, removal of these could lead to reductions in consumer prices of between 5 and 10 per cent. This corresponds to between 1.6 and 3.3 billion SEK, and should be regarded as a minimum estimate of the annual gain households can expect to receive from removal of quantitative restrictions.[15]

In conclusion, it may be pointed out that trade barriers have different effects on different groups of households. In 1988, an average Swedish household spent about 9,000 SEK on clothes. Such a household will save between 450 and 900 SEK per year when quantitative restrictions are abolished. It is likely that families with children and low-income households pay a disproportionately large share of the costs of textile policy. This disproportionate burden is attributable partly to the fact that such households spend a larger share of their income on clothing, and partly because they are likely to have a greater tendency than other groups to buy clothes made in low-cost countries.[16] As such, Sweden's system of trade restrictions had a doubly regressive taxation effect. It is also these groups that stand to gain the most from deregulation.

NOTES

1 In the following, termed 'textile policy'.
2 The expression 'MFN-tariff' refers to GATTs 'most-favoured nation' principle under which each country shall enjoy the same rights as the most-favoured nation.
3 For a summary and critique of previous objectives of the Swedish textile policy, see Hagström (1984).
4 If the underlying motives are traced back to concerns of labour or industrial policy, production volumes or employment rates would have been more relevant benchmarks than market share.
5 Most industrial countries are participants in the GSP, through which tariff preferences are granted to certain goods from developing countries. The preferences are unilateral and non-binding.
6 Exports from LDC's to Sweden have, however, been somewhat facilitated since 1987, when freedom from tariffs for all products was introduced for a very limited number of countries.
7 An example of this type of trade barrier is the Swedish requirement that imported clothing be labelled with its country of origin.
8 Between 1977 and 1984, Norway used a system of global import quotas for textile and clothing imports. Thereafter, Norway switched to export restriction agreements under the MFA. A study by Lindström (1987) shows the significant redistribution of scarcity rents from importers to exporters occurring in conjunction with the change in regulatory regimes.
9 Studies of Swedish clothing and textiles imports from low-cost producers indicate the existence of upgrading at the end of the 1970s and the outset of the 1980s, see Kommerskollegium (1988).
10 The liberalization carried out by Sweden pursuant to MFA IV has in several cases been directed at products that are not actual substitutes for Swedish products.
11 Price comparisons in Lindström (1987) indicate that exports from such countries as Italy, Great Britain, Denmark and, to some extent, Finland, fall within this price stratum.
12 See *Dagens Industri*, 30 September 1989.
13 The government has recently set up a commission to study whether competition legislation could be applied more extensively to the sectors of housing, food and transportation.

14 See Hamilton (1981) and (1984), Hagström (1984) and SPK (1988).
15 This estimate can be compared with the SPK's estimate of a 2 billion SEK annual saving at 1985 prices, see SPK (1988).
16 A study of the preferences of Norwegian consumers indicates that families with children and younger consumers have a higher tendency than other groups to buy low-cost products.

REFERENCES

Hagström, P. (1984) *Mål och medel i svensk tekopolitik – en översikt*, Arbetsrapport nr. 11, Stockholm: Utredningssekretariatet, Kommerskollegium.
Hamilton, C. (1981) 'A new approach to estimation of the effects of non-tariff barriers to trade: an application to the Swedish textile and clothing industry', *Weltwirtschaftsliches Archiv*, *117*, 2.
Hamilton, C. (1984) 'Voluntary export restraints on Asia: tariff equivalents, rents and trade barrier formation', Seminar Paper no. 276, Stockholm: Institute for International Economics Studies.
Industridepartementet (Ministry of Industry) (1989) Prop. 1988/89:100 Bilaga 14, Stockholm.
Kommerskollegium (Swedish Board of Trade) (1988) 'Handelspolitiska konsekvenser på tekoområdet och skyddseffekten av avtal slutna under regimen MFA IV', mimeo, 5 August.
Lindström, E. (1987) *Norges tekopolitik och hushållens ekonomi. Med jämförelse av svenska och danska förhållanden*, Forskningsrapport nr. 66, Oslo: Fondet for markeds- og distribusjonsforskning.
OECD (1983) *Textile and Clothing Industries*, Paris: OECD.
Pettersen, I. (1983) 'Teko-politikk i Norge och Sverige: Forholdet mellom handelspolitiske og industripolitiske virkemidler', *Internasjonal Politikk*, no. 4.
Silberston, Z.A. (1984) *The Multifibre-Arrangement and the UK Economy*, London: Imperial College of Science and Technology.
Statens pris- och konkurrensverk (SPK) (National Price and Competition Board) (1988) *Tekopolitikens effekter för konsumenter och producenter*, SPK's utredningsserie 4, Stockholm.
Wolf, M., Glismann, H.H., Pelzman, J. and Spinanger, D. (1984) *The Cost of Protecting Jobs in Textiles and Clothing*, London: Trade Policy Research Centre.

9 Economic regulation of domestic air transport in Sweden*

Siri Pettersen Strandenes

INTRODUCTION

Airlines are regulated so as to prevent them from exploiting their market power. In addition, the authorities aim to ensure a high level of safety in air transport. Authorities often favour cross-subsidization from economically viable routes to induce supply in unprofitable markets. Such motives do not, however, limit the ways in which control is exercised over the existing regulatory scheme. In addition, analyses show that entry regulation and regulation of price competition may by itself be a source of inefficiency. Posner (1975) discusses the social costs of regulated monopolies. In evaluating the regulated American airline industry he found that the estimated social costs of regulated airline monopolies exceeded estimates on costs of unregulated monopolies. This shows that there is every reason to discuss the existing regulatory scheme.

The airline industry in Sweden has been regulated from the beginning as in most other countries. Regulatory schemes have been virtually unchanged, both nationally and internationally, since the emergence of the industry in the 1930s up until the last ten years. The regulatory schemes have been quite similar in different parts of the world, although there has been some variation in details of rules in Europe and the United States. The last decade has seen deregulation of US domestic air transport and less strict rules in some international markets. This deregulation, or more correctly re-regulation, followed a period of discussion on the efficiency of traditional regulatory schemes in the airline industry.

In later years there have been important developments in the theory of regulation of industries and firms in imperfectly competitive markets. Demsetz (1968) proposed regulation of market access instead of market conduct. By opening up the market, negative

274

effects of lack of competition could be reduced. He suggested that the right to operate should be awarded to the company that offered to supply the product on the best terms. By repeating such bidding for the right to operate, the regulator could select the most efficient firm at any point in time. An important aspect of bidding systems is that they induce firms to operate more efficiently. This limits a firm's exercise of market power. Williamson (1976) commented on this approach and pointed to the problems of transferring capital equipment between firms when a new firm wins the right to operate. This means that the duration of the right to operate influences firms' willingness to invest. Another problem is for the authorities to ensure that the winning firm continues to operate in accordance with its (winning) bid. The theory of incentive contracts is developing, supported by contributions such as those of Laffont and Tirole (1987) and Riordan and Sappington (1987).

In this chapter the author will present and discuss aspects of auctions and bidding when used in regulating airlines. Before dealing with these questions, the existing regulation in the Swedish domestic market and the resulting market structure are discussed briefly. The section also includes a presentation of traditional arguments for regulation, and the usual effects of such regulation.

Discussions of airline regulation are especially interesting in the Nordic countries because of the relatively high intensity of airline travel in these countries. Figure 9.1 illustrates travel frequencies in domestic air travel in the Nordic countries and some European countries, in addition to North America in 1984. Travel intensity is seen to be high in Sweden, Iceland and Norway, and even in Denmark and Finland the intensity of demand relative to the population is above similar levels in the larger European countries.[1]

One result of the relatively high travel intensity is that some of Europe's denser 'city-pair' markets are found in Scandinavia. This counteracts conventional wisdom of market size in the Scandinavian airline industry. The major city-pair market, Stockholm–Gothenburg, in 1987 on weekdays offered eighteen daily departures from Stockholm and eighteen back.[2] The ten largest markets in Scandinavia had twelve to fourteen daily departures in each direction. This compares well with the number of departures in European city-pair markets when we take into account that several of the markets operate more than two airports. From the production point of view, it is most relevant to compare traffic between specific airports. The sum of flights per day from London to Paris totalled twenty-seven in 1987, but of this only sixteen flights left Heathrow

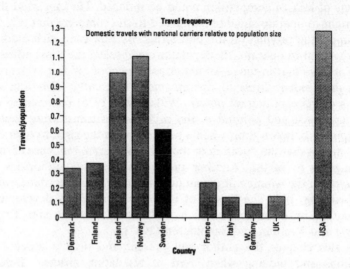

Figure 9.1 Travel frequencies: domestic travel with national carriers relative to population size, 1984

for Charles De Gaulle. The Heathrow–Schipol market totalled twenty daily departures in each direction. The important domestic German market, Frankfurt–Hamburg, offered sixteen daily flights. Similarly, Paris (Orly)–Marseille offered fourteen (fifteen) departures. On the other hand, Madrid–Barcelona is a denser market with twenty-four (twenty-two) daily departures. The number of seats offered, of course, is higher in the main European markets relative to the Scandinavian markets, since the airlines typically employ larger aircraft in these markets. The high frequency of flights in Scandinavia reflect passengers' willingness to pay for frequent flights.

TRADITIONAL REGULATION SCHEMES

The aim of regulating natural monopolies is manifold. The authorities may wish to extract the rents that accrue to the firm from operating a market with imperfect competition. To secure rents for the community the authorities may regulate the firm instead of nationalizing its operations. Authorities may alternatively choose to limit the firms' possibilities to extract rents. Production by a monopoly is inefficiently low. Another aim of regulation, therefore, is to increase production relative to the volume produced by an unregulated monopoly. A monopolist or a firm facing imperfect competition, furthermore, may have less incentive to maximize its internal efficiency than firms operating in a competitive environment. The extra cost may be imposed on the customers by higher prices, without attracting new suppliers. One aim of regulation thus is to reduce internal inefficiency.

If authorities had perfect information on demand and costs of production, they could decide on the quantity to be produced. But as authorities only have imperfect information of operations, it is possible for the monopoly to extract rents, restrict production or continue operations in spite of cost inefficiency. Regulation is introduced to limit this exercise of market power. Consumers may have imperfect information on the quality of service. As a remedy, regulation often specifies rules related to minimum quality such as safety. Yet another reason for regulating the firms is when there are externalities in the firm's operations.

Reasons for regulating airlines

All elements mentioned above may be in effect in the airline industry. Airlines often have a monopoly position in individual city-pair markets. They may be able to extract rents, when economies of scale hamper the profitable entry of a second airline.[3] The result is that market size limits profitable entry, except in city-pair markets with relatively heavy traffic. If there exists alternative routes they may limit the operating airline's market power, however. The efficiency of such competition depends on the structure of routes and whether or not one single airline operates all relevant routes. When there are few route alternatives, regulation is often introduced to counteract the operator's market power. On the other hand, the regulators often allocate competing routes alternatives to the national carrier.

When authorities have imperfect knowledge of operating costs, airlines may operate with inefficiently high costs and still be allowed to increase their prices. Similarly, airlines may not be forced by the authorities to reduce their prices if input prices fall. It is difficult for the authorities to evaluate arguments put forward by the firm that other cost elements have increased, thereby increasing total costs or not lowering them as much as the reduced input prices indicate. If so, regulation may induce higher prices.

The airlines gain information on their customers and the pattern of demand. They may exploit the resulting asymmetric information on demand between the regulators and themselves. Information from computer reservation systems in later years have been used by most large airlines in yield management. In this way the airlines may discriminate between different passengers and increase their revenue. In yield management schemes, airlines use self-selection to discriminate between passengers. They have detailed information on the distribution of passengers on specific flights registered in their computers. The information is used in deciding what number of seats to offer in different fare classes on a specific flight to maximize the yield and increase the cabin factor.[4] It should be pointed out, however, that such price discrimination helps allocating seats to passengers according to their willingness to pay.

But high fares also influence the cost level of the rest of the economy. Demand for air travel is derived from demand for output of other industries in addition to demand for personal visits or holidays. Higher prices reduce demand and are taken into acount by the airlines, but the authorities still may wish to limit the airlines' extraction of monopoly rents since it influences the competitiveness of other industries negatively.

In transport there are different types of externalities. Thus, this reason for regulation is relevant in the airline industry. For example, aircraft pollute the air and influence the environment surrounding airports negatively, because of the noise from the aircraft. Technological development has reduced these problems to a certain extent, however.

Different forms of regulation

Airline regulation may take on different forms. The authorities may focus on indirect control through positive or negative taxes. Both are seen in the airline industry. Airlines and passengers are taxed in different ways to pay for the airports and airport safety schemes.[5] At the same time, direct subsidies are often offered to smaller airlines operating unprofitable routes. Airlines also are expected to extract rents on some routes, and use them to cross-subsidize internally in favour of routes that cannot be profitably operated.

In addition to such indirect measures, most countries use direct regulation of airlines. Entry is restricted and the frequency and capacity offered in specific markets must be approved by the authorities. The authorities often set maximum prices and in some countries the detailed price structure should be approved by the authorities.

Direct ownership by governments in airlines is widespread. The United States is the major exception to this, whereas several of the European airlines are publicly owned, totally or in part. The 'flag' carrier usually obtains preferred treatment in the bilateral agreements that still dominate international scheduled air traffic.

Regulation of domestic air transport in Sweden

Air transport services in Sweden are regulated by law. The law sets the requirements regarding registration of aircraft, nationality, manning and safety. An airline is granted a concession to operate domestic markets upon application. Airlines, typically, are granted an exclusive concession for a specific route even though this is not required by law. Operations are regulated as regards the type of aircraft to be employed on a specific route. Frequency of flights also has to be approved by the authorities. In Sweden, contrary to the regulatory scheme of the other Scandinavian countries, the regulator specifies maximum prices only. Thus, firms specify prices and discount schemes themselves as long as they do not exceed the maximum price.

The primary domestic air transport market in Sweden is divided between Scandinavian Airlines System (SAS) and Linjeflyg AB. SAS operates the most prominent city-pairs like the routes from Stockholm to Gothenburg, Malmoe and Lulea/Kiruna, whereas Linjeflyg AB operates some thirty domestic city-pairs. Smaller routes are operated by different small firms. Each of these firms operate a small number of city-pair routes. Linjeflyg AB also operates routes in low density markets and is expected to cross-subsidize internally between routes. SAS supplies almost 40 per cent and Linjeflyg AB above 55 per cent of the domestic market. The rest is supplied by several small airlines.

The authorities in 1987 opened up some intra-Scandinavian routes to other airlines in cases where SAS stated that they were not interested in operating the route themselves. Routes to and from the main cities (Copenhagen, Stockholm, Oslo, Bergen, Stavanger, Gothenburg and Malmoe) are exempt from this liberalization, however. The rules are set to ensure that traffic is not diverted from the main airports and routes. Furthermore, no direct flights to Copenhagen from airports north of Gothenburg or Stockholm are allowed by other airlines. Even though this regulation applies to intra-Scandinavian flights, it affects domestic city-pair markets, since domestic routes also act as feeder routes to international flights, and SAS operates both domestic and other routes.

The resulting market structure

The existing regulatory scheme is similar to airline regulation in Norway and Denmark and reflects the tight co-operation in these markets caused by the co-ownership of SAS. SAS was set up and given favourable treatment in an agreement that was reached by the Scandinavian countries in 1951. This agreement favours SAS in international, intra-Scandinavian and domestic markets and has been prolonged several times. In 1987 it was prolonged to the year 2005.

SAS is owned by a national company in each of the Scandinavian countries.[6] The companies are 50 per cent government owned. Thus, SAS is regulated both directly in the market and indirectly through public ownership. Linjeflyg AB is the other major domestic airline in Sweden. SAS holds 50 per cent of Linjeflyg's shares. The rest is held directly by the Swedish government. The third airline, Swedair, does not operate its own routes, but is chartered by Linjeflyg AB to fly in low density markets in which its smaller aircraft are better suited. The relationships between these firms are illustrated in Figure 9.2. The airline industry is characterized by vertical integration. Most of the large airlines have their own computer reservation system or co-operate with a limited number of airlines on such systems. They typically integrate downstream into hotel chains, travel agencies and inclusive tour operators and upstream into catering. This is the case also in the Swedish airline industry.

SAS has built up a reservation system – SMART – in which the private Norwegian airline Braathens SAFE and the Swedish railway have shares. Together with other European airlines, SAS is building up an international reservation system – Amadeus.[7] The major inclusive tour operator in Scandinavia, Vingresor, is a subsidiary (100 per cent owned by SAS). The consortium that owns SAS also owns the charter operating airline Scanair. SAS, furthermore, has established a catering firm, SAS Service Partner, which is one of the larger international catering firms. About 30 per cent of its revenue is based on SAS operations. SAS International Hotels is another subsidiary with hotels in Scandinavia and abroad. SAS also bought the credit card firm Diners Club International some years ago. In 1988, SAS decided to set up Scandinavian Aero Engine Services together with Volvo Flymotor. This firm intends to specialize in the maintenance of engines for aircraft. SAS is engaged in travel agencies and has 30 per cent the shares in 'Travel Management

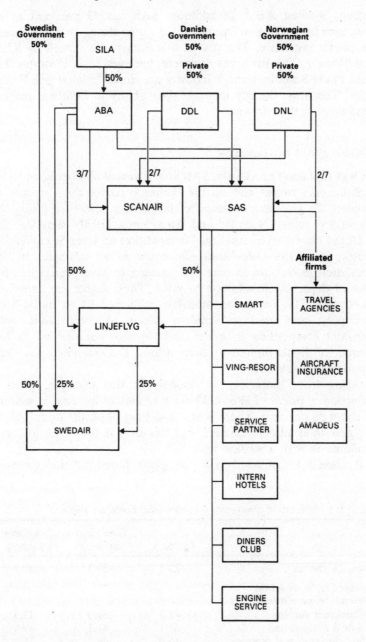

Figure 9.2 Ownership in the Swedish airline industry
Note: The figure is not complete as regards SAS daughter companies and affiliated companies.

Group, Sweden AB'.[8] In addition, SAS has 33 per cent in an insurance firm, Polygon Insurance Co., specializing in international air carrier insurance. The rest of this company is owned by KLM and Swissair. This list is not complete, but even so it illustrates that firms in the Scandinavian air industry are closely related (see Figure 9.2).[9] The firms thereby increase their ability to influence market conditions in their favour.

Welfare effects of regulation[10]

As was explained previously, SAS have a virtual monopoly on inter-Scandinavian routes and on the domestic routes they operate in Sweden. To give an assessment of the welfare effects of lifting the regulatory rules, Norman and Strandenes (1990) simulate the potential effects of international competition on inter-Scandinavian routes, using the Oslo–Stockholm route as an example. In the simulation model, we assume that passengers have preferences for time of departure in addition to price. Thus, flights are imperfect substitutes. The simulation model is calibrated to an initial SAS monopoly, and used to simulate effects of competition, with Bertrand competition in prices and Cournot competition in the number of flights offered by each airline. The estimated gains are reported in Table 9.1.

Going from monopoly to duopoly in this example, gives a reduction in prices of almost 30 per cent and an increase in welfare of about 36 per cent. There is also a shifting of profits from SAS to the new international carriers, but this shift is too small to leave Scandinavia with a welfare loss.

It should be stressed that the gains found in this example

Table 9.1 Effects of competition, Oslo–Stockholm air route

	Duopoly	Three-firm oligopoly	Four-firm oligopoly
Price, % change	−29.7	−39.5	−42.1
Change, as % of initial consumer expenditures:			
Consumer surplus	45.5	67.0	73.3
World real income	36.1	47.1	49.9
Scandinavian real income	16.9	28.3	31.4

Source: Norman and Strandenes (1990).
Note: New carriers are non-Scandinavian.

represent an upper estimate. Today there is competition on routes to and from Scandinavia and limited competition on some domestic routes with parallel concessions to alternative means of transportation where they exist. But even so, one would expect substantial gains from entries into other Scandinavian routes as well as from the Oslo–Stockholm route.

Price regulation is also known to reduce incentives to operate efficiently if operators are allowed to increase their price to cover rising costs. Such effects are not included in the model estimates, since we assume that all carriers operate at the same cost level. Low incentives may be the case in Sweden, since in the 1980s, for example, price increases in some instances were accepted to compensate for loss of revenue caused by labour conflicts.[11] Fares also seem to reflect fuel costs due to higher energy prices to a larger degree than energy cost reductions. This contrasts with the situation in the charter markets where prices are set without regulatory intervention.

Even though major domestic city-pair markets are allocated to only one airline, alternative routes with a shorter or longer detour operated by another airline may offer direct competition. A limit to the monopoly power of one airline can therefore be provided. In Sweden, as in the other Scandinavian countries, the total network is small and structured as a network with one major hub. This means that there are few, if any, alternatives to most routes. But as previously mentioned, Scandinavian airlines may also face competition from other modes of transport. If service quality does not reflect prices charged in air transport relative to the costs (including time costs) of travelling by railway or private car, the airline will lose passengers. The fact that the fare between Stockholm and Malmoe, where the train is a fairly attractive alternative, is lower than the Stockholm–Copenhagen fare may reflect this. Alternative methods of transport are less attractive for passengers to Copenhagen, one reason being that many passengers only wish to pass through Copenhagen. Because of the topological conditions, competition from other methods of transport is relevant only for a restricted number of city-pairs in Sweden.

Cross-subsidies from dense routes to city-pair markets with low density operated by the same airline is part of the regulatory regime. There are well-known negative effects of such policies. Evaluation of effects of cross-subsidization in Norway support the general result that gains to passengers in low density markets are outweighed by losses from distorted prices and cost inefficiency.[12]

Regulation also affects flexibility in supply. The regulated network of routes becomes less flexible in response to changing demand, when changes have to be approved by the regulators. The network, furthermore, reflects the authorities' beliefs as to what is the structure of demand. This may result in an inefficient network, when regulators have less knowledge of demand than the airlines. In the United States, deregulation changed the network towards a 'hub and spoke' network. It has been argued that this indicates that European regulation is less inefficient since hub and spoke is the dominating pattern of European networks. But this does not ensure that the existing network in Sweden is the most efficient hub and spoke network.

The capacity offered cannot typically be increased without allowances from the government. Thus reactions to rises in demand are postponed. Airlines also become reluctant to reduce capacity in a city-pair market, if they believe that reduction in demand is temporary, and fear they will not be allowed to increase supply in response to future rises in demand. This may increase costs compared to a situation with more flexibility in supply reactions to demand variations.

The division of routes between firms given by regulation, may reduce the flexibility to employ the appropriate aircraft in a specific city-pair market, since each firm typically have few types of aircraft. Airlines can go on operating routes by inefficient aircraft, when they can pass on the extra costs to the passengers without attracting competition. Linjeflyg AB operates most domestic primary routes, except routes that are operated by SAS, whereas secondary routes are operated by several smaller firms. It is not clear that this is the most efficient division of routes between firms. On the other hand, Linjeflyg AB charters Swedair's smaller aircraft for operations in their less dense routes.

The detailed regulation of domestic airline markets implies that the strategic variables left to the airlines are punctuality, discounts and number of rebated seats, service quality and the general image of the firm. As long as the airline is in a monopoly position, both in relation to other airlines and the other means of transportation, it may reduce punctuality to gain other results. An airline that operates both monopoly (domestic) and duopoly/oligopoly (international) routes, may find it worthwhile in the case of a technical breakdown, to reallocate aircraft to the city-pair operated in competition with other firms. It prefers to leave passengers waiting in one of its monopoly routes compared to losing passengers to other airlines in competitive city-pair markets.[13] Most larger airlines also are engaged in extensive yield management. By changing the number of discounted seats in each flight according to statistically expected demand by passengers with different time and price elasticities, the airline maximizes its revenue by what is an approximation to perfect price discrimination, as pointed out above. Another characteristic is that airline advertisements traditionally focus on the general image of the firm, whereas in competitive markets information on prices and schedules are more usual. Reflecting this, the introduction of parallel concessions between SAS and Braathens SAFE in Norway was followed by increased advertising of schedules and handling procedures in these markets.

AIRPORT POLICY AND AIRLINE COMPETITION[14]

Experience in the United States after deregulation of domestic air transport has shown that there is an important relationship between competition in air transport and airport policy.[15] Airlines need airport slots to enter into a new city-pair market or to expand their service on routes where they are already engaged. Inefficient distribution of airport capacity, therefore, limits competition between airlines as entry is hampered. In regulated markets where authorities restrict entry, they have to match airport capacity with the concessions they issue. If airport capacity is scarce, the regulators must divide the capacity on flights/routes, thereby favouring some regions and markets.

Airport policy influences air transport competition also in other ways. One example was the effects on SAS's competitiveness for Scandinavian (and other) passengers on intercontinental flights to the United States caused by congestion at John F. Kennedy International Airport. Scandinavian passengers had incentives to use another airline to avoid this airport. This also shows part of SAS's motivation for the agreement reached with Texas Air, which opened up the use of Newark Airport. Generally, efficiency at airports may influence passenger flows when there are alternative routes in the network. Passengers take departure times, frequencies and total travel time, as well as related services like tax-free shopping into account. The alternatives are limited, however, in the Swedish domestic market with its network centred around one major hub – Arlanda. In domestic markets, competition from other modes of transport may be more strongly felt by the airlines. Location of airports relative to the city centre will have an impact on competition between airlines and railways.

AUCTIONS AND BIDDING IN THE AIRLINE INDUSTRY[16]

Instead of regulating firms in the industry, the authorities may regulate competition between firms for the right to operate in the market. City-pair markets are markets with imperfect competition, since market size usually limits the number of airlines that can profitably operate the route. Competition for access to the market may be introduced to limit market power and increase welfare. This was argued by Demsetz (1968). He proposed to auction off rights to operate.

Bidding may be introduced to get a job done for the lowest possible price relative to the quality. When bidding is used by the authorities in distributing, for example, bus services or airline routes, the authorities act as an agent for the passengers and the aim is to have cost efficient operations and optimal fare/quality combinations. The main issue is to ensure that the bidder or the firm that gets the operation rights has incentives to provide efficient service and not to extract monopoly rent. Even though new operators cannot enter into the market between auctions, the firm will not be able to renew the concession to operate in the next bidding scheme unless offering the best bid.

Auctions often are used by a monopolist seller to secure maximum price for the item he wishes to sell, as in auctions of art or oil drilling licences. Auctions for the right to use congested infrastructure, for example, airports, are similar. The idea is to secure the scarcity rent which is then handed over to the authorities. Airlines' bids will reflect their evaluation of passengers' willingness to pay for flights to the airport and thereby will indicate the market value of investments in airport capacity.

If the auctions are organized as sealed bid auctions, the incumbent, or more correctly, the bidder who operated the route in the previous period cannot try to stop newcomers as may happen in a free market. The winner of the auction, furthermore, gets the entire concession at once and does not have to go through a period of gradually building up his market share. This means that auctions may increase contestability relative to an imperfectly competitive market with unregulated entry.

Asymmetric information is essential in motivating the use of auctions instead of traditional regulation. With symmetric information the authorities would know the operating costs and would have almost exactly the same information about demand as the firm itself. In such a case, the authorities would be able to regulate the operator directly. Asymmetric information exists either when it is impossible to get the information, or when the information in principle is general, but where it is costly or difficult to get. Information on costs from a firm often falls into the latter class. Even though the airline industry is an industry with extensive information on costs and profitability,[17] historic costs reflect the historical situation with direct regulation and reduced cost incentives. The authorities should, perhaps, design auctions to induce the airlines to reveal whether they belong in the high- or low-cost group of bidders for a concession or, if possible, to reveal their operating costs. Operators, typically, have better knowledge of demand than the regulators. This aspect has become more important following the extensive use of computer reservation systems (CRS) and the airlines' ability to use the registered information in statistical analysis of passenger flows. Airlines with CRS are probably better predictors on the distribution of passengers in fare groups for a specific flight.

Several problems arise when using auctioning in the airline industry, however. First, the authorities have to decide how often to arrange an auction or equivalently for what period to issue the concession to the winner. The duration of the concession will influence airlines' decisions, especially investment decisions, as some of the future income from an investment may accrue to the next operator. Such problems arise with repeated auctions.[18] Another problem is how to enforce the contract or ensure that the airline operates in accordance with its bid on price/quality combinations for the whole period. When deciding on which of the bids to accept, the authorities must compare different packages, minimum capacity, minimum frequency and maximum fares offered in the bids. There may be no clear ranking of bids as different passengers may favour different solutions.

Risk is a basic feature of auctions in that the bidders run the risk of getting the item or not. One aspect is the 'winner's curse'. The bid with the best fare/quality combination wins the concession. This implies that the winner has evaluated operating costs to be lower than the other bidders. He also may have higher expectations on demand for this service than have the failing bidders. If the winner's evaluation turns out to be wrong, he is in for a loss. This is relevant only when there is common value, i.e. when different bidders agree on the value from winning except for possible disagreement on the probability of the different future states. The potential income from operating a route is an example of common value. That is, airlines bidding for routes or airport slots may experience the winner's curse if their evaluation of the expected income is unrealistic. This may induce bidders to include a risk margin, so that the winning bid becomes less efficient.

As pointed out above, we have to discriminate between two situations when discussing auctions in this industry:

1 Using auctions to reduce negative effects for airline passengers of imperfect competition in city-pair markets;
2 Using auctions to ration too low capacity of airports, that is imperfections in the factor markets for airlines.

In the following sections, there is a discussion of which items to auction off, starting with a discussion of allocation of route concessions.

Bidding for the right to operate

In regulated air transport markets, regulators traditionally award concessions to operate a specific route between two airports. Auctioning off individual routes would be an alternative way to distribute specific routes. When routes are auctioned off the airline that wins the bid may be allowed to set the frequency and the capacity offered on that route above a minimum frequency specified in their bid. The airline then will have incentives to offer flights reflecting development in demand on that route. The authorities, of course, could auction off a set of flights on the route, thereby setting the frequency, but this will bind supply and reduce adjustment to changes in demand between auctions.

Airlines could be invited to bid for operations in a region or a country by specifying the network they would set up, both as regards routes and frequencies. The region could be large enough to represent total income for a (small) firm or expected to be part of a larger network operated by an existing airline. This would relieve the authorities of designing the network and may increase adjustments of supply to changes in demand. But this increases the problems regarding investment decisions. If the airline takes into account that they may win the concession only once, their offer could imply an inefficient fare/frequency combination. This would be a reasonable response if the airline did not have profitable alternative uses for the capital equipment or did not expect to get a fair price when selling the equipment. Similarly, human capital may reduce its value when moved into other activities. Such results are less likely for air services than in several other markets, however, because sunk costs are fairly small in an industry with viable second-hand markets for capital equipment. Airlines, on the other hand, have sunk costs in affilitated activities. The computer-assisted reservation system (CRS) is one example. Small firms, typically, do not have their own CRS and large airlines will experience only marginally increased costs from losing operations in one small city-pair market. This indicates that it may be more efficient to auction individual routes than networks of routes. First, the airline will experience higher costs by building up a network than by engaging in one single (additional) route and, more importantly, this increases the costs of not having the winning bid in the next auction. Second, bidding for networks of routes instead of individual routes may reduce the number of bidders. Empirical studies of auctions indicate that the winning bid is less favourable when the number of bidders falls.

Some concessions in low density markets are not economically viable and have to be subsidized by the authorities. If auctions are used to distribute such concessions, the airlines will have incentives to plan efficient production. This should reduce the subsidies needed. The auctioning of low density routes with subsidies has been used in Canada. There may be fewer bidders in auctions for low density routes, however. One reason is that the cost of operating such a route depends on whether it will represent an extension of the airlines' network or is disconnected from the bidder's existing routes. On the other hand, small airlines may be set up specifically to operate such a route.

Seats in an aircraft could be the item auctioned off. An airline could buy seats from another airline's flights. In this case, they do not have to offer the capacity of an aircraft at each point in time on every route. This could reduce the problems of adjusting capacity in each market, but may limit the airlines influence in the market. It may resemble the situation of airlines and hotels in inclusive tour markets, where the tour operator is the unit known in the market. Airlines, in this case, are contractors to the firms selling seats and setting up routes. This point is raised in Rassenti *et al.* (1982). Vickrey (1972) discussed auctioning off seats in over-booked flights. Passengers state how much they should be paid to leave their seat and take the next flight. This raises another type of problem. Over-booking is used to increase cabin factors. By auctioning, the airline gets the passengers to reveal their willingness to pay for a seat on that particular flight, or more correctly, how much the airline must pay the passenger to wait for the next flight. These examples are not directly related to questions on regulation of carriers, however.

In looking at which item – network, route or seat – to auction off, it can be seen that the narrower the definition of the item, the more decisions the authorities have to make as regards the structure of supply. Since routes usually are interdependent, except for some low density routes disconnected to or at the periphery of the network and for shuttle operations on the largest routes where several operators can operate with profit, it may be difficult to set up an auction system for individual routes. Auctions for networks, on the other hand, could result in a low number of bids. One could start using auctions in distributing routes that are most independent, i.e. low density routes at the fringe of the network. As auctions induce the airline to be more cost efficient, auctioning off subsidized low density routes should reduce subsidies. As pointed out previously, the authorities have to evaluate different fare/frequency combinations, however, and there may be no clear ranking of the bids.

Several operators

Denser markets may be operated by several airlines and, as we have seen, Scandinavia has some of the denser markets in Europe. If the concession to operate a route is divided between two or more airlines, there is a problem as to who should set capacity. It is possible for the authorities to decide how many firms should be allowed to establish themselves on a specific route and leave the division of traffic between the firms to the market. Another possibility is to auction off flights in the market one at a time and let the results in the auctioning of the first flight be known before the second is auctioned. In this case, the authorities will set the frequency indirectly, when they offer flights for 'sale'. Another possibility is to specify the number of flights to be auctioned off and let the airlines decide the number of flights each of them bids for. If the authorities set the number of airlines to be let into the market and lets them decide the capacity and flights they will offer, the only difference from full deregulation is that new airlines cannot enter between auctions.

The airlines that bid for parallel concession in the same city-pair market will have strong incentives to collude and thereby act as a monopoly. If so, the route may just as well be auctioned off to one airline in the first place.

Auctioning of airport slots

In markets with little or no congestion problems in airports, or air corridors, a concession to operate a route can be treated as an independent item as regards the capacity needed in airports and air corridors.[19] When there are capacity problems in one or both airports on the route, this is not so. If the items auctioned off are specific routes or flights, it implies that the authorities and not the market divides the limited airport capacity between the different markets. Restricted capacity in rush hours at, for example, Arlanda is then divided between traffic, for example, to and from north Sweden or the western part of the country and similarly between international and domestic transport by the authorities when they decide on the set of flights to be auctioned off. Even if the authorities correctly specify relative demand for the restricted airport capacity at the time when concessions are allocated, the system cannot adjust to changes in relative demand from the different geographical areas.

Grether *et al.* (1981) discuss problems of allocating scarce capacity at congested airports. They evaluate the system that was established at the four major congested airports in the United States[20] in the late 1960s. A committee was set up comprising representatives for the airlines that were certified to use the airports, to schedule the flights of the airlines. Allocations from such committees need not be economically efficient. The committee's decisions are influenced by the consequences of default or impossibility to agree on an allocation. If the committees fail the authorities allocate the slots themselves. Grether *et al.* recommended that these committees were replaced by auction schemes.

The auction system proposed by Grether *et al.* (1981) implied independent primary markets for landing slots at each airport. A 'one-shot' auction of all slots at airports with congestion will lead to competition, but not necessarily to efficient allocation. Airlines may end up with landing rights that do not constitute specific flights. Since landing rights by themselves are not enough for the airlines, they proposed an 'aftermarket' where airlines could sell or purchase among themselves the slots obtained in the primary market. Thus, airlines could obtain a combination of airport slots that fitted in with their network. The aftermarket as proposed by Grether *et al.* may match slots but will not in general lead to efficient allocation. The prices and allocation of the initial auction influence the aftermarket and inhibit this market from gaining an efficient solution. Companies, furthermore, have incentives to bid in the auction only to take part in the aftermarket. Rassenti *et al.* (1982) point out two disadvantages with this system. On the one hand, airlines may face losses in the aftermarket if the slots they lack to get a functioning route system are priced higher than the slots they can sell in return. In addition, trade in aftermarkets requires resources by itself.

Rassenti *et al.* (1982) instead proposed an auction system where airlines bid for packages of airport slots. These packages should be flight compatible so that the aftermarket becomes unnecessary. This means that the items indirectly are flights and not only individual slots. Rassenti *et al.* (1982) refers to experiments with this package auction system and found that it converges and is more efficient than the individual slot auction. Experiments indicate that the resulting primary market allocation tends to make aftermarkets unnecessary. Experience by the players increased the speed with which the process reaches an equilibrium. This auction system allows the airline to construct the product or network from the individual airport slots it obtains by bidding for the different packages.

Another possibility is a 'first choice' auction, where the winner has the right to choose any slot that is still available. Thus the airlines, in a sequence of auctions, can acquire slots that constitute routes and networks. One effect is, however, that prices paid for landing rights in specific slots may differ widely. Sequential auctions of the different slots in congested airports will give airlines more information as more auctions are performed, but earlier deals cannot be changed. It is well known that the allocations and prices are sensitive to the sequence used. Balinski and Sand (1985) propose repeated auctions instead. One starts off with conditional bids and the resulting aggregate demand for each slot is published. The airlines are conditionally awarded slots if their price offer is above the equilibrium price. The results indicate to each airline the demand pressure for the different slots and they may change their bids accordingly, taking their expected profit from the flight into account. The bidding is terminated when no airline wants to continue. Balinski and Sand (1985) comment that other stopping rules are necessary as there is no guarantee that the auction system will converge. This auction, typically, would not result in perfect equilibrium. In addition, demand facing the airline may change between auctions. Therefore, a continuous aftermarket should be open until the next auction.

The motivation for auctioning of airport slots is to find the airlines' willingness to pay for the capacity in the airport. This knowledge is of value to the authorities who must decide on the capacity, when investing in airports. Congested airports today are a limited problem in Sweden, but Scandinavian airlines face congestion problems on European routes. Changes in airline regulation that increases traffic may result in congestion on some domestic routes as well.

CONCLUSIONS

We have seen that the Swedish airline industry is highly concentrated. The major domestic city-pair markets are operated either by Scandinavian Airlines System (SAS) or Linjeflyg AB. Had they shared each city-pair market, they still could limit competition since Linjeflyg AB is affiliated to SAS, who has 50 per cent of the shares. The rest of the shares are held by the state – which also holds 50 per cent of the Swedish interests in SAS. This shows that entry regulation is associated by a high degree of concentration.

Air transport in Sweden is regulated in detail. Concessions specify maximum fares, capacity (both type of aircraft and frequency of flights) and safety measures. Thus, the strategic variables left to airlines in domestic transport are punctuality, discount structure, service quality and the general image of the firm. The airlines use yield management systems to increase their returns, but detailed regulations and maximum prices are set with the aim of limiting their exploitation of market power. But asymmetric information on demand and operating costs hampers regulation. Regulation by itself may be a source of inefficiency. When entry is regulated, airlines are not induced by competition to increase operating efficiency. Cross-subsidization between high- and low-density routes is part of that regulatory system. Generally, this is known to be a costly and inefficient way of supporting unprofitable markets.

Alternative routes operated by separate companies may restrict utilization of market power in specific city-pair markets and increase consumer welfare. But the Swedish domestic network of routes is a hub and spoke network with few alternative routes – and the two airlines operating the main routes are closely related. Other modes of transport, especially railroad and private car, are possible alternatives in some city-pair markets and may influence the suppliers of air transport services, so as to limit their market power.

In the brief discussion in the second part of this chapter, we tried to illustrate gains and problems by introducing auctions in distribution of concessions in the airline industry. A major gain is to limit the exercise of market power by airline companies. A positive effect of introducing auctions is that they give bidders incentives to reduce cost inefficiency. On the other hand, ranking of bids with different fare/frequency combinations may not be clear, since passengers will favour different combinations. The appropriate item to be auctioned off was discussed. This depends upon the conditions in the markets to be served. Independence between items poses problems. This indicates that auctions may be an interesting alternative first and foremost for smaller routes at the periphery of the networks. Auctioning off subsidized routes may minimize the support necessary to supply these routes. Congested airports pose problems in that auctioning of route concessions leaves the allocation of scarce airport capacity to the authorities, whereas auctioning of landing slots is complicated because of interdependence between allocating slots at different airports. But congested airports are less of a problem in the Swedish domestic air transport market than in Europe and in North American markets.

NOTES

* I wish to thank Geir B. Asheim, Yves Bourdet and Arnljot Strømme Svendsen for valuable comments to an earlier version.

1 Using domestic travel with national carriers as an indication of travel intensities poses problems, but as long as domestic transport is restricted to national carriers, passengers on domestic flights reported by these airlines should indicate traffic generated at home.
2 The source of all numbers of departures is *ABC World Airways Guide*, February 1987.
3 Whether airlines are natural monopolies is discussed in more detail in Strandenes (1987b).
4 The cabin factor measures occupied seats relative to total available seats on a flight.
5 This tax need not be proportional, but may be used to cross-subsidize between airports.
6 AB Aerotransport (ABA) in Sweden holds three-sevenths of SAS whereas Det Danske Luftfartsselskap (DDL) and Det Norske Luftfartsselskap (DNL) each hold two-sevenths.
7 Development was started in 1987 together with Iberia, Air France and Lufthansa. In 1988, Finnair, Air Inter, Braathens SAFE, Linjeflyg AB, Yugoslavian Airlines and Icelandair joined. The basis in the system is the American 'System One'.
8 SAS also holds 31 per cent in Bennett Reisebryå A/S, a Norwegian travel agency.
9 Accurate information on subsidiaries and affiliated firms is found in the

annual reports of SAS or DNL.
10 Effects of deregulation in the domestic market in the United States are discussed among others by Bailey *et al.* (1985), Meyer and Oster (1984), Morrison and Winston (1986) and Sletmo (1987).
11 For example, in September 1985 (SPK 1986, p. 43).
12 Estimates for Norway have been made both by Prisdirektoratet (1987) and Knudsen (1985).
13 Such reallocation of aircraft, of course, depends on the flexibility of the aircraft routing system set up by the airline, and the cost of repositioning aircraft.
14 For a more comprehensive discussion of the influence on airline competition of airport policy, see Strandenes (1987a).
15 Similar interdependence also exists with the other input markets. Some of the mergers in the US airline industry are thought to be based on lack of pilots and aircraft (Meyer *et al.*, 1981).
16 Waterson (1988) gives an introduction to questions of bidding schemes in regulation. McAfee and McMillan (1987) give a review of auctions and bidding.
17 The International Civil Aviation Organization (ICAO) reports fairly detailed cost and profitability data on the member airlines. ICAO (1985).
18 For a discussion, see Laffont and Tirole (1989).
19 But concessions are interdependent to the airlines even in this case, since the profits depend on the airlines' abilities to utilize aircraft and employed staff in their total network. A flight consists of both departing slot and landing slot and there are restrictions on the timing of the airport slots that must be made available.
20 La Guardia, Washington National, John F. Kennedy International and O'Hare International.

REFERENCES

Balinski, M.L. and Sand, F.M. (1985) 'Auctioning and landing rights at congested airports', in H. Peyton Young (ed.) *Cost Allocation: Methods, Principles, Applications*, Amsterdam: North-Holland.
Bailey, E.E. *et al.* (1985) *Deregulating the Airlines*, Cambridge, MA: MIT Press.
Demsetz, H. (1968) 'Why regulate utilities?', *Journal of Law and Economics*, 11, 55–66.
Det norske luftfartsselskap (DNL) (1989) *Annual Report 1988*, Oslo: DNL.
Grether, D., Isaac, M. and Plott, C. (1981) 'The allocation of landing rights by unanimity among competitors', *American Economic Review*, 71, 166–71.
ICAO (1985) *Financial Data. Commercial Carriers. Digest of Statistics* (yearly publication), Montreal: ICAO.
Knudsen, K. (1985) 'Mot en forbrukervennlig luftfartspolitikk', *Sosialøkonomen*, September 1985.
Laffont, J.-J. and Tirole, J. (1987) 'Auctioning incentive contracts', *Journal*

of Political Economy, 95, 921–37.
Laffont, J.-J. and Tirole, J. (1989) 'Repeated auctions and incentive contracts, investment, and bidding parity with an application to takeovers', *Rand Journal of Economics*, 19, 516–37.
Lommerud, K.E. (1989) 'Regulering av naturlige monopoler', Center for Applied Research, Bergen: Norwegian School of Economics and Business Administration.
McAfee, R.P. and McMillan, J. (1987) 'Auctions and bidding', *Journal of Economic Literature*, XXV, 699–738.
Meyer, J.R., Clinton, V., Oster, jnr., Morgan, I.P., Berman, B.A. and Strassman, D.L. (1981) *Airline Deregulation. The Early Experience*, Boston: Auburn House Publishing Company.
Meyer, J.R. and Oster, C.V. (1984) *Deregulation and the New Airline Entrepreneurs*, Cambridge, MA: MIT Press.
Morrison, S. and Winston, C. (1986) *The Economic Effects of Airborne Deregulation*, Washington DC: The Brookings Institution.
Norman, V.D. and Strandenes, S.P. (1990) 'Deregulating Scandinavian airlines: a case study of the Oslo–Stockholm route', CEPR discussion paper no. 403.
OECD (1988) *Deregulation and Airline Competition*, Paris: OECD.
Posner, R.A. (1975) 'The social costs of monopoly and regulation', *Journal of Political Economy*, vol. 81, 4, 807–27.
Prisdirektoratet (1987) 'Virkninger av økt konkurranse i innenriks luftfart', Notat no. 8, Marked og Konkurranse, Oslo: Prisdirektoratet.
Rassenti, S.J., Smith, V.L. and Bulfin, R.L. (1982) 'A combinational auction mechanism for airport time slot allocation', *Bell Journal of Economics*, 13, 402–17.
Riordan, M. and Sappington, D. (1987) 'Awarding monopoly franchises', *American Economic Review*, 77, 375–87.
Sletmo, G.K. (1987) 'The US Airline Deregulation Act of 1978 – its background and results', Center for Applied Research, Bergen: Norwegian School of Economics and Business Adminstration.
Statens Pris- och Kartellnämd (SPK) (1986) *Regulering på transportområdet. Behovet av ökad konkurrens*. SPK's PM serie 1986:17, Stockholm: SPK.
Strandenes, S.P. (1987a) 'Airport policy and airline competition', Center for Applied Research, Bergen: Norwegian School of Economics and Business Administration.
Strandenes, S.P. (1987b) 'Scandinavian airline industry: market structure and competition', Center for Applied Research, Bergen: Norwegian School of Economics and Business Administration.
Vickrey, W. (1972) 'Airline overbooking: some further solutions', *Journal of Transport Economics and Policy*, VI, 257–83.
Waterson, M. (1988) *Regulation of the Firm and Natural Monopoly*, Oxford: Blackwell.
Williamson, O.E. (1976) 'Franchise bidding for natural monopolies – are general and with respect to CATV', *Bell Journal of Economics*, 7, 55–65.

Part V

Competition policy, market power and economic efficiency

10 Policy toward market power and restrictive practices*

Yves Bourdet

> The concerns of competition policy must change to
> take account of the evolution of the competitive
> process.
>
> K.D. George and C.L. Joll[1]

INTRODUCTION

The main purpose of this chapter is to analyse the evolution and logic of Swedish competition policy. As far as consumer welfare is concerned, competition policy plays a crucial role. Actually it can be regarded as a form of voice, the aim of which is to favour competition and protect consumer welfare.[2] This form of protection may be especially decisive in those markets which are characterized by the presence of barriers to exit for consumers and which therefore are likely to develop non-competitive behaviour. On a priori grounds, such markets may be, for example, composed of only a small number of firms on the supply side or sheltered from international competition by high transport costs or the presence of some sort of barriers to trade. The non- or limited availability of the exit option makes the voice option the dominant way of maintaining competitive pressures on domestic firms and of curbing market power in these markets. On the other hand, competition policy and voice may be of little use in markets subject to international competition because of the availability of the exit option. The analysis of competition policy in a widely open economy like the Swedish one should undoubtedly shed some light on this issue. Answers to these questions are interesting, not only for the Swedish public, but also for small open economies. They are also of interest, for example, to the United States, where the role of competition policy has long been debated both in academic and policy circles and where it is often suggested nowadays that antitrust policy has lost its *raison d'être* because of the growing openness of the US economy.

The organization of this chapter is as follows. A first part briefly presents the Swedish legislation on restrictive practices and mergers.

299

Particular emphasis is put on the evolution of the legislation over time and on the respective place of conduct and structural considerations in it. A second part is devoted to the enforcement of the antitrust legislation in Sweden over the past two-and-a-half decades. Emphasis is laid on the practices of the enforcement authorities, on the forms taken by corporate restrictive practices and by mergers (or takeovers), and on their evolution over time. In this respect, two main issues are given particular attention. The first is whether the number of cases brought has increased, in relative as well as in absolute terms, over time. The second is whether the distribution of cases brought has changed during the same period. A third part concentrates on the logic of Swedish competition policy. It attempts to find the factors that have affected the intensity and the distribution of restrictive practices in Sweden. Among these, the most likely, on a priori grounds, are changing general economic conditions, the growing openness of the Swedish economy (in terms of real as well as potential competition), the fear of competition policy and changes in antitrust legislation. Another issue examined in the third part is whether the way competition policy is enforced can be explained by public choice arguments: does the enforcement agency select the cases that require most investigation and thus maximize its budget? Are there other factors behind the policy of the enforcement agency?

In the final section, an attempt is made to see whether the competition policy implemented over the past two decades in Sweden has succeeded in curbing market power and in protecting consumer welfare. No doubt an answer to this question, even if tentative, should shed some light on the effectiveness of the voice option in dealing with various forms of threat to competition.

THE SWEDISH ANTITRUST DOCTRINE

Two legislative areas are concerned with competition policy: laws against restrictive business practices and laws on mergers and takeovers.[3] The first aims to regulate non-competitive market conduct while the purpose of the second is to preserve 'competitive' market structures. The relative role of these laws in overall competition policy varies from country to country and over time. In the words of Alexis Jacquemin 'the antitrust policies pursued by industrial countries vary mainly in the emphasis laid on the roles of structure, conduct and performance, as criteria for determining the existence of monopoly power or for enforcing remedial measures'.[4]

The largest variation is to be found between the west European countries and the United States, where structural aspects are given much broader scope.[5] By and large, the Swedish legislation has placed emphasis on market conduct while it has devoted a minor role to structural aspects and has ignored performance. This seems to be broadly the case in most relatively small open west European economies. The economic philosophy behind such legislation is straightforward: market power is not regarded as a structural concept; its existence can only be proved by its exercise, i.e. by the appearance of non-competitive business practices.

Another variation in the competition laws between countries is the relative role of the rule of reason and the *per se* rule.[6] Under the former, competition authorities consider not only the restraint of trade, but also the reasons behind it as well as its effects on the competitive process and the public interest. Under the latter, on the other hand, competition authorities need only prove the existence of business practices, such as price fixing or market sharing, that are prohibited by legislation. Here, too, the largest range of variation is to be found between the United States, where the scope of the *per se* rule is large, and western Europe, where only limited legislative areas are inspired by the *per se* rule.[7] As will be seen, Sweden is no exception in this respect. Except for two restrictive practices, which are subject to the *per se* principle, the Swedish competition laws embody a case-by-case approach, where each situation is judged on its own merits.

The first legislation against restrictive trade practices in Sweden was enacted in 1925.[8] It was replaced by new legislation in 1946 that gave the government the power to investigate corporate restrictive practices. A striking feature of this legislation was the absence of sanctions at the disposal of the government. No fines could be imposed on firms involved in restrictive practices with harmful effects and no legislative provision existed that gave competition authorities the power to force firms to terminate restrictive practices agreements. Making information about these firms and their behaviour public was considered sufficient to convince them to respect the legislation and to adopt the competitive straitjacket.[9]

A new law was passed in 1953, the purpose of which was to prevent corporate practices not compatible with the public interest.[10] This law, which was amended in 1956, was in force until the beginning of the 1980s. It forbade a certain number of business conspiracies in restraint of trade that were considered to result in harmful effects. They occur either at a single stage of production or distribution, i.e. horizontally, or between different stages, i.e. vertically. Examples of such practices are price-fixing agreements, vertical restraints, predatory pricing, joint co-operation in tendering bids, price discrimination, excessively high prices, resale price maintenance and exclusive distribution agreements. Only two of these practices, resale price maintenance and joint co-operation in tendering bids, were regarded as criminal offences and brought with them fines.[11] Both restraints of trade were a matter for civil courts under the 1953 competition law. The concept of harmful effects was central to the 1953–6 legislation. It referred to situations where corporate restrictive practices unduly affected prices, restrained efficiency in business or impeded the competitive process by, for example, raising barriers to entry.[12] Note that the 1925 as well as the 1953 legislation did not prohibit restrictive practices *per se* but restrictive practices having harmful effects, except for the two above-mentioned criminal offences. Consideration was given to effects of collusion for good or ill.

A new Restrictive Trade Practices Act was adopted by the Swedish parliament in 1982 and entered into force on 1 January 1983.[13] The same rule of reason inspired it. The concept of harmful effects and the non-prohibition of restrictive practices not having harmful effects central to the 1953 legislation were carried through unchanged to the new Act.[14] Note, however, that the new legislation, by giving more attention to the interests of consumers, seems to put more emphasis on the protection of competition than on the protection of competitors. The same two restraints of trade, resale price maintenance and joint co-operation in tendering bids, are still considered criminal offences. Inspired by the recommendations of the Competition Commission, the new law advocated adding two additional practices to these two offences, namely price and market sharing agreements, and the setting of penalties for firms violating their prohibition.[15] These recommendations, which would have expanded the scope of the *per se* rule in Swedish competition policy were, however, rejected by the government and thus were not included in the new competition law. Another important change concerns the greater enforcement power given to the antitrust authorities, i.e. the Competition Commissioner and the Restrictive Practices Court.[16] The fact that the court could now force firms to terminate a restrictive agreement illustrates this change. This was further confirmed by the increased resources in terms of personnel allocated to the Competition Commissioner (from twenty to thirty staff members) and to the Restrictive

Practices Court (three new laymen) since the new law came into force in 1983.[17]

The new legislation also contained rules concerning merger control. This was a major development, since the 1953 legislation had not contained merger provisions in the strict sense of the word. Mergers could be examined, however, by the Competition Commissioner if they were expected to lead to harmful effects. In such cases, they were regarded as a form of restrictive practices. Thus, until 1982, there was no merger law in Sweden except for mergers involving foreign firms. But there existed fiscal incentives (tax exemptions) for merging firms.[18] The lack of a structural approach to market power in the Swedish antitrust policy was probably the result of the favourable climate to mergers that existed among politicians, trade unionists and most people[19] and of the competitive pressures that the high degree of trade exposure of the Swedish economy imposed on domestic firms. The efficiency effects of mergers were considered greater than their uncertain detrimental anti-competitive effects. It should be added that a long history of absence of merger control is not specific to Sweden. It is found in most other industrial countries as well. Before 1972, only four OECD countries – Canada, Japan, the United Kingdom and the United States – were equipped with legislative provisions to control merger activity.[20]

The new Swedish law concerns mergers that give the firms involved a dominant position in a market, or strengthen an already dominant position, and result in harmful effects.[21] The rule of reason inspires the legislation: the dominant position is not prohibited *per se* but only if it is against the public interest. There are provisions for exemption when the potential cost savings of a merger are larger than the monopoly dangers. A firm can be said to reach a dominant position when it enjoys such a large part of the market that it can, if it so wishes, restrict competition and abuse its position. The new law also provides a geographical and product defintion of a market, which is necessary to determine the products to be included in the market considered and the influence of the merger on competitive conditions: the output of the merging firms together with its good substitutes constitutes the output of the relevant market.[22] If the merger, or planned merger, is expected to be against the public interest, it is taken to the Restrictive Practices Court by the Competition Commissioner. The court is to remedy the merger's harmful effects through negotiations. If no agreement is reached between the parties involved, the court can forbid the merger.[23] However, the prohibition will come into force only if the government confirms the decision of the Restrictive Practices Court.

To conclude this overview, note that there is no provision in the new Swedish legislation for the dissolution of existing concentrations, even if these are found to have harmful effects and to be against the public interest, although a proposal in this direction was made by the 1978 Competition Commission, whose recommendations served as a basis for the new legislation.[24]

THE ENFORCEMENT OF THE SWEDISH COMPETITION POLICY

What the legislation on competition policy looks like is an issue which concerns mainly lawyers. For economists, a more important issue is the way this legislation is enforced in practice. Before turning to this issue, let us briefly introduce the authorities entrusted with the responsibility of enforcing Swedish competition policy.

Enforcers

There are three antitrust authorities in Sweden: the National Price and Cartel Board, the Competition Commissioner and the Restrictive Practices Court or Market Court.[25] The National Price and Cartel Board (statens pris- och kartellnämnd) was created in 1956. Its main task is to supervise changes in prices, to provide information on these changes to the general public and to keep registers on restrictive practices and mergers.[26] (The Swedish legislation requires registration of all agreements between two or more parties relating to prices to be charged, firms or geographical areas to be supplied, quantities to be supplied and conditions on which products are to be sold.) Another major task of the Board is to analyse the workings of competition in real world markets. Except for the banking and insurance sectors, which are a matter for other authorities, the Board selects on its own the markets to be investigated.[27] However, some of the inquiries are made at the instigation of the Competition Commissioner or the government, if there arises a presumption that competition is restricted in a market. New instructions given by the government in 1986 concern the analysis of the formation of prices in various markets and of the influence of public regulations on prices and competition.[28] This somewhat new orientation was further strengthened on 1 October 1988 when the Board received new government instructions and a new name, the National Price and Competition Board (statens pris-och konkurrensverk). According to these new instructions, more attention should be paid to the analysis of competitive conditions in goods and service markets, to the influence of public regulations or practices on these conditions and to the impact and workings of international competition.[29] Changes in the distribution of resources within the Board have been made to implement these new directives.[30] Finally, it should be stressed that the Board has no power to prohibit mergers or to take any action against restrictive practices.

The Competition Commissioner (näringsfrihetsombudsmannen) is an independent lawyer who acts as public prosecutor. His resources are limited, since his staff is composed of only thirty employees (twenty prior to 1983). The staff is divided into five investigative departments dealing with different economic sectors. The Commissioner selects certain corporate practices on his own initiative or as a result of complaints made by private parties, principally firms, and he initiates restrictive practice proceedings.[31] His own selection is made on the basis of the register of the National Price and Competition Board or of information chiefly collected in the media. If the corporate practices examined are found to have harmful effects and thus not be compatible with the antitrust legislation, the Commissioner will invite the firms concerned to terminate these practices and to adopt a competitive behaviour. (A negotiated solution is reached in the great majority of the cases investigated by the Commissioner.) If the recommendations of the Commissioner are rejected by the firms involved in the alleged business conspiracies, the case is brought before the Restrictive Practices Court for a decision. Very few cases are brought to court (some 1 per cent of the cases investigated each year), suggesting that the Competition Commissioner is the main authority in charge of the enforcement of the antitrust policy in Sweden.

The Restrictive Practices Court (marknadsdomstolen) is a special court dealing with, amongst other things, antitrust cases. The court is serviced by judges and by laymen representing business and consumer interests. Negotiations between the firms involved and the court is the first step when a case is taken to court. If the negotiations fail, the Restrictive Practices Court can issue an injunction restraining the firm(s) concerned. The decisions of the court are final, except for merger cases.

The cases examined: number, origin and outcome

As indicated by Table 10.1, the number of cases reported to the Competition Commissioner has increased rapidly over time, especially between the 1960s and the 1970s, when the number doubled. This increase does not mean, however, that restrictive practices cases are more common now than two-and-a-half decades ago, since the size of the economy and the number of business transactions have increased as well. A kind of 'deflator' is needed to estimate real changes in restrictive practices intensity. In the last row of Table 10.1 the number of cases examined by the Competition Commissioner has been 'deflated' by the real gross domestic product. Although much less pronounced, the increase in the number of cases is sizeable, especially between the 1960s and the 1970s. This increase concerns, in particular, cases selected by the Commissioner on the basis of information in the media, the number of which multiplied by three-and-a-half.

Table 10.1 Number of cases examined by the Competition Commissioner, 1960–87

	Average per year during period		
	1960–9	*1970–9*	*1980–7*
At the initiative of the Competition Commissioner	39	123	153
(in % of total cases)	(25)	(38)	(35)
Of which: on the basis of			
1 the register of the Price and Cartel Board	16	37	29
(in % of total cases)	(10)	(11)	(7)
2 information in the media	23	86	123
(in % of total cases)	(15)	(27)	(28)
As a result of complaints made by private parties[a]	117	200	290
(in % of total cases)	(75)	(62)	(65)
Total	156	323	443
Total 'deflated' by GDP	125	186	222

Sources: Computed from SPK (1970), (1978a), (1981a), (1984b); NO (1988a); GDP figures: OECD (various years).
Notes: [a] These figures over-estimate the number of private complaints because they include what can be considered inquiries rather than real complaints (some 20–25 per cent of the private complaints may be inquiries). The reason for including the latter is that both complaints and inquiries belong to the same item in the records of the Competition Commissioner since 1982.

Table 10.1 also shows that the majority of the cases were examined by the Competition Commissioner as a result of complaints made by private parties. However, the proportion of cases selected by the Competition Commissioner on his own initiative has increased over time, especially between the 1960s and the 1970s. In this respect, a striking feature is the rapid relative decrease in the number of cases selected by the Competition Commissioner on the basis of information in the register of the National Price and Cartel Board and the parallel increase in the number of cases selected on the basis of information collected in the media. No doubt this development reflects the decreasing role of the register as a source of information on restrictive practices for the conduct of competition policy in Sweden. The slight decrease in the proportion of cases selected by the Commissioner on his own initiative during the 1980s – from 38 to 35 per cent – reflects the more rapid increase in the number of complaints made by private parties over the past decade.

In many of the cases reported to the Competition Commissioner, restrictive practices cannot be established. After a first rapid investigation, many of the cases are abandoned either because the Commissioner cannot prove that they constitute restrictive practices having harmful effects or because the competition laws cannot be applied. Not surprisingly, it is among the cases referred to the Commissioner by private parties that one finds the largest proportion of cases abandoned after a first, rapid investigation. Surprisingly, the Commissioner dismissed 22 to 38 per cent of the cases brought by his own staff. (This figure has increased over the past decade.) Table 10.2 indicates that, between 1954 and 1981, between 31 and 42 per cent of the cases examined as a result of private complaints were abandoned after a first check by the Commissioner because no harmful effects could be found, while only 25–38 per cent and 22–30 per cent of the cases selected by the Commissioner himself on the basis of the Cartel register and information in the media respectively met with the same fate. This result is not surprising in view of the fact that the competition authorities are better informed about the content of the competition laws and the meaning of restraints of trade. The great majority of cases were cleared up without formal decisions. This applies especially to the cases selected by the Competition Commissioner, where the offending behaviour was eliminated through negotiations in some 60 per cent of the cases considered. As regards the private complaints, the parties involved undertook not to continue to operate restrictive agreements contrary to the public interest in only some 33–36 per cent of the cases that came up for examination by the Commissioner. Note that in most of the cases competition was restored without a contest on the part of the firms guilty of restraints of trade. A last striking result of Table 10.2 concerns the low and decreasing percentage of cases brought before the Restrictive Practices Court.[32]

Table 10.2 Distribution of cases examined by kind of outcome, 1954–87

	Average per year during period (%)		
Origin of information	*1954–69*	*1970–5*	*1976–81*[a]
Cartel register			
(a) Competition restored	65	64	58
(b) No harmful effect found	25	29	38
(c) Further investigation	5	1	3
(d) Brought to court	4	5	1
Media			
(a) Competition restored	47[b]	58	59
(b) No harmful effect found	22[b]	22	30
(c) Commissioner statement	12[b]	15	4
(d) Further investigation	19[b]	6	6
(e) Brought to court	2[b]	0	1
Private complaints			
(a) Competition restored	36	35	33
(b) Complaint withdrawn	14	8	7
(c) No harmful effect found	31	37	42
(d) Further investigation	5	5	6
(e) Competition laws not applicable	9	13	10
(f) Brought to court	4	3	2

Sources: Computed from SPK (1977), NO (1982) and (1988a).
Notes: [a] Since 1982 no difference is made in the records of the Competition Commissioner between the origin of information. Between 1982 and 1987 and for all the cases examined, the distribution is as follows: (i) competition restored: 34%; (ii) complaint withdrawn: 5%; (iii) no harmful effect found: 40%; (iv) commissioner's statement: 15%; (v) competition laws not applicable: 5%; (vi) brought to court: 1%.
[b] 1967–9 only.

The mix of cases

Another interesting aspect of the enforcement policy concerns the distribution of cases examined by type of restrictive practice. No systematic record is kept by the Competition Commissioner. However, the register of restrictive practice cases filed between 1970 and 1987 and appearing in the review of the National Price and Competition Board provides a valuable source of information on this distribution. Table 10.3 presents the main trade arrangements studied by the Commissioner and the number of cases brought to the Restrictive Practices Court. It shows that vertical restraints and horizontal price-fixing agreements clearly are the most common, followed in order of importance by mergers, various forms of barriers to entry, market sharing, price discrimination and predatory pricing. Except for vertical restraints, the number of cases brought to the court are few, confirming that in most cases the Competition Commissioner reaches an agreement through negotiations with the firms involved in restrictive practices. Some fifty cases concerned with the two restrictive practices that are explicitly prohibited by the law, i.e. bidding cartels and resale price maintenance, have been detected during the period 1970–87. Of this total, fourteen were

Table 10.3 Restrictive practices examined by the Competition Commissioner and the market court, reported in the review of the competition authorities, 1970–87

Practice	No. of cases investigated by the Commissioner	Court decisions
Vertical restraint	150	15
Price-fixing agreement	107	2
Mergers and takeovers	64	1
Entry barriers or control	45	3
Market sharing	42	0
Predatory pricing	38	1
Discriminatory pricing	37	2
Public regulation and discriminatory public information	35	0
Joint co-operation in tendering bids	33	8[a]
Resale price maintenance	31	6[b]
Monopoly pricing	20	3
Non-price discrimination	17	1
Ancillary covenant against competition	16	2
Joint selling venture	16	1
Excessively high pricing	16	0
Boycott	9	1
Exchange of price information	9	0
Buyer co-operative agreement	9	0
Discount	3	0

Sources: Computed from SPK (1986a) and NO (1988b).
Notes: [a] Six cases were brought to the civil court; [b] fourteen cases were brought to the civil court.

brought to the Restrictive Practices Court and twenty to the civil court. Assuming that the cases filed in Table 10.3 are representative of the cases examined by the Competition Commissioner, this means that the *per se* rule has applied to some 9 per cent of the restraints of trade.

As already stated, one of the sources of information used by the Competition Commissioner is the register kept by the National Price and Competition Board. On request from the Board, firms are legally obliged to register every agreement which contains restrictions on prices, quantities or quality of goods traded or on channels of distribution. The development of the number of registered restrictive practices agreements is given in the last column of Table 10.4. It shows that the number of new agreements registered each year decreased at the beginning of the 1970s and increased somewhat during the second half of the 1970s and increased sharply over the past five years.

Two interesting aspects of the enforcement policy concern the distribution of cases, i.e. the mix of restrictive practices examined by the Competition Commissioner and its evolution over time. The records of the Competition Commissioner provide insufficient information in both these respects. Nevertheless, there exist two sources that provide an idea of the distribution of cases and, for one of them, of its evolution over time. The cases considered in Table 10.3 is one of them. The other is the register of the National Price and Competition Board (Table 10.4). It is worth stressing that these figures should be considered with some care because they may not reflect the distribution of restrictive practices in the economy or the one emerging from the Competition Commissioner's enforcement policy, mainly because they ignore informal and tacit agreements. Table 10.4 shows that the most common restrictive practices registered are ancillary covenant against competition[33] and exclusive distribution agreements followed in order of importance by market sharing, price fixing and joint selling, buying or production ventures. A comparison of Tables 10.3 and 10.4 is difficult to make because of the different classifications that have been adopted. Nevertheless, vertical restraints and exclusive dealings, price fixing and market sharing appear to be common restraints of trade in both cases. The register of the Competition Board, on the other hand, exhibits a much larger proportion of ancillary covenants against competition.

Table 10.4 also shows that the mix of restrictive practices registered has changed over the past two-and-a-half decades. The

Table 10.4 Distribution of new agreements registered by the National Price and Cartel Board by kind of restrictive practices, 1947–87

Period	Market sharing (%)	Exclusive dealing (%)	Price fixing (%)	Ancillary convenant[a] (%)	Joint agreement[b] (%)	Others (%)	Average per year
1947–71[c]	12	14	37	27	8	3	116[d]
1971–4	14	10	23	44	9	1	84
1975–8	16	33	12	29	6	4	94
1979–82	16	30	7	40	7	0	98
1983–7	14	28	9	42	6	1	162
Average 1971–87	15	25	13	39	7	1.5	112

Sources: Computed from SPK (1971) and SPK, *Konkurrensbegränsande avtal* (1971–88).
Notes: [a] Agreement among firms not to compete with each other in a particular geographical area or line of business or during a certain period of time; [b] joint selling or buying agreements and joint ventures; [c] agreements registered over the period 1947–71 and still in force on 1 March 1971; [d] average number of new agreements registered per year over the period 1947–71.

two most striking changes are the sharp increase in vertical restraints and the rapid decrease in registered price-fixing agreements. The decrease in the number of price-fixing agreements is still more pronounced if the figures for 1947–71 are considered (see Table 10.4). As regards the other forms of restrictive practices, Table 10.4 indicates that their share has remained more or less constant over the past seventeen years.

Merger policy

A last area of intervention for competition policy concerns merger policy. As mentioned above, there existed no merger law in the strict sense of the word before 1983. However, the Competition Commissioner could examine mergers that were expected to lead to restrictive practices.[34] Despite this possibility, it was not until 1971 that the Commissioner investigated a merger.[35] No systematic register of the mergers examined is available. There exists, nevertheless, a certain number of indications regarding the extent of the activity of the Competition Commissioner with respect to mergers. Between 1971 and 1980, some forty mergers were investigated, half of them in 1980.[36] Table 10.3, on the other hand, indicates that the sixty-four mergers investigated by the Commissioner were reported in the review of the competition authorities. Since the new legislation entered into force in 1983, the number of mergers examined by the Competition Commissioner seems to have increased. In 1986 and 1987, for example, some 140 mergers were subject to some form of investigation by the Competition Commissioner.[37] The register of the mergers referred to in the review of the competition authorities provides further information. It suggests that the number of mergers investigated increased sharply in 1982 and 1983 and has decreased somewhat since then.[38] Most of the mergers investigated have been of the horizontal type.[39] Only a few conglomerate mergers have been considered and almost no vertical ones. The mergers investigated are selected by the Commissioner on his own. The information necessary to the investigation is collected by the Commissioner's staff members mainly from the National Price and Competition Board, merging firms, competitors, retailers, buyers or individuals with a justified interest in a specific case.[40] The firms concerned are obliged to furnish the required information.

The decision of the Competition Commissioner is based on an analysis of the effects of the merger. The rule of reason guides this analysis: the potential cost savings – and other perceived advantages

– are weighted against the monopoly dangers. In this respect, the new law has not introduced any change. The main aspects considered by the Commissioner in his investigation are:[41]

1 The impact on competition, i.e. whether the merger leads to a dominant position. Here attention is given to import competition, potential competition from domestic as well as foreign competitors, the existence or not of substitute products and the risks of monopoly and discriminatory pricing that the merger may bring about.
2 The expected effects on X-efficiency as well as technical efficiency and whether the merger permits the exploitation of large economies of scale and, hence, could result in lower average costs.
3 The effects of the merger on employment, in particular, whether the merger in question will help rescue employment in a failing firm.[42]

In the great majority of cases investigated, an agreement has been reached between the firms involved and the Competition Commissioner to remedy the expected harmful effects of the merger. In very few cases, the Commissioner has recommended a prohibition of the merger and taken the case further to the Restrictive Practices Court. Between 1971 and 1982, i.e. under the 1953 competition law, this only happened with two mergers. It is interesting to note that both these mergers eventually took place despite the opposition of the Commissioner. The government authorized one of those regarding two cement manufacturers, Cementa and AB Gullhögens Bruk, on the grounds that the expected efficiency effects of the merger were likely to be larger than the monopoly dangers.[43] After lengthy investigations and negotiations[44] the second one, between the two meat producers Slakteriförbundet and Samfod, was permitted to proceed provided that the overtaken firm, Samfod, maintain an independent distribution network.[45] Since the new law came into force in 1983, legal proceedings have been instigated in only three cases (two in 1986 and one in 1987).[46] In two of them, the recommendations of the Commissioner were accepted by the court and the firms involved. In one case, however, the decision taken by the court differed from the recommendation of the Competition Commissioner, which had advocated the prohibition of the merger.[47] A merger between two paint manufacturers, Alcro-Beckers and Alfort & Cronholms, was not considered to lead to a dominant position having harmful effects and, thus, was authorized by the

Restrictive Practices Court.[48] Two main arguments were put forward by the court for not prohibiting the merger.[49] First, the market share of the newly formed firm, 45–50 per cent of the consumer paint market, was not considered sufficient *per se* to reach a dominant position having harmful effects. Second, after the merger there would still be scope in this market for actual as well as potential competition from domestic and foreign producers.

Previously, we have used the number and the distribution of concerted practices cases investigated as well as the policy toward mergers to illustrate the way competition policy has been enforced in Sweden. It was argued that the Swedish policy has mostly intervened at the conduct stage and mainly prohibited certain anti-competitive business practices. This emphasis on the regulation of behaviour is not surprising in view of the greater emphasis placed on market conduct in the Swedish legislation. The new merger law has not enlarged the scope for structural considerations in competition policy. A second result has been the very limited scope of the *per se* rule in the enforcement of competition policy. A third result has been the paramount role of the Commissioner in enforcing competition policy. A fourth observation is that very few cases have been taken to court. This reflects the Commissioner's view that a more conciliatory policy of negotiating with firms who have violated the restrictive practices legislation will bring more positive effects for society than would court proceedings.

THE LOGIC OF COMPETITION POLICY

Once the changes in the number and the distribution of restrictive practices examined have been portrayed, one has to examine the underlying factors. There exist two main types of factors. First, we may expect changes in the intensity and the distribution of restrictive practices examined by the enforcement agency to be the result of changes in the number and the nature of restrictive arrangements between firms in the economy. Thus, factors that explain the latter also explain the former. Second, changes in the intensity and the distribution of restrictive practices examined can be the result of changes in the policy of the enforcement agency itself. Unfortunately, the overly aggregated nature of the available data on restrictive practices intensity by kind of economic activity does not allow us to perform any econometric test to disentangle the various explanatory factors. Thus, the discussion should only be seen as an indication of probable explanations, not of their order of magnitude.[50]

Restrictive practices intensity

One of the first concerns will be changes in the number of cases examined by the Competition Commissioner. This number, which gives a fair measure of the intensity of restrictive practices investigated, has increased rapidly over time, especially during the 1970s (Tables 10.1 and 10.5). In Table 10.1, (p. 306), it was shown that this number has increased in relative terms as well, albeit at a slower pace. Over the past five years, however, the trend seems to have been reversed and the number of cases investigated has dropped sharply from their 1983 peak value (Table 10.5). What, then, are the factors behind these changes? We will start by looking at the first type of factors, i.e. those that are likely to affect the concerted practices activities in the Swedish economy.

Table 10.5 Restrictive practices intensity and gross domestic product, 1960–87

	Average per year during period (%)		
	1960–70	*1970–83*	*1983–7*
Changes in the intensity of restrictive practices examined	3.8	6.9	−7.7
Changes in gross domestic product	4.5	1.7	2.6
Trade exposure			
(i) import competition[a]	27.4	34.7	38.3
(ii) export involvement[b]	20.5	25.8	29.4

Sources: Restrictive practices examined: see Table 10.1; GDP: OECD; Import and export figures: SCB (Statistics Sweden).
Notes: [a] Imports divided by domestic consumption; [b] exports divided by gross national product.

Growth patterns

A first probable factor is the general economic conditions and the shifting of demand over the business cycle. A high rate of growth of demand fosters competition and technical changes. It plays a destabilizing role in existing restrictive business agreements since it requires changes and exposes differences in preferred prices. The latter occur as a result of differences in costs that in turn are due to differences in the technology chosen by the firms, differences in the size of firms, differences in factor combinations in production, differences in the quality of management or in location.[51] In view of this, it is likely that the rapid growth rates of demand between the Second World War and the very beginning of the 1970s tended to keep down the intensity of restrictive practices in industrial countries. On the other hand, stagnating markets or slowly growing markets tend to affect firms' willingness to enter into some form of collusive agreement in the opposite direction. In such markets, every small price cut by a firm encroaches upon the sales of competitors in absolute terms, while it only leads to a limited fall in the relative market share of competitors in expanding markets. Stagnating markets make firms more aware of their interdependency and create an incentive for them to restrict supply and price competition. This is especially so for markets that consist of few firms and where some kind of barrier to entry limits the extent of potential competition. Demand and supply of concerted practices are indeed confined to particular circumstances and branches of the economy.

On these grounds, we may expect the slowdown of economic growth since the beginning of the 1970s to have encouraged restrictive practices activities. Presumably the slight increase in concentration noted during the first half of the 1970s has strengthened this tendency by making firms more aware of their interdependency.[52] The hypothesis about the impact of general economic conditions on concerted practices intensity can be examined by help of Table 10.5. As far as the rate of economic growth is concerned, there are three sub-periods with rather different patterns. During the first, between 1960 and 1970, the Swedish economy grew quickly and the number of restrictive practices examined by the Competition Commissioner increased more slowly than the rate of growth of the gross national product. This is roughly what we would expect on the basis of what we said above. During the second sub-period, between 1970 and 1983, restrictive practices intensity rose very rapidly, four times quicker than GDP. This is also in line with the above hypothesis, since the Swedish economy was experiencing slow growth and stagnating markets during this period. Finally, the number of restraints of trade examined has dropped sharply over the past four years when Swedish economic growth has increased rather rapidly. Taken together, all this suggests that general economic conditions provide a fair explanation for the changes in the intensity of restrictive practices investigated over the past two-and-a-half decades.

Trade exposure

On a priori grounds, a second likely factor is the degree of openness of the Swedish economy. The liberalization of trade since the 1950s and the growing integration of the Swedish economy in the world economy mean that the exit option for consumers dissatisfied with the price/quality of domestic products is more available nowadays. These consumers can buy imported products. The very existence of the exit option has undoubtedly put competitive pressure on domestic firms. They will be less willing to engage in some form of restrictive agreements because concerted practices intended to avoid or suppress competition are not very likely to be successful in open economies. (It is assumed that competition prevails on the import side and that no collusive practices take place between importing and domestic firms.) Table 10.5 provides figures on changes in the degree of import competition. At first sight, growing openness does not seem to have had any effect. Except for the past five years, restrictive practices activity as measured by the number of cases examined has experienced an upward trend although one would have expected a downward trend as a result of growing competition from imports.

The increase in import competition experienced during the 1970s is mainly the result of increasing oil prices, which hardly resulted in new competitive pressures on domestic firms. This may explain the absence of any effect of increasing import competition on restrictive practices intensity. On the other hand, the increase in import competition observed over the past five years might have increased competitive pressures on domestic firms because it took place while the price of oil dropped drastically. This may provide a complementary explanation for the rapid decrease in the number of restrictive practices investigated during the same sub-period (see Table 10.5).

Before turning to the next plausible explanatory factor, it should be pointed out that the import–consumption ratio only imperfectly reflects changes in the extent of competitive pressures, since it ignores potential competition. This is a serious shortcoming because potential competition has increased sharply over the past two-and-a-half decades due to the drastic drop in tariff protection and, to a much lesser extent, to non-tariff protection in the wake of (1) the formation of EFTA in the 1960s (2) the Kennedy Round at the very end of the 1960s and beginning of the 1970s (3) the formation of an enlarged free trade area in western Europe during the second half of the 1970s and (4) the Tokyo Round during the first half of the 1980s.

Foreign trade can influence restrictive practices activity in another way. Assuming that export firms cannot discriminate between the domestic and foreign markets, increasing participation in world trade tends to dilute market power on the domestic market. The larger the export involvement of domestic firms the more difficult it is for them to avoid the competitive straitjacket on their home market.[53] The reason for this is that competitive prices prevail in the world market and that discrimination is not possible because no barriers to arbitrage-induced reimports exist. Very little support is, however, provided for this hypothesis by the changes in the export–GDP ratio for the past two-and-a-half decades (see Table 10.5). There is a fair increase in the export involvement of the Swedish economy over the past two-and-a-half decades but, except for the past five years, this increase does not seem to have influenced restrictive practices enforcement intensity on the domestic market. That intensity has experienced an upward trend as well.

It may be that the increased trade exposure of the Swedish economy has prevented business conspiracies from being more numerous. Or it may be that our figures on restrictive practices intensity are too aggregated to highlight the impact of trade exposure. Another way to test the above hypothesis is to see whether the sectors with the highest practices intensity are the sectors that are most sheltered from international competition. Table 10.6 gives the number of registered restrictive arrangements by economic sector, as they are compiled in the register of the National Price and Competition Board. It shows that there were only two sectors of the economy free from such agreements, mining and electricity, gas and water. Restraints of trade are most common in wholesale and retail trade followed in order of importance by construction, services, manufacture of chemical and plastic products, machinery, manufacture of non-metallic mineral products and fabricated metal products. This data provides some support to the above hypothesis because the first three sectors, wholesale and retail trade, construction, and services, are sheltered from international competition.

Table 10.6 also gives figures on restrictive practices intensity that take into account the size of the economic sectors considered. These figures modify the picture that emerges from the unweighted figures. Six sectors exhibit a restrictive practices intensity that is equal to or greater than ten: manufacture of non-metallic mineral products, wholesale and retail trade, manufacture of chemical and plastic products, fabricated metal products, manufacture of food, bever-

Table 10.6 Registered restrictive practices by kind of economic activity, 1971–87

Activity	No. of restrictive practices	Restrictive practices intensity[a]
Mining	0	0
Manufacture of food, beverages and tobacco	130	9.6
Textile, wearing apparel and leather industries	31	8.3
Manufacture of wood and wood products	83	9.5
Manufacture of paper and paper products, printing and publishing	85	4.6
Manufacture of chemicals and plastic products	154	12.4
Manufacture of non-metallic mineral products except products of petroleum and coal	140	32.5
Basic metal industries	40	5.3
Fabricated metal products	136	11.1
Machinery	152	7.9
Electrical machinery	39	2.6
Transportation equipment	22	1.1
Electricity, gas and water	0	0
Construction	198	4.4
Wholesale and retail trade	877	14.5
Transport	71	2.7
Services including hotels and restaurants	170	8.1

Sources: Computed from SPK: *Marknad och fusioner* (1972–7); SPK (1978b), (1979), (1980), (1981b), (1982), (1983b), (1984b), (1985), (1986c), (1987b), (1988a); GDP by kind of economic activity; National accounts (SCB: Statistics Sweden).
Notes: [a] Number of restrictive practices divided by value added (in billions of SEK) in 1982.

ages and tobacco and manufacture of wood and wood products. Except for wholesale and retail sale, these sectors are subject to import competition. Moreover, some of them (like wood and fabricated metal products) are export-oriented. Among the sectors with a high degree of trade exposure, two sectors (transportation equipment and electrical machinery) have experienced low restrictive practices intensities between 1971 and 1987.

Sheltered economic sectors, especially wholesale and retail trade, contribute most to restrictive practices activities. Except for construction, these sectors also exhibit overly high restrictive practices intensities. When it comes to other sectors, no conclusive evidence on the diluting effect of international trade on domestic market power emerges from the restrictive practices register.

Enforcement policy preferences

As suggested above, the second type of factors may be found on the side of the enforcement agency. The implementation of the laws requires sufficient resources available to the authorities charged with the discovery and prosecution of collusive activities. This is particularly true where, as is the case in Sweden, a rule of reason inspires competition policy, because then detailed and prolonged economic investigations are necessary for the enforcement authorities. The *per se* rule, on the other hand, economizes on the costs of enforcement because the competition authorities only need to prove that firms conspire to restrain competition, but need not prove that the restraints of trade harm consumer welfare or result in absolute control over price or whatever. In most west European countries the competition agencies are small compared to their tasks. This is well illustrated by the limited personnel resources devoted to the Competition Commissioner in Sweden.[54] Between the mid-1960s and the beginnng of the 1980s, the personnel of the Competition Commissioner has doubled while the number of cases examined by the Commissioner has trebled. Against this background, one may wonder whether and how the budget constraint faced by the enforcement agency is likely to affect the number and the mix of cases examined.[55]

We may expect budget constraints to affect the number of restrictive practices selected by the Commissioner and those cases that are not reported by private persons or firms but selected by the competition authorities on the basis of information in newspapers. On the other hand, it is expected that the enforcement agency cannot influence the number of private complaints which therefore should have remained unaffected by the changes in the resources of the Competition Commissioner. Table 10.7 provides an idea of the impact of the size of the enforcement agency on the number of cases under examination. Large changes in the resources in terms of the personnel of the Commissioner between the three sub-periods considered motivate the division adopted. Table 10.7 shows that the number of cases selected by the Commissioner – in particular those selected on the basis of information in the media – increased much more quickly than the number of private complaints during the 1970s, when the resources of the Competition Commissioner doubled. Thus, it seems likely that increased resources constitute a complementary explanatory factor for the sharp increase in the number of cases brought during the 1970s. On the other hand, the changes in the number of restrictive practices examined observed during the 1980s do not seem to be the result of increased resources provided to the Competition Commissioner. Between 1983 and 1987, the number of cases selected by the Commissioner on the basis of information collected in the media decreased by 9.1 per cent per year on average and private complaints decreased by 7.2 per cent per year on average.

Table 10.7 Changes in the number of restrictive practices and in the resources of the Competition Commissioner, 1960–87

	Average per year during period		
	1960–9	1970–82	1983–7
Number of cases selected by the Commissioner on the basis of			
(i) media	23	94	126
(ii) register	16	36	27
Private complaints	117	217	299
Personnel resources of the Commissioner	11	19	30

Sources: Restrictive practices examined: see Table 10.1; Personnel resources: Holmberg (1981), pp. 38–9, and information provided by the Competition Commissioner.

Mix of cases

A related issue that is worth scrutinizing concerns the mix of cases and changes over time. In this respect, several striking features emerge from the analysis of enforcement policy in the former section. The first is the larger number of vertical restraints. The second is the growing number of ancillary covenants against competition and exclusive dealing in the register of the National Price and Competition Board. The third is the rapid decrease in the number of price-fixing agreements, especially horizontal ones, in the official register. The fourth is the stagnating number of registered agreements during the 1970s and the decreasing role of the official register in the Commissioner's policy. These are the main patterns we must explain. Explanatory factors may be found either on the side of the enforcement agency or on the side of firms or in the interaction between them.

The case-selection process

Beginning with the role of the competition authorities, a first issue concerns the impact of the policy of the Commissioner on the mix of cases investigated. Is this mix biased? Does it reflect the self-interest of the public enforcers? Does the competition agency select those cases that are most inimical to consumer welfare and to the aims of the legislation or those cases the investigation of which require a large amount of time and thus more resources of the enforcement agency? In a study covering a large number of cases examined by the enforcement agency, Stina Holmberg advances the view that one of the main objectives of the Commissioner has rather been to settle disputes between private parties than to promote competition and consumer welfare.[56] The large scope of negotiations in the enforcement of the Swedish policy is an indicator of this orientation. Another is the large number of cases investigated that are to a very limited extent a matter for competition policy and where the policy of the Commissioner has permitted small inefficient firms to survive. Examples of such cases are the numerous refusals to sell to small firms, especially in the wholesale and retail trade. Presumably a reason behind this orientation is that the time-consuming negotiations necessary to find agreements between private parties increase the tasks of the public enforcers and requires more resources for the enforcement agency.[57]

The distribution of restrictive practice agreements (see Table 10.3) suggests another explanatory factor: the enforcement agency seems rather to select those cases where collusive behaviour is more obvious than those cases that are most harmful to consumers and that require more resources because the non-competitive behaviour is less easily identified. As mentioned above, the majority of trade restraints are examined by the Competition Commissioner as a result of complaints made by private parties. The most common restrictive practices (exclusive dealing, market sharing and joint agency) are obvious to the buyers and therefore are more likely to be called to the attention of the Competition Commissioner. No doubt, once suspected, the existence of these restrictive practices can be easily proven. This may explain the distribution of cases between the various forms of business restraints of trade (see Tables 10.3 and 10.4). On the other hand, it is not so easy to detect, and thus to enforce, less obvious forms of collusion, such as price agreements. This may explain the relatively few number of price agreements (above all horizontal) detected by the enforcement agency[58] although the number of tacit price agreements investigated has increased.[59]

Competition policy and firms' concerted practices

As regards the distribution of cases, it is likely that the very existence of a competition policy affects the choice of restrictive practices by firms. Probably the prohibition of many forms of restrictive practices has caused firms to shift to other restrictive practices to keep the intensity of competition down. For example, the prohibition of formal cartel agreements may have led firms to substitute collusion without agreement, i.e. tacit collusion, for overt forms of collusion. This will not be reflected in the official register of restrictive practices, which will show a decrease in restrictive practice activity, albeit concerted practices may still have the same intensity as before in the economy. An illustrative example may be price-fixing agreements. According to the register of the competition authorities, the number of registered price-fixing agreements has decreased sharply during the 1970s (see Table 10.4), probably as a result of the tougher attitude adopted by the competition agency towards horizontal price fixing.[60] During the same period, empirical evidence suggests that the number of tacit price-fixing arrangements increased rapidly.[61] Another example is the distribution between registered restrictive practices and non-registered cases examined which can be regarded as an indicator of the intensity of restrictive practices in the economy. It is likely that a strict policy towards anti-competitive behaviour may lead firms that have entered restrictive practices agreements not to register them. Table 10.1 provides some support for this point. It suggests a decrease in the number of retrictive practices registered between the 1970s and the 1980s, while the number of unregistered restrictive practices examined by the Competition Commissioner increased during the same period. Between the 1960s and the 1970s, the number of registered agreements increased very slowly (or decreased if the figures are adjusted for changes in GDP) while the number of unregistered alleged restrictive practices increased rapidly.

A related topic concerns the substitution of mergers for restrictive practices. In lines of business where non-competitive conduct has been prosecuted, we may expect firms to 'internalize' restrictive practices through mergers and hence to economize on transaction costs. Such a pattern is most likely in countries like Sweden where there exists a positive attitude towards amalgamation of production.[62] The evidence on this issue is, however, mixed. A study concerned with the British economy suggests a faster rise in concentration, partly as a result of a higher merger intensity, in those industries where restrictive practices had operated.[63] This result was, however, questioned in a later study which showed that industries where price agreements had been removed were not more merger-intensive than other industries.[64]

Table 10.8   Restrictive practices and merger intensities by kind of activity, 1971–87

Activity	Restrictive practices intensity[a]	Merger intensity[b]	Ancillary covenant intensity[c]
Mining	0.0	5.1	0.0
Manufacture of food, beverages and tobacco	5.9	25.3	3.7
Textile, wearing apparel and leather industries	2.9	65.3	5.3
Manufacture of wood and wood products	6.3	58.7	3.2
Manufacture of paper and paper products, printing and publishing	2.4	20.1	2.2
Manufacture of chemicals and plastic products	6.7	40.8	5.7
Manufacture of non-metallic mineral products except products of petroleum and coal	20.2	74.8	12.3
Basic metal industries	3.7	8.0	1.6
Fabricated metal products	4.0	58.4	7.1
Machinery	3.5	36.1	4.4
Electrical machinery	1.0	19.9	1.6
Transportation equipment	0.1	7.3	0.9
Electricity, gas and water	0.0	7.3	0.0
Construction	2.4	20.5	1.9
Wholesale and retail trade	10.7	54.8	3.8
Transport	1.7	21.4	1.0
Services including hotels and restaurants	3.7	68.3	4.4

Sources: Restrictive practices: computed from SPK: *Marknad och fusioner* (1972–7), (1978b), (1979), (1980), (1981b), (1982), (1983b), (1984b), (1985), (1986c), (1987b), (1988a); Mergers: computed from the SPK register on mergers: GDP by kind of economic activity: national accounts (SB: Statistics Sweden).
Notes: [a] Number of restrictive practices exclusive of ancillary covenant against competition divided by value added (in billions of SEK) in 1982; [b] number of mergers divided by value added in 1982; [c] number of ancillary covenants against competition divided by value added in 1982.

In order to test this hypothesis, i.e. whether industries where concerted practices have operated are more merger-intensive than other industries, we have estimated the intensity of restrictive practices by kind of economic activity between 1971 and 1987 and the intensity of merger activity in the same sectors during the same period. Table 10.8 provides only weak support for the hypothesis which holds that incentives for mergers are created by competition policy that prohibits restrictive practices. Except for manufacture of non-metallic mineral, wood, chemical and plastic products, and wholesale and retail trade, high merger intensity is to a limited extent correlated with high restrictive practices intensity.[65]

$$\text{Ancillary covenant intensity} = -0.140 + 0.104 \text{ Merger intensity}$$
$$(0.176) \quad (5.487) \tag{1}$$

$$R^2 = 0.667$$

$$F_{1,15} = 30.11 \qquad nb = 17$$

Ancillary covenants against competition have been deducted from the number of restrictive practices because they cannot be regarded as substitutes for mergers but rather as a by-product of mergers.[66] This is supported by equation (1) (t statistics within parentheses) which regresses ancillary covenant intensity on merger intensity across sectors. The t statistic associated with the coefficient of the merger intensity variable is significant at the 1 per cent level and the R^2 of 0.667 implies that the variation in the level of merger intensity explains some 70 per cent of the variation in ancillary covenant intensity. Ancillary convenants against competition are more common in merger-intensive sectors. This applies in particular to sectors like manufacture of non-metallic mineral products, fabricated metal products, manufacture of chemical and plastic products and textile, wearing apparel and leather industries. It is, thus, the increasing number of mergers since the end of the 1960s[67] that lies behind the increasing proportion of ancillary covenants against competition among registered restrictive practices.

Trade exposure

Besides competition policy one may wonder what the factors are that are likely to influence the mix of restraints of trade selected by firms. A plausible factor is internatioal competition, actual as well as potential. We may expect increasing trade exposure to alter the distribution of cases because some restrictive practices are less likely to be successful in open economies. A striking feature of Table 10.4 concerns the sharp decrease in price-fixing agreements during the first half of the 1980s and a simultaneous increase in exclusive dealing. As suggested above, the tougher attitude adopted by the competition agency towards horizontal price fixing constitutes one explanatory factor.

Presumably another arises from the growing openness of the Swedish economy, which renders horizontal price agreements unlikely to be successful. A question is whether other restraints of trade are more suitable to limit competition from abroad. Table 10.9 shows the distribution of restrictive practices registered by kind of economic activity. It confirms that price fixing is most common in sectors that are sheltered from international competition and, surprisingly, in sectors not normally regarded as highly concentrated. Examples of such sectors are construction, wholesale and retail trade, transport and services. Roughly the same pattern can be observed for market sharing and exclusive dealing, although a larger share of the registered restrictive practices is found in sectors subject to some degree of international competition, such as manufacture of food, beverages and tobacco and manufacture of chemical and plastic products. On the other hand, joint agreements, i.e. joint selling and buying agreements and joint ventures, are distributed more evenly among the economic sectors. Ancillary covenants against competition seem to follow the same pattern, although to a lesser extent.[68]

By and large, changes in general economic conditions, in the resources of the enforcement authorities and, to a lesser extent, in trade exposure provide a firm explanation of the evolution of the number of restrictive practices examined in Sweden over the past two-and-a-half decades. As regards the mix of cases investigated, only tentative conclusions emerge from this study. The factors that have been put forward, mainly the policy of the enforcement agency and changes in trade exposure, perform rather well in explaining changes in horizontal price fixing and ancillary covenants against competition. The results are less conclusive when it comes to other changes observed in the distribution of restrictive practices over time. This applies in particular to the increasing number of vertical restraints, such as exclusive dealing, observed over the past fifteen years. Presumably other factors than the ones presented here have been at work.

Table 10.9 Registered restrictive practices by kind of economic activity, 1971–87 (%)

Activity	Market sharing	Exclusive dealing	Price fixing	Ancillary covenant against competition	Joint agreement	Others
Mining	0	0	0	0	0	0
Manufacture of food, beverages and tobacco	4.6	6.2	3.1	5.3	10.1	2.8
Textile, wearing apparel and leather industries	0.9	0.9	0	2.1	1.3	0
Manufacture of wood and wood products	3.7	2.3	4.7	2.9	8.2	8.3
Manufacture of paper and paper products, printing and publishing	2.5	2.8	2.3	4.3	5.7	8.3
Manufacture of chemicals and plastic products	7.7	4.7	0.8	7.5	9.4	30.6
Manufacture of non-metallic mineral products except products of petroleum and coal	6.5	3.9	4.3	5.6	17	8.3
Basic metal industries	4	0.9	2	1.3	2.5	0
Fabricated metal products	4.3	2.6	3.5	9.2	5.7	0
Machinery	6.5	3.4	2.3	8.9	10.1	5.6
Electrical machinery	0.6	1.2	0.4	2.5	1.9	2.8
Transportation equipment	0.3	0.2	0.4	0.2	0	0
Other manufacturing industries	0.6	1.4	0.4	2.9	0	2.8
Electricity, gas and water	0	0	0	0	0	0
Construction	2.8	5.3	23.4	9.1	5	2.8
Wholesale trade	32.5	38.8	21.5	21.1	5.7	11.1
Retail trade	17.3	18	15.6	2.9	5.7	13.9
Transport	0.9	1.4	8.6	2.6	6.9	2.8
Services including hotels and restaurants	4	6	6.6	9.8	5	0
Total	100	100	100	100	100	100
Total number (i.e. not %)	323	645	256	950	159	36

Sources: Computed from SPK: Marknad och fusioner (1972–7), (1978b), (1979), (1980), (1981b), (1982), (1983b), (1984b), (1985), (1986c), (1987b), (1988a).

CONCLUSION: COMPETITION POLICY AND CONSUMER WELFARE

Competition policy is a form of voice and a mechanism of recuperation, the aim of which is to avoid social losses. The way the enforcement of competition policy shapes the competitive process and affects consumer welfare is therefore a most crucial issue from the economist's point of view. It is, however, difficult to reach a clear conclusion as to how successful competition policy is in maintaining competition. 'No type of legislative endeavour is harder to measure in its effects than a prohibition of actions which can be concealed.'[69] The figures presented in this chapter do not reveal the whole effect of restrictive practices and merger laws on competition. Only tentative conclusions can, therefore, be drawn from them. The figures underestimate the effect on competition, mainly because of the lack of quantitative information on the deterrent effect of legislation on business behaviour.

The analysis of the deterrent effect of competition policy, e.g. agreements which would otherwise have been concluded, are not made or are voluntarily cancelled before registration, has been ignored in the course of our study. Tempering the exercise of market power and the intensity of concerted restrictive practices deterrence probably constitutes the most positive effect of antitrust laws. This should be kept in mind when the impact of competition policy is discussed. In Sweden, however, the deterrent effect of competition policy may be much less important than in a country like the United States, since in most cases no penalties are imposed on firms that are found guilty of restraints of trade.[70] From the deterrence perspective, one may question the Commissioner's view that there is not much to be gained from taking cases to court and that a more conciliatory policy of reprimanding firms who have violated the competition laws will bring about more positive effects for society.

On a priori grounds, there should also exist a deterrent effect of merger laws on merger activity. As illustrated in several empirical studies, market dominance is one of the major objectives of many merging firms.[71] The existence of strict anti-merger legislation is likely to deter those mergers which have as their main purpose market dominance. On the other hand, the Swedish legislation calls for a case-by-case cost-benefit approach in assessing the likely effects of a merger and allows mergers to proceed if the potential cost savings are expected to be greater than the monopoly dangers.

In an open economy like Sweden's, such dangers are in most cases considered minimal. This probably explains why the Competition Commissioner has allowed almost all mergers to proceed in Sweden with the consequence that the merger law is largely regarded as an empty threat.

Table 10.10 suggests that the deterrent effect, if any, of the new legislation on merger activity must have been minimal. In fact, the number of mergers in the Swedish economy has increased over the past five years. A large majority of the merged firms were small or medium-sized, often family-owned, enterprises. The merger activity of this type of firm since the new law came into force in 1983 has, however, increased less than that of larger firms which are more easily suspected of striving for market dominance. This, on a priori grounds, surprising result supports the view that the effect of the 1982 law on merger activity must have been very limited. This is further supported by the very limited number of mergers that have been forbidden by the Commissioner.

Table 10.10 Merger activity in Sweden, 1969–87

	Average per year	
Period	Firms of more than 200 employees	All firms
1969–72	46	319
1973–7	43	651
1978–82	38	636
1983–7	58	775

Sources: Computed from the SPK register on mergers.

There is little evidence on which to judge the effectiveness of competition policy in curbing market power and protecting consumer welfare. As indicated in Table 10.2, a substantial proportion of agreements are abandoned as a result of the intervention of the Competition Commissioner. The evidence, therefore, bears out that the competition policy implemented in Sweden over the past three decades might have furthered competition. It has most likely had a 'noticeable' positive effect on consumer welfare and has improved resource allocation. The relation between the number of cases coming up for examination by the Commissioner and the number of agreements registered suggests, however, that there is a fair (and increasing) amount of unregistered collusion. By its nature, it is difficult to gain information about this form of collusion.

A crucial issue that has been examined in the course of our study concerns the ability and the incentive of public enforcers to bring actions against non-competitive behaviour and what they regard as conspiracies in restraint of trade. This raises the question of the efficiency of competition policy, i.e. how the resources are allocated within the enforcement agency. A large part of the time-resources of the Competition Commissioner have been devoted to vertical restraints (see Table 10.3) and to cases involving small firms, especially in sectors like wholesale and retail trade.[72] Most of these cases, concerned with refusal to sell to a particular class of buyer, mainly small firms, are of minor importance from the point of view of consumer welfare. As suggested above, this selection is the result of the Commissioner's policy, which has protected competitors rather than promoted the welfare benefits of competition for consumers. Moreover, the pendulum seems to have swung regarding the economic reasons behind vertical restraints, questioning further the focus of the Swedish competition policy on vertical restraints. During the 1960s, vertical restraints were chiefly regarded as instruments for the exercise of market power by manufacturers and, to a lesser exetent, by dealers. Nowadays, they are rather considered to be responses to failures in the market for distribution services.[73]

Another factor that has impeded the efficiency of competition policy in Sweden is the conflicts between two objectives of public intervention, namely price control policy and competition policy. Price control policy to combat inflation was widely used during the 1970s and at the beginning of the 1980s in Sweden. The National Price and Competition Board is entrusted with the responsibility of enforcing price control policy. The same public agency is in charge of some aspects of competition policy. According to the Competition Commissioner, price control policy has furthered co-operation between firms and favoured the emergence of restrictive practices.[74] Thus, it has come into conflict with the main goal of competition policy and has had a negative effect on consumer welfare.

The distribution of cases across industries suggests that Swedish competition policy has played a non-negligible role in limiting the exercise of market power in those markets that are sheltered from international competition. But competition policy has its *raison d'être* in sectors subject to import competition too because usually restrictive practices are not absent in these sectors. In open economies, an even greater challenge to competition policy is the emergence of numerous impediments to trade. Often these are the result of efforts by various industries to insulate and immunize themselves from competition by utilizing the coercive power of the state. Examples of industries that benefit from such protective measures in Sweden are textiles, passenger cars and the food sector. These impediments to trade are, however, not regarded as restrictive practices and thus not a matter for competition policy. There is no doubt that the concern of competition policy must change to take into account this evolution of the competitive process if consumer welfare is considered as its main goal.

NOTES

* Reproduced, with permission, from *The Antitrust Bulletin*, XXXIV (1989), pp. 533–78, with amendments by the author. Thanks are due to Bo Lindörn, Mats Modin and Inga Persson for constructive comments on an earlier version. Most of the work in this chapter was carried out at the European University Institute in Florence, which provided a congenial research environment.

1 George and Joll (1975), p. 212.
2 Bourdet (1990), pp. 30–7.
3 This section on the evolution of the Swedish legislation concentrates on aspects of interest for economists, foregoing many points which lawyers would consider of major importance.
4 Jacquemin (1975), p. 130.
5 On the role of the structural aspects in the US competition policy, see Martin (1988), ch. 10. On competition policy in western Europe, see Walsh and Paxton (1975), chs 6 and 7, and OECD (1984b), pp. 25–49.
6 On the *per se* versus rule of reason issue, see, for example, Scherer (1980), pp. 497–502, 509–13.
7 Ibid., pp. 504–9.
8 Martenius (1985), pp. 17–18, and Walsh and Paxton (1975), pp. 161–4.
9 Although it is not a fine in the strict sense of the word, public information on business conspiracies may have a similar effect since it is very likely to result in a drop in the sales of the firms involved.
10 Martenius (1985), pp. 19–23, and Walsh and Paxton (1975), p. 162.
11 Martenius (1985), p. 20.
12 Ibid., p. 21.
13 For a short presentation of the new competition law in Sweden, see SPK (1983a), pp. 5–12, and with special emphasis on the merger law, OECD (1984b), p. 36.
14 SPK (1983a), p. 7, and Martenius (1985), p. 67.
15 Martenius (1985), p. 126.
16 SPK (1983a), p. 7, and Martenius (1985), p. 67.
17 Ibid., p. 12.
18 Rydén and Edberg (1980), p. 197.
19 See, for example, Rydén (1972), p. 172 and Rydén and Edberg (1980), pp. 196–7.

20 OECD (1984b), p. 7.
21 Martenius (1985), pp. 32–3, and SPK, 1983a, p. 8.
22 SPK (1983a), p. 10.
23 Note that the decision of the court must come within the first two years following a merger in order to prohibit it (SPK, 1983a, p. 9).
24 Martenius (1985), pp. 29, 32.
25 For a presentation in English, see Walsh and Paxton (1975), pp. 163–4.
26 Ibid., p. 163.
27 SPK (1986b), p. 4.
28 Ibid., pp. 3–4.
29 SPK (1988b), pp. 5–6.
30 Ibid., p. 5.
31 A report on the activity of the Competition Commissioner appears each year in the review of the antitrust authorities *Pris och konkurrens* (*Pris och kartellfrågor* before 1982).
32 Sweden seems to differ from other countries in this respect. For example, between 1954 and 1976 only 2 per cent of the cases examined were brought to the Restrictive Practices Court in Sweden while no less than 86 per cent of the cases examined were brought to court in Norway (computed from Table 25 in Holmberg, 1981, p. 180).
33 Such provisions are very common in contracts of sale or lease of business.
34 See, for example, Harding (1982), p. 334. It should be noted that there was some discussion about the conformity of this practice with the 1953 legislation (ibid., pp. 336–8).
35 Ibid., p. 340.
36 Ibid.
37 SPK (1987b), p. 40 and NO (1988a), p. 13.
38 According to the review of the competition agency, on average two mergers per year were investigated during the period 1974–82. This figure rose to about twelve in 1983–4 and dropped to around seven during 1985–7.
39 Harding (1982), p. 360.
40 Ibid., p. 140.
41 Ibid., pp. 340–61. See also the Competition Commissioner's own opinion in SPK (1975), pp. 134–42.
42 In 1975, beside the above-mentioned effects, the Commissioner said the effects on the balance of trade should be considered as well, see SPK (1975b), p. 137.
43 Harding (1982), p. 356 and Holmberg (1981), p. 157.
44 See SPK (1983a), pp. 48–103.
45 SPK (1984a), pp. 69–70.
46 SPK (1987b), pp. 40–1, and SPK (1988a), pp. 32–3.
47 See Competition Commissioner Yearly Report, SPK (1987b), pp. 40–1.
48 This was the first decision taken by the court in accordance with the new merger law.
49 For a detailed analysis of the reasons behind the court's decision, see SPK (1987a).
50 In a second stage we intend to build our own register based on a larger and more disaggregated sample in order to be able to test various

hypotheses with the help of econometric methods.

51 See, for example, Shepherd (1979), pp. 294–8.

52 The mean of the four-firm concentraiton ratio in Swedish manufacturing industry has increased from 0.50 in 1965 to 0.57 in 1975 and 0.58 in 1978 (Stålhammar, chapter 2, p. 80). In another study, it is suggested that no major changes in concentration took place between 1967 and 1970 (OECD, 1979, p. 72). Both studies, it should be stressed, tell us very little about the changes in the ability of firms to exercise market power in the Swedish market since they do not include foreign trade and thus do not reflect changes in market shares.

53 See Caves and Jones (1985), pp. 168–9 for a presentation of the argument. Note, however, that very little support has been given to the diluting effect of export opportunities on domestic market power in empirical studies. See, for example, Marvel (1980), pp. 118–19, Pagoulatos and Sorensen (1976), p. 264, Jacquemin *et al.* (1980), pp. 140–1.

54 Another illustrative example is France where the Commission in charge of the enforcement of competition policy was composed of only fourteen members working on a part-time basis in the mid-1970s, of which six were representatives of the business community (Jenny and Weber, 1977, p. 401).

55 For an analysis of this issue in the US context, see Katzmann (1980).

56 For an illustration, see Holmberg (1981), pp. 101–2.

57 Ibid., p. 101.

58 Between 1970 and 1975, the Commissioner investigated 31 cases concerned with non-registered price-fixing arrangements. In only three cases could the existence of price co-operation be proven. (Holmberg, 1981, pp. 133–8).

59 Ibid., p. 161.

60 See the yearly reports of the Competition Commissioner in SPK (1975a), p. 61, and SPK (1979), p. 78.

61 Holmberg (1981), p. 161.

62 See, for example, Rydén (1972), p. 130.

63 Elliot and Gribbin (1977).

64 Quoted by Sawyer (1981), p. 248.

65 Regressing merger intensity on restrictive practices intensity yields a regression coefficient of 3.23 (significant at the 1 per cent level) with R^2 = 0.44, i.e. 44 per cent of the variation in merger intensity across economic sectors are explained by the variation in restrictive practices intensity. The fact that merger activity in an industry is dependent upon other factors as well, such as the initial level of concentration, the rate of growth, the degree of trade exposure or the scope for economies of scale suggests, however, that this result should be taken with a pinch of salt. Actually a specification bias is extremely likely to occur since the included independent variable, restrictive practices intensity, is very probably correlated with some of the omitted independent variables, like the rate of growth or the degree of trade exposure. Note, moreover, that the causality may run in both directions since, on a priori grounds, anti-competitive behaviour may be associated with high concentration, i.e. high merger activity, on the seller's side as well.

334 *Internationalization, market power and consumer welfare*

66 Holmberg (1981), p. 161.
67 See, for example, Rydén and Edberg (1980), pp. 194–5.
68 Roughly the same picture emerges from the register on the restrictive practices appearing in the review of the competition authorities (see Table 10.3). It shows that most cases of suspected price-fixing arrangements and monopoly pricing are to be found in sectors sheltered from international competition while vertical restraints and provisions against competition are more evenly distributed among the economic sectors.
69 Stigler (1966), p. 267.
70 Holmberg (1981), p. 143–4.
71 See, for example, De Jong (1976), pp. 95–123, and George and Silberston (1976), pp. 124–42.
72 Holmberg (1981), p. 88.
73 On the two explanations, see Martin (1988), pp. 446–59, and Williamson (1987), ch. 6.
74 Quoted by Jonung (1984), p. 249. A simple comparison between changes in the extent of price control policy (Table 10.2, p. 223) and the intensity of concerted practices examined by the Commissioner only provides weak support for this conjecture. Actually, the number of restrictive practices examined increased marginally at the end of the 1970s and beginning of the 1980s when the degree of price control was highest. On the other hand, the number of restrictive practices examined as well as the extent of price control policy have decreased over the past five years.

REFERENCES

Adams, W. (1986) 'Public policy in a free enterprise economy', in W. Adams (ed.) *The Structure of American Industry*, 7th edn, New York and London: Macmillan.
Bjuggren, P.O. (1981) 'Brister i konkurrensutredningens betänkande', *Ekonomisk debatt*, no. 2.
Bourdet, Y. (1990) 'Market power and consumer welfare in open economies', ch. 1 of this volume.
Caves, R. and Jones, R. (1985) *World Trade and Payments*, 4th edn, Boston and Toronto: Little, Brown & Co.
Dalton, J. and Lewis, S. (1974) *The Antitrust Dilemma*, Lexington, VA: Lexington Books.
De Jong, H. (1976) 'Theory and evidence concerning mergers: an international comparison', in A. Jacquemin and H. de Jong (eds) *Markets, Corporate Behaviour and the State*, The Hague: Nijhoff.
Elliot, D.C. and Gribbin, J.D. (1977) 'The abolition of cartels and structural change in the United Kingdom', in A. Jacquemin and H. de Jong (eds) *Welfare Aspects of Industrial Markets*, The Hague: Nijhoff.
George, K. and Joll, C. (1975) *Competition Policy in the UK and the EEC*, Cambridge: Cambridge University Press.
George, K. and Silberston, A. (1976) 'The causes and effects of mergers', in A. Jacquemin and H. de Jong (eds), *Markets, Corporate Behaviour*

and the State, The Hague: Nijhoff.

Harding, L.-E. (1982) Kontroll av företagssammanslagningar, En konkurrensrättslig studie, Stockholm: LiberFörlag.

Holmberg, S. (1981) Mot monopolisering? NO:s verksamhet under 25 år, Lund: PA Norstedt & Söners förlag.

Jacquemin, A. (1975) 'Abuse of dominant position and changing European industrial structure', in K. George and C. Joll, Competition Policy in the UK and the EEC, Cambridge: Cambridge University Press.

Jacquemin, A., De Ghellinck, E. and Huveneers, C. (1980) 'Concentration and profitability in a small open economy', Journal of Industrial Economics, 29.

Jenny, F. and Weber, A.-P. (1977) 'French antitrust legislation: an exercise in futility', in A. Jacquemin and H. de Jong (eds) Welfare Aspects of Industrial Markets, The Hague: Nijhoff.

Jonung, L. (1984) Prisregleringen, företagen och förhandlingsekonomi, Stockholm: SNS.

Katzmann, R. (1980) Regulatory Bureaucracy: The Federal Trade Commission and Antitrust Policy, Cambridge, MA: MIT Press.

Martenius, Å. (1985) Konkurrenslagstiftningen, Stockholm: PA Norstedt & Söners förlag.

Martin, S. (1988) Industrial Economics, Economic Analysis and Public Policy, New York: Macmillan.

Marvel, H. (1980) 'Foreign trade and domestic competition', Economic Inquiry, 18.

NO (1982) 'Näringsfrihetsombudsmannens verksamhet åren 1954–1951', Bilaga 3, Stockholm.

NO (1988a) 'Näringsfrihetsombudsmannen, Verksamheten 1987', Stockholm.

NO (1988b) 'Näringsfrihetsombudsmannen, Register till PoK 1986–1987', Stockholm.

OECD (1979) Concentration and Competition Policy, Paris: OECD.

OECD (1984a) Competition and Trade Policy, Their Interaction, Paris: OECD.

OECD (1984b) Merger Policies and Recent Trends in Mergers, Paris: OECD.

Pagoulatos, E. and Sorensen, R. (1976) 'Foreign trade, concentration and profitability in open economies', European Economic Review, 8.

Posner, R. (1970) 'A statistical study of antitrust enforcement', Journal of Law and Economics, 13.

Posner, R. (1976) Antitrust Law An Economic Perspective, Chicago and London: The University of Chicago Press.

Rydén, B. (1972) Mergers in Swedish Industry, Stockholm: Almqvist & Wiksell.

Rydén, B. and Edberg, J. (1980) 'Large mergers in Sweden 1962–1976', in D. Mueller (ed.) The Determinants and Effects of Mergers, Cambridge, MA: Oelgeschlager, Gunn & Hain.

Sawyer, M. (1981) The Economics of Industries and Firms, Theory, Evidence and Policy, London: Croom Helm.

Scherer, F. (1980) Industrial Market Structure and Economic Performance, Boston: Houghton Mifflin Company.

Shepherd, W.G. (1979) *The Economics of Industrial Organization*, Englewood Cliffs, NJ: Prentice-Hall.
SPK (1970) *Pris och kartellfrågor*, nos 1–2.
SPK (1971) *Pris och kartellfrågor*, nos 8–9.
SPK (1975a) *Pris och kartellfrågor*, no. 2.
SPK (1975b) *Pris och kartellfrågor*, nos 6–7.
SPK (1977) *Pris och kartellfrågor*, no. 1.
SPK (1978a) *Pris och kartellfrågor*, no. 1.
SPK (1978b) *Pris och kartellfrågor*, nos 2–3.
SPK (1979) *Pris och kartellfrågor*, no. 2.
SPK (1980) *Pris och kartellfrågor*, no. 3.
SPK (1981a) *Pris och kartellfrågor*, nos 1–2.
SPK (1981b) *Pris och kartellfrågor*, no. 3.
SPK (1982) *Pris och konkurrens*, no. 3.
SPK (1983a) *Pris och konkurrens*, no. 1.
SPK (1983b) *Pris och konkurrens*, no. 3.
SPK (1984a) *Pris och konkurrens*, no. 1.
SPK (1984b) *Pris och konkurrens*, no. 2.
SPK (1985) *Pris och konkurrens*, no. 2.
SPK (1986a) *Avgöranden i konkurrensärenden 1970–1985*, Stockholm.
SPK (1986b) 'Verksamhetsberättelse 1986, Statens pris- och kartellnämnd', Stockholm.
SPK (1986c) *Pris och konkurrens*, no. 2.
SPK (1987a) *Pris och konkurrens*, no. 1.
SPK (1987b) *Pris och konkurrens*, no. 2.
SPK (1988a) *Pris och konkurrens*, no. 2.
SPK (1988b) *Pris och konkurrens*, no. 4.
Stigler, G. (1966) 'The economic effects of antitrust laws', *Journal of Law and Economics*, 9 reprinted in G. Stigler, *The Organization of Industry*, Chicago: The University of Chicago Press.
Stålhammar, N.-O. (1988) 'Concentration, prices and profitability in the Swedish manufacturng industry', ch. 2 of this volume.
Walsh, A.E. and Paxton, J. (1975) *Competition Policy, European and International Trends and Practices*, London: Macmillan
Williamson, O.E. (1987) *Antitrust Economics*, Oxford and New York: Basil Blackwell.

11 Competition policy and economic efficiency: efficiency trade-offs in industrial policy

Lennart Hjalmarsson

INTRODUCTION

In industrial economics there is a long and dominating tradition of research focusing primarily on different aspects of competitive failures in different markets on the basis of the so-called structure–conduct–performance (SCP) paradigm, providing a strong support for market interventions and antitrust policy. In this tradition, industrial policy has been almost synonymous with competition policy. What may seem surprising is the weak influence of this tradition in Swedish economic research (at least, until recently). Instead, research in industrial economics in Sweden has, to a large extent, dealt with productivity issues.

In examining policy, the same picture emerges with a minor role being assigned to competition policy and a strong role assigned to productivity-enhancing measures in industrial policy (see Bourdet, ch. 10, this volume for a discussion of Swedish competition policy). Even though there exists a competition law with some restrictions on mergers and restrictive practices, the emphasis in Swedish industrial policy has been on productive efficiency in general and scale efficiency and structural efficiency in particular. The keywords have been productivity, optimal structure and structural rationalization. Competition from abroad has been regarded as a substitute for competition policy.

It is particularly interesting to note the different meanings of 'structure' and 'structural policy' in the Swedish tradition compared to what might be termed the 'antitrust tradition'. In the latter, 'structure' usually refers to market concentration while structure in the Swedish tradition usually refers to the distribution of plant sizes and plant productivities. While in both traditions, size distribution of plants and firms are of interest, structural policy in the antitrust tradition has been aimed at limiting market concentration and, in the Swedish tradition, has been aimed at creating a structure of plants with high productivity.

Swedish industrial policy has tended to stress the importance of successful innovations and large firms that are able to survive international competition, and this policy has been supported by an active productivity-enhancing labour market policy. As a consequence, the attitude towards monopolies and 'big business' has been quite different in Sweden as compared to, for example, the United States. Industrial policy has been a protrust policy rather than an antitrust policy with fiscal incentives (tax exemptions) for merging firms. As shown by Bourdet (ch. 10, this volume) the Competition Commissioner did not investigate a merger case before 1971, the law to prohibit mergers before 1983 was severely limited, and after that, only two mergers have been 'avoided' through intervention by the Competition Commissioner.

In a Swedish merger case, the decision of the Competition Commissioner is based on an analysis wherein potential cost savings are weighted against increase in monopoly power. Thus, considering industrial policy in Sweden, the trade-off between exploitation of market power and exploitation of economies of scale, i.e. between allocative and productive efficiency is a very interesting issue. The purpose of this chapter is to address this issue. More specifically, I will first present a theoretical foundation for the Swedish policy, and second, I will discuss the trade-off between allocative and productive efficiency. This analysis rests on two models, a capacity expansion model under 'putty-clay' assumptions and Williamson's so-called trade-off model. Despite a growing literature there are still neglected points, which in the view of the author deserve more attention. One such aspect is the proper understanding of the importance of scale economies for productive efficiency and productivity growth.

This chapter has the following structure. The following section contrasts two traditions in industrial economics, one with emphasis on markets and allocative efficiency and the other with emphasis on productivity and scale efficiency. The section on pp. 341–3 discusses the importance and relevance of scale economies in industrial economics literature, while the next section (pp. 343–5) provides a brief survey of efficiency concepts. In a section on pp. 345–8, I present a capacity expansion model for an industrial company and exploit this model for a discussion about dynamic scale efficiency in the following section. A more formal trade-off model between allocative and scale efficiency is presented in the section on pp. 348–55, while dynamic aspects of scale efficiency are addressed in the following section (pp. 351–5), followed by policy conclusions in the final section (pp. 355–6).

TWO TRADITIONS IN INDUSTRIAL ECONOMICS AND INDUSTRIAL POLICY

One may distinguish between two old traditions in industrial policy and industrial economics, one based on neoclassical production theory and what is normally referred to as the structure–conduct–performance (SCP) paradigm and the other based on a dynamic, though not until recently very well-developed, production theory. In this section, I will briefly characterize these traditions.

For many years, research in industrial economics focused primarily on different aspects of competitive failures in different markets on the basis of the SCP paradigm. In this tradition, market structure (i.e. market concentration) largely determines the conduct of the firms in a market and conduct, in turn, yields predictable levels of performance. Since structure determines conduct, and conduct determines performance, there is a strong, albeit indirect, link between structure and performance. Hence policy can focus primarily on structure, seeking to prevent undesirable increases in concentration and market power and reducing barriers to entry through an active antitrust policy. Industrial policy in this setting would aim at achieving or, as in the case of direct monopoly regulation, replicating the price and cost structure associated with a competitive economy. Thus, in this tradition, industrial policy is focused on market failures of a particular kind, namely those connected with deviations of price from marginal cost, and the main objective of industrial policy is to reduce the social costs of monopoly power. From an efficiency point of view, the main focus is on static allocative efficiency obtained by an efficient competition and antitrust policy (or direct price regulation) yielding prices at marginal cost levels. Productive and dynamic efficiency is of less concern and is supposedly obtained by efficient monitoring inside firms and through capital market pressure, forcing the average firm to the efficient part of its production possibility set.

This tradition has a long history in economics with early

important contributions by, for example, Marshall and later developments in the neoclassical tradition with its focus on the behaviour of the representative or average firm.

The second tradition has a long history too, but, to the author's knowledge, it seems to be fairly limited to the history of Scandinavian and particularly Swedish economics and Swedish industrial policy. The industrial policy in Sweden has put a great emphasis on the productive efficiency of the manufacturing sector, and on the so-called 'structural rationalization' policy of less efficient industrial sectors. Here the interest is not so much in the average firm, but in the whole structure of the industrial company as regards technology and the size distribution of micro units. Thus, structural rationalization policy has been directed towards a more efficient utilization of resources, such as labour, by squeezing out less efficient firms and providing strong incentives for capacity expansion in new modern technology. From an efficiency point of view, the focus is on technical and scale efficiency of individual firms in general and on the structural efficiency of a whole industrial company in particular.

As early as 1918, the Swedish economist Eli Heckscher, in a book on Swedish industrial problems, introduced a diagram in which the firm's current average costs were sorted in increasing order. On the basis of such a diagram, Heckscher performed an analysis of the impact on industrial structure of tariff changes (see Heckscher, 1918). Other Swedish economists, e.g. Akerman and Svennilson, should also be mentioned. In a study in 1931, Akerman investigated the difference between the best-practice and average productivity of labour in Swedish saw mills. He showed that during the period 1923–6, the input coefficients of labour for the most modern plants were only 50 per cent of that for the average of the industry (see Akerman, 1931). The distance between best-practice and average practice is also discussed in an article by Svennilson (1944). It includes a thorough analysis of the determinants of the rate of growth of industrial productivity and a simple model from which 'ratios of inoptimality' are calculated. These ratios of inoptimality show the percentage ratio between the average and best-practice input coefficients for labour as a function of the rate of growth of production, the physical lifetime of equipment and the input-coefficients of labour for each vintage of capital. A main point is the relationship between the rate of growth of production and the rate of productivity growth, which is also studied in an empirical analysis of Swedish industries.

These early examples of industrial studies have been followed by a very large number of so-called structural studies of different industries, concentrating on productivity aspects, as a basis for the structural rationalization policy. Interest has chiefly focused on the modernity of capital equipment, the size of plants and the extent of division of labour and specialization. The keywords have been productivity, optimal structure and structural rationalization, not competition. For a discussion of theoretical aspects, see Hjalmarsson (1973) and for a brief history of Swedish industrial policy, see Hjalmarsson (1991).

ECONOMIES OF SCALE IN INDUSTRIAL ECONOMICS

Traditionally, there has been a strong bias towards constant returns to scale assumptions in industrial organization models. This has now changed, and economies of scale in imperfect competition models has emerged as an important topic in recent theoretical research into industrial economics and international trade; for a review see, for example, Venables and Smith (1986). The practical importance and the relevance for antitrust policy is less clear, and some economists seem to be very sceptical about the potential productivity gains from further exploitation of scale economies. See, for example, Prais (1981), Cowling *et al.* (1980), Geroski and Jacquemin (1985) and Geroski (1989). One reason for this scepticism is based on the results in Cowling *et al.* (1980) which conclude that efficiency was rarely increased by merger and sometimes actually declined after a merger.

According to my view, the short-term effects of mergers are not a convincing or not even a very relevant argument as regards the importance of scale economies. Mergers may enhance managerial efficiency, but, from a production function point of view, a merger between two firms in an industry with a rigid capital structure in the short term should be expected to yield a very moderate increase in technical or scale efficiency. The scope for improvement is in general very limited by the nature of technology; see Forsund and Hjalmarsson (1987, ch. 8) and Forsund *et al.* (1985, ch. 5).

On the other hand, a merger between two firms in the same industry is one way to buy market shares and increase the size of the buying firm's market and thereby influence the potential benefits of scale economies in the future development of the firm. In a dynamic perspective, in industries characterized by 'putty-clay' technology, the gains from economies of scale arise in the process of long-term capacity expansion, much less so in the more efficient utilization of existing capacity. The most relevant measures of scale economies are therefore engineering estimates of scale factors in the construction of new plants. Such engineering estimates usually indicate substantial scale economies in most manufacturing industries; see Haldi and Whitcomb (1967), Ribrant (1970), Pratten (1971), Hjalmarsson (1976), Scherer *et al.* (1975) and EEC (1988).

Usually, economies of scale relate to the effect on average cost of production of different rates of outputs, per unit of time, of a given commodity, when production at each scale is as efficient as possible. This is the 'scale curve'. The scale curve holds at a given point in time, and it assumes a given state of technological knowledge.

Considering that the scale curve changes over time, we are rather interested in the long-run scale curve, i.e. the envelope of the different vintage scale curves. At least for small countries, with a limited market and relatively small economically optimal plant sizes, this long-run scale curve seems to be the relevant 'choice of capacity' curve, i.e. the curve representing the actual possibilities from which the firm has to choose when a new plant is to be established. The impression one gets from a cursory glance at plant capacity data for small countries is that plant capacities for many industries are located on the steep part of the respective scale curves. On the other hand, for large countries such as the United Kingdom and the United States, the largest plants seem to be located on the flattest part of the respective scale curves. If this hypothesis is correct, small countries with small markets should have larger possibilities and gains from exploiting economies of scale than large countries. Thus, for such industries one should expect a faster rate of productivity growth *ceteris paribus* for small countries than for large.

In Scherer *et al.* (1975, ch. 3), the minimum optimal scales, MOS, of different industries in 1967 are compared to domestic consumption, where MOS is the smallest capacity or planned output volume at which all relevant economies of scale are achieved. As can be seen in the Table 11.1 there is a clear difference between Sweden and the other countries.

The importance of scale efficiency seems to be a minor problem in the United States and other large countries, but an important issue for small countries like Sweden.

Table 11.1 The number of MOS plants compatible with domestic consumption in six nations, c. 1967

Industry	US	Canada	UK	Sweden	France	Germany
Brewing	29.0	2.9	10.9	0.7	4.5	16.1
Cigarettes	15.2	1.3	3.3	0.3	1.6	2.8
Fabrics	451.7	17.4	57.0	10.4	56.9	52.1
Paints	69.8	6.3	9.8	2.0	6.6	8.4
Petroleum refining	51.6	6.0	8.6	2.5	7.7	9.9
Shoes	532.0	59.2	164.5	23.0	128.2	196.9
Glass bottles	65.5	7.2	11.1	1.7	6.6	7.9
Cement	59.0	6.6	16.5	3.5	21.7	28.8
Steel	38.9	2.6	6.5	1.5	5.5	10.1
Bearings	72.0	5.9	22.8	3.3	17.0	n.a.
Refrigerators	7.1	0.7	1.2	0.5	1.7	2.8
Storage batteries	53.2	4.6	7.7	1.4	12.8	10.5

Source: Scherer *et al.* (1975, p. 94).

THE CONCEPT OF EFFICIENCY

Efficiency is a multidimensional concept, and the terminology varies between different fields in economics such as production theory and traditional market theory. In the latter, the main distinction is between productive efficiency and allocative efficiency. Productive efficiency refers to the efficient use of resources inside the firms, as represented by the traditional average production function, while allocative efficiency refers to the economic optimization of inputs and outputs, i.e. allocative efficiency deals with the question of whether the input mix is cost-minimizing or not, and whether different outputs are produced in the right proportions, i.e. if prices are equal to marginal costs. One measure of allocative inefficiency is the well-known deadweight loss measure.

In one branch of production theory, productive efficiency is further subdivided into technical and scale efficiency. Technical efficiency concentrates on the physical utilization of resources inside a firm or an industry independent of relative prices, and the notion of best-practice technology and frontier production function serves as the measuring rod for performance. If the technology is not constant, returns to scale, scale efficiency of different production units becomes an important concept. These efficiency concepts are illustrated in Figure 11.1.

The input saving measure, E_1, is obtained when holding output constant at the observed level for a unit and measuring inputs

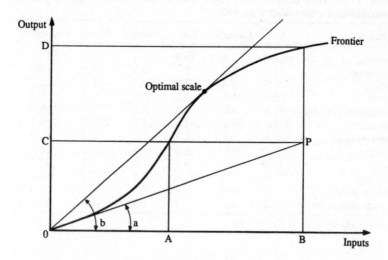

Figure 11.1   Measures of technical efficiency and scale efficiency relative to
a frontier production function
Notes:Efficiency measures for unit P: E_1 = OA/OB, E_2 = OC/OD, E_3 =
a/b.

required at the frontier compared to the observed inputs for the
observed factor ratio, OA/OB. The output increasing measure, E_2,
is obtained when observed inputs are utilized on the frontier
(yielding potential output) and observed and potential output are
compared, OC/OD. The scale efficiency measure, E_3, is defined as
the ratio between minimal input coefficients at optimal scale and the
observed input coefficients, a/b (see Forsund and Hjalmarsson,
1987, ch. 3).

To characterize the entire structure of an industry in a summary
way, different measures of structural efficiency are often used. One
type of such a measure is obtained by calculating the technical and
scale efficiency measures as defined in Figure 11.1 for the average
production unit. All these measures are purely static in nature.

When dynamic aspects are important, the empirical measurement
of efficiency becomes more complicated due to the difficulties of
observing expectation formation and attitudes towards risk and
uncertainty. In general, dynamic efficiency refers to the optimal use
of investment resources and the path of capacity expansion in an
industry. One measure of dynamic inefficiency is the ratio between
observed average costs and the average costs obtained had the

industry developed along an optimal path. Another aspect of dynamic efficiency, not discussed here concerns R&D and innovations.

What is of particular concern in this chapter is the dynamic aspects of scale efficiency. In the static market model with economies of scale, one large plant remains in long-term equilibrium, or a number of equal size plants in the case of a technically optimal scale. In a dynamic model (and 'reasonable' assumptions) with increasing returns to scale in the production function, this single large plant is never realized, since it is not profitable to build. The exploitation of economies of scale is limited by the market. Optimal scale becomes an endogeneous concept depending on several factors. In general, in an expanding market, an optimal path of capacity expansion implies a series of lumpy investments with a gradual increase in size, so an optimal structure, defined as a snapshot picture of an optimal development, would consist of a set of plants covering a whole range of sizes. In the next section, such a capacity expansion model is presented.

THE VINTAGE FRAMEWORK

Although the Swedish industrial policy was never based on an explicit theoretical model, the vintage or 'putty-clay' model is a good *ex post* rationalization of the main ideas. The vintage framework provides the possibility of insight into the structural change and optimal development of an industry and clearly illustrates the distinction between static and dynamic efficiency.

The vintage approach is concerned with the dynamic process of structural change in an industry producing a homogeneous good. Of particular interest is the difference between best-practice and average productivity and the origin of differences in the structure with regard to capacity and input coefficients; the development of the structure over time through the process of choice of new technique; and investments picked from the *ex ante* production function and the closing down of old equipment.

This dynamic theory of production is based on assumptions about *ex ante* versus *ex post* substitutability and embodied technical progress. Here the interest is not so much in the average firm, but rather in the whole structure of the industry as regards input coefficients and the size distributions of the micro units. In Johansen (1972) the vintage approach was developed into a formal production function framework, and it was further developed by Forsund and

Hjalmarsson in a series of articles and further elaborated in Forsund and Hjalmarsson (1987).

The basic idea can be described in the following way: let us consider an industry producing a homogeneous product. The firms in this industry face the same *ex ante* or choice of technique production function when new investments are performed. Technical progress is assumed to be capital embodied. *Ex ante* there are large substitution possibilities between different inputs and free choice of capacity. *Ex post*, when a new plant has been erected, capacity is fixed and substitution possibilities narrow. This *ex post* rigidity creates a rigid capital structure in the industry, in the short run. In the long run, this structure may be changed through a, usually gradual, process of investments in new capacity and scrapping of old capital.

The scale properties of the *ex ante* function are crucial for the size distribution of plants. As discussed above, in a static model economies of scale lead to one large plant. In a dynamic model, however, exploitation of economies of scale depends on the size of the market and a trade-off arises between the development of demand and scale economies. This trade-off was first illustrated by Manne (1967) in a simple cost function framework. Here I will use a production function framework and present a capacity expansion model based on Hjalmarsson (1973) and Forsund and Hjalmarsson (1987). This model will then be utilized in the analysis of dynamic scale efficiency.

Consider an industry producing a homogeneous product which serves demand that grows at a constant rate (g). All demand is to be satisfied by domestic production, and initially there is just capacity $(x(0))$, to meet the demand. Substitution possibilities between different inputs are present in the planning stage, but fixed capacity and technology obtain *ex post* (putty-clay).

The choice of technique function relevant in the planning stage exhibits increasing returns to scale and is a quasi concave function with capital equipment and one current input

$$x = Ae^{\delta t}L^{\alpha}K^{\beta} \qquad \alpha + \beta = \varepsilon \qquad (1)$$

The price of the current factor, as well as of capital, is continuously increasing, at a rate of 100 a and 100 b per cent per year, respectively.

Plant life is assumed to be infinite. This assumption is less realistic when economies of scale exist, which makes it profitable to scrap old plants with high unit costs and build new, somewhat larger plants, with low unit costs. However, as far as I can see, the results below are not biased by this assumption. For a more thorough discussion of this and the other assumptions below, see Hjalmarsson (1974).

The horizon is infinite and the discount rate (r) is positive. The capacity utilization of a plant completed at a certain investment point is zero at first, but grows correspondingly to demand until the next investment point, when there is no unutilized capacity. This assumption is made partly for convenience and is partly based on the following consideration: if the time period between two investments is not too long, we can regard it as a learning period. During this period utilization of capacity grows continuously.

With these assumptions it can be shown that an optimal policy consists of building successive plants at equidistant intervals of time (τ) (a proof for this can be found in Hjalmarsson, 1974).

This model yields a total cost function for the whole horizon of the following form:

$$C(\tau) = Hx(0)^{1/\varepsilon} \frac{(e^{g\tau} - 1)^{1/\varepsilon}}{1 - e^{\theta\tau}}, \qquad \theta > 0, \qquad H > 0 \qquad (2)$$

where τ is the constant time interval between two investments, g is the rate of growth of demand, ε is the elasticity of scale, H is a positive constant and θ is a parameter.

$$\theta = \frac{\alpha a + \beta b - \delta + g}{\varepsilon} - r \qquad (3)$$

Thus, the optimal time period between two investments, and accordingly the optimal capacity of a new plant, depends on a whole set of parameters reflecting the scale properties of the production function (α, β, ε), rate of embodied technical progress (δ), rate of demand growth (g) and the discount rate (r).

One interesting aspect of this model is the characteristics of technology and size structure generated during an optimal path of capacity expansion. A more recently constructed plant is larger than an older plant, so at a given time point there is a whole range of different plant sizes with different choices of input coefficients. The exact size distribution depends on all the model parameters, but the most crucial parameters are the scale elasticity and rate of demand growth. Thus, an important feature of this model is that the degree of exploitation of scale economies is endogenous, depending on a set of parameters. A typical size structure in the input coefficient space is shown in Figure 11.2.

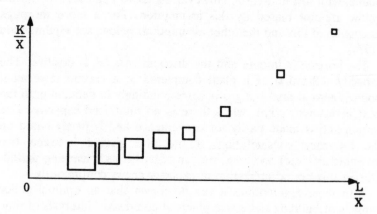

Figure 11.2   The size distribution of plants in a vintage model

This model can be used as a basis for an analysis of different aspects of dynamic efficiency closely connected with Swedish industrial policy and especially the importance of scale economies and scale efficiency and the determinants behind structural efficiency. Such an analysis is undertaken on pp. 351–5. For a further discussion of this model see Hjalmarsson (1973) and Forsund and Hjalmarsson (1987).

THE STATIC ALLOCATIVE EFFICIENCY: PRODUCTIVE EFFICIENCY TRADE-OFF

The social welfare loss (the deadweight loss) arising from monopoly refers to the net reduction of consumers' surplus, i.e. the excess of the loss of consumers' surplus over the monopolist's gain in profits, the latter being regarded as a transfer of income from the consumers.

The analysis of monopoly losses are usually based on cost curves which are independent of market structure. If a more concentrated industry leads to lower production costs due to scale economies, but also to a higher price level, a trade-off arises between productive and allocative efficiency. The purpose of this section is to present this welfare trade-off, between cost savings from economies of scale and the loss of consumer surplus, first analysed by Williamson (1968). Williamson restricted his analysis to the case of a merger which simultaneously provided cost savings and a price in excess of the competitive level. Williamson's approach is illustrated in Figure 11.3.

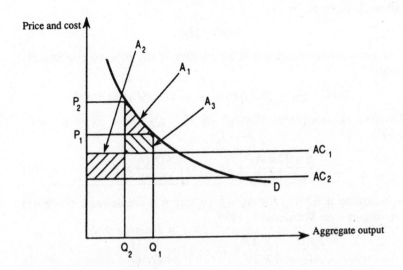

Figure 11.3 The trade-off between productive and allocative efficiency

It depicts the case of a proposed merger which would introduce market power into a previously more or less competitive situation. The horizontal line labelled AC_1 represents the level of average costs of the two (or more) firms before combination, while AC_2 shows the level of average costs after the merger. The price before the merger is given by P_1 and is equal to $k \cdot AC_1$, where k is an index of pre-merger market power and is greater than or equal to unity. The price after the merger is given by P_2 and is assumed to exceed P_1, i.e. the price is assumed to be higher than in the pre-merger case in spite of the scale economies. In such circumstances, a welfare trade-off is required between the loss of consumers' surplus A_1, and area A_3, due to the higher price and the cost saving gain to the producer, A_2 (see Figure 11.3).

Referring to Figure 11.3, the area A_1 is given approximately by

$$0.5(P_2 - P_1) \cdot (Q_1 - Q_2),$$

or

$$0.5 \Delta P \Delta Q$$

and A_3 by

$$(k - 1)AC_1 \cdot \Delta Q$$

while A_2 is given by

$$\Delta AC \cdot Q_2.$$

The net economic effect will be positive if the following inequality holds:

$$\Delta AC \cdot Q_2 - [0.5\Delta P + (k - 1) \cdot AC_1]\Delta Q > 0$$

Dividing the inequality through by $P_1 \cdot Q_2$ where $P_1 = k \cdot AC_1$ yields:

$$\frac{\Delta AC}{AC_1}\left[\frac{k}{2}\frac{\Delta P}{P_1} + (k - 1)\right]\frac{\Delta Q}{Q_1}\frac{Q_1}{Q_2} > 0 \qquad (4)$$

Substituting $\eta(\Delta P/P_1)$ for $\Delta Q/Q_1$ (where η is the demand elasticity) we obtain (see Williamson, 1969)

$$\frac{\Delta AC}{AC_1} - \left[\frac{k}{2}\frac{\Delta P}{P_1} + (k - 1)\right]\eta \frac{\Delta P}{Q_1}\frac{Q_1}{Q_2} > 0 \qquad (5)$$

Calculations are presented in Table 11.2.

Table 11.2 Percentage cost reductions $[(\Delta(AC)/(AC_1)) \times 100)]$ sufficient to offset percentage price increases $[(\Delta P/P_1) \times 100]$ for selected values of η

	Elasticity of demand: η								
	2			1			0.5		
$\Delta P/P_1$	Value of k			Value of k			Value of k		
(%)	1.00	1.05	1.10	1.00	1.05	1.10	1.00	1.05	1.10
5	0.3	0.8	1.4	0.1	0.4	0.6	0.1	0.2	0.5
10	1.1	2.2	3.3	0.5	1.0	1.7	0.2	0.5	0.8
20	4.4	6.8	9.3	2.0	3.1	4.2	1.0	1.5	2.0
30	10.4	14.3	18.3	4.5	6.2	7.9	2.1	2.9	3.7

Sources: Williamson (1969, p. 957) for $k = 1.00$ and $k = 1.05$ and own computations for $k = 1.10$.

Williamson's main conclusion was that 'a merger which yields nontrivial real economies must produce substantial market power and results in relatively large price increases for the net allocative effects to be negative'. For low to medium values of the price elasticity the required cost reductions sufficient to offset price increases are fairly small.

In the next section, the possible magnitude of such costs reductions in the capacity expansion model with scale economies in plant contructions will be calculated. These calculations will then be combined with Williamson's trade-off results.

DYNAMIC EFFICIENCY WITH SCALE ECONOMIES

The trade-off between cost savings due to economies of scale and the effects of increased market power, set out in the previous section, is purely static. Williamson claimed that when time is introduced 'significant economies will ordinarily be realized eventually through internal expansion if not by merger. Growth of demand can facilitate this internal adjustment process; the necessity for part of the industrial company to be displaced in order that efficient size be achieved is relieved in a growing market.' (see Williamson, 1968, p. 25). In my view, this comment misses the point. The point is that even if a certain level of scale economies is achieved eventually, it matters a lot for the cost level when this 'eventually' occurs. The exploitation of economies of scale is even more important in a growing market than in a stagnating one. A firm with a given market share will reach a certain cost level before a firm with a smaller market share. The purpose of this section is to investigate this point.

As stressed above if economies of scale are present over the entire range of potential capacities of new plants, a technically optimal scale does not exist or is very large compared to demand. However, an economically optimal scale, which differs from the technically optimal scale, may nevertheless exist. In such a case, economies of scale must be treated as an endogenous rather than as an exogenous concept. The main point now is not to achieve an optimal scale as in a comparative static analysis, but to achieve an optimal path of capacity expansion. The plant capacities generated by such an optimal process of capacity expansion are all economically optimal, even if they differ in size.

In this section we consider an industry which may consist of one or more firms, each with its own optimal process of capacity expansion and with specific market shares constant over time. The model set out on pp. 345–50 can be interpreted as a capacity expansion model for a multiplant firm producing a homogeneous product. This makes it possible to compare the costs of two different paths of capacity expansion for an industry, (1) when the capacity expansion takes place with only one, multiplant, monopoly firm, and (2) when the capacity expansion takes place in an industry producing the same output, but with two or more multiplant firms.

Let us then return to equation (2). $C(\tau)$ is the discounted total cost as a function of the time interval τ, of a process of capacity expansion for an industry with an initial capacity of $x(0)$ and growth in demand of 100 g per cent per year. Let us now assume that there exists only one firm in the industry, and that it follows the rule of an optimal capacity expansion process as outlined above. Let us compare this development with that of an industry embracing two or more firms, each following the same rule of optimal capacity expansion and keeping their original market shares constant over time. The ratio of discounted costs, between the 'decentralized' process of capacity expansion and the monopolistic one, is denoted by m.

Since g and θ are assumed equal for all firms both in the multifirm case and in the monopoly firm case, so also is τ. Furthermore, H is also assumed equal for all firms, i.e. the same *ex ante* function holds in both cases and the same initial factor prices. If all firms begin their process of capacity expansion at the same moment, they will later invest at the same points of time. This assumption is probably less realistic and tends to overestimate the value of m. A cost minimizing development for an industry embracing several investing firms would show that the investments should be spread over time, reducing temporary excess capacity. This may also be common in practice in many multifirm industries, even if there seems to be a lot of exceptions as, for example, the European chemical and pulp and paper industries, which seem to exhibit a very regular pattern of capacity expansion.

Let $x_1(0)$ be the initial capacity of firm no. i ($i = 1, \ldots, N$); $\Sigma x_i(0) = x(0)$, which means that the total capacity equals that of the industry with only one firm. From equation (2) one obtains a simple formula for the ratio of the discounted cost of the two capacity expansion regimes

$$m = \frac{\Sigma x_i(0)^{1/\varepsilon}}{x(0)^{1/\varepsilon}} \qquad (6)$$

where $x_i(0)$ is the initial capacity of firm no. i ($i = 1, \ldots, N$);

$$\sum_i x_i(0) = x(0)$$

which means that the total capacity equals that of the industry with one firm.

From equation (6) it can then be seen that m is also the ratio between the plants' costs at every time of investment, i.e. the costs of the plants to be constructed and operated in the multifirm case are m times those of the plant erected by the monopoly firm at the same investment point, when the capacity of the single plant belonging to the monopoly firm is equal to the aggregate capacity of the plants constructed by the multifirm industry. This also means that the average cost in the multifirm case is m times as high as the cost in the single firm case.

In Table 11.3 the value of m is calculated for different values of ε and different numbers of firms with equal market shares. The number of firms is denoted by N and $x(0) = 100$. Thus in Table 11.3 all firms are assumed to be of equal size with equal market shares.

Table 11.3 The value of m for different values of elasticity of scale

N	S_i	Elasticity of scale: ε							
		1.10	1.20	1.25	1.30	1.40	1.50	1.75	2.00
2	50	1.07	1.12	1.15	1.17	1.22	1.26	1.36	1.41
4	25	1.13	1.26	1.32	1.38	1.49	1.59	1.81	2.00
5	20	1.16	1.31	1.38	1.45	1.58	1.71	1.99	2.24
10	10	1.23	1.47	1.58	1.70	1.93	2.15	2.68	3.16
20	5	1.31	1.65	1.82	2.00	2.35	2.71	3.61	4.47
25	4	1.31	1.71	1.90	2.10	2.51	2.92	3.97	5.00
50	2	1.43	1.92	2.19	2.47	3.06	3.68	5.35	7.07
100	1	1.52	2.15	2.51	2.89	3.73	4.64	7.20	10.0

Note: All firms have equal market shares, S_1.

Table 11.3 shows considerable differences in costs between the monopoly case and the multifirm case. These costs of decentralization increase when the elasticity of scale increases, but decrease when the number of firms decreases.

If the market shares vary between the firms (see Table 11.4), the differences in costs decrease for the same number of firms. Thus, the more unequal market shares, the less to be gained by further centralization of capacity expansion. Fringe competition may be very important from a market power point of view and at the same time cheap in terms of potential productive efficiency losses.

If we still assume that the values of all the parameters are the same in both cases, different optimizing rules might be adopted by the firms. (In oligopolistic markets, strategic considerations are important.) In the multifirm case, equation (6) does not hold

Table 11.4 The value of *m* for different values of elasticity of scale when market shares differ between firms

N	S_1	S_2	S_3	S_4	S_5	S_6	1.10	1.25	1.50
			Percentage market shares				Elasticity of scale: ε		
2	1	99					1.01	1.02	1.04
2	2	98					1.01	1.03	1.06
2	5	95					1.02	1.05	1.10
2	10	90					1.03	1.08	1.15
2	20	80					1.05	1.11	1.20
2	25	75					1.05	1.12	1.22
3	5	5	90				1.04	1.10	1.20
4	5	5	5	85			1.06	1.15	1.30
3	10	10	80				1.06	1.15	1.29
4	10	10	10	70			1.09	1.23	1.43
3	20	20	60				1.09	1.22	1.36
4	20	20	20	40			1.13	1.31	1.57
5	5	10	20	25	40		1.14	1.34	1.63
6	5	5	10	20	25	35	1.16	1.38	1.72
5	15	15	20	25	25		1.16	1.37	1.70

because the time period between two investment points, τ, will now differ between firms and perhaps also for the same firm over time. If the number of firms are constant, such a development will result in higher costs compared with the case above, in which all firms follow a cost minimizing path of capacity expansion with constant market shares.

Thus, we can distinguish two different aspects of efficiency here. The first one is connected with a scale elasticity greater than one. Equation (6) shows that time does not bring anything essentially new into the analysis. The ratio *m* becomes independent of the time cycle. The same formula must hold, *ceteris paribus*, also when the assumption of 'putty-clay' is removed and a smooth capacity adjustment in pace with demand is possible. Inefficiency is here due to the number of firms and their market shares.

The second aspect is connected with the assumption of a 'putty-clay' production structure. When capacity expansion must take place step by step, the costs of different paths of capacity expansion become important. Inefficiency is here due to the lack of co-ordination of investment decisions both with regard to the size of the plants and the time points of investments.

As the last step in this analysis, a return will be made to Williamson's trade-off results. Comparing the trade-off values in Table 11.2 with our estimates of cost reductions in Table 11.3 and

11.4, we have shown that bringing dynamics into the analysis tends to make the possible gains from exploitation of scale economies even more important. My main conclusion is, therefore, that exploitation of scale economies are likely to result in substantial welfare gains even if a higher concentration leads to abuse of market power. Large price increases seem to be required in the monopoly case to offset the cost reductions due to centralization. If there arises a trade-off between scale efficiency and allocative efficiency, the scale efficiency aspects should get a heavy weighting.

Several reservations may be in order, however. The dynamic effects on innovations and R&D of changes in market power is not considered and neither the question of the degree of increasing X-inefficiency due to monopoly.

CONCLUDING REMARKS

As regards the inherent conflict in many countries between industrial policy and antitrust policy, theory is not enough. Empirical knowledge is necessary for an evaluation of the trade-off between scale efficiency and the effects of increased industrial concentration.

The analysis in this chapter has stressed the importance of scale efficiency. This does not imply that allocative efficiency should be neglected. However, for small open economies like Sweden, foreign trade exerts a strong competitive pressure diminishing the tension between scale efficiency and allocative efficiency. Stålhammar (chapter 2, this volume) concludes in his investigation of domestic market power in Swedish industry, that the most efficient way to stimulate competition is, whenever this is possible, to stimulate foreign trade and increase the exposure of the economy to world market competition rather than trying to reduce seller concentration. Taken together, these two studies imply the policy recommendation that Swedish industrial policy should continue to promote exploitation of scale economies, even when this results in high seller concentration, and rely on foreign trade as the most important source of competition. Internationally contestable domestic markets give dominant firms little scope for exploiting market power. Therefore, Swedish competition policy should be much more alert to the international dimension.

356   *Internationalization, market power and consumer welfare*

ACKNOWLEDGEMENTS

Comments on earlier drafts by Yves Bourdet and Nils-Olov Stålhammar are gratefully acknowledged.

REFERENCES

Akerman, G. (1931) 'Den industriella rationaliseringen och dess verkningar', Stockholm: SOU 1931:42.
Bourdet, Y. (1991) 'Policy toward market power and restrictive practices in Sweden', ch. 10, this volume.
Cowling, K., Stoneman, P., Cubbin, J., Cable, J., Hall, G., Domberger, S. and Dutton, P. (1980) *Mergers and Economic Performance*, Cambridge: Cambridge University Press.
EEC (1988) *The Economics of 1922*, Brussels: EEC Commission.
Forsund, F.R. and Hjalmarsson, L. (1987) *Analyses of Industrial Structure: A Putty-Clay Approach*, Stockholm: Almqvist & Wiksell International.
Forsund, F.R., Eitrheim, O., Karko, J. and Summa, T. (1985) 'An intercountry comparison of productivity and technical change in the Nordic cement industry', Helsinki: ETLA Report B44.
Geroski, P.A. (1986) 'Competition policy and the structure–performance paradigm', discussion paper, Berlin: IIM/IP 86-27 Wissenschaftszentrum Berlin für Sozialforschung.
Geroski, P.A. (1989) 'European industry policy and industry policy in Europe', *Oxford Review of Economic Policy*, 5(2), 20–36.
Geroski, P.A. and Jacquemin, A. (1985) 'Industrial change, barriers to mobility and European industrial policy', *Economic Policy*, no. 1, 169–204.
Haldi, J. and Whitcomb, D. (1967) 'Economies of scale in industrial plants', *Journal of Political Economy*, 75(4), 373–85.
Heckscher, E.F. (1918) *Svenska produktionsproblem*, Stockholm: Bonniers.
Hjalmarsson, L. (1973) 'Optimal structural change and related concepts', *Swedish Journal of Economics*, 75(2), 176–92.
Hjalmarsson, L. (1991) 'The Swedish model of industrial policy', in M. Blomström and P. Meller (eds) *Diverging Paths – A Century of Latin-American and Scandinavian Development*, Baltimore: Johns Hopkins University Press.
Johansen, L. (1972) *Production Functions*, Amsterdam: North Holland.
Leibenstein, H. (1966) 'Allocative efficiency vs X-efficiency', *American Economic Review*, 56(3), 392–415.
Manne, A.S. (ed.) (1967) *Investments for Capacity Expansion*, London: Allen & Unwin.
Melitz, J. and Messerlin, P. (1987) 'Export credit subsidies', *Economic Policy*, no. 4, 149–68.
Mueller, D.C. (1985) 'The persistence of profits', discussion paper, IIM/IP 85-21, Berlin: Wissenschaftszentrum Berlin.
Parry, T.G. (1974) 'Plant size, capacity utilization and economic efficiency: foreign investment in the Australian chemical industry', *Economic*

Record, 50(2), 218–44.

Prais, S.J. (1981) 'A new look at the growth of industry concentration', *Oxford Economic Papers*, 26, 273–88.

Pratten, C.F. (1971) 'Economies of scale in manufacturing industries', Department of Applied Economics, University of Cambridge, occasional papers, no. 28.

Ribrant, G. (1970) 'Stordriftsfördelar inom industriproduktionen', Stockholm: SOU 1970:30. (Economics of scale in industry production.) (The Swedish Government Committee on the Concentration of Economic Power.)

Scherer, F.M., Beckenstein, A., Kaufer, E. and Murphy, R.D. (1975) *The Economics of Multi-plant Operation*, Cambridge, MA: Harvard University Press.

Sleuwaegen, L. and Yamawaki, H. (1988) 'The formation of the European Common Market and changes in market structure and performance', *European Economic Review*, 32, 1451–75.

Stålhammar, N.-O. (1991) 'Collusion and concentration in Swedish manufacturing industry', ch. 3, this volume.

Svennilson, I. (1944) 'Industriarbetets växande avkastning i belysning av svenska erfarenheter', in *Studier i ekonomi och historia tillägnade Eli F. Heckscher, 24–11–1944*, Stockholm: Almqvist & Wiksell.

Venables, A.J. and Smith, A. (1986) University of Sussex and CEPR: 'Trade and industrial policy under imperfect competition', *Economic Policy*, 3, 621–59.

Williamson, O.E. (1968) 'Economies as an antitrust defense: the welfare trade-offs', *American Economic Review*, 58(1), 18–36.

Index

absolute cost advantages, barriers to market entry 17, 19
administered prices hypothesis xiv, 72–5, 78–9
advertising, barrier to market entry 18
AEG 121, 129
agricultural policy xv, 205–45; consumer groups' organization 237–9, 242; Consumer Subsidy Equivalent (CSE) 207–9; and consumer welfare 207–14; development of 220–1, 223–9, 243–4; efficiency of 216–18, 244; fairness 214–16; and organization of producers 28, 230–7, 242–3; and politics 219–20, 240–2, 243; reasons for 214–21; Sweden, institutions 205–7; testing explanatory models 222–42; values and ideology 240–2
air transport, domestic xvi, 274–94; airport policy and airline competition 285–6; auctions and bidding 286–93; consumers and regulation 282–5; demand for 278; reasons for regulation 277–8; Swedish regulation system 279–85
Akerman, G. 340
Albertson, J. 214
allocative efficiency, trade-off with productive efficiency 348–51
allocative inefficiency cost 8–9, 11–12, 32
Anderson, Å. 230
Anderson, K. 219–20, 223, 234, 245

Andersson, F. 163–4
Andersson, Y. 216
antitrust policy see restrictive practices policy
Apoteksbolaget xv, 146, 154, 156–7
auctions, airline industry 286–93

Bain, Joe xiii, 15, 17–19, 181
Baldwin, R.E. 219, 220
Balinski, M.L. 292
barriers to market entry 17–18, 181; cars 180–5; sunk costs 12–13
Berlin, H. 145, 161–3, 165
bidding, airline industry 286–93
Blair, J.M. 73
Bolin, O. 209, 212, 216, 235, 237, 241
Bosch-Siemens 121, 129, 132
Bourdet, Yves xi, xiv, xv, xvi, 3–41, 172–97, 299–331, 337, 338
bureaucracy, and protection 29

Canada 21
Carlsson, B. 68
cars see passenger car market
Caves, R.E. 23, 57, 64, 68, 70
Chou, T.C. 57, 64, 68
Clarke, R. 88, 90, 93, 95
clothing see textile and clothing market
collusion: and concentration, theory 89–96; degree of 99–109; between oligopolists 9–10, see also restrictive practices
competition: and economic efficiency, Sweden xvi, 337–56;

and innovation 5, 12; and liberalization of trade 20–2, 24; and market power 4–5, 7–8; monopolistic 10–11; perfect 4–5, 7–8; pharmaceuticals 156–68; research design 38–9; synonym 164–7; and welfare 32–3
Competition Commissioner 304–5
competition policy 31–7, 40–1, 299–331; and industrial policy 337, *see also* restrictive practices policy
concentration 14; and barriers to entry 13; and collusion xiv, 87–111; and collusion, theory 89–96; and market power 13–19; measures of 14, 15–16; and prices 56, 71–9; and prices and profitability xiv, 55–83; and profitability 16, 97–9; research design 38; structure-conduct-performance paradigm (*q.v.*) xiv, 15; and wages-profitability-trade 55–6, 57–70
consumers: and agricultural policy 237–9, 242; and competition 32–3; costs of market power to 11, 26, 32; costs of monopoly to 8–9, 348; and market power xiv, 3–41; and regulation 282–5; and restrictive practices policy 328–31; and textiles restrictions 269–72; voice or exit 31, 299; white goods industry 134–42
Contestable Markets, Theory of 12, 19
cooperation: degree of 92–3, *see also* collusion; restrictive practices
cost of market power: inefficiency 11–12; innovation loss 12; to consumers (*q.v.*) 8–9, 11, 26, 32
Cournot, xiv
Cowling, K. 14, 88, 341
CR4 15
Curry, B. 64

Davies, S.W. 88, 90, 95
deadweight welfare cost 8–9, 11–12, 32, 348
de Jong, H.W. 149, 151, 341
Demsetz, H. 16, 88, 91–2, 109, 274, 286

DePodwin, H.J. 74
de Wolf, P. 147, 154
Dickson, V.A. 88
differentiation, product *see* product differentiation
direct market power 4
Dixit, A. 19
Donsimoni, M.-P. 91
Drake, L. 213
drugs *see* pharmaceuticals market
dynamic efficiency 5–6, 339; and scale economies 351–5
dynamic production theory 339

Eckard, E.W. 71
economies of scale *see* scale economies
efficiency 343–5; allocative-productive trade-off 348–51; and competition xvi, 337–56; dynamic 339, 351–5; productive 339, 343; vintage model 345–8
Electrolux 117, 119–22, 125–7, 129, 134–42, 143
Encaoua, D. 14
entropy measure 14
entry, barriers to *see* barriers
Europe: investments in USA 23; microwave oven market 129, 131–2; white goods industry 121–2
European Community (EC): car regulations 183–5; Common Agricultural Policy 218; effects of import competition 21; pharmaceuticals market 160; restrictive practices policies 35; tariff reductions 20; textiles and clothing trade 252, 258, 267
exports: and market power 22–3; restriction agreements 183–4, 193–4, 259–60
extra-market power 26–7

Fahlbeck, E. 209–12, 214, 218
Finger, J.M. 219
Fisher, E. 59
foreign investment, and market power 23
Forsund, F.R. 341, 344, 346, 348

Galbraith, J.K. 73
Garbarino, J.W. 62
Garber, S. 76, 78
Gardner, B. 215, 220
General Agreement on Tariffs and
   Trade (GATT) 20; car tariffs 182;
   textiles 253
General System of Preferences
   (GSP) 258
George, K.D. 64, 299
Gerdtham, U. 153–4
Geroski, P.A. 341
Goldstein, J. 219, 220
government, intervention *see* policy
Grether, D. 291–2
Gulbrandsen, O. 228

Hagström, P. 269–70
Haldi, J. 342
Hamilton, C. 269
Harberger triangle 8–9
Hayami, Y. 219, 220, 223, 245
Heckscher, Eli 340
Heckscher-Ohlin theorem of
   international trade 59
Hedlund, S. 216, 224, 236
Herfindahl's index of concentration
   14, 15, 91–2, 98, 105–7, 110
Hernes, G. 25, 238
Hitachi 124–5, 132
Hjarlmarsson, Lennart xi, xvi,
   337–56
Holmberg, Stina 321–2
Hutchinson, R. 21

imports, restrictions on 262–5
Indesit 121
indirect market power 4, *see also*
   policy
inefficiency: allocative 8–9, 11–12;
   X- 11–12, 33
innovation 5, 12
internationalization of trade *see*
   liberalization of trade
investment, foreign *see* foreign
   investment

Jacquemin, Alexis 14, 21, 300, 341
Japan: car exports 184, 193–4;
   microwave oven market 130–3;

white goods industry 119, 124–5,
   126, 137
Jefferson, Thomas 240
Johansen, L. 345–6
Joll, C.L. 299
Jones, Daniel 193–4
Jönsson, Bengt vii, xi, 145–69

Kindahl, J.K. 74
Klepper, S. 76, 78
Korea, white goods industry 119,
   126, 132, 137
Krauz, J. 74
Krugman, P.R. 59, 68
Kuran, T. 244
Kwoka, J.E. 56

Laffont, J.-J. 275
Lavergne, R.P. 219, 220, 221
Leibenstein, Harvey 12
Lerner index of monopoly power
   13, 14, 91
liberalization of trade 20, 20–5; and
   competition 20–2, 24;
   pharmaceuticals 149–50; and
   politics 268–9; white goods
   industry 121–7
Lindbeck, A. 228
Lindström, Eva xi, xv–xvi, 250–72
Linjeflyg AB 279–82, 284, 293
lobbying 27–8; costs of 11, *see also*
   organization
Lundahl, M. 216, 224, 236
Lundberg, L. 68
Lustgarten, S. 76

Maddala, G. 63
Manne, A.S. 346
manufacturing industry:
   concentration and collusion xiv,
   87–111;
   concentration-prices-profitability
   xiv, 55–83
market, definition 5
market power 4–7; and competition
   4–5, 7–8; concentration and
   barriers to entry 13–19; and
   consumer welfare xiv, 3–41; and
   economic development 5–6;
   exaggerated extent of 19; and

exports 22–3; and foreign investment 23; and liberalization of trade 20–5; policies and consumer protection 37–41; and politics 26; and prices 71; and profitability 62; regulation and producer behaviour 25–31; social costs of 11, 26, 32; studies of 3, 19; theories of 7–13; time dimension 5–6; and wages 62
Martin, S. 87
Marvel, H.P. 57
Matsushita 124–5, 132–3, 141–2
Meadows, D.H. 241
Means, G. 72, 73
mergers 329, 338; pharmaceuticals industry 147; policy 33–4; policy, Sweden 303–4, 312–14; and scale economies 338–9, 341–2
Messerlin, P.A. 238
microwave ovens, market 127–33
Molander, P. 212, 213
Monopolies and Restrictive Practices Commission 41
monopolistic competition 10–11
monopoly 8–9, 10
'most-favoured nation' concept 258
Mueller, Dennis xi, xiii–xvi, 88, 92
Multi-Fibre Arrangement (MFA) 250, 253–5, 259
multinationals 23, *see also* liberalization of trade
Myrdal, G. 224

National Price and Cartel Board 304–5
non-tariff barriers to trade 25, 29; cars 183–5, 193–4
Norman, V.D. 282
Norwegian Commission of Power 25

Official Statistics of Sweden (SOS) 63, 65
Ohlsson, L. 68
oligopoly 8–9, 10
Olson, M. 27–8, 219, 234
organization of consumers 268; and agricultural policy 237–9, 242; and textiles 268–9
Organization for Economic

Cooperation and Development (OECD), study of Sweden 209–10, 218
Organization of Petroleum-Exporting Countries (OPEC) 25
organization of producers 27–8, 30; agriculture 230–7, 242–3; textiles 266–8

Pagoulatos, E. 21
Palmgren, A. 241
Panasonic 119, 120
passenger car market xv, 172–97; concentration and foreign competition 178–80; demand 175–8; entry barriers 182–5; entry conditions 180–2; performance 194–7; pricing 185–94
patents, drugs 145–6, 163–4
perfect competition 4–5, 7–8
Petit, M. 221–2, 223–4
pharmaceuticals market xv, 145–69; dynamic competition 161–8; hospitals, prescriptions, and OTC sales 153–6; internationalization 149–50; market size and concentration 146–53; mergers 147; price competition 156–61; products, leading 148
Philips 119, 120–2, 125–6, 129
Phlips, L. 78–9
policy: agricultural xi, 205–45; competition 31–3, 37, 40–1; competition and economic efficiency, Sweden xvi, 337–56; export 36–7; industrial 36–7; merger 33–4; protection 25–31; restrictive practices 34–6; restrictive practices, Sweden xvi, 299–331; structural 337–8; textiles 255–7
politics: and agricultural policy 219–20, 240–2, 243; and liberalization 268–9; and markets 26
Posner, R.A. 274
power 6, *see also* market power
Prais, S.J. 341
Pratten, C.F. 342

prescription drugs 154–6
prices: cars 185–94; and
concentration 56, 71–9; and
market power 71; in perfect
competition 7; pharmaceuticals
156–61
product differentiation 10; barriers
to market entry 17–18, 181; cars
173, 181, 185–6; theory 93–4
production theory, neoclassical 339
productive efficiency 339, 343;
trade-off with allocative efficiency
348–51
profit, maximization of 6
profitability: and concentration 16,
97–9; and market power 62; and
wages-concentration-trade 55–6,
57–70
protection, policy 25–31
public *see* consumers
public sphere *see* policy
Pugel, T.A. 57

Rabinowicz, Ewa xi, xv, 205–45
Rassenti, S.J. 289, 292
Ravenscroft, D.J. 56
regulation: air transport 276–85;
pharmaceuticals 145; textiles and
clothing 250–72
rent-seeking 26–7
Restrictive Practices Court 304, 305
restrictive practices policy 34–6; and
consumer welfare 328–31;
enforcement of 304–14; logic of
314–27; Sweden xii, 299–331;
Swedish legislation 300–4; and
trade 317–19, 325–7
Ribrant, G. 342
Riordan, M. 275
Rosenbluth index 15
Ross, H.N. 74

Saab 178–9, 187
Sand, F.M. 292
Sandberg 215–16
Sanyo 128–9, 132–3
Sappington, D. 275
Saving, T. 14
Sawyer, M.C. 87
scale economies 341–3; barriers to

market entry 17, 18–19; cars
181–2; and dynamic efficiency
351–5; pharmaceuticals 167–8
Scandinavian Airlines System (SAS)
279–82, 284, 293
Scherer, F.M. xiii, 342–3
Schmalensee, R. 90, 93
Schmitt, G. 240
Schumpeter, Joseph 5, 24
Sears, USA 128–9
second best, theory of 32
Selden, R.T. 74
Sharp 124–5, 130, 132–3
Smith, A. 341
social costs *see* consumers
social-organization theory 25
Sölvell, Örjan xi, xv, 117–42
Sorensen, R. 21
Spence, M. 36
Stålhammar, Nils-Olov vii, xiv,
55–83, 87–111, 355
Stigler, G. 18, 74, 105, 110
Strandenes, Siri Pettersen xi, xvi,
274–94
structure, and structural policy
337–8
structure–conduct–performance
paradigm (SCP) xiv, 15, 55–6, 87,
337, 339–41, 345–8
sunk costs 12–13
Svennilson, I. 340
Sweden xiv, 40; agricultural policy
xv, 205–45; air transport,
domestic xvi, 274–94; Antitrust
Ombudsman 167; competition
policy and economic efficiency
xvi, 337–56; international trade
59; manufacturing industry,
concentration and collusion xiv,
87–111; manufacturing industry,
concentration–prices–profitability
xiv, 55–83; passenger car market
xv, 172–97; pharmaceuticals
market xv, 145–69; restrictive
practices policies 35–6; restrictive
practices policy xvi, 299–331;
tariff reductions 20; textile and
clothing market xv–xvi, 250–72;
white goods industry xiv–xv,
117–42

synonym competition 164–7

tariffs: cars 182–3; reduction of 20;
    textiles and clothing 252, 258–9
textile and clothing market xv–xvi,
    250–72; costs to consumers
    269–72; effects of trade barriers
    260–5; government aid 257–8;
    interest groups 266–9;
    international scene 251–5; policy
    objectives 255–7; quantitative
    restrictions 259–60; tariffs 258–9
theory: administered prices
    hypothesis xiv, 72–5, 78–9;
    collusion and concentration
    89–96; dynamic production theory
    339; Heckscher–Ohlin theorem of
    international trade 59; market
    power 7–13; monopoly 8–9, 10;
    oligopoly 8, 9–10; product
    differentiation 93–4; production,
    neoclassical 339; of the second
    best 32; social-organization 25
Thomson 121, 129, 132
Thullberg, P. 236, 242
Tirole, J. 275
Toshiba 124–5, 132
Tracy, M. 224
trade: barriers to 260–5 (*see also*
    tariffs); and concentration-wages-
    profitability 55–6, 57–70;
    Heckscher-Ohlin theorem 59;
    liberalization (*q.v.*) of 20–5; and
    restrictive practices (*q.v.*) 317–19,
    325–7
trade-off analysis 33–4, *see also*
    efficiency
Turner, P. 21
Tweeten, L. 240
Tyers, T. 219–20, 234

United States of America (USA):
    air transport deregulation 274;

competition policy 299; effects of
    import competition 21; industrial
    economic research xiii, 15;
    investments in Europe 23;
    microwave oven market 127–9;
    tariff reductions 20; white goods
    industry 119, 122–4
Urata, S. 69, 94

Venables, A.J. 341
Vickrey, W. 289
voluntary export restraints (VERs),
    cars 183–4, 193–4
Volvo 178–9, 187
von Ehernheim, J. 242

wages: and capital–labour ratio 62;
    and concentration–profitability–
    trade 55–6, 57–70; and market
    power 62
Wahlroos, B. 21
Waterson, M. 14, 88
Weiss, L.W. 70, 73, 75, 78
Whitcomb, D. 342
White Consolidated Industries 119,
    123
white goods industry xiv–xv,
    117–42; consumer view, Sweden
    134–9; international scene 118–19;
    market power and consumer
    welfare 139–42; market structure,
    concentration and
    internationalization 121–7;
    microwave oven market 127–33;
    product characterization 119–20
White, L.J. 59–60
Williamson, O.E. 33, 275, 338,
    348–51, 355
Winters, A. 216, 217
Winters, L.A. 214, 223

X-inefficiency 11–12, 33